Building the Operatic Museum

Eastman Studies in Music

Ralph P. Locke, Senior Editor
Eastman School of Music

Additional Titles of Interest

*Analyzing Wagner's Operas:
Alfred Lorenz and German Nationalist Ideology*
Stephen McClatchie

The Ballet Collaborations of Richard Strauss
Wayne Heisler Jr.

French Music, Culture, and National Identity, 1870–1939
Edited by Barbara L. Kelly

*In Search of New Scales:
Prince Edmond de Polignac, Octatonic Explorer*
Sylvia Kahan

Janáček beyond the Borders
Derek Katz

Musical Encounters at the 1889 Paris World's Fair
Annegret Fauser

Pentatonicism from the Eighteenth Century to Debussy
Jeremy Day-O'Connell

Rethinking Hanslick: Music, Formalism, and Expression
Edited by Nicole Grimes, Siobhán Donovan, and Wolfgang Marx

Verdi's "Il trovatore": The Quintessential Italian Melodrama
Martin Chusid

Wagner and Venice
John W. Barker

A complete list of titles in the Eastman Studies in Music series
may be found on our website, www.urpress.com.

Building the Operatic Museum

Eighteenth-Century Opera in Fin-de-Siècle Paris

William Gibbons

UNIVERSITY OF ROCHESTER PRESS

Copyright © 2013 by William Gibbons

All Rights Reserved. Except as permitted under current legislation, no part of this work may be photocopied, stored in a retrieval system, published, performed in public, adapted, broadcast, transmitted, recorded, or reproduced in any form or by any means, without the prior permission of the copyright owner.

First published 2013
Transferred to digital printing and reprinted in paperback 2017

University of Rochester Press
668 Mt. Hope Avenue, Rochester, NY 14620, USA
www.urpress.com
and Boydell & Brewer Limited
PO Box 9, Woodbridge, Suffolk IP12 3DF, UK
www.boydellandbrewer.com

ISSN: 1071-9989

Hardcover ISBN: 978-1-58046-400-0
Paperback ISBN: 978-1-58046-587-8

Library of Congress Cataloging-in-Publication Data

Gibbons, William (William James), author.
  Building the operatic museum : eighteenth-century opera in fin-de-siècle Paris / William Gibbons.
     pages cm. — (Eastman studies in music, ISSN 1071-9989 ; v. 99)
  Includes bibliographical references and index.
ISBN 978-1-58046-400-0 (hardcover : alkaline paper) 1. Opera—France—Paris—19th century. 2. Opera—18th century. 3. Mozart, Wolfgang Amadeus, 1756–1791—Criticism and interpretation. 4. Gluck, Christoph Willibald, Ritter von, 1714–1787—Criticism and interpretation. 5. Rameau, Jean-Philippe, 1683–1764—Criticism and interpretation. I. Title. II. Series: Eastman studies in
music ; v. 99.
  ML1727.4.G53 2013
  792.50944'361—dc23
                                                                                2013006028

A catalogue record for this title is available from the British Library.

This publication is printed on acid-free paper.
Printed in the United States of America

For my mother

Contents

	List of Illustrations	ix
	Acknowledgments	xi
	Introduction	1
1	Museums	8

Part One: Mozart

2	Restorations	23
3	(De)Translations	47
4	Transitions	60

Part Two: Gluck

5	Resurrections	83
6	Tragedies	106
7	Symbols	120

Part Three: Rameau

8	Monuments	145
9	Quarrels	163
10	Archaeologies	177
	Notes	197
	Bibliography	251
	Index	263

Illustrations

Examples

8.1	Excerpt from the Entrance of the Zephyrs, *Hippolyte et Aricie*, act 5	159
8.2	Excerpt from the Entrance of the Zephyrs, *Hippolyte et Aricie*, act 5, without d'Indy's additions	160

Figures

1.1	"Paris: Inauguration of the Opéra, 1875" (ca. 1890–ca. 1900)	12
2.1	*Paris illustré*, October 29, 1887. Cover after portrait of Gounod by Delaunay	35
2.2	Jean-Antoine Watteau, *The French Comedians* (1721–22)	42
3.1	Edmond Clément as Tamino	52
3.2	Lucien Fugere as Papageno	53
6.1	Pierre Puvis de Chavannes, *Hope* (1872)	114
7.1	Félia Litvinne as Alceste	129
7.2	Félia Litvinne as Isolde	130
7.3	Gustave Moreau, *Orpheus at the Tomb of Eurydice* (ca. 1891)	133
7.4	Alexandre Séon, *Lamentation of Orpheus* (1896)	136
7.5	Jean Delville, *Orpheus* (1893)	136
7.6	Marie Delna as Orphée, ca. 1896	138
10.1	Costume from *Hippolyte et Aricie* (1742?)	180
10.2	Jean-François Delmas as Thésée	181
10.3	Costume from *Hippolyte et Aricie* (1742?)	182
10.4	Designs for *Castor et Pollux* (1918)	192

Tables

2.1	Major revivals of Mozart operas at the Opéra and Opéra-Comique, 1875–1918	24
5.1	Gluck at the Société des Concerts du Conservatoire, 1875–1914	90
5.2	Volumes in the Pelletan Gluck edition	94
5.3	Major revivals of Gluck's operas in Paris, 1896–1918	102
7.1	Wagner opera productions in Paris, 1891–1914	125
7.2	Prima donnas in selected Parisian productions of Gluck Operas, 1875–1918	128
8.1	Rameau at the Société des Concerts du Conservatoire, 1875–1918	150
8.2	Operas published in the Rameau *Œuvres complètes*	151
8.3	Rameau's operas at the Schola Cantorum	152

Acknowledgments

This book is the result of my time at three academic institutions scattered across the United States, and would not have been possible without the support of friends and colleagues at each.

I am deeply indebted to a number of people at the University of North Carolina at Chapel Hill for their continued guidance and advice, particularly Annegret Fauser, Mark Evan Bonds, Tim Carter, Jon Finson, and Lloyd Kramer. I am equally thankful to my many colleagues and friends from North Carolina, whose support, suggestions, and patience have extended far beyond state boundaries. During my time teaching at the University of Iowa I was fortunate to have access to colleagues and graduate students who gave me opportunities to present my work and who were willing to listen to me talk about it incessantly. Most recently, the support of my wonderful colleagues, friends, research assistants, and students at Texas Christian University (TCU) have been crucial to completing this final research and writing. I of course owe thanks also to the librarians and library staff at all three institutions for accommodating my frequent special requests and for regularly accomplishing the daunting task of making sure things were actually where they were supposed to be. I am also delighted to acknowledge a number of scholars outside these three institutions, each of whom has generously lent some combination of advice, research assistance, and support to this project: Charles Dill, Katharine Ellis, Mark Everist, Ralph Locke, Adeline Mueller, Jann Pasler, and William Weber. Kyle Roderick very professionally prepared the musical examples, and Katheryn Lawson graciously scanned many of the journal illustrations.

Several institutions have also offered their financial support for this project. Research in the Bibliothèque Nationale de France and the French Archives Nationales was enabled through the American Musicological Society's M. Elizabeth C. Bartlet Travel Grant in 2008. Some initial research was completed with the assistance of a fellowship from the American Council of Learned Societies and the Andrew W. Mellon Foundation in 2009–10. Final preparations on the book project and financial support for obtaining image permissions were facilitated through a Junior Faculty Summer Research Fellowship from TCU.

Portions of this book have been presented or published elsewhere, and I am extremely grateful for the comments and suggestions I have received at conferences and in the editorial process. I gave talks on the central idea of the Operatic Museum at the 2010 Meeting of the American Musicological Society (Indianapolis, Indiana) and at the University of Iowa's Colloquium series in the fall of the same year. Much of chapter 3 was contained in my paper "The Trials of Authenticity: *The Magic Flute* in 1909 Paris," presented at a joint meeting of the American Musicological Society Southeast and South Central Chapters in the fall of 2009, and at the *After The Magic Flute* conference at the University of California, Berkeley, in March 2010. Subsequently most of chapter 3 and portions of chapter 2 were published as "(De)Translating Mozart: *The Magic Flute* in 1909 Paris," *Opera Quarterly* 28, no. 4 (Winter 2012): 1–17. Some of the early work that has become part 2 was published as "*Iphigénie à Paris*: Positioning Gluck Historically in Early Twentieth-Century France." *Intersections: Canadian Journal of Music* 27 (2006): 3–15. There is also a small amount of tangential overlap between part 2 and my article "Music of the Future, Music of the Past: *Tannhäuser* and *Alceste* at the Paris Opéra." *19th-Century Music* 33, no. 3 (Spring 2010): 228–42. My talk for the University of Iowa Opera Studies Forum in the fall of 2010, "Gluck, Wagner, and Symbolism: Staging *Orphée* in 1896 Paris," comprises parts of chapter 7.

Introduction

In the quiet lodgings where the great aunt lives
Everything recalls the bygone days of olden times,
The courtyard with its sonorous wells, the old servant,
And the century-old tarnished mirrors.

The salon still has its Flemish tapestries,
Where nymphs and shepherds dance amid the woods;
When the sun is setting, one believes
A flash of old love is caught in their eyes.

From the dark corner where an antique spinet rests,
Sometimes a long sigh rises and falls at random,
Like the echo of days when, pretty and young,
The great aunt played Rameau, Gluck, and Mozart there.

A rosewood chest is at the heart of the chamber.
Its aromatic drawers hold more than one treasure:
Candy boxes, bottles, bags of iris and amber,
From which the breath of a century is still exhaled.

A book is alone amid these withered relics,
And under the thin, darkened paper of a page,
A dried flower has been sleeping for sixty years:
The book is Zaïre, and the flower, a carnation.

In summers, near the window, with the old volume,
The great aunt turns in her armchair . . .
Is it the bright sun or the hot air that rekindles
The color in her cheeks and the sparkle in her eyes?

She inclines her brow, yellowed like ivory
Towards the carnation, which she is afraid of breaking in her fingers:
A memory of love sings her in her memory,
While the songbirds twitter on the roofs.

> She dreams of the morning the flower was put
> In the old black book by the hand of a boyfriend,
> And her tears moisten like dew
> The page where the red carnation has slept for sixty years.[1]

The great aunt in André Theuriet's poem is a woman out of time.[2] Although she exists in the "present"—late nineteenth-century France—she lives in another time. Alone in her peaceful home, with only memories and an aged servant for company, she inhabits a constant reverie, a Proustian state avant la lettre. Faced with unbearable sadness and desolation, she retreats into the past, surrounding herself with objects from happier times. There are many ways to read this poem, but I see it as an allegory for the French nation in the 1870s.

The collapse of the Second Empire in 1870 and the subsequent political disaster of the Commune sent Paris into an unprecedented crisis of identity. As historian Robert Gildea puts it: "The defeat of 1870 probably inflicted more pain on the French nation than any other defeat in its history, even that of 1940. The defeat was sudden, unexpected, incomprehensible."[3] Faced with this cultural and physical destruction the French turned to their history in search of both hope and a shared cultural identity. Such a dramatic turn of events required substantial effort to maintain (at least in the minds of the French) the semblance of France's dominance on the international stage, if not militarily, then culturally. In response to this need, the Third Republic (1870–1940) emphasized what historian Pierre Nora has called "lieux de mémoire" (places of memory): objects, locations, and people imbued with great symbolic value, each one a nexus of national and cultural identity.[4] These *lieux* permeated every aspect of French culture as symbols for the historical authority and power of France.

Preserving—and in some cases establishing—a sense of French cultural and national identity assumed new importance in the decades after 1870.[5] The cosmopolitan artistic atmosphere that Parisians had cultivated in the midcentury began to wane, replaced by a nationalistic zeal for French artworks (and often a distaste for Germanic ones).[6] In historian Christophe Charle's words, France's military defeat and the subsequent shift in the European power distribution "repudiated the former French cultural hegemony which dated back to the Enlightenment as well as the universalist ideals of the French Revolution. As a result, a type of cultural nationalism emerged which gradually spread into many fields, including literature, music, and of course the fine and decorative arts."[7] Demonstrating the past and present greatness of French culture required the skillful weaving and reweaving of historical narratives—a task eminently suited to museums.

To that end, the late nineteenth century saw an explosion in the number and quality of state-sponsored museums throughout France.[8] The specific goals of these institutions varied widely, but they all united in serving a common purpose: the display of a shared heritage. Museums are in many ways dedicated to the preservation of cultural memory. Yet they also create that memory; putting "history" on display in the form of historical objects inevitably constructs narratives of the past, and the careful selection and manipulation of those objects controls how those narratives are interpreted. "A walk in an art museum," art historian David Carrier eloquently informs us, "is a narrative under another name, for you need but describe what you see as you walk to write a history."[9] Museum visitors construct narratives from the evidence at hand—a powerful tool in the hands of those who wish to shape public understanding of their national history and cultural identity.

With this museal context in mind, let us return to the great aunt's collection, her private museum. Far from being chosen at random, the collection reflects her nation's history as well as her own. Her salon is replete with imagery of the ancien régime and the early nineteenth century, a time when France's power and cultural influence were unquestionable. Consider the objects: the salon walls are covered by Franco-Flemish tapestries, evocative of the long French tradition in this art—a reference, perhaps to the famous Gobelins Manufactory in Paris, which produced tapestries since the early seventeenth century and was seriously damaged during the Commune in 1871. The book that contains the great aunt's most precious keepsake, the dried flower, is Voltaire's *Zaïre* (1732), one of the most enduringly successful works of this French historical luminary—another gem of the ancien régime. The candy boxes and perfume bottles exhale "the breath of a century," offering a sensory reminder of better days, evoking an era of frivolity and pleasant excess.

And, of course, the spinet piano softly echoes the music of Rameau, Gluck, and Mozart that once filled the house. These three composers were known above all for their operas, the true test of worth for composers in France. Theuriet again chose his poetic examples with great care. Each composer at one time captivated Paris with his music: Jean-Philippe Rameau's *Hippolyte et Aricie* (1733) and *Castor et Pollux* (1737/1754) were icons of ancien-régime musical culture, pinnacles of the classical *tragédie en musique* (or *tragédie lyrique*). Christoph Willibald Ritter von Gluck's French operas—most notably *Iphigénie en Tauride* (1779) and the adapted *Orphée et Eurydice* (1774) and *Alceste* (1776)—were equally beloved in the decades before the Revolution, as well as at the beginning of the nineteenth century. Wolfgang Amadeus Mozart's Parisian fame rested mainly on *Don Giovanni* (1787), a staple of the repertoire for most of the nineteenth century. Adapted into various forms as the romantic *Don Juan*, the opera was a symbol of the grandiosity and cosmopolitanism of nineteenth-century Paris. Taken together, these three composers were powerful reminders of

France's musical greatness—and its contributions to European culture as a whole—just as Voltaire suggested its literary and philosophical contributions and the tapestries suggested its rich artistic history.

Theuriet's poem was prescient. Each of these three composers became a focal point of French musical culture over the course of the fin de siècle, and operas by each received major new productions on the Parisian stages. With the exception of *Don Juan* and a few other works, reaching back into the eighteenth-century for repertoire was extremely uncommon on the major Parisian stages, and even in those circumstances the works were heavily adapted for modern audiences. The restored productions of Mozart, Gluck, and Rameau operas that Paris saw around 1900 heralded a fundamental shift in the role audiences and producers assigned to the opera houses—a transition from pure entertainment to a kind of retrospective. These three eighteenth-century composers became the core of what I call the "Operatic Museum," a simultaneously physical and conceptual space in which works from multiple time periods could coexist to create an overarching historical narrative. This book is dedicated to exploring the creation and varied manifestations of this concept from a variety of perspectives. In doing so I have several aims. First, the varied ways in which this repertoire affected musical culture in fin-de-siècle Paris are often overlooked. Examining in detail how critics and audiences understood eighteenth-century music reveals a great deal about fin-de-siècle aesthetic priorities. More generally, I am interested in the process of canon formation as well as the evolution of historical fidelity as a concept in opera. But fundamentally this is a book about history, how it comes to be (re)written, and its use as a tool for building national and cultural identities.

In chapter 1, I give an overview of the Operatic Museum mindset from roughly the 1870s to World War I—which I will cavalierly call the "fin de siècle." I trace the development of the idea in the French press, as critics—including many of the major composers of the times—gradually accepted and then championed the Museum. Here I also introduce many of the themes and concepts that are explored in more detail in further chapters. After this brief overview, the book is divided into three parts, each dedicated to a single composer. Although each part covers the entire fin-de-siècle time period, they are nonetheless arranged in a kind of chronology. In a typical historical narrative we would encounter the composers in the order Rameau, Gluck, and finally Mozart. I move in the opposite direction, beginning with Mozart and ending with Rameau, following the order in which productions were staged during the fin de siècle. As we will see, the Operatic Museum began with the most familiar (and thus chronologically latest) works before pushing backward in time, encompassing more historically remote composers as the museal mentality gained ground with producers, critics, and—most important—audiences.

Part 1 is dedicated to Mozart's French reception. Chapter 2, "Restorations," investigates the shift in how the composer's operas were viewed during the fin de siècle. Mostly using *Don Giovanni/Don Juan* as a case study, I chart the slow and often painful transition from romanticism to classicism, as the accumulated trappings of the nineteenth century were painstakingly removed, exposing the eighteenth-century work underneath. This process encapsulates many of the critical debates about the necessity (or not) for an Operatic Museum in the last decades of the nineteenth century. The following chapter, "(De)Translations," is an in-depth look at one particularly pivotal production of *The Magic Flute* in 1909, which set the tone for "historically faithful" versions of Mozart's operas. French audiences were accustomed to having foreign operas adapted into their own language, both literally speaking and in a more cultural sense. This production challenged that strongly held belief, confronting critics and audiences with rapidly changing ideas about the nature of translation and historical fidelity. Chapter 4, "Transitions," examines some effects of the Operatic Museum mentality on the interpretations of Mozart and his operas. In particular, I examine how gender and national identity came into play in the French understanding of Mozart's biography, and how these issues may have affected the way that French audiences understood his operas.

In part 2, I switch focus to Gluck, whose works were ubiquitous at the Opéra-Comique for over a decade beginning in 1896. "Resurrections," chapter 5, traces the winding path that brought those works back to the stage and their critical reception once there. In addition to the increasingly vocal support the composer received from critics, I address in some detail the important battles fought on two other fronts: concert performances of Gluck's music and the new French edition of his operas. Chapter 6, "Tragedies," investigates the classical (in both senses of the word) aspects of Gluck and his operas. The composer was situated as part of a pantheon of great artists in the French classical tradition; in particular, he drew frequent comparisons to the playwright Pierre Corneille in terms of dramatic style and temperament. His operas, on the other hand, were classical in the sense of Greek mythology—and consequently were able to tap into the fin-de-siècle vogue for antiquity that both validated French cultural worth and provided audiences with suitably cathartic subjects on the stage with which to express a national sense of mourning. "Symbols," my final chapter on Gluck, likewise deals simultaneously with the composer and the subject matter of his works. This time, rather than exploring Gluck's connection to the French past, I look to his associations with the aesthetic theories of Richard Wagner. Nearly all fin-de-siècle critics believed that the two composers had much in common from an aesthetic standpoint—operatic reformers, mythological subjects, psychological complexity, and so on—but the ramifications of those similarities polarized Parisian musical culture to a surprising degree. After surveying this complex web of connections, I consider how the Gluck-Wagner binary contributed to interpreting Gluck's operas in a modern way—a crucial factor in the success of the Operatic Museum. I offer the 1896 *Orphée et Eurydice* as an example of this trend, suggesting that the subject matter encouraged audiences to connect Gluck's music to Wagnerian-symbolist depictions of Orpheus.

The last part of the book centers on Rameau's resurgence in popularity, which is attributable in large part to his status as a French cultural icon—a symbol of the artistic glory of prerevolutionary France. Chapter 8, "Monuments," outlines Rameau's fairly abrupt return to prominence in the years around 1900, as nationalist fervor pushed the boundaries of the Operatic Museum further back into the eighteenth century. As was the case with Gluck's rediscovered popularity, Rameau benefited greatly from concert performances, but perhaps the single greatest factor in his reappearance was the monolithic complete edition of his works that began in the 1890s and continued through the first decades of the twentieth century. The next chapter, "Quarrels," covers approximately the same time period—the 1890s through about 1920—and deals with the relationship between Rameau and another eighteenth-century luminary: Jean-Jacques Rousseau. Rousseau's advocacy for Italian musical styles over Rameau's style of French *tragédie lyrique* had been at the center of the "Querelle des Bouffons," a series of polemic letters and pamphlets that occupied Parisian opera culture during the 1750s. As both Rameau and Rousseau became important *lieux de mémoire* in the early twentieth century, these issues resurfaced, causing French critics to reenact the Querelle in their efforts to shape music-historical narratives. Finally, I end this study with chapter 10, "Archaeologies," which deals with the two productions of Rameau's music at the Opéra during the fin de siècle: *Hippolyte et Aricie* in 1908 and *Castor et Pollux* a decade later, amid the closing months of World War I. These two productions highlight the gradual acceptance of the Operatic Museum mindset since the 1870s, and the nationalist necessity for its expansion into the early eighteenth century. What had begun as an idealistic notion became by 1918 an accepted fact, a fundamental shift in how critics and audiences understood the function of opera houses and in how narratives of operatic history could be created.

A brief note on translations: This book is heavily dependent on primary documents—newspaper reviews, scholarly monographs, journal articles, and so on—almost all of which, naturally enough, happen to be written in French. Much like the Operatic Museum process I spend the next ten chapters describing, any reception study will necessarily involve objects and documents chosen carefully for the purpose of constructing a particular narrative. We can also add the fact that I am putting these documents through the process of translation, during which I inevitably impose my own interpretations on the original texts. Unless otherwise noted, all translations are mine. I have of course aimed to keep the original sense of the text as much as possible (though I am all too aware of the lost multiple meanings of particular terms). For clarity, however, I have made frequent changes—mostly minor, but occasionally drastic—to punctuation. Nineteenth-century French writers were not known for the succinct quality of their prose, and paragraph-length sentences that have a poetic or rhetorical character in the original French have an often ungainly and occasionally obfuscating character in English. I strongly encourage francophone readers to consult the French texts I include throughout.

Chapter One

Museums

Reviewing the 1861 revival of Gluck's *Alceste*, the music critic A. Thurner made a radical suggestion: the Paris Opéra, the pinnacle of French musical culture, "must be an operatic Louvre, where Classical works—alternating with our great modern productions—would provide the invigorating energy necessary to give shape to a new generation of composers and artists."[1] In Thurner's scenario, the Opéra—the Académie Nationale de Musique—would serve the same cultural role as the Louvre museum, the model institution for preserving historical masterpieces. His comparison of the Opéra and the Louvre is in many ways apt. Both had origins in the ancien régime and were state-run institutions dedicated to displaying French artistic achievements.[2] Just as important, both aimed at demonstrating, as historian Jean-Pierre Babelon points out regarding the Louvre, "the centrality of the relationship between state power and the arts."[3] More specifically, in the words of art historians Carol Duncan and Alan Wallach, the Louvre "embodies the state and the ideology of the state . . . disguised in the spiritual forms of artistic genius."[4] Just as the Louvre was meant to house cultural treasures, the Opéra—followed closely by the Opéra-Comique, another state-subsidized theater founded with prerevolutionary origins—was the greatest stage in a nation obsessed with opera.[5] As one early biographer of Camille Saint-Saëns wrote:

> The French . . . completely like music only when it is allied with words. They seek, they demand of this music a drama or a comedy to accompany it, and scenery to frame it. This is no dream of some supreme ideal; it is the way things are. Hence, the obsession with the theater haunts every one of us who thinks and lives amidst the song of notes and sounds. Material profit, resounding glory, popularity: for us, these do not recompense the labors of the musician-composer except when in league with the theater.[6]

Because opera occupied such a prominent role in French musical culture, the Opéra and Opéra-Comique were equipped to provide audiences with authoritative narratives of music history—to be an "operatic Louvre," or in my more general term, an Operatic Museum.

The novelty of Thurner's suggestion lay not precisely in the idea of holding onto an older repertoire—after all, throughout the nineteenth century all the major music theaters of Paris revived works by Rossini, Donizetti,

Verdi, Mozart, and Meyerbeer (to name only a few) to the extent that the Opéra remained nearly inaccessible to young composers.[7] Instead, the subversive newness of Thurner's "operatic Louvre" stems from its demand that audiences and theater producers shift their perceptions regarding the fundamental nature of the Opéra as an artistic enterprise. Rossini's *Guillaume Tell* (1829), for example, remained in the repertoire throughout the nineteenth century because audiences loved it, so it was certain to sell tickets. The purpose of the "operatic Louvre," by contrast, was at least in part the education of operagoers—a documentary history of music, dramatized in living color.

The "new generation of composers and artists" required more than entertainment. To understand themselves they needed to understand their heritage. The influential critic Stéphen de La Madeleine, also writing on the 1861 *Alceste*, supported this educational approach to programming operas, calling the production a "magnificent lesson." He continued:

> It is by relying on the past that we take possession of the future....
>
> The forms art can take are—and must be—limitless; but to reach something new it is necessary to have a perfect understanding of what has already been done.
>
> Open up for study the doors to the shrine where the old glories sleep in their august immortality, and you will enlighten those geniuses who are ignorant of themselves.[8]

In other words, for French opera composers to understand themselves they must first understand their own history; showing them these past glories enables them to reach new heights in the present. Though de La Madeleine does not specifically mention a museum, his "shrine where the old glories sleep in their august immortality" certainly has a similarly museal purpose. As museum historian Donald Preziosi tells us, museums function partially "as documentary indices of a (narrative) history of the world and its people, construed as teleological dramaturgy ('evolution'), a 'story' having a direction and a point and leading up to the spectator in the present, at the apex of this development."[9] Each work in the Operatic Museum was a portion of a larger whole, a single act of a metadramatic retelling of French musical history, culminating in the present (whenever that happened to be for the listener).

Thurner, de La Madeleine, and critics like them were at the vanguard of a new way of thinking about opera culture that would profoundly alter both the repertoire and the way that audiences approached the theater. But in the 1860s, the idea was simply unsupportable—idealistic rather than practical. On the one hand, music from before 1800—what fin-de-siècle critics might call "musique ancienne," or we in the twenty-first century might loosely call "early music"—became fairly common at Parisian concerts after the midpoint of the nineteenth century.[10] A number of organizations created around this time began to sponsor the performance of early music, and performers such as Louis Diémer began to deal with historical instruments as more than quaint curiosities, gaining celebrity for their interpretation of seventeenth- and eighteenth-century keyboard music.[11] Early music even became a frequent sight on programs at major concert series such as the Concerts Lamoureux and Pasdeloup and at the Société des Concerts du Conservatoire, as well as large-scale national events such as the Paris Exposition Universelle in 1889.[12] The idea of preserving canonic works from earlier eras through museological performance—what Lydia Goehr famously termed the "Imaginary Museum of Musical Works"—was readily apparent in Parisian culture.[13]

On the other hand, as prominent as early music may have been during this time, it was all but absent from the Opéra and Opéra-Comique. There was, certainly, the odd (if important) exception. The 1861 revival of Gluck's *Alceste*—the impetus for Thurner's review—was enabled only through the production's association with two of the most beloved musicians in nineteenth-century Paris, both ardent supporters of Gluck's music: the composer and critic Hector Berlioz, who significantly adapted Gluck's music for the occasion, and the mezzo-soprano Pauline Viardot, who sang the title role. This unusual production (which I discuss more in part 2 of this book) was preceded by another Berlioz-Viardot effort: the well-known revival of *Orphée et Eurydice* at the Théâtre-Lyrique in 1859, by all accounts an extremely successful experiment in musical archaeology. The Théâtre-Lyrique was in many respects a precursor to the Operatic Museum; as Flora Willson points out in a recent study of the 1859 *Orphée*, it was "an institution with strong educational imperatives, albeit one set up to run (in principle at least) at no cost to the state."[14] The theater, which also presented less-heard works by Mozart in the 1850s, was even described by one critic in 1859 as "a museum of old composers."[15]

Yet it was a far cry from the Opéra or the Opéra-Comique. The theater did not have the international stature or the historical grandeur necessary to truly display these works to their greatest effect. The surroundings affect how the historical objects (artistic or otherwise) are perceived; the Louvre was a palace, after all, not a warehouse. Unfortunately for the Operatic Museum ideal in the 1860s, archaeological excursions were largely unthinkable to audience members at the Opéra or Opéra-Comique, and ruled out as unprofitable (if not outright ridiculous) by the directors. To attain the Operatic Museum ideal, something had to change. The symbolic importance of reviving earlier opera had to become more beneficial to the opera houses than the probability of lost revenue; or, to use Pierre Bourdieu's framework, the cultural capital (symbolic value) gained by producing such a work had to counterbalance any possible loss to monetary capital (economic value).[16]

Though the process had begun in the 1860s, the nationalism that pervaded the decades following the War of 1870 provided a necessary push, accelerating the building of the Operatic Museum. The Franco-Prussian War and the subsequent Commune were devastating to French identity, a blow that sent the French scrambling to salvage their national and cultural heritage. Museums were central to this effort because all types of them—military, art, science, and so on—are in some way history museums, revealing the past as their narrative unfolds. And a nation cannot survive without its mythology; as Preziosi distills it, "As an imaginary entity, the modern nation-state depended for its existence and maintenance on an apparatus of powerful . . . cultural fictions, principle amongst which were the *novel* and the *museum*."[17] "Museums," he continues, "were civic spaces designed for European ceremonial engagement with (and thus the evocation, fabrication, and preservation of) its own history and social memory."[18] Museums became a crucial way to retell France's history, stressing its historical greatness and, via teleological progression, reaffirming the magnificence of its present.

The Operatic Museum thus quickly transitioned from a naively impractical concept to a cultural necessity. French audiences (not just composers, as had been the focus in the 1860s) needed to see their music history enacted on their most prominent stages; their (re)education was a key part of maintaining narratives of French artistic dominance. Since the past led inexorably to the present, creating the "correct" historical narrative—shaping history in as favorable a light as possible—was essential. The first step was creating the right space for the museum, and the nation responded quickly. The opulent new Palais Garnier—the construction of which coincidentally began in 1861, the year of Thurner's appeal—became the home of the Opéra in 1875 (see fig. 1.1), putting a tangible and magnificent public face on French music. It is a building designed to mirror the glory of the composers whose works were contained within, and so it is no surprise that the edifice and entry to the Palais Garnier are adorned with representations of composers of the past. The building is designed to be in part a museum dedicated to their music—and a visual representation of the Opéra's long history as an institution.[19] As Duncan and Wallach tell us, "the museum stands as a symbol of the state, and those who pass through its doors enact a ritual that equates state authority with the idea of civilization."[20]

The doors to the Palais Garnier were a gateway to French music history, and it should be no surprise that shortly after its opening, critics again raised the call of the Operatic Museum—this time louder and in greater numbers. And this time, the Opéra began to listen. In 1879, Auguste

Figure 1.1. "Paris: Inauguration of the Opéra, 1875" (ca. 1890–ca. 1900).

Vaucorbeil was appointed director of the theater, necessitating a new *cahiers des charges* (license). Article 1 contained an interesting new addition: "The Opéra is not an experimental theater: it must be regarded as the musical museum."[21] Although this phrase was an acknowledgment of a growing shift in the mindset of the directorship, the wheels of change turned far too slowly for many critics. The organist and musicologist Félix Clément voiced this complaint in his 1885 *Histoire de la musique*, invoking the museum metaphor while voicing his exasperation with the Parisian operatic repertoire:

> How regrettable it is that music is not considered like the other arts, where masterworks are preserved in museums and palaces with such care, expense, and foresight! The smallest fragments of ancient statues, the sculptures of Michelangelo, the paintings of Raphael and Titian . . . are offered up for study and admiration to the judgment of connoisseurs, artists, and the public. Musical works that have been the object of enthusiasm for two or three generations, in which composers who equaled the great painters or the most perfect sculptors have proven their genius, are allowed to fall into the deepest obscurity, disappearing under dust in the libraries or growing mold [in the shops] on the quays, and no one cares enough to point out their beauties. There are objections based on the capriciousness of public taste, which would no longer support old-fashioned operas and outdated forms. How do we know that? And, moreover, a government does not maintain great institutions dedicated to the fine arts—the Louvre and Cluny museums, the Sèvres and the Gobelins factories—for amusing or distracting the masses. . . . For some years now, I have demanded a sort of retrospective theater, which would be for the great geniuses of the musical art what the Louvre is for Classic artists. It would create a much larger audience than one would think, composed of elite connoisseurs—people of delicate and practiced taste.[22]

Clément makes a number of interesting points in this brief passage. Most obviously, he reinforces the Operatic Museum concept we have already seen—now expanded outward to encompass more than just the Louvre as a point of comparison.

Established in 1843 and housed in the fourteenth-century hôtel de Cluny, the Cluny Museum—officially the National Museum of the Middle Ages—displays French treasures from the distant past, including (since the 1880s) the famous *Lady and the Unicorn* tapestry and a number of illuminated manuscripts. The museums associated with the Sèvres and Gobelins factories likewise showcase France's long history of artistic achievements in the fields of porcelain and tapestry, respectively. Each museum provides a historical narrative that showed France in its best possible light, illustrating an unbroken chain of accomplishments from the Middle Ages on—even earlier, if one considers the classical works housed in the Louvre (a topic to which I return in chapter 6). Clément's choice of museums is suggestive. The Operatic Museum is still (like the Louvre) an art museum, yet it is also more; like the Sèvres and Gobelins examples, it was a factory-museum, a place where objects are not only housed but made. This concept both allowed for the display and celebration of classic works and called attention to the methods of production—the musicians, certainly, but also the French "national arts of music, décor, and costuming," as one critic would write about a Rameau production in 1918.[23]

Aside from outlining the aesthetic necessity of the Operatic Museum, Clément's musings also raise the issue of its audience. He suggests that the financial burdens of maintaining the Museum would not be insurmountable, with sales buoyed by "elite connoisseurs—people of delicate and practiced taste." Historically, many members of the Opéra's audience were after entertainment (not always of the musical sort), rather than education; clearly, and with good reason, opera producers were concerned about audiences' rejection of aesthetically unfamiliar works. The theater was dependent on ticket sales, particularly to wealthy patrons. In contrast to the majority of art museums in France, admission to the opera houses was not free, or even, in many cases, affordable: in the 1880s a subscription to one of the boxes at the Opéra might cost up to 25,000 francs per year, and individual seats could be 16 or 20 francs—at a time when 90 percent of the population of France earned below 2,500 francs per year.[24] Even seats at the Opéra-Comique, less expensive and more populist than the Opéra, were beyond the finances of much of the Parisian population.

Clément's assertion that sales might not suffer significantly with works in the Operatic Museum calls attention to a change in the mindset of both opera audiences and producers, one in which the museal function of the Opéra overrode its financial imperatives. "A government does not maintain great institutions dedicated to the fine arts . . . for amusing or distracting the masses," as Clément wrote. A new (or newly empowered) group of educated opera lovers could at least partially compensate for subscribers disinterested in a museum experience. To some extent, producers at the Opéra supported this change—in the late 1870s and 1880s, the Palais Garnier became (at least some of the time) a much more egalitarian space, opening the doors—literally and in de La Madeleine's more poetic sense—to audiences curious about their musical history.[25] The effects of the Operatic Museum were in fact even more widespread than the altered makeup of Opéra audiences. Excerpts from successful works at the Opéra were often performed in more public, and sometimes unexpected, locations—the Bon Marché department store, for example—and the sheet-music industry allowed the wide dissemination of successful operas (both old and new) in transcriptions.[26] Cultivating an interest in the works produced at the Opéra and Opéra-Comique—including the masterpieces that filled the Operatic Museum—allowed the middle class to emulate the cultural elites who were able to afford attending the full performances, enhancing the cultural cachet of the works and educating audiences in music history, thus fulfilling the Museum's function.[27]

As audiences began to embrace the underlying principle of the Operatic Museum, opera producers were faced with an obvious yet critical question: what objects should be displayed? What works, in other words, could uphold France's claims to operatic greatness? Certainly, some operas by contemporary composers were exploited for this purpose during the Third Republic. Important works by Saint-Saëns, Massenet, Debussy, and others received their premieres during the time period between 1875 and 1914, and were exported to other nations as evidence of French musical achievements.[28] But tracing a narrative through the past was the crux of the museum; without context, even these modern masterpieces could not save France's cultural reputation. As museum historian Daniel Sherman reminds us, "History . . . is the plot that weaves together the museum's objects, infusing them with meaning, constituting them as representations; objects, with the access to the real they promise, in turn help to legitimate history's truth-claim."[29] Historical context makes the works in the Operatic Museum *mean* something aside from their own artistic merits; a strong grounding in the classics was crucial to understanding the present as well as the past.

Tracing a path through nineteenth-century operatic history proved simple enough; the inaugural season at the Palais Garnier presented revivals of midcentury works, including Ambroise Thomas's *Hamlet* (1868) and Charles Gounod's *Faust* (1859) as well as favorites from the earlier nineteenth century, such as Gioachino Rossini's *Guillaume Tell* (1829) and Fromental Halévy's *La Juive* (1835), with Meyerbeer's *Le Prophète* (1849) and *Robert le diable* (1831) added to the list in the following year.[30] These popular works (among others) sufficed to demonstrate the nation's great nineteenth-century accomplishments, but the farther the lineage went back in time, the more problematic it became. Each work included as an artifact in the museum had to be a masterpiece, and recognized by the audience as such. Aside from the considerable financial ramifications of an unsuccessful production, putting on works that audiences found boring or aesthetically incomprehensible was tantamount to admitting that French music history was lacking.

Opera producers thus had to walk a fine line between historical significance and dramatic viability; in Katharine Ellis's words, "culture is not the same as practice, and heightened symbolic value does not necessarily make a repertory acceptable for professional or other public use."[31] Many works of clear historical importance were simply too divergent from listeners' expectations from opera. Despite being described by the nineteenth-century critic François-Joseph Fétis as the "oldest *opéra-comique* in existence," for example, the musical and dramatic style of Adam de la Halle's thirteenth-century *Jeu de Robin et de Marion* would obviously have alienated fin-de-siècle audiences at the Opéra or Opéra-Comique (though it *was* performed at a festival in 1896 by performers from the latter theater). Despite the opportunity to showcase French contributions to music history by putting on display a "lyrical people's opera written in France by a Frenchman a heart-warming three centuries before Monteverdi," reviving the *Jeu* at the major theaters was an impossibility.[32] The operas of Jean-Baptiste Lully (1632–87)—the court composer of Louis XIV and founder of the *tragédie lyrique*—were closer in style to modern expectations, but evidently still too distant; only short excerpts of his operas appeared on concert series, and there was no fin-de-siècle attempt to stage one of his works at the Opéra or Opéra-Comique despite the composer's cultural cachet.

The eighteenth century proved to be the ideal compromise, a point of convergence between historical importance and aesthetic comprehensibility. Not surprisingly, critics began to clamor for more performances of works from this period, turning first to Mozart's more familiar works of the late classical era before pushing the boundaries of the Operatic Museum by advocating for the inclusion of operas by Gluck and eventually Rameau. Some critics explicitly returned to the Operatic Museum metaphor to justify and explain this process. One of the most vocal and consistent advocates for the concept was the composer Paul Dukas, who invoked the museum on several occasions in his criticism during the 1890s. In an 1894 article in favor of creating an edition of Rameau's operas—a project to which Dukas would contribute his editorial talents (see chapter 8)—the composer complained that the Opéra was not living up to its museal responsibilities: "We dare not ask the Opéra to attempt the restoration of one of Rameau's masterworks, since it is already impossible to have Gluck in the repertoire of this theater—which should be, given its title and its sumptuous subvention, like the Louvre of music."[33] More than three decades after Thurner's review, Dukas echoed his call for an "operatic Louvre." As Clément suggested, the Opéra's position (and funding) as an arm of the state—the Académie Nationale de Musique—meant that like the Louvre it had a fundamental civic obligation, an educational task that superseded issues of funding or even entertainment.

Two years later, as the theaters were beginning to respond in earnest to their newly museal role, Dukas returned to the Louvre example, this time with regard to Mozart's *Don Giovanni* (*Don Juan* in France):

> It has already been several years since we have seen *Don Juan*. It is, perhaps, only in France that we could have these long absences of musical

masterworks without anyone dreaming of taking offense. Suppose that tomorrow someone put certain canvases by Rembrandt or Velasquez back into the attic at the Louvre. What a furor! But if one should banish from our opera houses *Der Freischütz, Fidelio, Alceste, Armide, Iphigénie, Les Troyens*, etc., etc., who would take notice?[34]

Here again we have the suggestion that France treated its visual art collections much better than its musical works, casting aspersions on the French national character by noting that this type of egregious neglect took place "only in France." Maintaining these works in the standard repertoire—not simply bringing them out for special occasions every few decades—was absolutely essential to understanding music history. Notably, this was to be a universal narrative rather than a purely nationalist one; Dukas expanded his definition of classic works beyond the French repertoire (or even adopted French, in the case of *Don Juan*) to include two German works— Carl Maria von Weber's *Der Freischütz* and Beethoven's *Fidelio*—alongside works by Gluck and Berlioz.

Although Dukas's position is fairly unusual in its cosmopolitism, around 1900, more and more critics espoused similar views on the need for a reliable Operatic Museum. In 1898, the prominent daily newspaper *Le Figaro* ran a series of articles by various authors in which they discussed the role of the Opéra-Comique in French society. In his entry, the composer Gabriel Pierné brought up the Operatic Museum, combining the metaphor with a concrete example of a theater that was effectively putting the concept into action: "The Opéra-Comique must be a sort of museum for the operatic repertoire, like the Comédie-Française is for the dramatic repertoire; it would even be reasonable to augment it, drawing on more works by Lully, Rameau, Gluck, Mozart, Méhul, and Grétry."[35] The Comédie-Française, as a state-run theater—and one with a history as long and storied as the Opéra's—was a perfect counterpart to the Operatic Museum, an example of an institution that cared for its historical masterpieces in an appropriately reverential fashion. Referring to the Comédie-Française as a model for the Opéra-Comique, the Opéra, or both, was fairly common for fin-de-siècle critics, basically interchangeably with the Operatic Museum concept. In other words, rather than referring to the Louvre or a similar brick-and-mortar museum, they cited the abstract Theatrical Museum that the Comédie-Française represented.

Not surprisingly, the comparison crops up in Dukas's writings, this time surrounding the 1896 production of Gluck's *Orphée* at the Opéra-Comique. "Must [classic works] not alternate in an ongoing fashion with modern works," he asked, "and form the core of the repertoire of the Opéra and the Opéra-Comique, as one sees Racine, Corneille, and Molière alongside Dumas, d'Augier, and Pailleron at the Comédie Française?"[36] The artistic achievements of composers like Gluck were put alongside the Golden Age of French theater (a subject to which I return in chapter 6). Dukas was not alone in the comparison, which was remarkably long-lived. Gabriel Fauré—distinguished composer and director of the Paris Conservatoire—echoed Dukas almost verbatim in a review of Rameau's *Hippolyte et Aricie* at the Opéra in 1908, noting that the state-run theaters must produce classic works "just as the works of Corneille, Racine, and Molière are permanently in the repertoire of the Comédie-Française and the Odéon." Fauré continued with two pointed rhetorical questions that acknowledged the dependence of French identity on an understanding of its past: "Is equal treatment of our past glories not simple fairness? And would our sense of a unique national culture not have everything to gain?"[37] A shared cultural history is a large part of what bound together the "imagined political community" that *was* France, to use Benedict Anderson's famous term—and we must surely agree with Anderson when he observes that "museums, and the museumizing imagination, are both profoundly political."[38]

Thus far we have seen this "museumizing imagination," as we might describe the nationalist weaving of historical narratives from the museum objects displayed at the Opéra and Opéra-Comique, manifested mostly in the critical writings of fin-de-siècle composer-critics. Yet other aspects of French musical culture worked in a symbiotic relationship with the Operatic Museum, both benefiting from and contributing to its efforts. We might look to the concert series such as those I mentioned above, for example, which performed excerpts of these eighteenth-century operas in an effort to prepare audiences for their museum experiences. The rise of French musicology around 1900 presented another avenue for venerating the works in the Museum, while the displays at the Opéra and Opéra-Comique drew attention to scholarly studies of the works and their composers—a process of mutual validation that solidified narratives of the French operatic past. It should be no surprise that a number of French biographical and stylistic studies of Mozart, Gluck, and Rameau appeared in the fin de siècle, from many of the most notable musicologists of the time: Julien Tiersot, Henri Quittard, Louis Laloy, and Romain Rolland, just to mention a few of the names that we will encounter throughout the following chapters. As Pierre Bourdieu reminds us, "the discourse of celebration, notably the biography, also plays a determining role [in the creation of symbolic value] . . . the biography establishes the artist as a memorable character, worthy of historical account, much like statesmen and poets."[39]

Closely related to these musicological endeavors was the process of creating scholarly editions of the music that formed the Operatic Museum. French nationalist pride manifested itself in the form of new and lavish editions of Gluck's French operas and Rameau's complete works (to which I return in detail in chapters 5 and 8, respectively). These volumes were necessary preparations to the display of the composers' works in the Museum, particularly in Rameau's case—because without a usable edition, performances were difficult if not impossible. But the editions were also concretizations of the Operatic Museum displays, a corporeal incarnation of the inherently ephemeral museum experience. Many of the best-known French composers were involved; the Rameau Complete Edition, for example, was directed by Camille Saint-Saëns and featured editorial contributions from Paul Dukas, Claude Debussy, and Vincent d'Indy, among other mainstays of Parisian culture.

Composers—even those who typically had little interest in editions—were eager to get involved with the project because they understood its importance for the way that audiences understood the musical past, present, and future. These editions, like the Opéra itself, were monuments in many senses. They looked backward in time, of course, designed to glorify musical luminaries and the country that produced them, yet they also reminded audiences of the shared French history and culture that led to the present day. Just as important, they were warnings—to draw on "monere," the Latin root of "monument"—of the dangers of neglecting that culture in the future. The editions fed back into the Operatic Museum, supporting its mission both by providing the Opéra and Opéra-Comique (and other venues, for that matter) with performance materials and by convincing French citizens that it was their duty to support the Museum as an expression of their "unique national culture," to use Fauré's words.

In the most basic sense, the Operatic Museum was a shift in the repertoire of Paris's main opera houses, but such a description captures none of the museum's importance. The changing repertoire was both a causal factor and a reaction to a radical transformation of how and why theaters produced opera—and why audiences attended. Building the Operatic Museum was a task that occupied the whole of the musical world of fin-de-siècle Paris. It was a decades-long project involving countless performers, opera administrators, stage designers, conductors, composers, critics, scholars, and audience members. I do not claim that my understanding or depiction of the museum is comprehensive; a complete picture of this widespread phenomenon would be impossible in a volume twice the size of this one. In chapters that follow, however, I offer windows onto various aspects of the Operatic Museum and the "museumizing imagination" that surrounded it as manifested in the fin-de-siècle receptions of Mozart, Gluck, and Rameau. We turn first to Mozart—whose *Don Giovanni/Don Juan* was easily the eighteenth-century opera best known to French audiences. The process by which Mozart and his works were "museumized" highlights the Operatic Museum's capacity to shape new historical narratives, often with unexpected (and not always welcome) consequences.

Part One

Mozart

Chapter Two

Restorations

By 1875 Mozart held a unique position in the French operatic canon: the sole eighteenth-century composer whose works were regularly staged in Parisian opera houses. Even then, his fame rested largely on three operas: *Le Nozze di Figaro, Die Zauberflöte,* and most important, *Don Giovanni,* known as *Don Juan*—a work that attained a near-legendary quality in France over the course of the nineteenth century. After fifty years of uninterrupted success in France, it seemed that nothing could topple Mozart's position as the lone eighteenth-century figure in the upper echelon of the operatic canon. So secure was Mozart's status that in 1875, the critic Adolphe Jullien was bewildered by the lackluster early reception of Mozart's operas in France:

> At present, when admiration for *Don Juan* has become an article of faith in the musical religion, and when this opinion generally spells trouble for those who do not find this work to be one of the most dazzling manifestations of genius, it is strange to think back sometimes to when Mozart's works were first introduced in France, and to realize what a sad welcome they received.[1]

Around 1900, however, as critics and audiences gradually became more chauvinistic in their efforts to demonstrate France's great music history, Mozart's continued prominence at the Opéra and Opéra-Comique came into question. By 1904, musicologist Jean d'Udine told a story much different from Jullien's, and lamented that audiences had turned away from Mozart toward other composers, particularly Beethoven and Wagner:

> Until the last quarter of the nineteenth century, Mozart passed, in the opinion of the dilettantes, as the ruling genius of music, and, like Raphael in painting, his name became almost dogmatically a synonym for perfection, grace, an unsurpassable ideal.... The cult of Beethoven, followed by the cult of Wagner, would quickly shake this article of faith. In the face of the formidable worlds that these two belatedly recognized geniuses opened to lovers of great art, the musician of Salzburg was all but forgotten.[2]

Table 2.1. Major revivals of Mozart operas at the Opéra and Opéra-Comique, 1875–1918

Opera	Theater	Year
Don Juan	Opéra	1875
Les Noces de Figaro	Opéra-Comique	1886
Don Juan	Opéra	1887
La Flûte enchantée	Opéra-Comique	1893
Don Juan	Opéra	1896
Don Juan	Opéra-Comique	1896
Bastien et Bastienne	Opéra-Comique	1900
L'Enlèvement au sérail	Opéra	1903
Don Juan	Opéra	1904
Don Juan	Opéra-Comique	1904
La Flûte enchantée	Opéra-Comique	1909
Don Juan	Opéra-Comique	1912

There was a limit, it appears, to how much Germanic music could be tolerated in the nationalistic environment of fin-de-siècle France. With Beethoven's domination of the concert hall and, more important, Wagner's of the Opéra, maintaining another Germanic composer in the permanent repertoire came dangerously close to suggesting that France lacked capable composers.

After the 1890s, as Wagner's music became ubiquitous in Paris, performances of *Don Juan* decreased dramatically at the Opéra and Opéra-Comique. There were brief revivals at both theaters in 1904, a single revival at the latter in 1912, and then nothing until well after World War I (see table 2.1). Nor was *Don Juan* replaced by Mozart's other operas, as only isolated productions appeared during this time, and rarely to great acclaim. This chapter explores the dramatic shift in Mozart's popularity in the opera house, which was a reflection of changing perceptions about both the composer and the nature of his works.

After the stage is set with an overview of Mozart's French reception to 1875, I will focus on *Don Juan* at the fin de siècle, since for most of that time Mozart's success or failure at the opera house was directly tied to that work in particular. From there we can begin to unravel three underlying threads woven throughout critics' visions of Mozart's identity: the transition from the nineteenth-century perception of Mozart as a romantic composer to the twentieth-century view of him as classical figure, the conflict between viewing him as a universal composer versus a Germanic one, and gender issues of masculinity and femininity surrounding the composer and his works.

Adapting to Romanticism

The key to Mozart's ultimate success in nineteenth-century France lay in creating adaptations of his operas that would resonate with the aesthetic preferences of French audiences. The question was initially not one of authenticity, but rather of *whose* adaptation was the most entertaining, and put Mozart's music to the best use. Not surprisingly, the composer's reception became more positive as new adaptations gradually minimized his Germanic musical identity and stressed the (proto)romantic aspects of his works—or created romantic aspects where none existed before. Many of the issues that affected Mozart reception at the end of the nineteenth century mirrored the initial critical response to the composer in France. At both times, Mozart's Germanic identity proved to be a stumbling block for some critics, and the question of adaptation versus authenticity in his works was an oft-repeated chorus throughout the century. Thus, any close examination of Mozart's position fin de siècle must be grounded in at least a cursory understanding of how French critics and audiences arrived at that point. The topic of Mozart's French reception from his life until 1875 is broad, and could (and should) easily fill a volume. The section that follows is necessarily a broad overview, synthesizing some of the significant body of scholarship on Mozart in France.

From the beginning, Mozart's French fortunes rested almost entirely on his dramatic works. Yet, despite the prominence they would later achieve, the early French reception of his operas was not particularly auspicious. Most of the composer's mature operas appeared in Paris during the first decades of the century, but in an effort to make the operas more palatable to audiences accustomed to French works, they featured heavily adapted librettos, scores, or both.[3] The first Mozart opera to reach the Parisian stage was *Le nozze di Figaro* (1786), which was produced at the Opéra in 1793, only two years after the composer's death. Because the source of Lorenzo da Ponte's libretto was Pierre Beaumarchais's popular (and scandalous) play *Le Mariage de Figaro* (1778), *Figaro* was a natural choice for introducing Parisian audiences to Mozart's operas. To make the Beaumarchais-Mozart connection as clear as possible—and to avoid any accusations of bastardizing Beaumarchais's universally admired text—for the purpose of the 1793 Opéra production, the recitatives were removed and replaced by the *entire* spoken text of *Le Mariage de Figaro*, in addition to the standard translation of the arias into French and a host of other changes.[4] The end result was a hybrid that failed both dramatically and musically. The singers of the Opéra were untrained in spoken theater, which led to a butchering of Beaumarchais's verse, and to make matters worse the quantity was as much a problem as the quality. Many audience members understandably found that adding most of an opera to a full-length play was intolerable; one critic observed in the *Journal de Paris* that "the work has been found excessively long, and ... in the final acts the most beautiful pieces of music no longer produced any effect."[5] Despite these considerable limitations, Parisian audiences were at least exposed to Mozart's operatic works in French, and this production set the standard for the types of alterations to his music that would continue over the next decades.

Perhaps the most extensive revisions to a Mozart opera were made in 1801, when a version of *Die Zauberflöte* (1791) titled *Les Mystères d'Isis* was produced at the Opéra.[6] The plot of *Les Mystères* retained only a distant kinship to Emanuel Schikaneder's singspiel, expounding instead on the subtle Egyptian elements of the original, which were much *en vogue* in early nineteenth-century France.[7] The opera's score was almost as altered as its libretto; along with much of Mozart's original music it included a potpourri of selections from his other operas as well as works by Haydn. Despite—or perhaps because of—these significant changes, *Les Mystères* was quite successful, and continued to be performed (although later cut in length somewhat) until its final performance in 1827. "And frankly," wrote Adolphe Jullien in the fin de siècle, "it was about time."[8]

The string of Mozart premieres at the Opéra continued in 1805, with *Don Juan*.[9] As we might expect by this point, the Opéra's version was quite different from the *Don Giovanni* Mozart's audiences had seen in Prague or Vienna. The identities and personalities of the main characters were freely altered, and the music was "arranged" (quite drastically) by the well-known piano virtuoso Friedrich Kalkbrenner.[10] Jullien again provides us with some commentary on this production: "A single piece was left in its place—a single one—and that was the overture."[11] Critics initially had a mixed reaction to *Don Juan*, with some praising the production as a masterpiece and others complaining of "too much music" and disparaging the work as too German for French audiences.[12] It was not until several decades after this initial performance that the work began to hold the position it was to achieve later in the century.

Beginning in 1807, when *Le Nozze di Figaro* appeared at the Théâtre Italien, audiences began to have a chance to hear Mozart's operas in versions a bit closer to the originals. Although this production was still significantly adapted, it was nonetheless the least altered version available onstage in nineteenth-century Paris. The same is true of the theater's productions of *Così fan tutte* (1809), *Don Giovanni* (1811), and *La clemenza di Tito* (1816). Despite some favorable critical response—the critic Salgues, for example, wondered about the 1807 *Figaro* "How did this same work, put on some years ago at the Opéra, have so little success?"[13]—Parisian audiences by and large preferred the more characteristically French versions offered by the Opéra. An anonymous critic at the *Journal de l'Empire*, for example, complained that "numerous *opéras comiques* by Grétry, Sacchini's *La Colonie*, Piccini's *La Bonne Fille*, and even several of the comic operas put on at the théâtre de l'Impératrice [i.e., at the Théâtre-Italien] are superior to Mozart's *Figaro*, but the disciples of the German school will not even allow the comparison."[14] Significantly, aspects of this chauvinistic tone would reappear at the fin de siècle, as long-buried questions of Germanic national identity began to resurface. All controversy in the press aside, Jullien could write in the 1880s that the 1807 *Figaro* "definitively established the great composer's reputation in Paris."[15] An overstatement, perhaps, but it is clear from the reviews of the Théâtre-Italien's production of *Così fan tutte* (1790) in 1809 that the French opinion of Mozart as an opera composer was rising. One reviewer for the *Journal de l'Empire* wrote that "everything that Mozart wrote is sure to please in Paris: he is the fashionable musician now," and Salgues opined that "when one names Mozart, one immediately has the idea of everything that is the most perfect in music."[16]

Don Giovanni arrived the Théâtre-Italien in 1811, where it was directed by no less a figure than Gaspare Spontini. The performance was a combination of the Prague and Vienna versions of Mozart's work, but nonetheless remained far closer to the original libretto than did the Opéra's 1805 production.[17] Critics remained generally skeptical of the work. The conservative Julien-Louis Geoffroy, for one, was openly hostile to the production:

> It has been several years since *Don Juan*, translated into French, was produced at the Opéra; despite the vogue for Mozart, the effect was mediocre: the masterwork was admired while producing yawns, and quickly abandoned. Enthusiasts placed all the blame on the performance; they claimed that Mozart had been massacred; they cried sacrilege. Here is the same *Don Juan* put on in Italian at the Opéra-Buffa [Théâtre-Italien] by an excellent troupe; and boredom, the faithful companion of this masterwork, still insists on following it all the way to the theater where it ought to receive the most spectacular justice.[18]

Less vitriolic reviewers found merit in the opera's music, at least, though the libretto was largely maligned—one reviewer reported that "this opera's libretto is, like the majority of Italian productions in this genre, a network of bizarre actions that strain credibility: it is [Molière's] *Festin de Pierre*, not translated, but travestied."[19] Again, there is a nationalistic tinge to the commentary: the poor quality of da Ponte's libretto is contrasted with the perfection of Molière's treatment of the Don Juan legend.

To the list of Mozart operas performed at the Opéra and the Théâtre-Italien, one may add a few performances of Mozart operas given at the Théâtre-Royal de l'Odéon, which performed musical theater in the period from 1824 to 1828. In 1825, the Odéon put on a pasticcio of Mozart's operas, titled *Louis XII, ou La Route de Reims*, which contained music drawn from *La clemenza di Tito*, *Idomeneo*, and *Die Entführung aus dem Serail*—in short, from the operas that had received comparatively little exposure in Paris (although *Die Entführung* was produced in Paris in 1802 by a German troupe).[20] *Les Noces de Figaro* was "surprisingly successful" during the hot summer months of 1826, and *Don Juan* followed in 1827, only a few months before the Odéon's opera troupe disbanded. Both operas were given in translations by François-Henri-Joseph Blaze (known as Castil-Blaze), whose importance to French music criticism during this time period can hardly be overstated.

After the first few decades of the nineteenth century, Mozart's reception history in Paris would become largely synonymous with that of *Don Juan*, which developed over the following decades from being a reasonably successful opera with "too much music" to being a masterwork. By 1846, Gustave Flaubert could write that the "three most beautiful things God has made are the sea, *Hamlet*, and Mozart's *Don Juan*."[21] Through the rest of the century, it remained by far Mozart's most popular opera in Paris, as it was in the rest of Europe, as well. The first significant step down this path was likely the 1820 production at the Théâtre-Italien, which finally achieved the success that had eluded previous productions of Mozart's works.[22] The tenor Manuel Garcia took on the role of the Don (originally written for a baritone voice), to great critical acclaim; for example, the influential critic and author François-Joseph Fétis wrote in the *Revue musicale* that "Garcia shaped the title role in a way that will for a long time linger in the memories of the musicians as the example of perfection."[23] Afterward, *Don Giovanni* was produced nearly every year at the Théâtre-Italien, always in the same 1820 version, and for several decades the theater remained the best place to hear the opera in Paris.

Leaving aside the largely unremarkable 1827 production at the Odéon, the Théâtre-Italien held a monopoly on *Don Giovanni* until 1834, at which time the work appeared at the Opéra (again as *Don Juan*) after an absence of nearly thirty years. The managers of the Opéra no doubt hoped that the Théâtre-Italien had done their work for them by popularizing Mozart's work, and that consequently audiences would be receptive to hearing the now well-known work in their native tongue. In Katharine Ellis's words, however, the 1834 production was "a commercial and artistic failure of immense cultural significance."[24] For once, the libretto (a further modification of Castil-Blaze's 1820s adaptation) was not the problem. It incorporated the *Don Juan* interpretations of E. T. A. Hoffmann and Alfred de Musset, whose works on the subject of Don Juan proved influential throughout Europe, and probably as a result, the libretto met with general approval. The alterations to the score, however, did not fare so well. The lead role was given to the famous tenor Adolphe Nourrit, necessitating the transposition of much of the opera, and several scenes were added to the score, including the use of music from *Idomeneo* and the "Dies Irae" from the *Requiem* in the rewritten *scena ultima*.[25] The opera's constant repetition at the Théâtre-Italien over the decade and a half leading up to the 1834 version seems to have cemented a particular version—one fairly close to Mozart's own—of the score to *Don Giovanni* in the minds of Parisian operagoers (who conveniently forgot that Garcia, also a tenor, had sung the role in 1820). Deviations from the familiar version opera audiences had heard repeated over the preceding decades met with general outrage at the lack of "authenticity" that one could find at the Théâtre-Italien. The Opéra tried once more to revive the opera in 1841, with a baritone in the title role for the first time at the Opéra, but audiences still stubbornly refused to be wowed.[26] The Opéra then abandoned *Don Juan* for a quarter century, leaving Mozart to the other theaters, including the newly opened Théâtre-Lyrique.

This new arrival, helmed by director Léon Carvalho, produced several of Mozart's operas during its two-decade lifespan. In 1858 *Les Noces de Figaro* (in French) finally met with some degree of success in Paris outside the Théâtre-Italien.[27] A production of *Die Zauberflöte*, titled *La Flûte enchantée*, followed in 1865, with a libretto somewhat closer to the original than *Les Mystères d'Isis*, and was an enormous success for the theater.[28] These productions did much to popularize these non–*Don Juan* operas in Paris, mostly by walking a careful line between adapting them to French tastes while not going to the excesses seen earlier in the century, thus avoiding alienating either purists or more general audiences.

These productions aside, however, *Don Giovanni* maintained its reputation as Mozart's chief masterwork, a position that culminated in 1866, when the opera was produced more or less simultaneously in three prominent operatic venues: the Opéra, the Théâtre-Italien, and the Théâtre-Lyrique—an event that Jullien referred to in retrospect as the "grand tournoi musical."[29] For the first time, the Opéra came out on top of its perennial quarrel with the Théâtre-Italien, thanks to the near-unanimous public acclaim of baritone Jean-Baptiste Faure, who played the title character at the Opéra, a role he continued to perform with great success for more than a decade. As Pauline Girard points out, Manuel Garcia ceased to be the "Don Juan de référence," and the Opéra's version began to be the definitive *Don Juan*.[30] In fact, for some critics the real struggle seems to have been between the two French-langauge productions (at the Opéra and the Théâtre-Lyrique), in which the victory seems to have been divided. According to critic Gustave Bertrand, for example: "Since it is a battle—a duel—who holds the advantage? If all's well that ends well, the Opéra wins with the admirable final scene. But for the entire first half of the evening— and even after—general agreement accords the victory to the Théâtre-Lyrique."[31] Bertrand does go on, however, to give high praise to Faure, "who sings *Don Juan* like no one else, taking the role with authority, distinction, and elegance."[32]

Though they were not the last revivals of Mozart operas before 1875, the 1866 productions of *Don Giovanni* are a fitting end to the overview of the composer's early nineteenth-century reception in Paris. After the slow beginnings around the turn of the century, Mozart began a meteoric rise in popularity in the 1820s that receded only in the final decades of the century. One of the major factors that supported the rise of *Don Giovanni* and its composer in French consciousness in the nineteenth century was the perception of the opera as being somehow romantic in sentiment. Certainly the widespread French popularity of E. T. A. Hoffmann's writings about the opera helped fuel the blaze of interest in the work, and, closer to home, the writings of Fétis in the *Revue musicale* did the same.[33] In fact, the romanticization of Mozart had begun in the 1810s, with Stendhal's emphasis on Mozart's dark and brooding musical qualities in his *Lettres écrites de Vienne* (1814) and the *Vies de Haydn, de Mozart et de Métastase* (1817).[34] The fact that *Don Giovanni* was perceived as a romantic, and thus, modern work allowed it to escape the fate that befell most other eighteenth-century works during the following century. Not only did it become a canonic work in the sense that it was preserved and venerated for historical reasons, but its extreme popularity remained essentially unabated from 1820 to nearly the end of the century, which is more than one can say about any other eighteenth-century opera in Paris.

Mozart's nationality makes this unique position all the more surprising, particularly given that some early critics were opposed to the composer's Germanic musical character. By the midcentury, though, French critics at least could speak of "our *Don Juan*," suggesting that not only had the work become de-Germanized, but ownership of it had somehow been transferred, mirabile dictu, to France. In one sense, at least, the physical incarnation of the opera did reside in Paris. In 1855, the soprano Pauline Viardot purchased the autograph manuscript of the work and brought it to France. Viardot became, in fact, something like the priestess of a Mozart "cult," presiding over the holy relic of the autograph—complete with reliquary case—housed in what amounts to a shrine in her Paris home.[35] The fact that such a cult emerged around not just a composer, but a specific work, highlights the unusual place that *Don Giovanni* and its composer occupied in Parisian society by the mid-nineteenth century. During much of the last half of the century, the cultural ubiquity of *Don Juan/Don Giovanni* led to its being conceived—at least in France—as French cultural property, if not precisely as a French work. it was this interpretation of Mozart and his operas that would be challenged in the years after 1875. By this time, the cosmopolitan atmosphere of Parisian artistic life had begun, in Anselm Gerhard's somewhat hyperbolic words, a "slow decline toward a poorly disguised provincialism," eventually leading to a reevaluation of the prominence that Mozart should enjoy in Paris.[36]

Romantic to Classical: *Don Juan* After 1875

The decades around 1900 saw a fundamental shift in the way that both critics and audiences perceived Mozart and his operas. For most of the nineteenth century, the composer was largely seen as a romantic (that is, up to date) figure, but during the fin de siècle, Mozart gradually evolved into a classical composer, and as such his works demanded a kind of "authenticity" in performance that was unnecessary for contemporary works. This transition is most visible in the changing attitudes toward *Don Juan*. As table 2.1 demonstrates, despite a decline in the number of productions during the first years of the twentieth century, *Don Juan* appeared substantially more often than any of Mozart's other works. This popularity resulted mostly from the opera's historical connection with French audiences. The oft-reworked 1822 Castil-Blaze version incorporated significant elements of Molière's *Dom Juan* (1665), leading to a kind of intellectual ownership of the work on behalf of France.[37] Though this version was superseded by the 1834 *Don Juan* created by Henri Blaze de Bury (Castil-Blaze's son) and Emile Deschamps, the connection between Mozart's opera and Molière lingered, no doubt luring critics and audience members into a kind of authorial slippage in which *Don Juan* became an inherently French opera. Even as late as 1925, in Reynaldo Hahn's operetta *Mozart* (libretto by Sacha Guitry), the titular composer specifically claims that he had read Molière's *Dom Juan* while in Paris (in 1778) and had been inspired by the play to compose an opera on the subject.

This intellectual lineage, combined with both near-constant performances of *Don Juan* in Paris and the sense of physical possession of the opera that Viardot's "cult" of the autograph score provided, encouraged French audiences to perceive *Don Giovanni* as their own cultural property. The critic Paul Bernard, for example, in response to Wagner's invasion of the Opéra in 1861, contrasted *Tannhäuser* with "our [French] masterworks... our *Guillaume Tell*, our *Don Juan*, our *Lucie*, our *Juive*, and our *Huguenots*."[38] Of these "French" masterpieces, only Halévy's *La*

Juive was written by an unquestionably French composer. In the case of Rossini's *Guillaume Tell*, Donizetti's *Lucia di Lammermoor*, and Meyerbeer's *Les Huguenots*, their Frenchness seems to result from being composed or adapted by the composer for French audiences. But *Don Juan* still does not fit. Mozart certainly had no hand in the sweeping changes made to the work for performance in Paris. In the minds of critics and audiences, however, *Don Juan* had become a French opera by the 1860s.

Because of this position as a "French" work, *Don Juan* enjoyed a unique position after 1875. While nearly all Mozart's other works receded into the background of Parisian operatic life, *Don Juan* continued to attract audiences for decades after the Franco-Prussian War. In 1875, the opera was performed as part of the inaugural season at the Palais Garnier, the new home of the Opéra; it was, in fact, the only non-French opera produced that season. Jullien later reported that Émile Perrin, the Opéra director, initially intended to perform *Don Juan* at the opening gala on January 5, but that he had been overruled for nationalist reasons—a hint, perhaps, of the simmering uneasiness about having a Germanic composer in such a lofty canonic position.[39] When the opera did appear onstage, the music itself seems to have taken a backseat to the opportunity it created for spectacle in the new theater. As François de Lagenevais (a pseudonym for Henri Blaze de Bury), for example, noted in the *Revue musicale* of the opera's ball scene:

> As for the party at Don Juan's home, with its masked dances, its new costumes from the old Comédie Italienne, its ballets, parading and prancing with the driving rhythm of the Turkish march amid a flood of light and in the immense space of the theater, one cannot imagine such a spectacle—"blinding" does not do it justice; it is above all highly entertaining to see the sparkling of the fabrics, the picturesque quality and variety of the groups [on stage].[40]

Other critics took a similar approach in their own reviews. H. Moreno (a pseudonym for Henri Heugel), for example, spent several long paragraphs in *Le Ménestrel* discussing the elaborate staging, which he found to be a "splendid spectacle."[41] This emphasis on the visual aspects of the evening rather than on Mozart's music essentially allowed critics to avoid addressing the work itself, or its composer, in the postwar environment of the 1870s, while at the same time celebrating French stagecraft.

In 1887, on the centenary of the Prague premiere of *Don Giovanni*, Moreno again had occasion to write about *Don Juan* in *Le Ménestrel*. This time, he was not so pleased with the work's changing fortunes: "My God, how the Opéra has neglected this incomparable masterwork for some years now. . . . It was still loved, without doubt, but with a purely platonic love. . . . It was a respected ancestor, to whom one gave the best seat . . . in the library, but for whom one didn't bother to light the lamps."[42] The 1887 *Don Juan* was a disappointment to critics despite its aims to rectify this neglect, mostly because of a perceived miscasting. The general consensus was that Jean Lassalle's performance of the title role was simply not up to the standards set by Faure in decades past. Moreno's hopes that the Opéra could rekindle audiences' appreciation for Mozart were frustrated, and he placed the blame squarely on the directors and performers of the theater: "The Parisian celebration of the centenary of *Don Juan* has been all it could be, given the current resources [i.e., singers] of the Académie nationale de musique: nothing but an agreeable parody of Mozart's masterpiece. The directors of the Opéra certainly have a unique way of *celebrating* people; it's a good thing the dead don't leave their tombs!"[43] For Moreno, it was unthinkable that the work itself could be at fault for the public's lukewarm reception. Any deficiency had to be the result of poor singers and incompetent direction. Other critics singled out the singers' difficulty with Mozart's music, as well. Johannès Weber began the final paragraph of his review in *Le Temps* with "One can anticipate what I am forced to say about the performance" before turning to the numerous faults of individual singers, suggesting that the poor quality was common knowledge.[44] Weber seems almost hesitant to mention the performance at all, as though a bad performance of *Don Juan* at the Opéra was an embarrassment to France.

The 1890s proved to be a more successful decade for Mozart's opera in Paris. One marker of this success came in 1890, when Charles Gounod published an analysis of the opera, *Le Don Juan de Mozart*, which is essentially an extended celebration of the perfect opera and its composer. "There are in history certain men," Gounod wrote in his preface, "who seem destined to mark, in their own sphere, a pinnacle beyond which it is impossible to advance. . . . Mozart is one of these men; *Don Juan* is such a pinnacle."[45] Gounod seems determined to preserve the romantic vision of the "divine Mozart," capable of musical miracles unattained since his death. Nearly every page of Gounod's text is aimed at reiterating this message, reminding the reader at every opportunity of Mozart's unique musical prowess. In the midst of a brief discussion of Zerlina's "Pace, pace, o vita mia," for example, Gounod breaks into a seemingly unprovoked apostrophe to the composer: "Mozart, divine Mozart! To know thee is to worship thee. Thou art the personification of perpetual truth, perfect beauty, inexhaustible charm; always profound, yet always clear; combining the entire knowledge of humanity with the simplicity of childhood! Thou hast experienced all things, and expressed them in a musical language that has never been, and never will be, surpassed."[46] Gounod's book exudes a desperate fervency, as though he felt Mozart's position in the operatic canon threatened and had to make some effort to restore him to his rightful place. Jullien certainly sensed Gounod's desperation, and wasted no time in suggesting in 1890 that "Gounod, disheartened to see that the journals are silent about him whereas they still speak continually about Richard Wagner, calls Mozart to the rescue."[47]

The Wagnerian Jullien (also a Mozart lover, as we have already seen) felt that Gounod misused the eighteenth-century composer in an attempt to claim a compositional lineage and thus validate his own aesthetic position as opposed to Wagner's. For Jullien, Gounod's absolute faith in the composer of *Don Juan* was misplaced; a more tempered and less zealous "worship" of Mozart was required. For this reason, Jullien's ultimate opinion of Gounod's work was anything but positive: "Conclusion: this book, with its infantile rhetoric and alleged explanations, at which Mozart himself would be appalled, is of no use whatsoever, either to those who admire *Don Juan* and who have a much less biased concept of the work, or to those who have no taste for it at all and for whom this interminable exegesis instead separates them even further from the master."[48] Gounod's tenacious hold on the romantic Don Giovanni (both the character and the work) is illustrative. If *Don Juan* lost its position as the paragon of romantic operatic perfection, it would be subjected to the same types of criticism leveled at other eighteenth-century works—old-fashioned, boring, irrelevant—a fate Gounod could not allow. Jullien's barbs also likely had some truth in them: Gounod was indeed attempting to position himself as Mozart's heir.[49] Such a supposition is supported by, for example, an 1879 portrait of Gounod by Élie Delaunay in which the composer appears almost in a trance, protectively clutching a score of Mozart's opera to his breast as though it were a religious icon. The portrait was widely disseminated in journals and books—see the cover of the journal *Paris illustré* in figure 2.1, for example—suggesting that Gounod's reputation as defender and descendant of Mozart was well established in French musical culture. Steven Huebner has pointed out that during this time Gounod "brandished *Don Giovanni* as a sword and shield to combat *wagnérisme*," suggesting that he drew a chronological line from Mozart's opera to himself and Saint-Saëns, who followed the true path of operatic enlightenment.[50] If Gounod was Mozart's true heir (or thought he was), then any challenge to *Don Juan* was a challenge to Gounod's own dominant position on the fin-de-siècle stage. Holding tenaciously to the romantic vision of Mozart was thus indirectly an effort to retain the primacy of Gounod's romantic aesthetic. In other words, the heir to a romantic Mozart would be a romantic composer like Gounod, whereas a classical composer would require a classical heir.

Luckily for Gounod, by 1896 Mozart's position looked somewhat improved. After nearly a decade away from the Paris stages, *Don Juan* was produced at both the Opéra and the Opéra-Comique in the same month, with no significant alterations to the French version of the work with which

Figure 2.1. *Paris illustré*, October 29, 1887. Cover after an 1879 portrait of Gounod by Élie Delaunay.

audiences were familiar. The work's unusually long absence was noted by critics, some of whom argued that the opera houses were irresponsible in their treatment of Mozart and other classical composers. As we will recall from the previous chapter, Paul Dukas was among the most vociferous of these:

> It has already been several years since we have seen *Don Juan*. It is, perhaps, only in France that we could have these long absences of musical masterworks without anyone dreaming of taking offense. Suppose that tomorrow someone put certain canvases by Rembrandt or Velasquez back into the attic at the Louvre. What a furor! But if one should banish from our opera houses *Der Freischütz, Fidelio, Alceste, Armide, Iphigénie, Les Troyens*, etc., etc., who would take notice? *Don Juan* was one of these ostracized scores. It will be restored to its rank and no one will complain about it. And we even have two *Don Juans* in place of one, with the Opéra and the Opéra-Comique competing for the glory of performing for us this masterwork by Mozart, who must without doubt be quite dumbfounded with this resurgence of enthusiasm. This is the way of the world: old or young, dead or alive, one never performs you unless one plays you too much.[51]

At this point, echoes of the Operatic Museum begin to come into focus. Like other critics we have seen (see chapter 1), Dukas compares the opera houses to the Louvre, with works by Mozart, Gluck, Weber, and Berlioz as metaphorical exhibits akin to Rembrandt or Velazquez. The idea that these musical works needed to be produced not only once every few decades but on a kind of rotating permanent display was rapidly gaining ground around 1900. Dukas's review also reveals a subtle appeal to nationalism when he chastises French theaters for being the only ones to neglect great masterworks in this fashion. This mentality, in which respect for classical composers became an international competition, came into play in particular with regard to Rameau, as we will see in part 3 of this book.

Dukas's wish for a renewed interest in Mozart was granted, a fact that did not go unremarked by other critics. M.-P. Pascal-Estienne, writing in *L'Europe artiste*, certainly noticed something brewing: "Mozart is played, sung, and praised in Paris at the end of 1896.... Mozart is in relief, and we take the opportunity to offer him our own homage in our columns."[52] The unusual double production of 1896 was encouraged by both the popularity of Gounod's monograph and the success of Gluck's *Orphée et Eurydice* at the Opéra-Comique earlier that year (see part 2), which demonstrated the possibilities of eighteenth-century opera on the modern stage. Both *Don Juan* productions were received with more enthusiasm than any production of the opera since the 1860s. Dukas, at least, was hopeful that the performances signaled a more permanent position for Mozart (and other eighteenth-century composers) on Parisian stages:

> We know that the most authentic musical masterpieces are not performed as routinely in our theaters as one might suppose; they are subjected to eclipses, the frequency of which is deplorable. The revival of Gluck's *Orphée* was a resounding event last season, and the simultaneous performance Mozart's *Don Juan* at the Opéra and the Opéra-Comique at the beginning of the present season has taken on an importance that calls attention to the offhand manner with which the classical masters are treated; must their fundamental works always leave the stage for such a long time? Is it acceptable for them to retake their place there about every ten years for a series of several performances, after which nothing more is said of them? Must they not alternate in an ongoing fashion with modern works and form the core of the repertoire of the Opéra and the Opéra-Comique, as one sees Racine, Corneille, and Molière alongside Dumas, d'Augier, and Pailleron at the Comédie Française?[53]

These attitudes are revealing. Dukas returns to the Operatic Museum, but from a different perspective, noting that the stage of the Comédie Française was far ahead of the opera houses in terms of respecting older repertoire. In his vision, shared by many critics, *Don Juan* would never be too far from performance, but would enter into a dialogue with modern works. This expansion, or perhaps revision, of the canon created a museum gallery of sorts, the purpose of which would be to establish music-historical narratives. Similar claims would be put forward over the course of the fin de siècle on behalf of Gluck and Rameau (see parts 2 and 3), always with this same educational goal in mind. Dukas's aims in this regard were not, of course, entirely altruistic; he, like many other French composers of his time, seems to have felt that his musical style had a special kinship with classical values and forms.[54] Presenting Mozart's operas more regularly was a way of highlighting this connection, thus endorsing by association Dukas's own aesthetic.

Dukas also highlights changing perspectives on the modernity of *Don Juan*. Returning for a moment to Paul Bernard's list of French masterworks, which included "our *Guillaume Tell*, our *Don Juan*, our *Lucie*, our *Juive*, and our *Huguenots*," it is clear that Bernard perceived *Don Juan* as a fundamentally nineteenth-century work, placing Mozart alongside Rossini, Donizetti, and Meyerbeer in the pantheon of romantic composers. By 1896, however, Dukas unequivocally identifies Mozart as a classical composer—he had, in short, transitioned from a composer of the nineteenth to one of the eighteenth century, at least for some critics. This change in perception carried with it a large amount of baggage. Nineteenth-century works could be treated with some flexibility; they were, after all, modern, and could be altered with impunity for the needs of each production. Classical works, however, as befitting their status as "museum pieces," required a certain degree of "authenticity" in performance.

Yet, ideas of what an "authentic" production might entail were anything but clear. The 1887 production—the centenary of the opera's Prague premiere—had purported to be an "authentic" presentation of the score, although a version of Castil-Blaze's translation of the libretto was still in use.[55] The Wagnerian critic and Mozart biographer Victor Wilder took issue with this version's claim to authenticity, wryly noting in *Gil Blas*:

> Except for the aria *Ah! fuggi traditore*, replaced by a different aria that was written for the Vienna Elvira; except for Don Juan's aria (*Metà di voi*), cut as if useless; except for Leporello's (*Ah! pieta, Signori*), crossed out as if making the opera too long; except for a large ballet, constructed from bits and pieces, introduced forcibly into the first finale; except for a tenor aria (*Dalla sua pace*), transformed into a clarinet aria to accompany the raising of the curtain; except for the denouement, which has been changed; except for the original recitatives, replaced by Castil-Blaze's; except finally for some other modifications, all of little importance; the score is now entirely intact.[56]

Clearly Wilder felt that the Opéra's "authentic" production wrought havoc with Mozart's original score, a feeling shared by a number of critics in the following decades.[57] Even as early as 1875, a few heretical critics began to suggest that perhaps the Opéra should turn to the original Italian version of Mozart's opera rather than persisting in French adaptations. In response, Moreno felt compelled to outline the reasons in favor of the Opéra's decision to perform the nineteenth-century French adaptation:

> Some downhearted spirits still yet do not find at the French Opéra their Italian *Don Juan*. They add that the work has become too large, too important, too pretentious, that the tempos are too grand in it, too slow, and that the joviality, the spirit, and the verve have finally disappeared in Mozart's masterwork as it is performed at our grand Opéra.
>
> It is evident that in changing the setting [i.e., the theater] of Mozart's sublime score, one must enlarge the design—but are we quite sure that the style of *Don Juan* is not, on the contrary, more at ease in the grand setting of the Opéra? I would willingly wager that it is. It is not that I approve, in principle, of the Opéra's regrettable tendencies to slow down indefinitely the recitatives and most of the numbers in our operatic masterworks, but I am inclined to believe that, apart from this just reproach—applicable to the entire repertoire at the Opéra—the score

of *Don Juan* would suffer from being interpreted in the Italian version on our premiere operatic stage. That is at least my humble opinion.[58]

Moreno seems to argue that the grand stage of the new Opéra, built for the huge forces of grand opera, demanded an equally large interpretation of Mozart's work—and one that reflected an appropriately romantic sense of gravitas. The nineteenth-century *Don Juan* was not only acceptable—it was to be preferable to the "authentic" Italian version. The idea that the Opéra could simply stop performing *Don Juan* in its French form is unsupportable to Moreno. Instead, the ever-flexible masterwork had to adapt to the time and place (i.e., French) conditions in which it found itself.

Critics of later decades rejected this line of reasoning. In an 1894 article titled "Charles Gounod and Mozart's *Don Juan*," Camille Saint-Saëns encouraged even those who believed themselves quite familiar with the opera to read Gounod's text: "Most of those people who think they know *Don Juan*, from having gone through it rapidly or heard it at the Opéra—where it is split up into five Acts, defiled by the translation and Castil-Blaze's sacrilegious alterations and even additions, and performed in that vast building so unsuited to either the delicate orchestra or to the subject-matter—are in reality completely ignorant of it."[59] Ironically, Saint-Saëns suggested that those who sought to learn more about the "authentic" version of Mozart's opera should turn to his mentor, Gounod, who (while acknowledging the differences between the Italian and French versions) maintained a staunchly nineteenth-century perspective on *Don Juan*. Many critics and audience members joined Saint-Saëns in lambasting the productions at the Opéra. Martine Kahane has pointed out that the 1896 "dueling" productions at the Opéra and Opéra-Comique resulted in a "pressing demand from music lovers for another type of production, conforming to the original version."[60]

A few years later, the composer and pedagogue Gabriel Fauré emerged as one of the leading critical voices in favor of doing away with the overblown romantic Mozart. He felt that the 1903 concert performances of *Don Juan* that Reynaldo Hahn organized at the Nouveau Théâtre offered a refreshing change from the Opéra: "the performance was alert, lighthearted, tender, moving, and dramatic, but totally devoid of the unwarranted tone of solemnity that normally weighs down this masterpiece under the pretext of better honoring it."[61] For Fauré, Hahn's production—which lasted only three performances—was the exception rather than the rule. Normally, Fauré implies, the work was staged in an unsatisfactorily romanticized, and thus inauthentic, fashion. To a certain extent, Fauré's perspective could be reconciled with Moreno's: the Nouveau Théâtre was a much smaller stage, with a smaller audience, allowing (according to Moreno's standards) a more intimate, classical staging than did the Opéra's cavernous hall.

The following year, Fauré was the only major critic to dwell at any length on the revivals of *Don Juan* at the Opéra and Opéra-Comique, which seem to have been in essence replicas of the 1896 productions. *Le Ménestrel*, for example, which usually covered Mozart operas in some depth, published only brief "nouvelles"—cast lists and such—on the 1904 productions. Similarly, the popular music journal *Musica*, usually keen to print production stills of the famous singers, published only a brief article on famous Don Juans at the Opéra.[62] In short, the Opéra and the Opéra-Comique were content to rely on the nineteenth-century version of *Don Juan* to which audiences had become accustomed, and the critics barely took note. Fauré, however, seized the opportunity to loudly complain again about the production style at the Opéra:

> The Opéra took up *Don Juan* again last night, which is to say a *Don Juan* unique to the Académie nationale de musique that unfortunately differs from *Don Giovanni* . . . on a number of points besides the replacement of the Italian text with a French one. It is an enlarged *Don Juan* because it was necessary for it to take up the entire evening, and it is rendered solemn because for a long time we have noted a propensity to envelop masterworks in a pomp that they do not in the least demand.
>
> To enumerate the travesties to which Mozart's *Don Giovanni* has been subjected would take too long. To research the multiple causes of these travesties would lead to conclusions unflattering to our [national] taste.[63]

Fauré lamented the "travesties" that had been inflicted on Mozart's original score at the Opéra, but he did not suggest that the theater was running contrary to popular opinion by doing so. Rather, he takes aim squarely at the preferences of French audiences, even going so far as to suggest that the continued mistreatment of Mozart at the national opera theater was a bad reflection on the nation's musical taste. A week later, the critic found the production at the Opéra-Comique to be a marginal improvement, but only because of the smaller size of the hall.[64] The main criticism for Fauré still seems to have been the "French" adaptation of Mozart's opera, a problem that could be rectified only by reverting entirely back to the original, "authentic" version. Audiences could not continue to adapt these masterworks to their own whims, but must learn to respect and admire them in their original, natural, forms.

Fauré's highly public position on the necessity for restoring classical Mozart is not surprising. Like Gounod, Fauré was (intentionally or not) emphasizing a historical narrative that would place him as the logical successor of Mozart. His career was, in fact, shaped to a large extent through his understanding and advocacy of eighteenth-century music. He attended the École Niedermeyer, which required extensive study of the classics, and as director of the Conservatoire he instituted reforms that mandated similar study.⁶⁵ As a composer, Fauré was heavily influenced by eighteenth-century musical techniques, and in general a deeply classical aesthetic ideology. His settings of Verlaine's "Fêtes galantes" reflect the classical idyll as depicted by the painter Jean-Antoine Watteau's renderings of eighteenth-century courtly life (see fig. 2.2). Similarly, the *Masques et bergamasques* (Op. 112, 1919) included modern versions of eighteenth-century dances (minuet and gavotte), and Fauré himself described these dances as being akin to Watteau's paintings.⁶⁶ Although these paintings were produced three-quarters of a century before Mozart's operas, Fauré's use of them nonetheless demonstrates his willingness to accept eighteenth-century works as artistic influences, and, consequently, to position himself as an extension of the classical environment from which they emerged. At least a few others made connections between the *Masques et Bergamasques* and Mozart: Fauré reported in a letter that "Reynaldo Hahn says it [the work] is as if Mozart had *imitated* Fauré! It's a funny idea, but not in the least banal!"⁶⁷ Fauré's self-positioning as the descendant of an eighteenth-century artistic tradition—one that encompassed Mozart as well as earlier figures—created for him a situation analogous to Gounod's. But while Gounod positioned Mozart firmly as a nineteenth-century composer in order to maintain his own status as an heir to the great composer, Fauré was required to return Mozart to the eighteenth century in order to accomplish the same task. For the (neo)classical Fauré to connect himself with the Mozartean eighteenth century, Mozart himself had to throw off his romantic trappings and enter the classical realm populated by artists like Watteau.

Eventually, Fauré's opinions began to spread, and less than a decade later the Opéra-Comique, if not yet the Opéra, could acknowledge the need for a new classical interpretation of the opera. The Opéra-Comique director, Albert Carré, was a major proponent of returning eighteenth-century operas to modern stages in something closer to their original forms to which French audiences were accustomed. He played a major role in the Gluck revival as well as in Mozart's changing fortunes. In 1906, in response to a small Mozart festival organized by Hahn, the critic Jean Chantavoine opined: "I hope above all that this demonstration [the Mozart Festival] piques the zeal of Albert Carré, who would benefit by replacing in his repertoire *Le Domino noir* [by Auber] with *Don Juan*, *Mignon* [by Thomas] with *Les Noces*, *Mireille* [by Gounod] with *La Flûte enchantée*, *Les Dragons de Villars* [by Maillart] with *La Flûte enchantée*, and *Fra Diavolo* [by Auber] with *Così fan tutti*."⁶⁸ Chantavoine, in short, wanted to replace the Opéra-Comique's traditional nineteenth-century repertoire with eighteenth-century works by Mozart, paradoxically updating the selection by pushing it further back chronologically.

Figure 2.2. Jean-Antoine Watteau, *The French Comedians* (1721–22). © The Metropolitan Museum of Art.

To a certain extent, this transition was precisely what happened. In 1912, thanks largely to the combined efforts of Hahn and Carré, the Opéra-Comique produced a new version of *Don Juan*, closer to the original than anything seen in Paris (except at the Théâtre-Italien in the nineteenth century). The libretto, although still in French, was retranslated by the dramatist and librettist Paul Ferrier into a form substantially closer to da Ponte's, and the score was similarly adjusted to reflect Mozart's original. Hahn restored the opera's recitatives (which were accompanied at the piano) and original structure (two acts, rather than the five that had become traditional in France), and also made a number of other musical alterations to further align the opera with Mozart's score, including, in Carré's words, "an orchestra reduced to the same proportions as [the one] Mozart conducted in Prague on October 29, 1787."[69] This production was not the first example of a Mozart "restoration" at the Opéra-Comique. As we will explore in detail in the following chapter, the theater had staged *The Magic Flute* in 1909 with a much-touted "authentic" translation of the libretto for the first time in France. The relative success of the *Magic Flute* in a classical version demonstrated to Carré that *Don Juan* might be equally, if not more, successful. Writing years later, Carré reminisced on the importance and lasting effects of his 1912 production:

> Three years [after *The Magic Flute* production], *Don Juan* was presented for the first time in Paris complete, in its original form. . . .
> The Opéra presented *Don Juan* again in this form in 1934, but the author of that new version, Adolphe Boschot, proclaimed that this version was the first complete restoration of the work in France. I was quite obliged to refute this claim, especially because in 1928 I had restaged the *Don Juan* from the Opéra-Comique to great success at the Conservatoire, with Henri Rabaud conducting the orchestra.[70]

In Carré's version of events—spoken from the perspective of looking back decades later—the Opéra-Comique had been more than twenty years ahead of the Opéra in terms of staging eighteenth-century works in an "authentic" way, as part of the Operatic Museum.

Carré was certainly not the only one to view the 1912 *Don Juan* as a major milestone in the opera's French reception, with enormous artistic issues at stake. Could modern critics and audiences, so used to the romantic vision of the opera and its composer, understand and appreciate an "eighteenth-century" *Don Juan*? Some critics, notably Arthur Pougin of *Le Ménestrel*, were skeptical, particularly regarding the dramatic validity of the newly restored finale:

> Among the innovations—or restitutions, if you wish—there is one that I do not support at all: it consists of, after Don Juan's *foudroiement*, all the characters of the drama who had disappeared for a long while returning to the stage, and they suddenly sing a final ensemble that has nothing to do with a suitably completed plot. This recalls the "couplet au public" that once served as a sort of moral in old vaudevilles, and, not to upset the memory of da Ponte and Mozart, it is perfectly ridiculous from a dramatic point of view. Molière would never have had such a burlesque idea.[71]

For Pougin, the restoration (a term he only grudgingly applies) of the final scene renders the opera too antiquated, leaving it ill-equipped to support comparison with modern operas. Again we see the implicit comparison to Molière's *Dom Juan, ou le Festin de pierre*, a similarity that had helped Mozart gain traction with French audiences—recall that aspects of the seventeenth-century play had been incorporated into Castil-Blaze's *Don Juan* adaptation. Rather than making a link to facilitate the French "ownership" of the opera, however, in Pougin's review the comparison accomplishes the opposite effect: separating *Don Juan* from the French tradition. Stripping away the French romanticism that da Ponte and Mozart's opera had accumulated at the Opéra and Opéra-Comique also removed the "Frenchness" that had been a crucial aspect of the work's reception since the mid-nineteenth century.

The influential Wagnerian and symbolist author Téodor de Wyzewa—who also wrote a monumental Mozart biography—penned a particularly enlightening review of the 1912 production in *La Revue musicale S.I.M.*, revealing the extent to which many attitudes toward Mozart changed after the turn of the century. De Wyzewa began by thanking Carré and Hahn for providing a "faithful resurrection of Mozart's work." After listing a few quibbles with the production, he then turns to the substantial benefits it provided to French audiences:

> What are these slight imperfections in comparison to the enormous number of new things—or rather happily renewed after the original score—that we see thanks to the providential "Mozartian" collaboration of R. Hahn and Albert Carré? An orchestra reduced to its natural proportions, the last scenes of the second finale restored to life after more than a century of being completely abandoned ... the original division into two acts scrupulously maintained (at least in the program and in theory), and the installation of three small "real" orchestras in the middle of the dancers during the first finale; many true victories have been won over a tradition that is most often foolish, without counting twenty other victories, less apparent, perhaps, but still better for deliciously touching every concerned soul with the pure and subtle perfume of Mozart's genius. I will add that, to say nothing of the excellent behavior of the orchestra under Hahn's personal direction, the interpretation of the roles attests to a considerable progress from those we have been accustomed to at the same theater in the past.[72]

For de Wyzewa, the 1912 *Don Juan* was clearly revelatory—a substantial step forward from the previous productions at the Opéra or Opéra-Comique. The score and libretto were better organized, and the performers under Hahn's direction played in a style more suited to Mozart's music. Given this glowing review, we might assume that de Wyzewa saw in this production a new future for Mozart's opera in Paris—something akin to the kind of Operatic Museum that Dukas had been writing about for almost a decade.

Despite these ringing endorsements of the Opéra-Comique's efforts, however, de Wyzewa's ultimate assessment of the production was fairly bleak. Because this passage is so clearly indicative of the critical ambivalence toward the Operatic Museum, and the conflict between practical and idealist positions, it is worth quoting at some length:

If someone asked me for my opinion on the practical results and the future possibilities for this admirable reprise of *Don Juan*, I would express the most pessimistic prognosis. Because I am all but certain that, once again, Mozart's masterwork is going to disappear quickly from the stage of the Opéra-Comique—just as *La Flûte enchantée* did last year. Again, the public will soon grow tired of *Don Juan*, which will confirm the directors' totally erroneous belief that there is no life possible in our country for Mozart's dramatic genius. And why? Because *Don Juan*, with all its immortal beauty, is more than a century old, and so cannot be presented in the same fashion as a work written today. . . .

Here is what our musical-theater directors seem not to want to understand, much to the detriment of their own efforts and of the glory of the old masters! Thus, *Don Juan*, on the poster, consists of only two acts: in reality, it condemns us to suffer, in addition to one regular entr'acte, a half-dozen slightly shorter entr'actes, which are quite tedious for listeners who are not encouraged to be patient by a curiosity to discover what will happen next onstage. The first finale, for example, is cut after the "masked trio" in a way that alters its musical unity. In the second act, we have to wait ten minutes for the little "cemetery duet" then another ten minutes for Donna Anna's aria—so unfortunate from a dramatic point of view, one must admit!—and, after this aria, ten more minutes of waiting before being admitted to the pleasure of the second finale. And one should not allege that these small breaks are not true "entr'actes" (i.e., intermissions), since one is not invited to move from one's place! I affirm, on the contrary, that this obligation to wait in place is unconsciously even more annoying for us than an intermission when we can exchange our impressions with our friends. I saw this at the dress rehearsal: all around me, from the middle of the second act on, listeners began rereading their programs—during one or the other of these disastrous breaks—and then, mechanically, tired of waiting, they took their hats and returned to their homes.[73]

Here, in sum, is the central conflict of the Operatic Museum. Although many critics and some educated audience members sought a return to an authentic, classical *Don Juan*, could such a work be successful with general fin-de-siècle audiences? De Wyzewa's answer was clearly "no," and that posed a significant problem. By his own account, the 1912 *Don Juan* was a near-perfect production, a sentiment shared by a number of other critics. Yet he felt sure that the production would quickly run its course and be removed from the stage, because despite the work's symbolic cultural capital it was simply too old-fashioned for modern audiences. In sharp contrast to the perspectives on the "divine Mozart" and his "French" opera *Don Juan* from the 1870s and 1880s, de Wyzewa had the audacity to find the work too long and to allege that audiences were bored to tears in their seats at a performance of "notre *Don Juan*."

Theater producers just could not win with *Don Juan*, it would seem. For a decade, critics had been lambasting the Opéra and Opéra-Comique for their overblown, romantic versions of Mozart's opera on an enormous stage, being forced to fill a larger space and a longer period of time than it was originally intended to. An attempt at a more "authentic" production, such as Hahn's in 1912, should have rectified the trouble, yet audiences were at least somewhat unreceptive to seeing a favorite work in a new—or rather, very old—way. For at least some critics and audience members, it may be that the problem lay deeper than superficial aesthetics. In this chapter, I have painted Mozart's reception with broad strokes, giving an overview of the composer's position in the Parisian Operatic Museum, and, in chapter 4, I will delve into several intersecting currents in fin-de-siècle Mozart reception, each affected to some extent by the complex issues of French identity—national, sexual, and otherwise.

Before continuing, however, I would like to turn to a more in-depth study of a production that was particularly significant for Mozart's French fate: the 1909 *The Magic Flute* at the Opéra-Comique. So far, I have been treating Mozart's fin-de-siècle decline and rehabilitation as an aspect of "restoration" in the sense of a work of visual art or a historical object. The similarities between these processes are indeed quite close, and, of course, the analogy resonates with my central concept of the Operatic Museum. The following interlude, however, takes a slightly different approach, examining the trials Mozart's operas faced through a lens of "translation" rather than "restoration." The process by which *Don Giovanni* became *Don Juan*, for example, was both a linguistic and—inevitably—a cultural translation, mediating distances of time and geography in an effort to bring a comprehensible artwork to nineteenth-century French audiences. In *The Magic Flute*, as the issues of fidelity that surrounded the Operatic Museum took hold, this process of translation came to the forefront of critical awareness, profoundly affecting the presentation of eighteenth-century opera in Paris.

Chapter Three

(De)Translations

All translation seems to me simply an attempt to solve an impossible task. Every translator is doomed to be done in by one of two stumbling blocks: he will either stay too close to the original, at the cost of taste and the language of his nation, or he will adhere too closely to the characteristics peculiar to his nation, at the cost of the original. The medium between the two is not only difficult, but downright impossible.

—Wilhelm von Humboldt, 1796[1]

Once upon a time, there was a young fisherman who lived on the bank of the Nile River, and who was in love with the beautiful girl next door. The happy couple made plans to marry, but one night the fisherman serenaded his fiancée with his pan-flute. This fateful little bit of night music attracted the attention of a voluptuous nocturnal deity, a Queen who became enamored of the fisherman and whisked him off to her magical realm for a night of wanton pleasure. In the cold light of day, the fisherman realized his mistake and begged his fiancée for forgiveness. Unfortunately, his night with the Queen had corrupted his spirit, requiring him to undergo a ritual purification at a distant temple. Along the way, the intrepid fisherman met a charming bird-catcher (and *his* fiancée) and learned that his beloved had been kidnapped and sold into slavery. After a series of trials and with the assistance of the benevolent High Priest of Isis, the young fisherman rescued the maiden and was finally purged of his corruption, and all was again well for the young lovers.

This story—as unfamiliar as it may be to us—is the plot that late nineteenth-century French audiences associated with Mozart's *Magic Flute*. Penned in 1865 by Charles Nuitter and Alexandre Beaumont for a production at the Théâtre-Lyrique in Paris, the loose adaptation of Schikaneder's libretto was an immediate success. Critics and audiences alike extolled Mozart's music as a model of clarity and simplicity, and the libretto appealed to a generation of operagoers who had grown accustomed to the convoluted plots and spectacles of *grand opéra*. Gustave Bertrand's review in *Le Ménestrel* was typical in this regard, lauding the Théâtre-Lyrique's Léon Carvalho as a "faithful and devoted restorer of Gluck, Weber, and Mozart."[2] Bertrand derided Schikaneder's original libretto at length, concluding that "the new appropriation is as apt and agreeable as possible; we only wish that Nuitter and Beaumont would further strengthen their dialogue."[3] The dismissal of Schikaneder extends to the published version of the libretto, which does not even mention him; the title page declares *"La Flûte enchantée: Opéra fantastique en quatre actes et sept tableaux par MM. Nuitter et Beaumont, Musique de Mozart."* Critics and audiences were both satisfied with this new version of the opera, and it seemed that France finally had its definitive version of *The Magic Flute*.

This version was as much a cultural translation as a linguistic one. The peculiar idioms of the singspiel—and *The Magic Flute* is perhaps more peculiar than most—were made intelligible through translating not only the libretto but the entire opera; the plot became as French as the text. David Levin has pointed out (regarding Peter Sellars's 1988 staging of *Le nozze di Figaro*) that translation often "aims to *erase* difference by transporting a text from a source language to a target language. From this point of view, the most successful translation is one in which the temporal and referential gaps—are rendered invisible."[4] Such was, presumably, the goal sought by Nuitter and Beaumont in their version of *The Magic Flute*: a production that minimized the cultural and chronological distance between composer and audience, essentially remaking Mozart into a French romantic composer. Linguist Lawrence Venuti describes the process: "Translation never communicates in an untroubled fashion because the translator negotiates the linguistic and cultural differences of the foreign text by reducing them and supplying another set of differences, basically domestic, drawn from the receiving language and culture to enable the foreign to be received there."[5] Thus, in order for *The Magic Flute* to make a successful transition to France, its content had to be read through a French cultural lens, remaking its subject into something understandable to domestic audiences.

This remaking was done, ironically, under the guise of making it acceptably "faithful" to Mozart's (if not Schikaneder's) original work. After all, this new version was substantially closer to the original *Magic Flute* than the first French productions had been. The Nuitter-Beaumont version of the opera was understood as faithful enough to the original; certainly by this 1865 version, Mozart's score was largely intact and free of interpolations. The libretto, on the other hand, was still a far cry from Schikaneder's original German. Compare, for instance, the original German text of the Queen of the Night's celebrated aria "Der Hölle Rache" to the Nuitter-Beaumont edition. Although the music for both versions is the same, here the Queen's majestic, and violent, rage over her daughter's betrayal is transformed into the banal machinations of a jealous rival, substantially diluting the effect of Mozart's score. This transformation of the Queen's character and her role in the plot also alters the conflict between light and dark (and, more ambiguously, good and evil) that forms the backbone of *The Magic Flute*'s narrative.

[Original Schikaneder version]

> Der Hölle Rache kocht in meinem Herzen,
> Tot und Verzweiflung flammet um mich her!
> Fühlt nicht durch dich Sarastro Todesschmerzen,
> So bist du meine Tochter nimmermehr.
> Verstoßen sei auf ewig,
> Verlassen sei auf ewig,
> Zertrümmert sei'n auf ewig
> Alle Bande der Natur
> Wenn nicht durch dich
> Sarastro wird erblassen!
> Hört, Rachegötter!
> Hört der Mutter Schwur!

> [Hell's vengeance boils in my heart,
> Death and despair blaze around me!
> If Sarastro does not by your hand feel the pain of death,
> Then you will no longer be my daughter.
> May you be forever disowned,
> May you be forever abandoned,
> Be forever shattered
> All the bonds of nature,
> If Sarastro does not by your hand
> Become pale [as death]!
> Hear, Gods of Vengeance,
> Hear a mother's oath!]

[1865 Nuitter-Beaumont version]

> Oui, devant toi tu vois une rivale,
> Son amour même est un crime à mes yeux!
> Et ma fureur, à mon amour égale,
> Abaissera ton front audacieux!
> Bientôt c'est moi qu'il aimera!
> Oui, ma haine vous perdra!
> Oui, tous deux vous frappera,
> En moi je sens d'avance
> L'espoir de la vengeance,
> Le traître qui m'offense
> Périra, j'en fais serment,

Non, rien, ne peut fléchir ma haine!
Sa perte est certaine,
Oui, la mort t'attend!

[Yes, you see before you a rival,
Your very love is a crime in my eyes!
And my rage, at my equal love,
Will bring down your audacious façade!
Soon it is I who will love him!
Yes, my hatred will defeat you!
Yes, you will both be struck,
I feel in advance
The hope of vengeance,
The traitor who offends me
Will perish, I swear it,
No, nothing can weaken my hatred!
Your defeat is certain,
Yes, death awaits you!]

In 1879, the Opéra-Comique staged *The Magic Flute* with Nuitter and Beaumont's 1865 libretto, to great acclaim. A subsequent attempt at a revival at the same theater in 1893, however, met with much less success. As we have seen in the previous chapter, by that time, French perceptions of Mozart and his operas had significantly changed, eventually leading to a concept of "authenticity" in opera unlike anything seen during the nineteenth century. I have previously painted this process with fairly wide brushstrokes, sketching the monumental changes in productions of *Don Juan* from the 1870s to the 1910s. In this section I would like to zoom in on the cultural politics of one particular production: the 1909 production of *The Magic Flute* at the Opéra-Comique. This production played a major role in establishing Mozart's position in the French Operatic Museum, and it exemplifies a shift in mindset between classical and romantic visions of the composer and his works that would have major implications for Mozart's French reception in the early twentieth century.

That *The Magic Flute* would assume such importance for Mozart's historical position might seem odd. After all, it was at best in a distant second place to *Don Juan* in the race for the hearts of the French audience. With *Don Juan*, however, perhaps too much was at stake; it was simply too familiar, too recent, and too hotly debated to take any chances in "restoring" it to its original condition. Given that *The Magic Flute* had not been produced in a state-sponsored theater for some time, it provided a welcome measure of distance for heavily invested critics and audience members. It thus could have served as a sort of trial for Carré to gauge audience reaction to a Mozart opera that had not been adapted and translated with French audiences in mind. If *The Magic Flute* passed the test, it would pave the way for further restorations; if it failed, no great harm done—or at least less harm than a disastrous production of *Don Giovanni* might cause. The 1909 production was thus less about *The Magic Flute* in particular than it was about testing the waters for a new concept of historicity in Parisian Mozart production.

As critics, audiences, and Albert Carré no doubt expected, the issue of textual fidelity was still a nexus of critical discourse around the 1909 production of *The Magic Flute*. But in contrast to what one might expect in a debate regarding an opera, critics were largely unconcerned about *The Magic Flute*'s musical bona fides. Few critics of the 1909 production felt obliged to mention the singers' performances save for a few perfunctory lines at the end of reviews (fairly typical practice for opera criticism of the time), and stylistic fidelity was seldom a major concern.[6] The size and style of the orchestra and performers seem to have been standard for the Opéra-Comique, which was to be expected; performance practice was still a contentious idea, particularly on the operatic stage. Audiences and critics had reacted badly, for example, to performances of Rameau's *Hippolyte et Aricie* at the Opéra in 1908 with a reduced orchestra and a harpsichord. In fact, the absence of recitative in favor of spoken dialogue was likely a factor in Carré's choice of *The Magic Flute*, since it avoided the firestorm of debate over *secco* versus *accompagnato* recitatives that had plagued the Rameau production.

In other words, as long as the music was by Mozart and did not deviate significantly from critics' expectations of the Opéra-Comique orchestra and singers, they were willing to accept the music of the 1909 *Magic Flute* without too much debate. Even sticklers for historical fidelity such as Fauré were pleased. Lavishing the work with praise, he asked rhetorically: "Does there exist a music that can give us impressions at once so immediate and so profound, a music that, without exerting the least effort, keeps the spirit in such joy, such tranquility, and which, at the same time as the strongest, or most exquisite, or most serene emotions, results in such great learning?"[7] Reviews of the costumes and sets were similarly laudatory. The mythical and exotic setting of *The Magic Flute* offered the opportunity to please (or at least distract) the audience with elaborate costumes and sets, which were well received in the press (see figs. 3.1 and 3.2). The critic Adhéaume de Chevigné, for example, praised the stagecraft (and only the stagecraft) in *Le Courrier musical*, claiming that the décor at the Opéra-Comique attained "quasi-perfection," and that "never, surely, has Mozart's masterwork known such splendor or equal éclat."[8] The chief bone of contention, in fact, was the new production's libretto. Carré had made the difficult decision to commission a new, "faithful" translation from veteran librettists Paul Ferrier and Alexandre Bisson, one designed to rectify the perceived failings of the 1865 version, which were becoming increasingly obvious to critics.[9]

Figure 3.1. "Edmond Clément in the role of Tamino in *The Magic Flute*, which he reprised with great success." *Musica*, July 1909.

Figure 3.2. "Lucien Fugere in the role of Papageno, which earned him great success at the revival of Mozart's *The Magic Flute* at the Opéra-Comique." *Musica*, July 1909.

Of course, saying a new translation is faithful does not necessarily make it so, and French audiences had been duped before. But in this case, Carré's claims were not far from the truth, and the translation is for the most part quite close to Schikaneder's original—in contrast to typical practice in France at the time. As an example, we may again compare Ferrier and Bisson's treatment of the Queen of the Night's "Der Hölle Rache" to Schikaneder's original. The sense of the text is clearly much closer now to the original German. Just as in Schikaneder, the Queen commands Pamina to assassinate Sarastro or risk losing her mother's love. The Ferrier-Bisson translation does focus on the weapon itself (the dagger, or, intriguingly, perhaps Pamina herself as an instrument of vengeance), which is not directly mentioned in the German, but otherwise the departures from the original text are minimal.

[1909 Ferrier-Bisson translation of "Der Hölle Rache"]

> Sers ma vengeance en châtiant l'infâme!
> Va, prends cette arme et frappe sans effroi!
> Sers vaillamment la haine qui m'enflamme,
> Où c'en est fait, tu n'es plus rien pour moi.
> Ou mon amour se détournera de toi![10]
> Venge-moi! va sans effroi!
> Ou mon amour s'écartera de toi!
> La haine qui m'anime
> Dénonce la victime.
> Mon cœur bénit ton crime!
> Le maudit succombera,
> Cette arme vengeresse
> Sans pitié le frappera,
> Sous cette arme il tombera!
> Ou bien alors, malheur à toi, traitresse!
> Dieux! Dieux!
> Fille indigne, Dieux! maudissez-la!

> [Serve my revenge by punishing the villain!
> Go, take this weapon and strike without fear!
> Valiantly serve the hatred that enflames me,
> When it is done, you'll belong to me alone.
> Or my love will turn away from you!
> Avenge me! go without fear!
> Or my love will abandon you!
> The hatred that fuels me
> Condemns the victim.
> My heart blesses your crime!

The accursed one will perish,
This avenging weapon
Will strike without pity,
By this weapon he will fall!
Or else, woe to you, traitor!
Gods! Gods!
Unworthy daughter, gods! curse her!]

With any new translation, particularly one determined to stay close to the original meaning of the text, comes the danger of poor text setting. If the accentuation failed to seem natural in French, critics would surely have condemned the new libretto. Those of a more classical bent would have maintained that the Opéra-Comique erred by not performing the work in the original Italian, while the more romantically inclined would have derided the theater for straying from the Nuitter-Beaumont version. On this issue, Carré again demonstrated himself to be a clever politician by soliciting a potentially dangerous critic: Fauré himself. In a letter to his wife on September 1, 1908, Fauré—already director of the Paris Conservatoire—found himself with another project: "The director of the Opéra-Comique, perhaps thinking that I am just loafing around during the holidays, sent me a new translation of Mozart's *Magic Flute*, with a request to review it from the point of view of the text setting. Alas! there are so many mistakes to correct! Ah well, I will try."[11]

Fauré was, of course, well known as a master of setting the French language to music, a skill revealed in his numerous art songs and choral works, making him a natural choice for such a task. But more was at stake here than just the subtleties of text setting. Fauré's involvement was a tacit testimonial for Carré's production from the director of the Conservatoire and the most vocal critic in favor of a classical Mozart. To hear Carré himself tell it, Fauré was an essential element of the production, without whom it would never have come to fruition: "For a long time I put off the project closest to my heart: staging the works of Mozart. I managed to achieve it all the same by soliciting the help of two of our greatest musicians: Gabriel Fauré for *la Flûte enchantée* and Reynaldo Hahn for *Don Juan*. . . . Gabriel Fauré brought to these studies an impassioned care."[12] Whether or not Fauré himself was aware of it, his involvement with the libretto lent to the production the imprimatur of perhaps the most influential musical voice in France—and probably secured a positive review in *Le Figaro*, to boot.

This plan succeeded admirably. Fauré pointed out with relish (and perhaps a bit of self-satisfaction) that the 1909 production was "a work restored to its original severity, thanks to a new and faithful version . . . that is finally and forever going to distance us from the extraordinarily arbitrary fantasies of Nuitter and Beaumont."[13] Although he might have been the most invested, Fauré was far from the only critic to voice such opinions. The Mozart scholar Henri de Curzon, for example, noted that "the principal interest of this new production is to provide us *for the first time* in France with the authentic state of this radiant masterwork."[14] De Curzon went on to praise Carré personally for risking the public's displeasure for the sake of fidelity to the sources:

> It was up to Albert Carré . . . not to allow an ill-informed public to persist in misunderstanding [*The Magic Flute*] any longer. Rejecting the previous version, he sought the help of Paul Ferrier and Alexandre Bisson in preparing a complete translation of the German text, simply cleared up in places or cut. . . . *The Magic Flute* is presented to us in all its poetry and original character. We cannot thank the director of the Opéra-Comique enough.[15]

At the same time, not all critics liked this new *Magic Flute*, and, ironically, the very idea of the work's "authenticity" created the stumbling block. The Ferrier and Bisson version was still, of course, a linguistic translation from the German original, but in a sense it was also a detranslation of the comfortably familiar version in favor of a culturally unfamiliar alternative. In other words, audiences were suddenly forced to try to comprehend a previously accessible work in a foreign dramatic language—a fundamental shift many listeners were unable or unwilling to accept. A number of fin-de-siècle critics expressed a genuine fondness for the 1865 version, even while acknowledging its distance from the original German. Jullien, for example, who had looked back in disbelief on the sacrilegious adaptations of *Les Mystères d'Isis*, nonetheless waxed nostalgic about the 1865 production as well as its revival at the Opéra-Comique in 1879. He opened his review of the 1909 *Flûte enchantée* by reminiscing wistfully on these older productions, "Alas, how long ago this was!"[16] To Jullien, evidently, the 1865 adaptation was the "real" *Magic Flute*, at least for French audiences. Given their degree of attachment to the Nuitter-Beaumont libretto, many critics like Jullien were probably predisposed to dislike any new translation. The serious alterations of the 1865 libretto were either ignored or actively preferred to the 1909 version.

Once the gloss of romanticism that had protected *The Magic Flute* during the nineteenth century was removed, the oddities of the work's plot simply could not resonate with modern tastes. Victor Debay, a critic for *Le Courrier musical*, singled out the libretto as the cause of his "ennui" during the 1909 production:

> The first [reason] is the insanity of Schikaneder's libretto, which has been reworked without wit by Paul Ferrier and Alexandre Bisson. One

should expect from them something aside from flat physical humor that would not even make the schoolboys at the Sunday matinees smile.... [Carré] agreed to be indulgent toward the adapters who sought, out of respect that it does not deserve, to come closer to the original version. Who can be interested in the quarrel between Monsieur the Sun and Madame the Moon as they argue over their daughter Pamina, or in the trials imposed on the lover Tamino in order to win over the gracious child of the Day and the Night? . . . [The libretto] is nothing more today than tedious verbosity that damages the exquisite pages of music that it separates. Between some heavenly minutes it imposes quarter-hours of yawns. The supreme intervention of Ferrier and Bisson would have been more useful by way of energetic scissor cuts, cutting everything in Schikaneder's dialogue that is unnecessary or makes no sense—and since there is almost no action, there would be nothing left except the sung part, which has the delicate and ideal meaning that Mozart's genius adds to the hollow words.[17]

Debay's diatribe blames Emanuel Schikaneder's libretto, rather than Mozart's "heavenly" music, for the opera's failures. In Debay's view, the historical fidelity sought by Carré, Ferrier, and Bisson—and supported by critics like Fauré and de Curzon—was a serious mistake from an aesthetic stance. What modern spectator, Debay asks, could possibly be interested in the opera's actual plot? Mozart's music deserved something better than the "real" libretto to which it had been set, which was not only nonsensical but also boring—the ultimate fin-de-siècle condemnation. Several influential critics made this later claim, including Jullien, who pronounced in *Le Journal des débats* that "there is not a single interesting scene to be found in *La Flûte enchantée*."[18]

Other critics expressed similar sentiments. Chevigné, despite his praise for the stagecraft, found that the excellence of the staging only set the libretto's inadequacy in greater relief. Mozart's music, he opined, "is reduced too easily to a second-rate accompaniment to the dull drollery that springs from Schikaneder's imagination. There was no need to collaborate with such a great musician to achieve this result."[19] The critic Georges Pioch went so far as to assert that the main problem with the 1909 production must be the translation, since surely Mozart would not have been involved with such a trivial work:

French adapters always refuse to discern the true strength of will to which Mozart attests. Bisson and Ferrier have sought above all to amuse, to "modernize." . . . Without doubt, the adaptation by Bisson and Ferrier constitutes, as far as the clarity of the conversation is concerned, progress over the version by Nuitter and Beaumont. But this progress is cruelly compensated by the stupefying language spoken by Tamino, Pamina, and all the other inhabitants of this poetic Fairyland. Is there no "serious" adaptation of *la Flûte enchantée?*[20]

Here the critic refuses to believe that the new translation of the work could possibly be faithful to the original German, preferring the view that French adapters have always been unable to understand the work fully. In search of a deeper message to the music of *The Magic Flute*, Pioch demanded a "serious" adaptation that could match the sublimity of Mozart's music.

Even Henri de Curzon was willing to admit *The Magic Flute*'s faults, but refused to allow critics to place the blame on any perceived "infidelity" of the production: "In order to maintain giving a *faithful* impression of the original spoken text in the German work—because it was much more faithful than certain 'informed' critics who have certainly not read the German have affected to believe; it was faithful all the way until its faults, its clumsiness, and its needless length—Albert Carré has demanded a bit too much of the attention, easily lost, of the modern public."[21] De Curzon lambastes those critics who doubted the accuracy of the Ferrier-Bisson translation; if they found the plot ridiculous, it was because it was that way in the original. Carré was even grudgingly willing to acknowledge its flaws, admitting that *The Magic Flute* was "the last—and perhaps the most beautiful—of the master who was dying at thirty-six years old. But the poem, it must be said, is inane to the point of incoherence."[22]

This was a hard truth for some critics to accept. The contrast between the fidelity they desired from *The Magic Flute* and the debatably incoherent spectacle they saw onstage was a major problem for fin-de-siècle critics. The primary—if unspoken—issue was the conflict between classical and romantic interpretations of Mozart, along with their attendant aesthetic binaries ("low" and "high," "comic" and "tragic"). Critics and audiences were certain that *The Magic Flute* deserved a place in the Operatic Museum, but whose *Magic Flute* should it be? The familiar 1865 version, with its typical Opéra-Comique plot conventions and heavily adapted score, situated the work comfortably within French historical traditions, and triggered nostalgia in critics like Jullien who had enjoyed the translation in the midcentury. On the other hand, the 1909 libretto and score suggested a classical Mozart—which, paradoxically, was also a modern Mozart.[23] This view was complemented, of course, by the number of fin-de-siècle composers who embraced neoclassical styles and forms—including many who, like Hahn and Fauré, were ardent in their advocacy for a "restored," museum-quality Mozart. But, of course, this classical vision required more work on the part of audiences. Although the language of the production was French, they were nonetheless required to translate the eighteenth-century German aesthetics of the singspiel (and of Schikaneder in particular) in order to have any hope of understanding the work.

Eventually, of course, those in favor of a museal Mozart won out. The 1909 *Magic Flute* demonstrated that such interpretations of a Mozart opera could be both financially viable and at least relatively successful with critics. Although the Ferrier-Bisson libretto was actually fairly short-lived in its use—apparently replaced in the 1920s by a new translation for the Opéra— the Opéra-Comique production had a significant impact. In 1912, only three years after *The Magic Flute* brought these issues into the spotlight, *Don Giovanni* received the same "restorations." Reynaldo Hahn served as musical director and dramaturgical consultant, and Ferrier was once again called upon to retranslate the libretto in accordance with the original. Hahn restored the opera's hitherto abandoned recitatives (accompanied at the piano) and its original structure (two acts, rather than the five that had become traditional in France), as well as making a number of other musical alterations to further align the opera with Mozart's score, such as restoring the long-omitted final scene.[24]

While some critics remained skeptical about these efforts at "restoring" Mozart's operas, none doubted that doing so was the new trend in staging canonical operas. Throughout the nineteenth century, works had been adapted to suit Parisian theatrical preferences. Beginning with the 1909 *Magic Flute*, however, historical works worthy of inclusion in the Operatic Museum required a different approach. These same producers, critics, and audience members had to adapt *themselves* to these works, and to understand them in their "original" forms. The trial was over, and the initiates survived; the 1909 Opéra-Comique production of *The Magic Flute* helped tip the scales in favor of a new concept of historicism at the opera house.

Chapter Four

Transitions

In chapters 2 and 3 we traced Mozart's gradual transition from a romantic composer to a classical figure—a restoration of his "original" state that accompanied his introduction into the Operatic Museum. This transition had a number of consequences for the way that audiences and critics understood the composer. Not only did stripping Mozart of his romantic veneer make his works challenging to Parisian audience members more accustomed to Wagner's or Massenet's theatrical language, it also raised a number of issues that Mozart's quasi-divinity had kept at bay. To put it another way, once the illusion of universality that had been attached to *Don Juan* was dispelled, audiences and critics were forced to situate the work in its geographical and chronological location, revealing the odd eighteenth-century Germanic composer lurking behind the mythology. In this chapter, I pick up some threads of French cultural identity running through Mozart's fin-de-siècle reception. As critics struggled to redefine Mozart and his historical position, they reflected the cultural preoccupations of their own time: in this case, larger issues of national identity, gender identity, and aesthetic priorities. We can begin this investigation with a look at perceptions of Mozart's Austro-German nationality, which proved a major stumbling block for those seeking to reconcile Mozart's position atop the musical canon with the idea of France's artistic superiority.

Cosmopolitanism versus Nationalism

Over the course of the nineteenth century, Mozart came to be regarded as the quintessential cosmopolitan composer. The European tours undertaken by the Mozart family when Wolfgang was a child were always a major topic of French critics (although they frequently, and often disproportionately, emphasized the stops in Paris). Furthermore, at least some critics—François-Joseph Fétis most prominent among them—found in Mozart's style a synthesis of German, Italian, and French national styles, ultimately creating "a new and universal musical language," in Katharine Ellis's words.[1] This cosmopolitan reputation served Mozart well in Paris throughout most of the nineteenth century. The city itself was a highly international setting during that time, a feature that virtually defined its character. As the Polish émigré Charles Forster, for example, wrote of Paris in 1848: "There is no country in the world where a foreigner, an émigré, will find hearts that are warmer or more compassionate to his suffering.... As soon as he touches French soil, he becomes, as it were, a citizen of the country.... No one demands of him an accounting of his opinions or his nationality. He is an exile and that is enough."[2]

This hospitable atmosphere was equally visible on the operatic stages of Paris. Italian composers like Gioacchino Rossini, Vincenzo Bellini, Gaetano Donizetti, and Giuseppi Verdi were welcomed at the Opéra with (mostly) open arms, and their works were extremely popular for much of the century.[3] Likewise, the German operas of Carl Maria von Weber were well received (though nearly always performed in French adaptations), and performances continued through the 1860s.[4] Even the failure of Wagner's *Tannhäuser* in 1861 had less to do with the composer's nationality than with his refusal to capitulate to French artistic preferences.[5] In such an environment, it is little wonder that the Austrian Mozart's works were featured so prominently on Parisian opera stages. Hospitality toward foreigners was a fundamental aspect of Parisian culture, and one on which the French prided themselves highly. Producing works by foreign composers became, in fact, an ironic type of nationalism, where the magnanimity and taste of the French people were celebrated—in contrast to the often cool reception French composers received outside their own national borders.

After 1870, however, Paris's spirit of cosmopolitanism began to evaporate. Only a society that was secure in its position of cultural dominance—as France was until the Franco-Prussian War—could afford to be so accommodating to foreign artists. The war severely compromised that security, forcing the French to question their military and cultural supremacy in a way they had not done since the ancien régime. To many critics, the rampant cosmopolitanism of the midcentury suddenly began to look less like a utopian display of transnational artistry and more like a foreign theatrical invasion. Consequently, French stages sought reaffirmation of their cultural glory through the production and celebration of unambiguously French artists, leaving little room for hospitality to foreign artists, including Mozart.[6] Philippe Blay, for example, examined a push in the 1890s for the Opéra-Comique to become an "entirely French" theater, which led to the rejection of the works that had dominated the repertoire there for much of the nineteenth century.[7] But such a change in perspective was not immediate, nor was it complete. Despite the rampant musical nationalism that governed many aspects of French musical life at the fin de siècle, Wagner's music (after an initial ban in the concert halls after the war) became increasingly popular with opera audiences. Steven Huebner pointed out the tension surrounding performances of Wagner's operas, as "perceptions that his art encapsulated the essence of the German nation coexisted, often within the same person, with the enormous appeal of his music."[8] This same tension, though less publicly debated, governed the reception of Mozart's operas during this time, when his Austro-German identity was brought into conflict with the public interest in—and the critical respect for—his music.

The primary difficulty lay in the fact that Mozart had spent little time in France (at least as an adult) and thus his stage works were neither in French nor written with a French audience in mind. Unlike Gluck, who had adapted to French musical traditions, Mozart had composed in a more international language. This difference made it difficult to successfully claim him as a "French" composer in the increasingly nationalist climate emerging in the years leading up to 1900. Some critics nonetheless made valiant attempts: Félix Clement, for example, acknowledged the issue of Mozart's nationality in his *Histoire de la musique*, but made an effort to rescue Mozart for France:

> Gluck naturalized himself as a French composer. He separated himself from the German symphonists and the Italian melodists. Mozart never made a single concession to our taste. We have admired and loved him nevertheless, because of the French qualities of his heart, of his effusive nature, of the limpid clarity of his style and of his ideas, and finally because of the supreme beauty of his genius. At such a height, borders are erased. I will go farther: the divine Mozart, dethroned by the sectarians of the new German school, will retain his altar in France.[9]

Although Mozart the man made no efforts to assimilate in France either culturally or musically, in this construction of French musical identity his music nonetheless possessed qualities that rendered it inherently French. Furthermore, Clément emphasized that in modern times it was France—not Germany—that embraced Mozart's music with open arms, and showed his genius the respect it deserved. There was another, less explicit, assumption underlying Clément's representations of Mozart. The critic seems to say that it was the very beauty of Mozart's music that made it French—in contrast, again, to the implied "ugliness" of German music. This flawed logic would certainly be convenient for aggrandizing French musical styles: French music is beautiful, therefore any composer who composes beautiful music must necessarily be in some fundamental way French, regardless of geographical boundaries.

This refusal to acknowledge Mozart's foreign origins colored the writings of other critics, as well. The composer Gabriel Pierné, for example, inexplicably included Mozart in a list of French (or adopted French) composers that should be included in the Operatic Museum: "The Opéra-Comique should become a sort of museum for the operatic repertoire . . . it should even be reasonable to extend it by drawing more than we have thus far on works by Lully, Rameau, Gluck, Mozart, Méhul, Grétry."[10] The implication is clear: Mozart is a part of this French pantheon of composers, and his music belongs at the "eminently French" Opéra-Comique. Nowhere does Pierné acknowledge that Mozart was not French, or that he composed no operas for France. This position is essentially an extension of the nineteenth-century myth of the French *Don Juan*—Mozart belonged to France because his operas belonged to France, and had for nearly a century.

After 1900, as nationalist tensions reached a fevered pitch, this perspective became increasingly rare. But even critics who acknowledged Mozart's Germanic identity lamented the composer's lost "French" potential. In a 1906 article on the subject of Mozart in France, Henri de Curzon placed all blame for Mozart's distaste for France on the shoulders of the author Melchior Grimm:

> There are those types of *faux bonshommes* who must be unmasked: Melchior Grimm, in a fit of pique that one imagines to be his habit, played the most nefarious role in Mozart's career, from our point of view at least. It is thanks to him that Mozart did not become, like Gluck, a *French composer*. . . .
>
> Grimm, exasperated by Gluck's success, bitter from seeing his musical authority badly beaten, was in a spiritual excitation without bounds at the moment when Mozart fell into his arms. And he would sustain another German composer? *A d'autres!*
>
> . . . He certainly had the talent to instill in the young man his hatred or disdain for the French taste, of the French public, of French music—and the defiance, or the foolishness, that Mozart demonstrated on this subject in his letters, which are attributable to Grimm's malicious spirit. . . .
>
> He would have written the scores that we already know for us: *Les Noces de Figaro* and *Don Juan*, and he would have added many others, with our French librettos, so much "according to his spirit."[11]

If Mozart did not become a French composer in the way that Gluck had, de Curzon tells us, it is because his immanently Gallic sprit was corrupted, tainted by the jealousy and chauvinism of Melchoir Grimm. Furthermore, Curzon emphasizes that French librettos were "according to [Mozart's] spirit," reaffirming that the composer somehow had a natural connection to French musical traditions despite being so tragically misled. If this argument does not precisely redeem Mozart for France, it at least saves the composer from accusations of being too anti-French.

Even Debussy, who was normally staunchly opposed to all things Germanic (except Bach—but including the adopted Frenchman Gluck), had positive things to say about Mozart, reflecting on his "good taste" (a high compliment from Debussy) as late as 1913.¹² By this time, the effort to adopt Mozart as a French composer had failed—he was inextricably German. But later in the same year, in an article on modern directions in French music, Debussy could not help but express regret that Mozart was lost to France and its composers: "What a pity Mozart wasn't French. He would really have been worth imitating!"¹³

The Raphael of Music

The late nineteenth-century attempt to position Mozart as an adopted "French" artist not by any biographical evidence (e.g., as in Gluck's case) but rather by the inherent "Frenchness" of his works, while unusual, was not entirely unique. But as his national identity was called into question in the press, critics needed to be able to point to an exemplar of another adopted French artist who had spent little time in France. The perfect precedent was the Renaissance painter Raphael, who had for centuries been adopted as a French artist despite his having spent literally no time in France.¹⁴ In the early nineteenth century Raphael assumed a position of particular importance in French society, as his works formed the centerpiece of the Musée Napoléon, established in 1803. Much of his art was looted from its native Italy (and some from Spain) and taken to Paris because, the argument ran, "the French were more willing and able to preserve these masterpieces than their present owners."¹⁵ Only the French, it would seem, could truly appreciate the genius of Raphael, and so they essentially adopted him—a situation analogous to Mozart's later in the century.

French critics were not the first to compare Mozart to Raphael. That distinction seems to belong to Franz Xaver Niemetschek, who in his early biography of the composer (1798) described him as "our Raphael in music." Art historian Thomas Tolley points to the root of this comparison: it bestowed on Mozart "notions of pure classical form, ideal beauty, noble simplicity, and perfection" usually associated with the Renaissance master.¹⁶ This correlation between Mozart and Raphael rapidly caught on in German-language biographies and criticism, and the two became connected in the nineteenth century as paragons of classical artistic style. After a few decades this comparison reached France, where it took hold on critics as tightly as it had elsewhere. As early as 1855, for example, Henri Blaze de Bury pointed to a comment attributed to Lorenzo da Ponte, hailing Mozart as the return of Raphael.¹⁷ In late nineteenth-century France, however, the same strengths Niemetschek's original comparison was designed to highlight—Mozart's pure form, beauty, simplicity, and perfection—were becoming those traits with which French composers were associated. Thus began a kind of slippage, wherein Raphael's French temperament was transferred to Mozart, allowing him to be similarly adopted.

In the following years this connection became particularly useful for more poetic descriptions of Mozart. The poet and author Alfred Tonnellé, for example, noted in his posthumous aesthetic treatise that "Mozart is one of those rare geniuses in the same family as Raphael, who have the gift to equally move the heart, charm the imagination, to satisfy both taste and spirit, and to spread over everything a certain flower of beauty and ideal grace."[18] Though this passage is a bit vague on specifics, it captures the fundamental points: grace, charm, taste, and something of a sublime spirituality. An 1869 collection of poems by Marquis Anatole de Ségur (who also dedicated a poem to Charles Gounod) featured a poem titled "Raphaël et Mozart," which captures many of Tonellé's points in an even more florid fashion:

> Quand Mozart, désertant la terre,
> Montait radieux vers le ciel,
> L'âme heureuse de Raphaël
> Vint à l'encontre de son frère.
>
> Pareil à l'enfant qui croit voir
> Dans l'onde pure son visage,
> Chacun d'eux crut voir son image
> En l'autre, comme en un miroir.
>
> Ils mêlèrent en un sourire
> Leurs cœurs et se donnant la main,
> Vers le paradis sans rien dire
> Ils poursuivirent leur chemin.
>
> Et quand leurs deux âmes jumelles
> Entrèrent au divin séjour,
> Pourtant des grâces immortelles,
> Rayonnantes du même amour,
>
> Le chœur des célestes louanges
> Résonna plus harmonieux,
> Comme si de nouveaux archanges
> Venaient d'éclore dans les cieux.[19]

> [When Mozart, abandoning the earth,
> Radiantly rose to heaven,
> Raphael's happy soul
> Encountered his brother's.

Like the child who thinks he sees
His face in the pure waters,
Each thought he saw his image
In the other, as in a mirror.

They mingled their hearts in a smile;
Joining hands,
And saying nothing,
They continued toward Paradise,

And when their twin souls
Entered the divine abode,
Even by the immortal graces
Radiating the same love,

The chorus of celestial praise
Sounded more harmonious,
As if new archangels
Were born in the heavens.]

In this poem—which was reprinted in 1899 in the Marquis de Ségur's complete works—Mozart and Raphael are as more than "in the same family." They were spiritual brothers, bound by a force stronger than blood: the essential character of their art. But the poet never reveals precisely what this unifying characteristic is—as if the similarity is simply too obvious to merit comment. Instead, their relationship as "twin souls," implies that any greatness recognized in the one could be equally applied to the other.

By the fin de siècle, references to Mozart as a musical Raphael were frequent; recall Jean d'Udine's invocation of Raphael when the critic opined that "Mozart passed, in the opinion of the dilettantes, as the ruling genius of music, and, like Raphael in painting, his name became almost dogmatically a synonym for perfection, grace, an unsurpassable ideal."[20] In 1873, Gustave Choquet wrote in his *Histoire de la musique dramatique en France* that "Mozart drove musical comedy to its highest degree of perfection in *Le Nozze de Figaro*, in writing *Die Zauberflöte* he created the *drame fantastique*, and in composing *Don Giovanni* he delved into the depths of the supernatural world and opened the door to opera for Romanticism. These last three scores are those in which the Raphael of music delivered to us the secrets of his reverent, melancholy, and tender soul."[21]

In his biography of Mozart, Camille Bellaigue also emphasized this connection: "It is the secret of the great idealists, that of the composer of *Don Juan* as well as that of the painter of *Héliodore* and of *la Messe de Bolsène* [both by Raphael], to set aside until the grandiose pages, a sanctuary, like a familiar corner of intimate life, to the most modest, the most humble reality."[22]

More succinctly, Bellaigue opined that, "if the figures of Raphael could sing, they would sing Mozart's melodies."[23] By linking him to Raphael, the adopted French artist, critics subtly tied Mozart to French artistic culture, an important step in maintaining the composer in the French operatic canon during an increasingly nationalist period.

Thankfully, other critics were more explicit. In an article on the classical symphony, for example, the critic Émile Michel offered a similar concrete explanation of the constant comparison between the two figures:

> Many times he [Mozart] has already been compared to Raphael, and if, because of the evident similarities between their genius and their destinies, the comparison presents itself to the spirit, the recent critical works on the one or the other have only confirmed the numerous analogies that have been remarked upon. Not only, in effect, was their calling marked by clear enough indications, but, both sons of artists, they found from their cradle an intelligent direction from which their powers of assimilation apparently allowed them to continually benefit. Through the most diverse and happiest influences combined, they each retained all that originality, that taste, that sense of beauty and proportion, that fecundity of inexhaustible invention, that rare mélange of elegance and force, of knowledge and inspiration, that flexibility and that universality of abilities that we admire in them and that allowed them to excel in every branch of their art.[24]

The essence of these perspectives on Mozart seems to be that the primary quality of his music, like that of Raphael's painting, is the grace and elegance of the execution—the sheer beauty of the music. Grace, in particular, was the uniting factor between these two artists. After all, we might change only the name, and Eugène Delacroix's 1830 assessment of Raphael would be right at home among these exaltations of Mozart: "[Raphael] alone has carried to the highest degree those qualities which are the most captivating and which exert the most influence on men: an irresistible charm in his style, and a truly divine grace, which breathes throughout all his works, and masks the defects and makes us excuse all his excesses."[25]

Yet the same musical grace that maintained Mozart's position in the French artistic pantheon also had its negative effects, invoking coded phrases in use in the French press for decades that singled out Mozart as a "feminine," or even "frivolous" composer. "Feminine grace" (or the lack thereof), as Katharine Ellis has amply demonstrated, was a major feature in the rhetoric attached to female pianists from the 1840s through the end of the century.[26] Female performers were "graceful" and "sweet," while male performers were "powerful" and "expressive." Certainly the former adjectives were attached to Mozart more often than the latter, at least after 1900.

The increasingly prevalent perception of Mozart as a feminine composer would have had a significant effect on performances of his work during the fin de siècle, as mainstream French society experienced a push toward traditionally masculine qualities. A number of scholars have noted the "crisis of masculinity" that developed in the aftermath of the Franco-Prussian War.[27] This crisis was created by a combination of factors, the two most important being the rapid increase in the prominence of women in French society and the feeling of emasculation that plagued men after the War of 1870.[28] This backlash against feminine qualities extended into music, as well. Annegret Fauser has demonstrated that the concept of masculine music culture served to highlight "accepted cultural values that met a need for reassurance in threatening times." Fauser continues: "Given that the shared notion of 'masculinity' represented the highest and healthiest concept in the cultural and social hierarchy of Republican France, its constant presence in the cultural discourses of the fin de siècle is anything but unexpected. It played an important role in refining and appropriating French music past and present for the endeavor of patriotic and nationalist self-definition of both the French right and left in all their different shades."[29] Parisian audiences during this time of crisis would have been significantly less willing to accept operas by a feminine composer than by a masculine one—a bias that surely had a negative impact on the frequency with which Mozart's operas were staged.

As with so many trends in music aesthetics of the late nineteenth century, the notion of a feminine Mozart may have had its roots in Wagner's writings. As I discuss more fully in chapter 7, Wagner frequently characterized music as feminine and poetry as masculine—when combined, these elements produced a perfectly balanced offspring in Wagner's own music dramas. In *Oper und Drama*, Wagner specifically addressed the feminine nature of Mozart's music for *Don Giovanni*, as Gernot Gruber has pointed out:

> The resolution of the dialectical tension [between masculine poetry and feminine music] emerges at the end of the first part of *Oper und Drama*, when Wagner returns yet again to *Don Giovanni* and finally establishes the happy coincidence of music and poetry with the emphatic exclamation: "Where else has music achieved such infinitely rich individuality, where else has it been able to characterize in such a richly exuberant plenitude as here, where the musician, according to the nature of his art, is nothing less than a woman whose love is unconditional?" Wagner also speaks at the end of the second part about "music as a woman, splendid in her love": Mozart, apparently, stands for the feminine, the devoted, the emotional, the naïvely unconscious, and for the musical as such.[30]

This characterization of Mozart as "feminine," "devoted," "emotional," and "naïvely unconscious" found frequent echoes in his French fin-de-siècle reception. From the 1870s to the 1890s, descriptions of Mozart that included feminine qualities usually made some effort to redeem the composer by highlighting his masculine characteristics, as well. In his 1873 history, Choquet, for example, emphasized Mozart's apparently feminine characteristics but followed up with a disclaimer:

> A poet at once *fanciful,* elegiac, and Christian, Mozart shines still more by the *grace* and the *tenderness* than by the gift of infectious joviality: he loved so much, and he suffered so much! . . . The artist remained *faithful* to his particular style, the *elegance* and perfection of which one cannot help but admire. This style makes itself remarkable by its obvious *spontaneity*; nevertheless it carries at the same time the mark of *mature reflection.* (emphasis added)[31]

In this brief passage, Choquet describes the "fanciful" nature of Mozart's music as well its "grace" and "tenderness," and "obvious spontaneity"; the composer himself is described as being "faithful" to his musical style. These descriptions are all clearly qualities attributed to feminine music and its performers. Choquet, however, balances his description by pointing out that, despite these feminine elements, the music demonstrates "mature reflection," a masculine-coded term. The end result of the passage is a kind of androgynous reading of Mozart, possessing the (arguably) positive elements of feminine music, enhanced (or mitigated) by more serious masculine elements.[32]

By the early twentieth century, however, this androgynous view of Mozart had begun to shift toward an entirely feminine perspective on the composer. Téodor de Wyzewa, for example, wrote in the introduction to the first volume of his enormous Mozart biography (1912; coauthored with Georges de Saint-Foix) that Mozart differed from Beethoven primarily in the character of his spirit. While Beethoven's masculine nature allowed the composer to basically generate his own music from within, Mozart had to look outside himself: "With his essentially 'feminine' nature, this poetic genius always had to look elsewhere for the spirit necessary to employ his art in new ways—except for him to transfigure immediately, in animating them with an importance and with a beauty at once much higher [than the source] and entirely original, the ideas or the processes he discovered in the work of this or that musician, encountered in passing."[33] Wyzewa offers no evidence for Mozart's supposedly feminine essence. Rather, it is simply assumed to be a self-evident characteristic of the composer and his music. Even after World War I, Mozart was perceived as a somehow effeminate figure. In 1925, for example,

Reynaldo Hahn's operetta *Mozart* featured the composer—at twenty-two years old—performed by a female soprano.[34]

Like Mozart's transition in the press from universal to Germanic, the underlying causes for this shift to the feminine side lie in the transition from the romantic to the classical Mozart. The nineteenth-century vision of *Don Juan* as romantic masterwork imbued the work's creator with some aspect of the (hyper)masculine Beethovenian suffering artist. As the romantic Mozart was gradually supplanted by his classical doppelgänger in the years after 1900, however, this protective masculinity was stripped away, exposing his long-ignored feminine qualities. Whereas in the mid-nineteenth century the composer was masculinized and divorced from his historical and geographical context, by World War I, Mozart was clearly a feminized German composer, and he and his operas were readily identified as products of the eighteenth century. The net result of all these changes was to open the composer to a new and damaging criticism: irrelevance to modern French audiences. After the War of 1870 and the Commune, the atmosphere in France became significantly more somber, reflecting the nation's crisis in identity during this time. Mozart's operas, with their happy endings and comic characters, simply did not reflect the prevailing aesthetic of post-1870 France, and neither did they provide confirmation for Republican ideals of masculinity and femininity. Without the cloak of "universality" protecting him, Mozart's works began to appear in some ways frivolous. Romain Rolland, for example, pointed to Mozart's decidedly unromantic life in contrast to Beethoven or Wagner:

> As Mozart himself did not suffer from passion, so his heroes are not troubled with broken hearts. The sadness of Anna, or even the jealousy of Elektra in *Idomeneo*, bear no resemblance to the spirit let loose by Beethoven and Wagner. The only passions that Mozart knew well were anger and pride. The greatest of all passions—"the entire Venus"—never appeared in him. It is this lack which gives his whole work a character of ineffable peace.[35]

Because Mozart's life lacked drama, or at least the romantic type of drama cultivated in the nineteenth century, his characters could not be interpreted as reflecting deep emotional situations. For Rolland, such a situation was not necessarily a negative aspect of Mozart's operas, but what Rolland saw as their "ineffable peace" was viewed by other critics as a fundamental lack of necessary dramatic focus. As early as 1878, Wagner—whose opinions never failed to have an impact on the French—had leveled such an accusation at Mozart:

> Intelligent people praised the way in which the roughly sketched and incomplete nature of his texts, for example in *Don Juan*, lent itself to a masque, which corresponded so agreeably with his music, a music that reflected the most passionate aspects of the human situation in a charmingly delightful game.
>
> If this opinion could be easily misunderstood, and could even be disparaging and harmful, well, it was meant seriously and contained within itself the generally current opinion of our aesthetic experts regarding the proper activity of music, against which it is difficult to fight, even today. But I believe that Mozart completely exhausted this form of art, a form which, in a very deep sense, may be open to the charge of frivolity.[36]

Wagner does not deny that *Don Juan* dealt in some way with "the most passionate aspects of the human situation," but only as a "game," and not in a deeper way. Consequently, Mozart's type of opera was "open to the charge of frivolity."

Perceptions of the composer as somehow feminine likely did not help matters in this regard. As Katharine Ellis reminds us, for nineteenth-century music critics, the feminine was inextricably tied to the idea of *broderie*, frivolous ornament in music—style without substance.[37] As Mozart's image became tinged with an aura of femininity so too did his music, opening it to the charge of being nothing more than *broderie*, bereft of deeper meaning. The counterpart to this frivolity was the sublime, a characteristic that would allow the music to touch on the higher mysteries of human nature and transcend any claim of emptiness or femininity.

What Mozart needed to succeed in the fin de siècle was an opera that could demonstrate his sublimity, proving that music was not only serious but fundamentally moral, and could thus provide the sense of pathos that many audience members (and critics) sought onstage. This issue took center stage with one particular early twentieth-century production: the 1909 *Magic Flute* at the Opéra-Comique. This staging offered fin-de-siècle critics, producers, and audiences a new chance to find relevance in Mozart's operas, saving these works from the obscurity that loomed threateningly on the horizon. Not all critics jumped at this chance, however, so *The Magic Flute* presents a clear example of critical discord regarding how, precisely, Mozart's works should be featured in the Operatic Museum.

Sublimity, Religion, and Gender in *The Magic Flute*

In yet another comparison between Mozart and Raphael, Camille Bellaigue found that the link between the two artists lay in the "grace" of their artworks, a quality shared with the ancient Greeks: "The genius of Mozart is at once ideal and familiar, superior and approachable, without a single shock, or even a strain, resulting from this encounter. He arrives at the sublime sometimes by grandeur, sometimes—more often—by grace. I do not know anyone else besides the Greeks, or Raphael after them, who were able to achieve sublimity by this latter path."[38] Grace—ironically, the very element that led to Mozart's feminine reputation—is thus the key to unlocking the sublime in music. In a way, then, Bellaigue used sublimity as a shield, defending the composer against charges of femininity and frivolity. If Mozart's music was sublime, it automatically transcended such considerations. *The Magic Flute*, with its vaguely religious plot and suitably heroic characters, offered critics and audience members a chance to see this side of Mozart's music, one that might better resonate with fin-de-siècle ideologies.

Unique among Mozart's popular operas, throughout the nineteenth century, *The Magic Flute* had a reputation as an inherently moral work. Despite the significant differences between the work's widely varying French adaptations, the plot was always an epic tale of good triumphing over evil, and the superiority of the virtuous over the wicked. Unlike *Le nozze di Figaro*, for example, where even the noblest of characters is capable of deception and duplicity when serving a higher purpose, in *The Magic Flute* the characters of Pamina, Sarastro, and Tamino epitomize purity and simplicity of spirit. Through these qualities—descriptive of both the characters and their music—the work appealed directly to the French ideal of the musical sublime. The idea of the sublime, the modern French origins of which can be traced to Diderot, was crystallized in musical criticism by Berlioz. As Ellis has pointed out, the sublime was a major topic in Berlioz's criticism, where he used the term to identify "the noblest of human sentiments and the loftiest of human aspirations"—a definition that later writers adopted.[39]

French critics took note of this quality fairly early in the history of *The Magic Flute*'s reception. In his review of the 1855 production (reprinted in a collection of writings on music in 1880), for example, Henri Blaze de Bury wrote of the pure and noble character of the romance between Tamino and Pamina: "Of all the sentiments that men experience, the purest and most divine is that which women engender in them. But the kind of love that Tamino speaks about is not at all passion, as in *Don Juan* or *les Noces de Figaro*—it is something more moral, more sublime, a goal that one can only reach through initiation."[40] According to Blaze de Bury, the emotions expressed in Mozart's Italian operas were mere passion, while the love expressed in *The Magic Flute* was of a more sublime character, unburdened by either the worldliness of Susanna and Figaro or the depredations of Don Giovanni.

Notions of *The Magic Flute*'s sublime qualities did not end with the nineteenth century, and the issue became a focal point of critical discussion around the 1909 production at the Opéra-Comique, which we have already discussed at length in the preceding chapter. For many critics, the nobility of the *The Magic Flute*'s story—presented in a totally new translation for the occasion, and one quite close to the original German—was matched by the sublime clarity, purity, and simplicity of its music. Fauré found sublimity not only in the opera's central romance, but in the work as a whole. For him, it was an expression of "the purest and most ideal perfection." He continued: "Does a music exist that can give us impressions at once so immediate and so profound, a music that, without exerting the least effort, keeps the spirit in such joy, such tranquility, and which, at the same time, as the strongest, or most exquisite, or most serene emotions, results in such great learning?"[41] Here again, Fauré ties *The Magic Flute* to nineteenth-century notions of the sublime in music. The contradictory descriptions of the work—simplicity-profundity, joy-tranquility, strongest–most serene emotions—are essential elements of Berliozian notions of the sublime. Identifying *The Magic Flute* as a "sublime" work, whether explicitly or implicitly, would go a long way in defending Mozart against the charges of frivolity—associated with *broderie*, as I have already discussed. Sublimity and *broderie* were regarded in the nineteenth century as oxymoronic (though some music rested uncomfortably on the border), and thus any composer capable of creating such sublime masterpieces was at least to some extent shielded from reproach for more seemingly frivolous works.

At the very least, *The Magic Flute* is an unquestionably moral opera. In fact, it is a work that self-consciously delights in its own heavy-handed moralizing, manifested most obviously in the maxims that occur at regular intervals throughout the work.[42] In this sense, *The Magic Flute* is educational in its focus, less a moral opera than an opera *about* morality. This aspect of the world would undoubtedly have resonated with the portion of fin-de-siècle French audiences who looked to the theater for moral affirmation rather than decadence. Some critics, in fact, took opera's moralizing a step further, crossing over the line into religion. In the popular journal *Musica*, for example, Georges Pioch wrote:

> It is certain that Sarastro's sublime phrases, the religious scenes that confer on *La Flûte enchantée* a sacred value, surpass the beauties where Mozart's clear genius had flourished before 1791. We know that *La Flûte enchantée* is his final dramatic work. In it, he seemed animated by that emotion of thought that raises all the arts to the highest summit of human consciousness.... The libretto of *La Flûte enchantée*, by its dual nature as both magical and religious, was perfect for evoking his effusions, which are at once thoughtful and enjoyable.[43]

For Pioch, *The Magic Flute* had a "sacred value" above any of Mozart's other works. This additional element seems to have conferred on the work a special dramatic significance, allowing it to ascend to "the highest summit of human consciousness." Regardless of the plot details, on some fundamental level the opera was a religious work, and thus attained a special kind of sublimity. And its composer—given special insight, Pioch suggests obliquely, by virtue of his proximity to death—was far beyond his arguably frivolous earlier works.

This conflation of metaphysical religious content with aesthetic value was not unknown to fin-de-siècle audiences. Operas that espoused moral values in the form of religious or quasi-religious plots were fairly common. Several of Wagner's operas focused on issues of religious redemption and values, particularly *Tannhäuser* and *Parsifal*. In France, Gounod's *Jeanne d'Arc* (1873) and *Polyeucte* (1878) dealt with the subject of early Christian martyrdom. Slightly later, Vincent d'Indy's *Fervaal* (1897, Parisian premiere at the Opéra-Comique in 1898) was focused on the influence of religious morality on the title character. D'Indy and others like him were adamant that opera (and music in general) should provide a moral compass for audience members, keeping them on a righteous, religious path.[44] Though not explicitly Christian (the setting of the 1909 production was an ambiguously mythological Egypt), *The Magic Flute* nevertheless represented the type of moralistic work that could play into this trend.

In fact, *The Magic Flute*'s abstract religious qualities may have assisted some critics in viewing it as a moral work. Several major fin-de-siècle works, notably those by Fauré, toyed with the boundaries between the Christian values and a more "pagan" religious sensibility. Despite its traditionally Catholic genre, the composer's popular *Requiem*, for example, was viewed by many critics as being only partially a Christian work, more in keeping with the religions of antiquity than with modern French Catholicism.[45] The song cycle *La Chanson d'Ève* (1910), which Fauré was composing during the 1909 *Magic Flute* production, combines elements of pantheism and Catholicism even more explicitly, while still displaying religious sentiment.[46] The agnostic (or at least idiosyncratically theist) Fauré, and many other critics, found that these quasi-Christian works nonetheless contained a deep religious sentiment outside of a specific orthodoxy. Some critics treated *The Magic Flute* similarly. Bellaigue, for example, in his review of the 1909 production in *La Revue des deux mondes*, opined that although the religion of the priests in *The Magic Flute* was unspecified (i.e., only quasi-Christian at best), the transcendental emotions their music expressed were clear. "Who can deny," he asked, "that their sublime songs breathe the very essence, or the ideal, of religious sentiment!"[47] This pantheist sentiment toward the work allowed *The Magic Flute* to offer a moral message not only from an orthodox standpoint but also from a more generally religious, or quasi-religious, perspective.

Although most of *The Magic Flute* centers around Tamino's searches—first for Pamina and then for Enlightenment—I believe that for fin-de-siècle audiences the sublimity and morality of the opera would have been highly evident in the gender roles enacted on the stage, and, particularly, in Pamina. As traditional gender roles were beginning to erode around 1900, many, if not most, of the questions regarding onstage morality revolved around the female characters. Central in the discussion of gender in turn-of-the-century Paris was the dichotomy of the "Real Woman" (*la vraie femme*) versus the "New Woman" (*la femme nouvelle*). As the French feminist movement began to gain more momentum in the 1890s, the dangerously masculine New Woman posed a threat to traditional power structures and family structures.[48] As art historian Debora Silverman has pointed out, in the politically and socially unstable atmosphere of the fin de siècle, "even slight tampering with female identity and female activity was experienced as a threat to the entire structure; the menace of the *femme nouvelle* was therefore met with an active campaign to relegitimate women's procreative and moral role."[49] Certainly, many critics complained loudly enough about the increasingly prevalent images of the "New Woman" onstage; Jules Lemaître (who reviewed operas as well) wrote of Jules Case's influential play *La Vassale* (1897) that the work presented only "yet another woman beating our ears with demands for her rights."[50]

Unlike the New Woman, the Real Woman posed no threat to French masculinity, and, in fact, supported it. As Edward Berenson explains:

> *La femme, la vraie femme,* was for most French men of the era a creature governed by her emotions. Her intellect was limited, her practical and technical abilities restrained. The real woman acted not in the exterior world of politics and business, or even of literature and the arts, but in the inner sanctum of the home. She did not make a spectacle of herself... nor did she seek to upstage her husband. This womanly woman had no ambition beyond that of caring for her husband, her home, and most important of all her children. She was frail and frivolous, given to transports of childlike sentiment. But her disposition, frustrating as it might occasionally be, was as it should be. For the real woman needed not to shape the world, but to secure the family.[51]

It stands to reason that more conservative audience members, seeking validation of their traditional social power structures, would turn to theatrical stages for examples.[52] Male audience members sought more traditional depictions of women both to reaffirm their own masculinity and to serve as models for their wives and daughters. Many female audience members likewise found equal reassurance in seeing their own conservative values reflected onstage, or at least in finding solidarity with other women whose male-dominated lives to some extent mirrored their own. Producers and composers were happy to oblige them, and opera houses were filled with depictions of either "real women"—who often die a sacrificial death—or transgressive women, who are suitably punished by the final curtain.[53] But femininity was not the only gender issue at play on the fin-de-siècle stage. Demoralized and demasculinized men (and, again, traditionally minded women) of the Third Republic also turned to the theater for strong male role models.[54] Mozart's operas, however, mostly failed to offer suitable models for either sex.

Socially acceptable (at least by nineteenth-century standards) female roles do not appear with any frequency in Mozart's works, and most of the male characters are either feminized or challenged in their authority. *Le nozze di Figaro* (*Les Noces de Figaro* in France), conspicuously absent from the stages of both the Opéra and Opéra-Comqiue after 1886, features two main female roles (leaving aside the cross-dressed Cherubino, who is a problematic figure in the best of times): Susanna and the Countess. The former spends most of the opera avoiding the Count's unwanted advances, and generally outsmarting the male characters (including her fiancé). The Countess, while a paragon of faithfulness (in Mozart's opera, at least), is almost equally crafty, and by the end of the opera has reduced her ostensibly powerful husband to begging for forgiveness, literally on his knees. And, as Mary Hunter has pointed out, the Countess's authority is largely tied to the decline of her husband's: "Her trajectory rises just as the Count's begins to fall. Within the world of the plot she exercises very little power. . . . But in the auditorium, to the audience (at least in modern times), the Countess's power is unparalleled; she is the one who literally stops the show with 'Porgi amor,' and who provides the literal coup de grace at the end by agreeing to pardon the Count for his transgressions."[55]

Although the opera ends with what David Levin calls a "flurry of domestication," in which all major characters (save, arguably, Cherubino and Barberina) are systematically paired off into "normal" couples, this happy resolution is brought about almost entirely by the efforts of Susanna and the Countess.[56] We must surely agree with Charles Ford when he points out that in Mozart's operas, "women are never again allowed the strength of Susanna and the Contessa together in *Le Nozze di Figaro*."[57] Neither of these figures could be described in any way as "frail and frivolous," and both are anything but submissive to the Count's demands. Furthermore, far from being punished for their disruptions of the proper social order, they are rewarded with apologies and vows of love and devotion. Susanna and the Countess, in fact, bear more in common with the "New Woman" than with her antithesis.

Fin-de-siècle audiences were faced with a similar situation with *Don Giovanni*, where, once again, none of the opera's female characters could reasonably be interpreted as a "Real Woman." Donna Anna, physically violated and orphaned by the Don in a single night, had the potential to appeal to the sympathies of fin-de-siècle male audiences. Not content to play the powerless victim in need of male rescuing, in her feverish quest for vengeance she drags Ottavio behind her for most of the opera, rendering him almost totally feminized. Worse still, perhaps (from a fin-de-siècle perspective), is the fact that, despite his efforts on her behalf, she refuses (at least temporarily) to marry him at the work's conclusion, and thus rejects the true occupations of the "Real Woman": wifehood and motherhood. Her lust for revenge, and subsequent refusal to be suitably domesticated, was decidedly unfeminine.[58] Donna Elvira is driven to near madness by the sheer force of her passion and hatred for Don Giovanni—embodying the emotional aspect of the "Real Woman" but with none of the mitigating docility. The peasant girl Zerlina makes a cuckold of her husband Masetto on their wedding day, leaving her own party with Don Giovanni (thought she does later repent and beg Masetto for forgiveness). Again, none of these women are punished for their dangerous lack of femininity. Only Don Giovanni suffers for his misdeeds—which may themselves be perceived as resulting only from the expression of extreme (one might say pathological) masculinity. The Don, the paragon of the romantic (anti)hero, was in danger of giving ground to more moral alternatives.

Because of these transgressive female characters and the woes they cause their male counterparts, Mozart's libretti were equally unlikely to provide Republican men with suitable role models. In *Le Nozze di Figaro*, by the end of the day, both the Count and Figaro have clearly been bested by their wives. In *Don Giovanni*, Masetto has been abandoned (if only briefly) and is utterly powerless to exact any revenge on the Don, an impotence shared by Don Ottavio. The wily Leporello is essentially a slave to his master, and the Don himself is a slave to his desires. The only possible virtuous and strong male character in the opera is the Commendatore, who dies in the work's first scene, defending the virtue of his daughter.

Mozart's other operas offered no better alternatives, either for men or women. *Così fan tutte*, at its very heart a work hinging on female infidelity—infidelity that goes entirely unpunished, at that—was viewed in France as an almost entirely immoral work, and was not revived until 1920. *Idomeneo*, although performed in a concert version at the Schola Cantorum in 1902, remained virtually unknown to French audiences, as did *La clemenza di Tito* and Mozart's early works. *The Abduction from the Seraglio*, performed at the Opéra-Comique in 1903, was by all accounts an unsuccessful production, leaving critics and audiences alike bored.[59] In short, audiences in search of traditional gender roles in Mozart's operas were, for the most part, bound to be disappointed. I do not mean to suggest that French audiences consciously interpreted Mozart's operas in this fashion, nor that characters like

Susanna or Donna Elvira were necessarily perceived as subversive, though neither would I rule out such a response. Mozart's operas simply did not offer the unambiguous morality and gender roles that audiences found in Gluck's, as we will see in part 2.

Except, that is, for *The Magic Flute*, which could hardly be clearer in terms of gender roles.[60] Though fin-de-siècle critics are almost entirely silent on the matter—they seldom engaged with character analysis at all— the images of male and female power relations that audiences would have seen in 1909 were unmistakable. Jacques Chailley, for example, sees the entire opera as the conflict between the Masculine, embodied in Sarastro, and the Feminine, represented by the Queen of the Night.[61] The dominant positive personality of the work is clearly Sarastro, the wise and benevolent priest figure. Here (essentially alone in Mozart's oeuvre) is a male figure without flaw, upholding purity and morality at all costs while at the same time presenting a clearly powerful and masculine figure. He provides Tamino with a strong role model, steering the young prince to the light and helping him to achieve Enlightenment. Indeed, part of that path seems to be the rejection of the Feminine, as the Prince's most painful trial is the rejection of Pamina in order to enter Sarastro's (masculine) order. As Kristi Brown-Montesano puts it, Pamina "may be his betrothed, but his faithfulness to the tenets of manliness must come first."[62]

Like her father, Pamina is without flaw, prominently displaying *la vraie femme* onstage for all to see. She accedes without question to the demands of both Sarastro and Tamino, and seems to exist primarily to support them in their endeavors. Her character is, in fact, in large part defined by her relationships to these two male figures, one father, one husband. When Tamino seemingly rejects her during his trials, she does not turn to anger or seek revenge on the prince for spurning her; rather, without him her life is simply devoid of meaning, not worth living at all. Her focus on making herself useful to both husband and father—her focus, in short, on domesticity rather than on her own ambition—makes her the very image of the Real Woman so highly sought after in fin-de-siècle France.

Historian David Pomfret has pointed out the extent to which the young female body became an object of French national pride in the form of Coronation of the People's Muse, a recurring large-scale event held throughout France in the early 1900s, which centered on the selection of an adolescent girl (aged sixteen to twenty-one) to serve as an embodiment of the Muse.[63] "Muses" were chosen for their physical beauty, as might be expected, but also for their virtuous behavior. They were subjected to rigorous investigations before being chosen, assuring that they upheld the highest moral standards of femininity, chastity, and so on. They were chosen, in short, for their capacity to serve as models—resulting, intentionally or not, in reinforced traditional gender and power structures by putting a public face on acceptable behavior.[64] This choice of a young girl was significant for French culture of the time, as the morals of young women were increasingly called into question. As Pomfret reveals, newspaper reports of the Muse often described how young women in danger of becoming immoral "New Women" could be "rescued" and held up as paragons of Republican morality.[65] Celebrations of the "People's Muse" drew thousands of spectators across France, and became a kind of national emblem for the sublimity of young womanhood.

Returning now to *The Magic Flute*, we may start to see the striking similarities between these young Muses and Pamina. Just as these young women were often rescued from their immoral lifestyles as "New Girls," Tamino and Sarastro liberate Pamina from her mother's grasp and make sure she is indoctrinated in the "correct" lifestyle; by the end of the opera, she has rejected her mother entirely and undergoes the trials herself, cementing her position as subservient to both Sarastro and (presumably) Tamino. In doing so, Pamina also evokes the archetype of the young woman who rebels against an overbearing mother, played out time and again in the literature, theater, and music of the fin de siècle.

The contrast between the *femme nouvelle* and the *vraie femme* was a typical stage device of the time, although usually with daughters cast as the former. In *The Magic Flute*, however, Pamina may be read as a young woman saved from the toxic transgressions of her mother. As such, Pamina is the perfect foil for the Queen of the Night. The polar opposite of her daughter, the Queen seeks power for herself, meaning that she must overcome her (ex-?)husband Sarastro, upsetting the "rightful" masculine domination of the home. As Brown-Montesano summarizes, the Queen is "vengeful, scheming, defiant toward male authority, proud, violent, and stubborn"; in short, she was (from a male perspective) the very image of the *femme nouvelle*.[66] She thus represented onstage the fears of socially conservative audience members in fin-de-siècle France, threatening traditional hierarchical structures in both the family and the workplace. We may think here of Louise in *La Vassale*, who—much to the astonishment and derision of French critics—rejected her motherly duties in favor of ambition. "In me," she declares, "there is the pride of someone who wants to use all her forces, faculties, who wants to develop, grow, belong and devote myself only to myself."[67] Such staged representations of the "New Woman" were wont to abandon the sacred duties of the home, often leading to the downfall (if not deaths) of family members and friends, rendering them for many audience members into cautionary tales.

From a fin-de-siècle perspective, such is the plight of the Queen of the Night. By ambitiously stepping outside her traditional duties as mother and wife, she damns herself, and for transgressing such sacrosanct boundaries she is duly punished in the end. Furthermore, far from the "purity" and "simplicity" that many critics praised in *The Magic Flute*, the Queen's music is filled with empty coloratura passages—it is, in Carolyn Abbate's words, "the degradation of melodic line, which has the capacity to represent passion, into that which should have been supplementary: into the ornament."[68] The Queen, in stark contrast to the sublimity of much of the rest of the opera, is pure *broderie*. Thus, she vilified not only the *nouvelle femme* but also the feminine ornamental style of music that nineteenth- and early twentieth-century French critics (particularly Berlioz) rejected. The New Woman is cast down, the Real Woman triumphant, and balance—that is, a patriarchal society that privileges reason as opposed to an emotion-dominated matriarchy—is restored.

Again, I do not mean to suggest that audiences or critics explicitly understood these issues of morality, religion, and gender in fin-de-siècle terms. Yet, consciously or not, Mozart's works presented operagoers with concerns that were very much at the forefront of French thought—which was crucial to Mozart's continued success. He was, as we have seen, in a dangerous position. Stripped of his romantic, universalist reputation, he became a classical and perhaps feminized figure, open to allegations of frivolity and irrelevance to modern audiences. His works had to demonstrate that despite (or perhaps because of) their classicism, they could yet resonate with contemporary concerns. Therein lay the key to success in the Operatic Museum: works had to be, above all, *relevant*. The ideal of a theater in which classical works could enter into dialogue with new music depended on the audience's having something to gain from the exchange.

But the restoration of Mozart's operas had some antecedents, as well, that helped prepare audiences to understand a classical opera in a new context. The Gluck revival that began at the Opéra-Comique in the 1890s undoubtedly affected Mozart's reception, too. Not coincidentally, the pivotal 1909 production of *The Magic Flute* appeared only two years after the last of Gluck's five French operas to be revived in fin-de-siècle Paris appeared at the theater. Gluck's operas came to the forefront of the repertoire just as Mozart's were in decline, providing a substitute that possessed the exact qualities many critics found lacking in the latter composer, at least until the 1909 *Magic Flute* production: gravitas and morality. In many ways, it was the changing perceptions of classical opera's relevance to modern audiences that emerged from the Gluck productions at the Opéra-Comique (and, on one occasion, at the Opéra) that allowed Mozart's triumphant entry into the Operatic Museum in the first decades of the twentieth century. In the following chapter, we turn to Gluck's gradual rise to prominence, and how the sustained popularity of his operas during the 1890s and 1900s profoundly shaped the development of the Operatic Museum.

Part Two

Gluck

Chapter Five

Resurrections

For Parisian critics and audiences of the fin de siècle, Gluck was without doubt one of the great luminaries of music history, a name worthy of mention alongside Mozart or Rameau. As a cornerstone of French music history, he was a crucial to establishing and interpreting narratives of France's musical past. But just as important was Gluck's central role in defining the nation's musical present and shaping its future; in addition to being touted by many critics as a model for French opera composers, he frequently served as a focal point for aesthetic debates. More than either of the other composers this book examines, Gluck's sudden revival and sustained popularity illustrated the Operatic Museum's potential to French audiences and critics, providing a concrete rather than hypothetical example of how works from France's past could connect with audiences and artistic trends of the present.

The reasons for the resurgence of Gluck's music were both manifold and complex, and every critic and composer had different reasons for supporting (or decrying) the composer. These positions often drew upon Gluck's earlier nineteenth-century reception, and so I begin this chapter with an overview of the composer's historical position. We can then turn to the Gluck revival that steadily gained momentum after the 1870s, focusing on two main sources of interest in his music: the Pelletan Edition of his "French" operas and the frequent performance of his music in Parisian concert series. Finally, I will examine critical response to the culmination of these efforts in the 1890s and 1900s, when each of Gluck's great French operas received a new production on the Parisian stages.

"Gluck Is Dead, and His Music Is Sick": Reception to 1875

Largely because his status as a "French" composer had been definitively established during the composer's own lifetime, Gluck's early reception in France was a much smoother process than Mozart's. Though not French by birth, Gluck adapted several of his operas—the most important being *Orfeo ed Euridice* (1762) and *Alceste* (1767)—for the Parisian stage (in 1774 and 1776, respectively), and also composed major new works for Paris, including *Iphigénie en Aulide* (1774), *Armide* (1777), *Iphigénie en Tauride* (1779), and *Echo et Narcisse* (1779). Gluck thus faced none of the initial chauvinism that plagued the reception of Mozart's operas in the early nineteenth century (see chapter 2). On the contrary, Gluck's operas remained popular through the end of the eighteenth century and well into the 1820s, with the exception of a brief hiatus in their performance during the Terror following the Revolution.[1] Not only were the works still performed at the turn of the century, but they occupied a place of honor, essentially the cornerstone of the Opéra repertoire.[2]

In the first decades of the nineteenth century, however, the Parisian predilection for Gluck began to wane."[3] As was the case with Mozart's reception in the same time period, issues of national identity subtly (and occasionally overtly) crept into the discourse surrounding Gluck's operas. For some critics his Germanic origins simply outweighed even the composer's considerable concessions to French taste. In his review of an 1810 performance of *Iphigénie en Aulide*, for example, the well-known critic Julien Louis Geoffroy accused Gluck of not fully understanding the libretto, based on Jean Racine's play *Iphigénie* (1674). "It is likely," Geoffroy opined, "that the German musician did not understand French well enough to be sensitive to the melody of the most harmonious of our poets."[4] By suggesting that Gluck did not—and actually *could* not—understand Racine's text, Geoffroy goes beyond undermining the composer's mastery of the French language: he implies that Gluck lacked an understanding of the French spirit, and thus could not create "French" artworks. Gluck was effectively cut off from the great artists of French history (such as Racine), fundamentally unable to enter into their pantheon. No critic dared deny Gluck's importance as a composer, but even many of those who accorded him a place of distinction in French music history clamored for new productions on the stage. After decades atop the operatic canon, Gluck's position was giving way to newer composers with less dangerously Germanic works. "Gluck is dead," one reviewer wrote of the 1810 *Iphigénie en Aulide*, "and his music is sick."[5]

Gluck's problematic historical positioning in Paris during the first half of the nineteenth century is neatly reflected in the writings of Hector Berlioz and François-Henri-Joseph Blaze (Castil-Blaze), the first of whom saw the eighteenth-century master as a model worthy of maintaining on the stage, while the latter saw him as a relic of another time, respectable but not fit for modern audiences.[6] For Castil-Blaze it was Mozart, not Gluck, who led the way to the future; as we have already seen in chapter 2, the critic was instrumental in the adaptation and presentation of Mozart's operas in Paris. With Mozart as the symbol for artistic progress, it is little wonder that Gluck's continued dominance at the Opéra might seem counterproductive. While he could admire Gluck's music from afar, Castil-Blaze nonetheless believed the eighteenth-century *tragédie lyrique* had—through sheer overexposure if nothing else—lost its ability to affect a nineteenth-century Parisian audience, and consequently bored the public. The critic's comments on the Opéra's 1825 revival of *Armide* are revealing: "*Armide* continually contradicts the taste of the day, and the superannuated, gothic turns found on every page do not encourage music-lovers to listen without impatience."[7] Even as early as 1801, one critic could report "now high society arrives at the Opéra only for the ballet. A fly could be heard when Vestris, Mademoiselle Clotide, or Madame Gardel dance, but the patrons cough, spit, chat, or smirk when Alcestis or Iphigenia sing."[8] To combat this operatic ennui, Castil-Blaze called for either the adaptation of Gluck for modern audiences, or the programming of newer works—Mozart, for example. Thus, the rise of Mozart's operatic star in Paris was to some extent linked to the fall of Gluck's.

Most audience members shared Castil-Blaze's opinion until the late nineteenth century, and Gluck's operas were shelved, revered but not staged. But while Castil-Blaze adopted a realist view of French audiences' demands, Berlioz perceived Gluck's works as the pinnacle of French operatic achievement, models for emulation rather than ossified holdovers from a previous era. Faced with criticism like Castil-Blaze's, Berlioz became the chief champion of Gluck's music in the nineteenth century. From the 1820s on, he routinely turned to Gluck as the high point of operatic composition in his criticism, and attempted to position himself as the heir apparent to the eighteenth-century master's reforms (much as we saw with Gounod and Mozart in chapter 2). In Joël-Marie Fauquet's words, "Berlioz denounced the abandon into which the works of Gluck had fallen, urged that the integrity of his idol's musical texts be respected, and thus invoked a tradition of which he considered himself the primary keeper."[9] Berlioz's entreaties fell largely on deaf ears, however, and by the 1830s, Gluck's operas were nearly absent from the Parisian stages, aside from a revival of *Orphée* in 1848.

During this time, however, performances of fragments of the operas appeared regularly on concert programs, distilling the essence of each work into a few favorite morceaux. At the Société des Concerts at the Paris Conservatoire, for example, hardly a concert season went by in the mid-century without some of the popular excerpts from *Orphée* or *Alceste*.[10] But reducing Gluck's dramatic works to a few choruses, one or two arias, and the "Scène des Enfers" from *Orphée* was not enough for Berlioz. The admiration he felt for the older composer remained undimmed, as did his musical and critical efforts on Gluck's behalf. Perhaps the single most important event in Gluck reception during the nineteenth century is the well-known revival of *Orphée* at the Théâtre-Lyrique in 1859 (under the direction of Léon Carvalho), for which Berlioz was largely responsible.[11] The opera faded in popularity after the 1824 revival featuring the debut of tenor Adolphe Nourrit (who became known for his portrayal of the title character in Mozart's *Don Juan*), and was seldom performed after the end of the 1820s.[12] For the 1859 production, Berlioz rewrote the role of Orphée for the mezzo-soprano Pauline Viardot, whose reputation as a singer was well established by that time, as was her status as an authority on eighteenth-century opera, as we have already seen from her association with the autograph score of *Don Giovanni*.[13] This production was well received by Parisian critics—Berlioz's became the new standard version of the opera—and succeeded in rekindling some interest in Gluck and his works. The reviewer Philippe Martin, for example, presents a very different scene from the distracted audiences of the 1820s: "*Orphée*, one of Gluck's immortal masterworks, was sung before a room replete with musical and artistic illustrations, which listened with a religious silence to the admirable recitatives, in which one finds tenderness, sadness, and the most exalted passion expressed with an indescribable eloquence, without noise, but simply and naturally."[14]

Léon Escudier, writing in *La France musicale*, was even more laudatory, setting the "simplicity" of Gluck's music against more complicated modern music:

> The most touching simplicity restrains the music drama. There is nothing disjointed, nothing false, nothing banal; it is dramatic inspiration in all its grace and power. It is the purity of the melodic line; it is the charm of Raphael combined with the grandeur and the energy of Corneille! Everything is divine in this eternal masterwork, clarified by the rays of immortality, and the song and orchestra. The years will pass—the centuries as well.... Gluck will never pass; he will remain on his antique bronze pedestal, upright, like the gods of antiquity.[15]

Here Gluck's works have gone from being outdated to being immortal, and his artistic achievements, far from impeding the progress of music in France, are put onto the same level as the great artists of French art and literature. Significantly, by emphasizing the "simplicity" and "naturalness" of the opera, critics borrowed Gluck's own terminology, drawing from the composer's preface to *Alceste* (1767), which famously called for a reform from the perceived excesses of baroque opera seria. Gluck's operas—and the aesthetic vision they represented—were regaining ground they had lost in the first half of the nineteenth century.

Not surprisingly, the Opéra jumped relatively quickly on the success of *Orphée* at the Théâtre-Lyrique, and produced *Alceste* in 1861 (for the first time since 1826). Berlioz again adapted the title role for Viardot, albeit with some hesitation. The appearance of *Alceste* in 1861 is significant, immediately following the failure of Wagner's *Tannhäuser* and his new compositional "système" to win over critics and audiences. In the post-*Tannhäuser* atmosphere of late 1861 Paris, comparisons between Gluck and Wagner were on the tip of nearly every critic's tongue, and reviews routinely reprinted and analyzed the preface to *Alceste*, exploring in detail how the composer applied his musico-dramatic theories to the opera's composition.[16] A prominent three-part article series by A. Thurner in *La France musicale* focused on Gluck's artistic principles, for example, and Berlioz himself addressed the issue in the *Journal des débats*.[17] This trend continued through the 1860s and affected the reception of both composers well into the twentieth century. As Wagnerism infiltrated Paris in the 1880s and 1890s, Gluck's music became a battleground between those who saw Gluck as the predecessor to Wagner and those who saw him as an alternative, setting the stage for the fin-de-siècle positioning of the two composers, which I discuss in detail in chapter 6.

Despite the aesthetic importance and relative commercial success of the 1861 *Alceste*, the production failed to maintain the momentum established with *Orphée*, and although *Alceste* was revived at the Opéra again in 1866, Gluck's return to prominence seemed to have stalled. The problem with a sustained success for Gluck's operas, at least according to Fétis, rested more with nineteenth-century audiences than with the works themselves. Writing to the *Revue et Gazette musicale* in response to the 1861 *Alceste*, Fétis argued in favor of presenting Gluck's music in concert excerpts (as in Fétis's own *Concerts historiques*) rather than onstage; modern audiences simply found Gluck's austere dramatic style boring—beautiful, but without content.[18] Fétis's perspective seems to have been the dominant one in the decades that followed, and as a result of this surprisingly lukewarm reception in 1866, Gluck's works again retreated from the opera theaters of Paris. By the fin de siècle, however, the stage was set for a major return of Gluck's operas to the forefront of the Parisian musical scene. France began to seek its own musical champions to combat outside influences, a trend that would continue through the turn of the century. The city was primed to set up a French composer in opposition to Germanic (i.e., Wagnerian) influence, and Gluck was the natural choice.

Beginning in 1896, Gluck's operas returned in force to the Parisian music scene, and over the course of little more than a decade, each of his five major operas—*Orphée et Eurydice, Alceste, Armide, Iphigénie en Tauride,* and *Iphigénie en Aulide*—received a high-profile revival. Something had changed between 1866 and 1896, allowing Gluck's operas to strike a newly sympathetic chord with fin-de-siècle French audiences. In the intervening decades, the preparatory groundwork for Gluck's return took place on two fronts simultaneously: in the concert hall, with frequent performances of beloved excerpts, and in the library, with a monumental new edition of Gluck's operas. We can now explore these two subjects in some detail, revealing the tireless work on Gluck's behalf to prepare audiences to understand and appreciate Gluck's masterworks onstage.

Gluck in the Concert Hall

Although Gluck disappeared again from the operatic stages of Paris for the second time following the less-than-successful 1866 production of *Alceste*, audiences nonetheless had ample opportunity to hear his music in the concert hall. The nineteenth century saw a proliferation of major concert series, several of which offered weekly concerts of orchestral and operatic works during much of the year. The Société des Concerts du Conservatoire, begun in 1828, was the oldest of these; historically fairly conservative in its repertoire, it continued to toe the canonical line through the end of the century. Newer concert societies offered more daring programming choices in their efforts to attract audiences—most notably the Concerts Pasdeloup, Concerts Colonne, and the Concerts Lamoureux (begun in 1861, 1873, and 1881, respectively).[19] Each of these series contributed to bringing Parisian audiences not only new music—most notably Wagner—but also seldom-heard excerpts of *musique ancienne*, a problematically nebulous category that seems to have stretched from the Renaissance to, in some cases, the middle of the nineteenth century.

The importance of concert series in spreading and popularizing these works to a large middle-class audience can hardly be overstated. The low price of concert tickets as opposed to either the Opéra or Opéra-Comique encouraged audience members to take chances on unfamiliar repertoire, and allowed for a wider distribution of music across class boundaries. Furthermore, concerts offered a crucial opportunity to prepare Parisian audiences for new or unusual works at the Opéra or Opéra-Comique. Although opera houses presented only one work per night (usually), concerts could—and usually did—include excerpts of new or lesser-known works amid familiar favorites, preparing audiences for exposure to full-length operas. Wagner is the archetypical example in Paris; excerpts from his music dramas were played more or less constantly at Parisian concerts from the late 1870s on, with the assumption that the public, once sufficiently acquainted with Wagner's music, would be eager—or at least willing—to hear complete productions at the Opéra.

Early music, aside from the few excerpts from Gluck's operas that had been endlessly recycled since the early nineteenth century, was featured in a similar way. Often, selected examples of *musique ancienne* were presented as an educational, if also entertaining, aspect of programs, with the goals (occasionally stated explicitly) of improving the popular taste and instructing listeners in the glories of French music history—and France itself.[20] As Jane Fulcher succinctly puts it, toward the end of the century, "Nationalists... turned to culture as an effective but oblique means through which pertinaciously to disseminate and subtly insinuate the political values they still hoped to diffuse." In music, this process relied heavily on concert series to reach fruition. "By the time of World War I," Fulcher continues, "the results of such precedents would be clearly evident in a proliferation of politically pedagogical concerts designed to inseminate a sense of 'French values.'"[21]

Gluck's music played a major role in this process. In this context, where entertainment and education went hand in hand (we might neologistically call this type of concert programming "edutainment"), audiences saw short excerpts from the composer's operas, most often removed from any dramatic context. The composer was a regular feature on the programs of the influential Société des Concerts, for example, throughout the 1870s and 1880s (see table 5.1). The most popular selections on that series were instrumental: the "Entrée d'Orphée aux Champs-Elysées," the Overture to *Iphigénie en Aulide,* and excerpts from the ballet of the same opera. These excerpts by and large skirted the main focus of Gluck reception in the 1860s: Gluck's dramatic principles and their proximity (or lack thereof) to those of Wagner. Gradually, however, the instrumental excerpts began to give way to longer sections of Gluck's works, although the "fragments du ballet" from *Iphigénie en Aulide* remained popular until the turn of the century. In the 1890s, as the clamoring for Gluck's operas grew louder and complete productions appeared at the Opéra-Comique and the Opéra, the concert series often presented complete acts drawn from the works audiences could see at the opera house, much as we might see a teaser for an upcoming film at a theater.

But even these lengthier excerpts (or, on rare occasions, complete unstaged performances) lacked the dramatic possibilities of fully staged productions. Edme-Marie-Ernest Deldevez, who was for many years the director of the Société des Concerts, wrote in 1887:

> One regrets, it is endlessly repeated, that the Opéra does not busy itself with reviving *Armide, La Vestale* [by Spontini], and *Fernand Cortez* [also by Spontini], as well as other masterworks. But at least as far as our concerts go, one would hope that performance of excerpts from these same highly anticipated works would be favorably received by the same amateur public who would like to see the works performed at the theater. Well! no, the public remains cold to these advances....[22]

This "cold" reception may be a result of the works' context rather than indifference from those audience members who wished to see eighteenth-century opera returned to the theaters. Removed from their original

Table 5.1. Gluck at the Société des Concerts du Conservatoire, 1875–1914

Opera	Excerpt	Years
Alceste	Air ("Divinités du Styx")	1875, 1887
Iphigénie en Aulide	Fragments du Ballet (Prelude-Andantino-Gavotte)	1875, 1877 (two times), 1882, 1883, 1885, 1890, 1897, 1899
Orphée	Entrée d'Orphée aux Champs-Elysées	1876, 1878, 1879, 1884, 1888
Iphigénie en Aulide	Air de Danse	1876
Armide	Scène et Air	1877
Orphée	Air (probably "J'ai perdu mon Euridice")	1877
Armide	Choeur	1878
Iphigénie en Aulide	Overture	1880, 1882, 1884, 1898
Orphée	Recit, Air, Scène des Enfers	1880
Orphée	Fragment symphonique (probably Entrée aux Champs-Elysées)	1882
Orphée	Scène des Enfers	1883
Armide	Choeur ("Voici la charmante retraite")	1884
Orphée	Fragments (numerous)	1892
Alceste	Scenes from act 1	1895
Orphée	Act 2	1896
Armide	Act 3	1901
Orphée	Scène des Champs-Elysées	1904
Alceste	Fragments from act 1	1908

Source: The source for the information in this table is the online database of concerts maintained by D. Kern Holoman, available at http://hector.ucdavis.edu/sdc/. This Web site is the companion to Holoman's text *The Société des Concerts du Conservatoire, 1828–1967* (Berkeley and Los Angeles: University of California Press, 2004), which remains largely silent on the prevalence of early music on the concert series during the time period of this study.

setting—the opera house—these isolated arias and choruses were limited in their ability to convey the dramatic possibilities of the complete works to modern Parisian audiences. Deldevez's frustration aside, it is clear that many audience members did find these examples of *musique ancienne* appealing, since most of the major concert series of the fin de siècle continued to perform works by Gluck on a frequent basis—including (in addition to the Société des Concerts) the Colonne, Lamoureux, and Pasdeloup concert series.[23] Concerts featuring the Opéra soprano Gabrielle Krauss performing "Divinités du Styx" from *Alceste* (along with works by other composers) brought in the most ticket sales of 1886 on the Concerts Colonne, for example, prompting the popular excerpt of Gluck's opera to be repeated a number of times over the following seasons.[24] His works also appeared occasionally at the salon of the Princesse de Polignac for about a decade beginning in 1896, as well as on programs of the Société des Grandes Auditions Musicales de France (led by the Comtesse Greffulhe), including a production of *Iphigénie en Tauride* in 1893.[25] These concerts in the 1880s and 1890s clearly whetted the appetites of many audience members. The musicologist Julien Tiersot, a major figure in fin-de-siècle Gluck revival, pointed out in 1896 that "if those from my generation still have not been able to see Gluck's works in a single Parisian theater, at least we have been students in the cult of the old master, and his music has become familiar to us thanks to the frequent performances that have been given at symphonic concerts."[26]

Beginning around the turn of the century, another important source for the dissemination of Gluck's works was the Schola Cantorum, largely due to the influence of its director, Vincent d'Indy, whose relationship to Gluck's works I will treat in more detail later. Although in its early years the Schola focused almost exclusively on early sacred music, by the turn of the century its focus had expanded to include a wide range of musical styles before approximately 1800.[27] Gluck was a pivotal figure in music history for d'Indy; the older composer's works were staples of the Schola curriculum and were regularly featured in its concerts. As with other concert series, Gluck's presence at the Schola began with shorter excerpts and enlarged to include entire acts—a progression that culminated in a complete production of *Orphée* in 1910. By this time, however, Gluck's works had been regularly revived at the Opéra and Opéra-Comique for over a decade. Before turning our attention to these long-awaited productions, however, we should first take into account preparatory efforts running parallel to these concert series but in a very different venue: the library.

Gluck in the Library: The Pelletan Edition

As Gluck's works were gaining ground on various concert series during the decades around the turn of the century, an equally crucial (if much quieter) revolution was taking place. This revolution was the brainchild of Fanny Pelletan (1830–76), whose status as an outsider to the Parisian musical world did not deter her effort to create a complete Gluck edition—or rather, a complete edition of Gluck's *French* works. Details about Pelletan's life are scarce. She came from a well-to-do background; her father and grandfather were both high-society surgeons and professors of medicine; and she never married. (Fascinatingly, her grandfather, Philippe-Jean Pelletan, performed the autopsy on the "Lost Dauphin," Louis XVII, in 1795; he preserved the heart of the child in alcohol and placed it in a crystal urn, after which it became a morbid Pelletan family heirloom until 1879.)[28]

By all accounts, Pelletan's willingness to undertake the daunting task of creating a Gluck edition came as a direct result of her immense admiration for Berlioz, an affection that was apparently returned to an extent. In a 1906 article on Berlioz, for example, the musicologist Julien Tiersot—who later became associated with the Gluck edition himself—referred to Pelletan as an "authorized admirer" of Berlioz, and reported that the composer had given her the original manuscript of the surviving material of his unfinished opera *Les Francs-Juges* as a souvenir. A lavish gift, to be sure, but evidently not the only such that Pelletan received; Tiersot continued: "having already received from the master's hands the fragments of another equally incomplete opera, *La Nonne sanglante*, and the autograph of two parts of *L'Enfance du Christ*, [Pelletan] in turn gave all of this precious collection to the Bibliothèque Nationale."[29] Pelletan was clearly an ardent supporter of Berlioz, and it would seem that she took it very seriously indeed when the composer decried the lack of reliable Gluck editions in his *Les Grotesques de la musique* (1859):

> And as ill-fortune would have it, the old French edition, the only one in which the master's thoughts are to be found intact (I'm referring to the full scores), is becoming rarer by the day, and is very poor in respect of both layout and accuracy. It's marred by a lamentable lack of coherence and innumerable faults of every kind.
>
> In a few years' time two or three copies of these vast dramatic poems, these inimitable models of expressive music, will be all that remain in our great libraries, incomprehensible débris of another age.... No one in Europe has ventured to undertake a new edition of Gluck's six great operas which is at the same time scholarly, properly laid out and annotated, and well translated into both German and Italian. No serious attempt has been made to raise a subscription for this purpose. No one has considered risking 20,000 francs (it would cost no more than that) to combat in this way the ever more numerous agents of destruction which threaten these masterpieces. And despite the resources at the disposal of art and industry, this monstrous universal indifference to the key interests of musical art will cause these masterpieces to perish.[30]

Galvanized by this plea, Pelletan set to work on the project, financing it with her personal wealth (eliminating the vexing need for subscribers). Probably seeking a partner who was already ensconced in musical circles, she enlisted the aid of Berlioz's friend Berthold Damcke. Damcke was also acquainted with Pauline Viardot—another of Gluck's midcentury advocates—who exerted her influence to have some of Damcke's works performed in Paris.[31] Damcke's status as composer and well-known pedagogue no doubt laid to rest any doubts among the musical establishment about the scholarly bona fides of the Gluck edition, and possibly opened doors to the project that might have remained closed to Pelletan alone.

We can see some evidence of Pelletan's and Damcke's hard work in the former's correspondence with Charles Nuitter (1828–99), a librettist, frequent translator of librettos, and the archivist at the Opéra beginning in the 1860s. (Nuitter translated Wagner's works for the Opéra, and his 1865 translation of *The Magic Flute* with Alexandre Beaumont remained the dominant version until the twentieth century, as we saw in chapter 3 of this book.) On July 5, 1870, Nuitter received a letter from Camille Doucet, a playwright who was at the time the director of Theater Administration for Paris. As the note reveals, Pelletan contacted Doucet for help in creating a Gluck edition, and Doucet asked Nuitter to do everything in his power to help her "carry out this fine project."[32] Pelletan evidently went to work fairly soon thereafter; by the summer of 1872, she was (politely and deferentially) writing to Nuitter regarding details of manuscripts and scheduling appointments at the Opéra to view materials (though the parts for *Alceste* were allowed to leave the Opéra and were temporarily delivered to Pelletan's home—a rare privilege indeed).[33]

The first published results from the edition—*Iphigénie en Aulide*—appeared in 1873, with *Iphigénie en Tauride* and *Alceste* following quickly in the next year (see table 5.2). This rapid progress was tragically interrupted, however, by Damcke's death in 1875; in the words of Damcke's early biographer Prince Alexandre Bibesco, "first and foremost this death dealt a cruel blow to the artistic projects of Mlle. Fanny Pelletan."[34] To get the edition back on track and to restore the credibility that Damcke had provided, Pelletan turned to Camille Saint-Saëns, known to be an advocate for Gluck's music (and for eighteenth-century music in general). Exactly how much editorial work Damcke had completed before his death and how much remained to be done is unclear. Bibesco claimed (in 1894) that "the main materials are amassed for the three remaining tragedies: *Paris et Hélène, Armide*, and *Orphée*: the critical principles of the deceased great editor remain engraved on the memory of his successor [Pelletan?], who had learned them by heart."[35] In this revisionist view, Damcke had been the chief architect of the edition—with Pelletan, one supposes, providing mostly funds—and had completed most of the work for each of Gluck's French

Table 5.2. Volumes in the Pelletan Gluck edition

Opera title	Editors	Date of publication
Iphigénie en Aulide	Pelletan and Damcke	1873
Iphigénie en Tauride	Pelletan and Damcke	1874
Alceste	Pelletan and Damcke	1874
Armide	Pelletan (posthumous), Saint-Saëns, Tiersot	1890
Orphée et Eurydice	Pelletan (posthumous), Saint-Saëns, Tiersot	1898
Echo et Narcisse	Pelletan (posthumous), Saint-Saëns, Tiersot	1902

works before his death (barring *Echo et Narcisse*, which was the last opera published and likely not part of the original plan). Pelletan is relegated to the role of Damcke's "successor," implying that Damcke had been the principal agent from the start.

Whatever groundwork had already been laid, however, it would be more than a decade before another volume in the series would appear. Saint-Saëns had hardly begun work when tragedy again forestalled the process, this time in the form of Pelletan's untimely death in 1876. With the loss of her driving impetus, the edition languished for the next decade and a half before Saint-Saëns returned to the project in full force, releasing *Armide* in 1890. Saint-Saëns, evidently finding the edition to be a two-person job, sought out Julien Tiersot—assistant librarian at the Conservatoire—as a collaborator on issues of a musicological or bibliographic nature. The final volumes in the series were released sporadically, with *Orphée* appearing nearly a decade later in 1898 and *Echo et Narcisse* following in 1902, tacked on almost as an afterthought to the five primary masterworks. Even on the latest of these volumes, written more than a quarter century after her death, Pelletan was still listed as the primary editor, presiding over the monument to which she had so tenaciously dedicated the final years of her life.

Damcke's name, however, is absent from the later volumes, despite the large amount of preparatory work he had already undertaken on these works. Saint-Saëns strongly opposed Damcke's editorial methods, suggesting in a 1919 article on the Pelletan Edition that Damcke had been entirely too free with a "zeal for 'improvements'—a zeal that can do so much harm," and complaining "it took an enormous amount of time to undo this mischief, for I somewhat distrusted my own lights and Mlle Pelletan had too high an opinion of Damcke's work and did not dare to override his judgment."[36] Damcke's editorial sins were legion, in Saint-Saëns's opinion, but none more egregious than his reorchestrations of the ballet music, "in the naïve belief that he was bringing out the author's real meaning better than he had done himself."[37] Just as we saw with Mozart's operas in the first decade of the twentieth century, battle lines were drawn between those who felt, as Damcke evidently did, that eighteenth-century opera needed to be "updated" for inclusion in the Operatic Museum (and let us not forget that Berlioz, who initially spurred the Pelletan Edition, might have agreed with this position, given his adaptations of *Orphée* and *Alceste* around 1860) and those like Saint-Saëns, who espoused a new dogma of fidelity to original sources.

No doubt, the total absence of Damcke's name from the later volumes in the edition resulted to a large extent from these differences between his and Saint-Saëns's editorial styles, between Damcke's efforts to "modernize" Gluck and Saint-Saëns to "preserve" him. Another possible factor is that "Berthold Damcke" added a bit too much of a German accent to a project so important to narratives of French music-historical narratives. Not surprisingly, Saint-Saëns praised Pelletan at every turn (in his typically patriarchal way) and suggested that all errors and editorial policies that disagreed with his own, "correct" methods could be laid directly at Damcke's feet:

> Mlle Pelletan was an unusually intelligent woman and an accomplished musician, but she needed someone to help her in this large and formidable task. She was unassuming and distrusted her own powers, so that she secured as a collaborator a German musician named Damcke, who had lived in Paris a long time and who was highly esteemed. He gave her the moral support she needed but some bad advice as well, which she felt obliged to follow.[38]

The French Pelletan, mistrusting her own considerable talents, had unfortunately fallen under the spell of the "German musician" Damcke, who seduced her via "moral support" into bad (i.e., "German") editorial policies.

As though this statement were not clear enough, Saint-Saëns continued his chauvinist tirade against Damcke, who "belonged to the tribe of German professors who have since become legion. Due to their baleful influence, in a short time, when the old editions have disappeared, the works of Haydn, Mozart, and Beethoven, even of Chopin, will be all but unrecognizable. The works of Sebastian Bach and Handel will be the only ones in existence in their pristine purity of form, thanks to the admirable editions of the *Bach und Händel Gesellschaft*."[39] Again, the subtext here is that as a German, Damcke is incapable of editing Gluck's music well; the French alone (meaning Saint-Saëns and, possibly to a lesser extent, Pelletan) possessed the necessary understanding of his operas. The composer also unequivocally derides Germany and its scholars for not similarly treating the music of the classical school with the same acumen as they had addressed (German) composers like Bach and Handel. Under his direction, Saint-Saëns suggests, the Gluck edition was proof positive that France was equal or superior to Germany in treating its composers with the reverence that they deserved.

Saint-Saëns's attitude is hardly surprising. From its inception, and despite Damcke's involvement—Pelletan was evidently cosmopolitan in her musical outlook—many critics and scholars understood the Pelletan Edition as an object of French nationalist pride. As such, it was immediately held up as a French equivalent of the German Bach and Handel editions of the late nineteenth century. One review of the first two volumes of the Gluck edition (the two *Iphigénie* operas), for example, pointed out that "Bach, Handel, and Beethoven have theirs in the guise of magnificent editions published by the Leipzig *Bachgesellschaft*, by Chrysander, and by Breitkopf and Härtel. Here is Gluck in their company, receiving at last the homage he has been due for so long."[40] Nearly a half century later in 1922, Saint-Saëns's early biographer Jean Bonnerot expressed a very similar sentiment: "It had taken thirty years of work to bring this Gluck edition to fruition, one of the richest monuments that France has raised to music, worthy of the great edition of Bach and Handel that Germany has published."[41] Although bearing in mind Bonnerot's post–World War I perspective, it is nonetheless significant that he compares the French Gluck edition specifically to key editions of German composers.

The word "monument" is further indication that this edition was seen as—and likely was intended to be—a nationalist statement; it was the academic equivalent of the statues of Jeanne d'Arc and other notable French figures that spread throughout the nation at the turn of the century. Just as these statues did for historical figures, this new edition created a physical representation of Gluck's musical greatness, allowing him to better serve as a symbol of France's musical past. Gluck's historical importance is underscored here also by the fact that Pelletan's Gluck edition was the first of its kind; a similar Rameau edition—again led by Saint-Saëns—was not begun until 1895 (see chapter 8).[42] The implied historical importance granted to a composer who merited such a luxurious edition, especially one under the auspices of musical figure as notable as Saint-Saëns, seems to have had a galvanizing effect on Gluck's place in the opera house. It was only a small step from the monumentalizing effect of the Pelletan Gluck edition to the composer's inclusion in the Operatic Museum.

But however important the Pelletan Edition was for national pride, it would seem that performers felt no compulsion to make use of it exclusively. With *Orphée* and *Alceste*, particularly, choosing performance materials was a problem, since Berlioz—another hero of French music history—had prepared a more modern adaptation of both works. The solution to this problem seems to have been a compromise, at least to some extent, with elements of the newer edition incorporated into the framework of Berlioz's adaptation. The choice to use Berlioz's edition as the basic material for new productions was a natural one. The connection to a composer who, by 1896, was generally regarded as one of France's greatest musical figures could only help *Orphée*'s chances of success. Furthermore, it was almost certainly Berlioz's version that was heard so frequently in the concert hall excerpts, and the Opéra-Comique might not have been willing to take a chance on audiences being pleased to hear "new" versions of favorite arias and choruses.[43]

Other productions followed *Orphée*'s lead whenever possible, and Berlioz's modern versions were preferred throughout the turn of the century. But with the works Berlioz had not adapted (*Armide* and the two *Iphigénie* operas), the most likely approach was to alter the Pelletan Edition wherever necessary. Even with the elements of the Pelletan score that were used in the 1896 *Orphée*, some changes were made to create a more modern sound, a task that fell to Tiersot, as Hughes Imbert clarified in *Le Guide musical*: "Helping himself to the reconstructive work done with such attention and intelligence by Mlle. Pelletan, with the purpose of removing editorial and copying mistakes, and also (it must be said) Gluck's oversights, M. Tiersot, the knowledgeable assistant librarian of the Conservatoire, has modified somewhat the orchestration, which still left something to be desired."[44] Thus, though the sources (archival and critical) are often somewhat unclear about the specifics of what edition was used for performance, the general approach to Gluck's operas during the fin de siècle was to modernize the works somewhat, whether through adapting Berlioz's version or by other hands.

Gluck at the Opera House

By the mid-1890s, all the pieces had fallen into place for Gluck's return to the stage. The Pelletan Edition had produced its first three volumes, and excerpts performed on concert series programs had tantalized audiences for decades, setting the stage for them to embrace full productions. Yet, economic concerns still plagued the Operatic Muesum. As Paul Dukas frustratedly wrote in 1895:

> Works signed by glorious names who in their own time were the subject of discussions they surely would no longer raise today are classified in advance as operas that would not bring in money—which is to say, works condemned to be forgotten; the Opéra, in effect, cannot voluntarily take

unpredictable risks in its selections, its existence being dependent strictly on its commercial prosperity and its traditions having created exigencies of luxury that it cannot strip away, under pain of bankruptcy. And so we must renounce the hope of seeing the Opéra form a truly classic repertoire, composed of the most important works of the great masters, French and foreign. Furthermore, it is likely that the public's interest in such works would be platonic; we have clearly seen the productions of *Don Juan* and *Der Freischütz*, which the Opéra has finally had to abandon.[45]

But while these works may tragically have been anathema at the Opéra, Dukas notably fails to mention the Opéra-Comique, suggesting that perhaps he yet clung to some hope for a Museum after all, even if it could not be housed at France's grandest music theater.

On the subject of Gluck, in fact, Dukas took on a significantly more optimistic tone: "As concerns Gluck, he has come back into fashion for some time now, and with the wind blowing in his favor, it would not be surprising if the promise—given by three generations of directors—to return one of his works to the stage will finally be realized."[46] Dukas's excitement at the prospect of a Gluck opera returning to the Parisian stage is palpable, but he raises a few questions at the same time. What factors had made Gluck's operas so suddenly appealing to French audiences that a major theater would take such a financial risk? Certainly the edition had done its part (although probably more with the musical elite than with the average operagoer), and the performances of excerpts contributed to this effort. But these were not enough. This work was to be the cornerstone of the Operatic Museum; for it to succeed in this effort, it had to appeal to fin-de-siècle audiences. It must be a *modern* work as much as a classical one.

Dukas's optimism was ultimately justified, and in 1896 the Opéra-Comique's production of *Orphée et Eurydice* was the first complete Gluck opera seen on a major Parisian stage since the 1860s. This production was tremendously important for the burgeoning concept of the Operatic Museum, and spurred a major shift in the repertoire at the Opéra-Comique (and, to a lesser extent, the Opéra) for over a decade. We can also find in the critical reception of this production the seeds for the sociocultural factors that separated Gluck's works from those of other eighteenth-century composers, and allowed them to be viewed as unusually relevant to fin-de-siècle audiences. Fittingly, an opera about resurrection led to Gluck's return to Parisian stages, when, in March 1896, *Orphée* appeared at the Opéra-Comique after an absence of three decades. The production was an event of considerable artistic importance—the critic Léon Garnier lauded it in his review as "the greatest and most powerful dramatic effort of modern times."[47]

For many older critics the 1896 production was a direct link to the past, calling to mind the revivals of *Orphée* and *Alceste* at the Théâtre-Lyrique in 1859 and 1861, respectively—the only staged versions of those works that would have been in living memory for fin-de-siècle audiences. These productions, starring Pauline Viardot and created under Berlioz's musical supervision, significantly affected how the 1896 *Orphée* was received.[48] Marie Delna, the soprano charged with the opera's title role, was compared in almost every review to Viardot, whose interpretation of Orphée was legendary by the end of the century. The director, Léon Carvalho, provided further common ground between the 1859 *Orphée* and the 1896 revival: the Viardot *Orphée* and *Alceste* emerged from his savvy business mind during his time at the Théâtre-Lyrique, and the 1896 *Orphée* offered him a chance—though by no means a guarantee—of repeating his earlier successes only a few years after his move to the Opéra-Comique.

The last decades of the nineteenth century were financially difficult for that theater, not least because of the 1887 fire that destroyed the Salle Favart (where the Opéra-Comique was located), resulting in a temporary relocation to the Place du Châtelet, which had previously housed the Théâtre-Lyrique.[49] Perhaps the financial hardships of the Opéra-Comique and the familiar location encouraged Carvalho to revisit one of his greatest successes at the Théâtre-Lyrique. As Paul Rameau points out in *Le Temps*, however, these two productions had their differences: "The *Orphée* with which Carvalho has presented us is not precisely the *Orphée* he presented in 1859. There are differences in the text and the sets, and the interpretation is quite different. In 1859, Pauline Viardot—who was Orphée before, an inimitable Orphée—sang at the end of the first act an aria that Nourrit in the past and Mlle. Delna today replaced with an aria taken from *Echo et Narcisse*."[50] Despite these changes, critics found the productions to be similar—memories had no doubt dimmed in the interceding decades. Hughes Imbert, for example, noted clearly in *Le Guide musical* that "This production reminds us also of the superb performance given by Mme. Viardot in the role of Orphée in 1859."[51]

The 1896 revival of *Orphée* was by all accounts an enormous success. Carvalho's gambit at the Opéra-Comique paid off, and he was able to replicate the success of his 1859 production. In a serialized history of Gluck's work, Tiersot wrote in *Le Ménestrel*:

> Finally, in the same year these lines are being written, a new production of [*Orphée*] has taken place, also under Carvalho's direction, at the Opéra-Comique, conforming to the traditions previously established at the Théâtre-Lyrique [in 1859]. Its success has been no less complete this time, and without doubt will continue.

> The public's sustained admiration is certainly the most beautiful homage that has been given to Gluck's genius and to the principles of his art. And this homage is made all the more significant by the fact that it is unique, *Orphée* being the sole work of dramatic music from this period to which such a fortune is due.[52]

For Tiersot at least, *Orphée* held a special place in the operatic canon as the only work from its "period" [époque] that possessed a sustained artistic following in the late nineteenth century. This is a somewhat surprising assertion, particularly since the French version of *Orphée* was created in 1774—only thirteen years before Mozart's *Don Giovanni*, which was clearly a favorite in Paris throughout the nineteenth century. The subtext is thus somewhat unclear: Is Tiersot suggesting that Gluck had replaced Mozart in the public's affections, or is he conveniently forgetting that *Don Giovanni* (or *Don Juan*) was an eighteenth-century work at all? Both possibilities have some merit, and likely influenced Tiersot's modes of thinking. As we have already seen, until the early 1900s, *Don Giovanni* in particular was often viewed as a romantic work. And Gluck's return to prominence from 1896 though the 1900s seems to have emerged at Mozart's expense, and the much-lauded returns of *The Magic Flute* and *Don Juan* in 1909 and 1912 did not occur until each of Gluck's main operas had received a staging.

Despite Tiersot's assertions that *Orphée* was the unique darling of the Parisian public, several critics pointed to the fact that the opera may not have been Gluck's best, but that it was nonetheless enough of a masterpiece to stand the test of time. Paul Rameau wrote in *Le Temps*, for example, that "*Orphée* is neither *Alceste* nor *Iphigénie en Tauride*. But, without being Gluck's masterpiece, it is still a masterpiece nonetheless." Rameau continued: "Give a man dying of thirst a glass of water: would he dream of asking you first if you have . . . fitted your container with a perfect filter? No, the unlucky man to whom you have given life will not be too difficult. He will thank you—even if you do not deserve it at all, or if your help is late or incomplete—and he will drink eagerly."[53] In this particularly vivid analogy, the Parisian musical scene is parched, dying for lack of the operatic classics that it so desperately needs, and in the absence of better choices, *Orphée* would do. Audiences could wait no longer for the Operatic Museum to open its doors.

Orphée allowed critics and audiences to connect the glories of France's past to the achievements of its present, creating a lineage of French masterpieces stretching back more than a century. Given the success of this juxtaposition of the ancient and the modern—a clear demonstration of the important educational and cultural roles the Operatic Museum was beginning to play—some critics dared to hope that the 1896 production might be the harbinger of a full-scale revival of Gluck's operas. Dukas, writing in the *Revue hebdomadaire*, expressed such a sentiment in strong language:

How many times have we predicted the triumph of these sublime creations if they were to be performed, and on how many occasions have we insisted on the opportunity to return to our theaters the most authentic masterworks they can pride themselves on! Gluck has triumphed this time just as he will always triumph, by his force alone and without the help of prior publicity. Is it permitted to hope that we will not stop on this excellent path, and that after the production of *Orphée* at the Opéra-Comique, we are right to expect the Opéra to present us with *Alceste, Armide,* or one of the two *Iphigénies*?[54]

Others had hoped for a similar revival before and had been disappointed. This time, however, *Orphée* opened a door through which Gluck's remaining operas could enter the Parisian music scene.

Once *Orphée* awoke French audiences' thirst for Gluck, subsequent stagings followed with surprising alacrity, with critics essentially unanimous in their approval for this new (old) development. Productions of Gluck's works appeared about once every four years (see table 5.3): *Iphigénie en Tauride* was produced at the Opéra-Comique in 1900, starring the soprano Rose Caron. *Alceste* followed four years later, featuring Félia Litvinne in the title role. After this point, however, the pace of revivals began to quicken. In 1905—nearly a decade after the Opéra-Comique began to feature Gluck's works prominently—the Opéra finally took notice, mounting a production of *Armide*. This production marks that theater's sole contribution to the Gluck revival; the *Armide* production was continued there over a number of years, but the theater made no attempts to produce other Gluck works. Thus, it was again at the Opéra-Comique that the collection of Gluck's "masterworks" was completed with *Iphigénie en Aulide*.

Gluck's works were staged occasionally in venues aside from the two major opera theaters, but never for very long; for all intents and purposes Gluck remained the property of the Opéra-Comique.[55] In explaining the predominance of Gluck's works there, it is tempting to draw connections between the traditional repertoire of the theater (i.e., opéra comique as a genre)—usually characterized as "eminémment français"—and the equally French identity of Gluck and his genre, the *tragédie lyrique*.[56] This French character is entirely in keeping with the fin-de-siècle goals of the theater. In an 1898 issue of *Le Figaro* largely devoted to the topic of the role of the Opéra-Comique in French society, a number of composers wrote columns that called for the institution to demonstrate the glories of French music of the past (as well as the present) and to become, in this way, an overtly nationalistic entity.[57] For example, the composer and critic Alfred Bruneau wrote in *Le Figaro* that the Opéra-Comique should be "a French theater, entirely French. And by that I do not mean reserved for only our composers appropriate to be placed in the first rank, but guided by a spirit of large

Table 5.3. Major revivals of Gluck's operas in Paris, 1896–1918

Opera	Year	Theater
Orphée et Eurydice	1896	Opéra-Comique
Iphigénie en Tauride	1900	Opéra-Comique
Alceste	1904	Opéra-Comique
Armide	1905	Opéra
Orphée	1905	Opéra-Comique
Iphigénie en Aulide	1907	Opéra-Comique
Orphée et Eurydice	1910/1911	Schola Cantorum
Orphée et Eurydice	1912	Opéra-Comique

and proud French generosity, which is to say respectful to the same degree of our authentic past glories and of the indisputable universal glories; curator of the national genius so that we may transmit it to the true masters of today."[58] Given the prominence of the idea that a major role of the Opéra-Comique was the preservation of French operatic triumphs, echoed time and again at the turn of the century, it is hardly surprising that Gluck's works began to appear in earnest only a few years later.

Furthermore, although Gluck's operas do not conform to the traditional guidelines of the Opéra-Comique (which required spoken dialogue), the nature of the genre was in flux during this time, as was its status as the "true national genre" of France. Saint-Saëns, for example, explicitly stated, "The true national genre, we have forgotten, is the great French opera created by Quinault . . . the *tragédie lyrique* whose most prominent quality was beauty of declamation, a tradition faithfully upheld until the Italian invasion of the beginning of this century. In returning to declaimed singing, to the *drame lyrique*, France has done nothing else but to retake what is rightfully hers, with a more modern appearance."[59] Far from being unpatriotic by focusing on the eighteenth-century *tragédies lyriques* of Gluck, the Opéra-Comique was in fact serving a nationalistic role by creating a place where this genre could be preserved for display as an antecedent of the modern French *drame lyrique*.

Nearly all critics shared the opinion that the revival of these works was appropriate, and not only as a one-off exercise in novelty programming. Critics envisioned a future where modern music and classical music would exist side by side in dialogue, an attitude that demonstrated how thoroughly the idea of an Operatic Museum had taken hold by this time. By

1905, Gluck's works were so ubiquitous in Paris that a biographical article on the composer in the popular journal *Musica* maintained that "although generations pass, and with them faddish repertoires, *Alceste, Orphée, Armide,* and the two *Iphigénies* feature today on the bill of nearly all of the opera theaters. If ever a past composer was continuously current, and deserved eternal tributes, it is this one."[60] The irony of this passage (written by M.-D. Calvocoressi) is palpable; in describing Gluck as "continually current," the critic glosses over the decades of neglect to which the composer's operas had been subjected. By the early years of the twentieth century, such a rejection of the composer was entirely unthinkable, tantamount to heresy, and critics usually took the aesthetic value of Gluck's works for granted. Rather than spending precious time rehashing the impeccable merits of the composer, reviewers tended to dwell on the quality of the production. If any productions failed to please critics the blame fell entirely on the interpretation. Dukas, Gluck's tireless defender, wrote in *La Revue hebdomadaire* in 1900 that he was consistently disappointed in the quality of productions of Gluck's works, which deserved better.[61]

Inevitably, critical discussion turned to the proper way to perform Gluck's music for modern audiences, and so debates over the merits of individual productions became a major issue in the composer's reception. This question of performance practice came to a head in many ways in 1907, with the production of *Iphigénie en Aulide* at the Opéra-Comique. Vincent d'Indy was so incensed by that interpretation that he wrote a vitriolic letter to the editor of the journal *Comoedia* (later reprinted in *Le Guide Musical*). This letter—d'Indy biographer Léon Vallas describes it as "sévère à l'extrême"[62]—harshly criticized director Albert Carré, saying that nothing "is on point in this interpretation: neither the recitatives, too solemn; nor the arias, totally lacking life and expression; nor the orchestra, perfect from the point of view of the notes, but absolutely off the mark from the point of view of the tone and style; nor even the ballet."[63]

Within weeks of the Opéra-Comique performance, d'Indy responded by conducting the opera's overture at the Concerts Lamoureux (to which he had recently been appointed to the position of deputy to Chevillard). Such a direct challenge to the Opéra-Comique was a dangerous course of action for an opera composer, and it set in motion d'Indy's estrangement from the institution.[64] These events caused quite a stir in the music periodicals in 1907 and 1908, highlighting the issues surrounding the importance of Gluck's historical placement at the fin de siècle.[65] Gabriel Fauré and Camille Saint-Saëns, never ones to stay aloof from aesthetic debates, joined the fray by taking varying positions on the proper interpretation of Gluck's works, much as they did with Mozart's in the same time period. With Gluck's works part of the pinnacle of operatic composition, the partisan debates for and against the production of *Iphigénie* at the Opéra-Comique found any possible fault almost always with the interpretation rather than with the quality or style of the work itself, the quality of which, typically for Gluck reception, appeared beyond question. The notion that Gluck's operas were not only high-quality music but were also dramatically viable in the modern opera house is a striking contrast to perceptions about nearly every other classical French composer.

The critic Victor Debay was an exception in that he placed blame on Gluck's music as well as on its interpreters. The trepidation with which he criticized the construction of *Iphigénie en Aulide* is revealing: "Despite our admiration for the works of Gluck ... it is our duty, through concern for the truth and above all our scruples, to confess here the impression of cold indifference—we will not be bold enough to say boredom—that we have taken away from the revival of this opera, not seen in Paris since 1824. For this we will blame both the dramatic conception of the work and its modern interpretation."[66]

Debay makes sure to reveal the high esteem in which he holds Gluck's operas before reluctantly suggesting that *Iphigénie en Aulide* might be in some ways a flawed work. Only rarely did critics condemn Gluck's works outright. Jean Marnold scathingly reviewed *Iphigénie en Aulide* in *Le Mercure de France* in 1908: "Hearing it, one perceives a heap of confusingly dissimilar impressions of which the worst is the total impossibility of taking seriously for a moment the action that one sees unfold onstage."[67] Significantly, Marnold goes on to reveal that the opera's ultimate fault lay in not conforming to the standards of post-Wagnerian music drama in the manner that he perceived *Orphée* had done (see chapter 7). The fact that he, or any critic, would expect Gluck's works to reflect modern tastes illustrates both the power and the problems inherent in the Operatic Museum. On the one hand, Gluck's opera could be—and had to be—perceived as a modern work, able to exist in dialogue with more contemporary works, most particularly Wagner's. On the other hand, judged purely by modern standards, *Orphée, Alceste,* and their siblings were doomed to fail, their musical and dramatic language too foreign to Parisian audiences.

The broader reasons for the resurgence of interest in producing Gluck's works on the main operatic stages of Paris are complex, and resist any attempts at a simple cause-and-effect narrative. The two chapters that follow are principally concerned with how fin-de-siècle audiences were able to find relevance in Gluck and his music—how they were able to find modernity in the classical. Chapter 6 deals with Gluck and his music as a part of French historical and cultural identity, and how creating a sense of shared identity shaped the way that audiences may have interpreted Gluck's music. By establishing Gluck as a quintessentially French composer (at least stylistically), it was possible for critics and audiences to associate the composer with golden-age playwrights such as Corneille and Racine, allowing the composer to serve as a *lieu de mémoire*—essentially as a national treasure—extolling the glories of eighteenth-century France. And the subject material of Gluck's operas allowed Parisian audiences and critics to indulge in the French cultural obsession for all things Greek, a preoccupation with serious political ramifications. In chapter 7, I address the continuing critical connections between Gluck and Wagner, exploited by both Wagnerians and anti-Wagnerians around the turn of the century, either tracing a history of music that led from Gluck directly to Bayreuth or setting the two figures in opposition. Finally, using the 1896 *Orphée* as a focal point, I offer a glimpse into how the Wagnerian symbolist movement may have affected Gluck's Parisian reception.

Chapter Six

Tragedies

A crucial, if obvious, part of securing Gluck's reputation in French music history was to establish definitively that the composer was in fact French, by style if not by birth. Fin-de-siècle critics consequently spent a fair amount of time reinforcing Gluck's Frenchness and minimizing his German "otherness." In the introduction to his 1882 book on Gluck (drawn from articles he wrote for *Le Ménestrel*), for example, Hippolyte Barbedette asks, "Can one not say that in matters of art, nationality does not depend on an act of birth?—Gluck is and will remain the founder of the French *drame lyrique*; with this title, he is French in the same way as Meyerbeer, and France should have the right to lay claim to him. Germans, when they are honest about it, acknowledge this themselves."[1] This attitude toward the composer is typical; while acknowledging Gluck's Germanic roots, Barbedette nonetheless regarded him as French by naturalization. The critic also points to France's historical tradition of adopting composers, such as the similarly German Meyerbeer (or, for that matter, the Italian Lully—the founder of the French *tragédie lyrique*). Félix Clément, in his *Histoire de la musique* (1885), argued at least for the inherent Frenchness of Gluck's ideas, if not the composer himself: "Gluck's theory . . . opposed exclusively the tendencies of Italian dramatic art. . . . The ideas published by the famous Bohemian composer in his letters and developed by his partisans were in essence French, and had been put into practice by Lully, Campra, and even Rameau, especially in *Castor et Pollux*."[2] Clément chooses his words carefully, identifying Gluck as "Bohemian," rather than the more culturally dangerous "German." And as Clément's argument demonstrates, a central aspect Gluck's French identity was preserved musically through positioning the composer's style in a direct historical line through the French *tragédie lyrique* composers Lully, André Campra, and Rameau. Composers were not the only historical figures at play in contextualizing Gluck, however; it was equally important to Gluck's French identity to place the composer's aesthetic ideals in the context of the historical luminaries in other disciplines. In an effort to emphasize the French aspects of his life and music, Parisian critics frequently connected Gluck to two high points of their nation's artistic achievement: to the Encyclopedist tradition of the eighteenth century and to the playwright Pierre Corneille.

Gluck and the French Classical Tradition

One of Gluck's most passionate defenders in the early twentieth century was the Nobel Prize-winning polymath Romain Rolland. Best known for his ten-volume novel *Jean-Christophe* (1903–12), Rolland also completed a doctorate with a dissertation on early opera and taught music history at the Sorbonne. In his *Musiciens d'autrefois* (1908), Rolland spent a great deal of time connecting Gluck to the traditions of the Encyclopedists—the widely respected group of intellectuals and philosophers who typified French Enlightenment thought. "Gluck's revolution," Rolland points out early on, "was not the work of Gluck's genius alone, but of an entire century of thought as well. It had been prepared for, announced, and awaited by the Encyclopedists for twenty years."[3] Like a musical Messiah, Gluck fulfilled the operatic prophesies of the Enlightenment foretold by Denis Diderot, Jean-Jacques Rousseau, and their compatriots. Rolland offers *Iphigénie en Aulide* as the perfect opera for encouraging such an interpretation, and in particular Gluck's choices of the topic and libretto. Though written by the playwright Marie François Louis Gand Leblanc Roullet, the libretto was based on Racine's play of the same name, which facilitated a connection to the golden age of French theater.[4] Diderot's *Troisième entretien sur le fils naturel* (1757) cites Racine's text as its example of a play that could be set fruitfully by a reformer of opera due to its expressivity and lyric qualities, a fact Rolland was quick to point out in 1908.[5] Furthermore, Rolland asserts, Gluck was probably familiar with Francesco Algarotti's 1755 *Saggio sopra l'opera in musica* (published in the May 1757 *Mercure de France* as *Essai sur l'opéra*), which included a libretto based on both Euripides and Racine as an example of future operatic reforms.[6]

Connecting Gluck to eighteenth-century French thought as Rolland did, however, also raised the specter of Rousseau. Given Rousseau's loud derision of the *tragédie lyrique* as a genre, this association ran the risk of distancing Gluck irrevocably from the French genre. By minimizing the significance of the infamous *Querelle des Bouffons*, however, Rolland was able associate Gluck with both Rameau and Rousseau: "If . . . the Encyclopedists were quick to vehemently take Rousseau's side in favor of Italian opera [i.e., against Rameau], it is because they were exasperated by the scandalous brutality with which the partisans of French opera opposed them."[7] The Encyclopedists were thus not actually opposed to French opera, only to the manner in which Rousseau was treated by its defenders. This convenient conjecture sidesteps the necessity of allying Gluck with either side of this conflict, depicting the composer as both faithfully following in Rameau's footsteps and eagerly responding to Rousseau's call for operatic reform.

Many critics were quick to pick up this association with Rameau, whose cultural capital was making significant gains in the early 1900s (culminating in the 1908 production of *Hippolyte et Aricie* at the Opéra in 1908, discussed in chapter 10). Gabriel Fauré, for example, wrote in response to the 1907 production of *Iphigénie en Aulide* at the Opéra that "Lully and Rameau had marked the path; Gluck, with his ardent, passionate, and profoundly human genius, widened it."[8] Similarly, in his review of the same production, the music historian Henri Quittard opined that, by the 1774 premiere of *Iphigénie*, "the art of Lully, of Campra, and Rameau is already the art of Gluck. . . . *Iphigénie en Aulide* is the first homage of Gluck's genius to the genius of the French masters, in whom he recognized his true precursors and whom he overshadowed in realizing more completely what they had conceived."[9]

Quittard went on to name *Iphigénie* as "the masterpiece of Classical French opera," a grand claim that suggests the work and its composer were looking backward as opposed to toward the future.[10] As early as 1877, Henri Lavoix's *Histoire de la musique* maintained that Gluck's operas "mark the culmination of the old *drame lyrique*, which began in France with Lully and arrived at its apogee with Gluck."[11] Positioning Gluck as the logical outcome of the musical developments of seventeenth- and eighteenth-century France minimizes his Austro-German (or Italianate) identity, reinforcing instead his Frenchness. Just as important, this narrative also enhances France's role in the operatic history of opera after Gluck; if we interpret Gluck as a French classical composer, any composer influenced by him would have been emulating an inherently French style. At this point, I would like to focus on one continuing effort to situate Gluck in this French classical mold, much like Mozart's enduring association with Raphael: the recurring image of Gluck as the musical version of the tragedian Pierre Corneille.

Gluck's position as the musical equivalent of Racine or Corneille was well established by 1900. We might recall, for example, Léon Escudier's review of the 1859 *Orphée* (which I briefly examined in the previous chapter), in which he referred to the work as "the charm of Raphael combined with the grandeur and the energy of Corneille."[12] Gustave Chouquet, in his *Histoire de la musique dramatique en France* (1873), contended that "like Pierre Corneille, [Gluck] endowed our stage with sublime tragedies. . . . Between these two masculine geniuses, more reflective than spontaneous, we find this point of resemblance: their tragedies have in common a type of grandeur, but they differ from one another in appearance—by their forms and characters. Finally, their theater does not soften the heart, but entirely to the contrary, it elevates and fortifies it."[13] The gender tropes in this passage, though not my primary focus here, are too evident to ignore. Choquet explicitly refers to Gluck and Corneille as "masculine geniuses," and reinforces this with stereotypically male characteristics: they are "reflective" not "spontaneous," they have "grandeur," and their dramas are aimed at "elevating" and "fortifying" the audience rather than "softening" them.[14] Katharine Ellis has pointed out the feminization of Racine during the fin de siècle, which suggests that perhaps here Gluck was being connected with Corneille in order to preserve the composer's masculinity.[15] This seems to be what Escudier was hinting at in the passage above, uniting the feminine grace of Raphael with the masculine powers of Corneille. (This unison of masculine and feminine qualities in the interpretation of *Orphée* is a topic to which we will return in the next chapter.)

Although still focused on linking Gluck to the French Golden Age, some critics were less focused on Corneille in particular.[16] In his own *Histoire*, Lavoix opines that "Gluck is the most faithful musical translator of the great *tragédie* of Racine and Corneille."[17] Julien Tiersot likewise referred in 1907 to Gluck's operas as the "musical equivalent" of the tragedies of Corneille and Racine.[18] In fact, numerous reviews of Gluck's works as early as the 1860s, particularly the full operatic productions, constantly reinforced the image of the composer as a part of Paris's intellectual and artistic history, placing him squarely as a part of a French artistic heritage.

Comparing Gluck to Corneille, in particular, was high praise indeed, as classical French theater was in the midst of a major revival around the turn of the century. Corneille was the subject of a number of academic and popular studies during this time, and—with the exception of a brief decline in popularity in the immediate aftermath of the Franco-Prussian War—his tragedies were almost never absent from Parisian stages.[19] Victor Cousin wrote in his influential *Du vrai, du beau, et du bien* (1853) that "Aeschylus, Sophocles, and Euripides all together do not come close to balancing Corneille alone. . . . Corneille is the creator of a *pathétique nouveau*, unknown in antiquity and to all the moderns before him."[20] Similarly, Victor de Laprade opined in 1882 that "if France were forced in some shipwreck to sacrifice all its poets except for one, the one that she would have to save is Corneille."[21] In his fin-de-siècle text on the playwright's life and works, Gustave Lanson succinctly summarized Corneille's importance to the fin de siècle: "Before [Corneille], the *tragédie classique* did not exist. Thanks to him, it existed."[22]

French music was very much in need of an equivalent, someone who could demonstrate the greatness of the operatic stage just as Corneille proved the glory of French theater—a role Gluck was uniquely capable of taking. Mozart, despite his popularity until around 1900, was not a good fit. As we saw in part 1, he was (almost) irredeemably Germanic and thus unavailable for adoption by the French in the same manner as Gluck. Furthermore, Mozart's operas did not fit into the tragic mold that typified classical French opera and theater.[23] Even the omnipresent *Don Giovanni* was tragicomic, not set in antiquity (as good tragedy nearly always was), and featured a protagonist who was anything but heroic.

At least at first glance, Rameau should have been a more likely contender for this position than Gluck. Rameau was French by birth, and his works were clearly written in the *tragédie lyrique* style. The main complaint against Rameau, as we will see more fully in part 3, was that his works were not readily understood by modern audiences—a charitable way of saying that people were not likely to pay to see them. If seventeenth-century theatrical works like Corneille's remained capable of being understood by modern audiences and even retained some measure of popularity, it would reflect poorly on the history of French music if the "Corneille lyrique" could not claim the same distinction. Gluck's operas, in contrast to Rameau's, were both dramatically viable and consistently lauded by fin-de-siècle critics. As one critic pointed out as late as 1914, "Rameau is no more than the pleasant reflection of an epoch—one must listen to him with the ears of a historian; Gluck is eternal."[24]

There are several reasons for Gluck's sustained dramatic viability. One straightforward reason lay in the relative familiarity of his musical language, much closer to Mozart's accessible style than Rameau was. Neither did Gluck's operas demand the nontraditional (by nineteenth-century standards) orchestration that Rameau's work would—particularly harpsichord continuo. *Orphée* and *Alceste*, at least, existed in Berlioz's modernized orchestrations, meaning that they could be performed by the usual instrumental and vocal forces of the Opéra-Comique; the other works could be (and were) adapted similarly. Another and perhaps more significant reason, however, lay not in Gluck's music but in the subject matter of his librettos: Greek Antiquity. Here we must shift from one definition of classical to another, examining how the mythological Greek themes of these operas paradoxically helped audiences perceive them as both modern and French.

Mythologies

From the very beginning, Gluck's operas were inextricably tied up with ancient Greece.

Ranieri de' Calzabigi, for example, the Italian librettist for *Orfeo ed Euridice* and *Alceste*, argued extensively that his texts were a rejection of the overwrought opera seria librettos of the period in favor of a return to Greek values. To this end, the role of the chorus was expanded dramatically, and complex plots were pared down to the essentials. As classicist Simon Goldhill has pointed out, in Calzabigi's hands, *Orfeo*'s resurrection-driven plot "became a self-reflexive and self-authorizing image for the recovery of a dead classical tradition through the power of art."[25] When

Gluck's works first appeared in eighteenth-century Paris, French critics quickly seized upon this classical aspect of the works, frequently comparing the composer and his works to ancient Greek authors and tragedies.[26]

In the nineteenth century, Gluck's brief return to the limelight in 1859 and 1861 was again accompanied by the specter of Greek tragedy. In his analysis of *Alceste*, for example, Berlioz points to the opera's third scene, which takes place in Apollo's temple: "Enter the high-priest and the sacrificers; bringing with them the burning tripods and instruments of sacrifice; whilst, following them, comes Alceste, conducting her children; the courtiers, and then the crowd. Here Gluck gives us local color, if anyone ever did; for it is literally ancient Greece which he reveals to us, in all its majestic and beautiful simplicity."[27] For Berlioz, the Greek quality of the scene went far beyond the setting, permeating the drama and enabling Gluck to "literally" put ancient Greece on display.

Not surprisingly, when Gluck's operas reappeared at the fin de siècle, the topic of their antiquity resurfaced immediately, and in full force. The critic Édouard Schuré ardently argued for this classicism in his history of opera—which tellingly begins with ancient Greece and culminates in Wagner. Schuré, like Berlioz before him, pointed to an essentially Greek character to Gluck's operas that penetrated deeper than the libretto, pervading the music itself: "if Beethoven found the universal language of modern humanity, Gluck rediscovered in the language of sounds the immortal essence of the Greek soul and recreated the *tragédie classique* across the world of harmony."[28] Hippolyte Barbedette expressed a similar sentiment in his study of Gluck's operas: "At forty years old, Gluck began to learn the ancient languages.... He penetrated the thoughts of the ancients; he knew the holy majesty of the Hellenic temples; he saw the sweetness of the Elysian fields and the horrors of Tartarus."[29] Unlike other composers (except Wagner, of course, as we will see in the next chapter), Gluck actually *understood* the ancient authors and their ideas on a level that transcended the superficiality of subject matter.

Camille Bellaigue joined in this same chorus (or perhaps *khoros* is more appropriate here), applying this ineffable "Greek" quality directly to the composer himself, noting that as a result of his "magnificence and economy, the composer of *Orphée* is ancient [*antique*]. Finally, by pursuit and constant creation of a beauty that, even at the climax, is never distorted, in a word, by all his genius and his soul, he was more a Greek—the last— than Willibald the Bohemian."[30] This perspective has a dual purpose; most obviously, it imbues Gluck with the Greek qualities that were so fashionable in fin-de-siècle Paris. As an added benefit, however, it further distances Gluck from his Germanic origins by positioning him as "more a Greek... than Willibald the Bohemian." In case the message were not clear enough, Bellaigue later pointed out that from "this German, or this Bohemian, three masterworks—the last—were written in French and for France."[31] Given the German-French dichotomy running rampant in the French press, pointing out qualities that overruled Gluck's "Bohemian" place of birth helped to turn Gluck into a more "French" composer; ironically, connecting the composer to Greece contributed indirectly to this effort.

Although Bellaigue's simultaneous reinforcing of Greek and French identities for Gluck seems at first glance contradictory, there is method to his apparent madness. Greek antiquity was a topic with which fin-de-siècle Paris was nothing short of obsessed. During this time the French increasingly came to view themselves as the new incarnation of ancient Greek culture.[32] This interpretation came about partially as a result of the revision of their history to reflect a Gallic, rather than Germanic, past—a process begun in the 1850s and 1860s by Napoleon III.[33] The historical linking of the Gauls to the Greeks resulted in a French self-perception as direct descendants of the ancients. As sociologist Athena Leoussi tells us, the Greek origin of Marseilles was particularly important in creating "an unbroken connection with the ancient Greeks—a link which justified French self-esteem and also suggested that the well-known virtues of the Greeks were the inherited elements of the French nation."[34]

A visual example of the growing ideology of France as the new Greece (or, perhaps, as the continuation of the *old* Greece) is Pierre Puvis de Chavannes's painting *Massalia, colonie Grecque* (1869), which presents a vision of a "Greek" Marseilles. The implication of such a work, of course, is again that the culture of Greece was transferred to France via this connection. After the defeat of 1870, the ties (illusory or not) between France and Greece became critical to maintaining French national identity. Consequently, interpretations of ancient Greece abounded in literature and visual art as well as in music. Many of the leading composers of the time composed works on mythological subjects: Debussy, Ravel, Saint-Saëns, Massenet, and Fauré, to cite only a few examples.[35] Outside the concert halls, Julien Tiersot and other musicologists placed great importance on tracing French music history back to its Greek (and Roman) influence, and both the influential music critic Louis Laloy and the composer and musicologist Maurice Emmanuel completed dissertations on ancient Greek musical subjects in the last decade of the nineteenth century.[36]

Some composers turned to the idyllic side of classicism, focusing on the idealized (and sensualized) pastoral lifestyle found in the *Idylls* of Theocritus. The most notable composer to be strongly influenced by this aesthetic was Debussy, who incorporated aspects of Greek pastoral into his *Prélude à l'après-midi d'un faune, Trois chansons de Bilitis, Syrinx,* and other works.[37] But even as this carefree, pleasure-seeking vision of antiquity attracted more "decadent" artists like Debussy, other composers focused on more restrained classical themes in order to oppose the perceived moral decay of French society at the turn of the century. As historian Eugen Weber has amply demonstrated, around 1900, even the very term "fin de siècle" came to connote the decline of traditional values, and among those "who discussed such things, or listened to the discussion, the debasement and decrepitude of the society and of its values seemed beyond argument."[38] As one might imagine, French culture saw a backlash against this perceived moral lassitude—a trend reflected in a second, more Hellenistic method of approaching Greek subject material.

It is within this latter category that we can locate the revivals of Gluck's operas; composers and critics could point to the aspects of Greek tragedy in his operas that upheld conservative values and culture, while at the same time embracing the "exotic" aspects of ancient Greek culture. In the face of the ostensibly declining importance of the family in French culture, for example, audiences and critics could turn to the *Iphigénie* operas for works that would highlight the importance of family bonds. Similarly, in comparison with the increasing menace of adultery (mostly a fear of empowered women), *Orphée* and *Alceste* focus on the successful lengths gone to restore a married couple, complete with happy ending—a sharp contrast to the protagonists of *Tristan und Isolde* or *Pelléas et Mélisande*, to name only two operas popular at the fin de siècle.[39]

The subject matter of Gluck's operas also suggests a more directly political reading in the context of fin-de-siècle Paris, which was in many ways still in a state of national mourning following its defeat in the Franco-Prussian War—a state that lasted essentially until the end of World War I. The events of 1870 were not commonly addressed directly in opera, with the notable exception of Alfred Bruneau's *L'Attaque du moulin*, based on the literary work by Émile Zola, in which a rural Alsatian village and its occupants are devastated by the effects of the war. Such realist subject matter was largely foreign (literally and figuratively) to the stages of the Opéra, and even to those of the more progressive Opéra-Comique. In the case of *L'Attaque du moulin*, the setting was pushed back 100 years for the first Parisian production—becoming a tale of the Revolution rather than of the Franco-Prussian War—at least partially in order to avoid unduly upsetting the audience.[40] Given the implicit restrictions on depicting images likely to stir all-too-fresh emotions in audiences, opera producers and composers who sought to tap into the postwar national grief had to find another way.

Allegorical subject material, or at least subject material that could be read allegorically, was a common method of depicting the horrors of the Franco-Prussian War.[41] Another look at Puvis de Chavannes, for example, reveals two allegorical representations of Paris's isolation while under siege: *Le Ballon* and *Le Pigeon voyageur* (1870–71).[42] In the years that followed, he continued to paint works that may refer to the Franco-Prussian War. The painting *Hope* (1872), for example, depicts a woman (nude in

Figure 6.1. Pierre Puvis de Chavannes, *Hope* (1872). Reproduced with permission from Erich Lessing / Art Resource, New York.

the smaller version of the work, clad in a white dress in the larger) holding aloft a sapling as dawn breaks on the horizon, with ruins and graves visible in the background of the painting. The time period reflected in the painting is ambiguous; the woman's clothing is caught between antiquity and modernity, and the ruins in the background are ambiguously classical in origin. Any (deliberate) temporal confusion aside, the clear subject of the painting is the rebirth of France in the wake of disaster, with the young woman representing France (see fig. 6.1).

A similar argument might be made for the same artist's *Death and the Maidens* (1872), in which Death approaches a group of women in the same ambiguously Greek white dresses we saw in *Hope*. As art historian Brian Petrie has pointed out, "it may well be felt that here was a comment on the irresponsible France of the years immediately preceding the War."[43] Here again France is represented by the Greek female form. Puvis's placement of his allegorical works in ancient Greece (or, arguably, a France that evokes ancient Greece) is effective only in the event that his audience would understand the connection between Greek and French cultures. Puvis's work for the Hôtel de Ville, reconstructed in the 1880s after its destruction in the war, further illustrates this connection. His mural *Summer* (1891) presents the viewer with yet another idyllic Greek scene, this time of men, women, and children in various states of undress, bathing in a river. Given the placement of the work in the Hôtel de Ville, the work was "universally assumed to be an image of France."[44] Art historian Jennifer Shaw makes clear the republican stake in such classical imagery:

> The degree and kind of classical heritage pictured in *Summer* became one issue around which debates over the ideal nature of France crystallized. In the 1890s classicism came to signify much more than a painterly or literary style. It became a politically embattled category, appropriated (like nationalism) by a variety of groups on the Right even while republicans tried to reclaim it and transmute its meanings back to their own purposes.... As the numerous examples of classical subject matter in the Hôtel de Ville make clear, the state still wanted to promote its possession of the classical legacy.[45]

Clearly, many French critics at the fin de siècle understood that representations of Greece were representations of early France (avant la lettre). Greek themes in fin-de-siècle art, therefore, could often be interpreted as coded representations of modern France.

The prevalence of Greek subject matter was not limited to visual media, as a look at Parisian theaters quickly reveals. One critic of an 1893 production of Sophocles's *Antigone* at the Comédie-Française—featuring incidental music by Saint-Saëns, a recognized authority on Greek music—wrote in *Le Figaro* that the production was "one of the most instructive and most moving demonstrations of art of the past few years."[46] Even more important, between 1896 and 1912 the Odéon ran a series of Greek works on their "Classical Thursdays," designed to both entertain and educate audiences in ancient theater. The theater's directors made it abundantly clear that the presentation of classical repertoire was a major issue: "*Classical Repertoire*. We consider this to be an important point in our mission, and this repertoire will be the object of all our attention.... We will make, if we can express ourselves this way, a sort of permanent theatrical exhibition."[47] Toward this museum-making goal, the Odéon produced works by Aeschylus, Sophocles, and Euripides (the last adapted by the prominent Parnassian poet Leconte de Lisle).

In addition to these revivals, a number of modern playwrights reworked classical tragedies in modern ways. As Sylvie Humbert-Mougin points out, "the years from 1890 to 1910 saw a flourishing of symbolic or allegorical plays, in which myth is liberally reworked in view of an edifying, moral, or political message."[48] An example of this trend is André Gide's *Philoctète, ou Le Traité des trois morales* (1899), an adaptation of Sophocles's play (which was itself translated for the stage in 1896 and 1900). In Gide's version, the idea of sacrifice becomes the focus of the tragedy. This quasi-symbolist adaptation was widely interpreted as allegorical, although interpretations varied widely, including the possibility that the work was a reflection of the tumultuous Dreyfus affair.[49]

Lest we think the Parisian opera stages immune to this type of allegorical statement, Steven Huebner has proffered Saint-Saëns's *Étienne Marcel* (1879) as an example of a musical drama that can be read in a similar way.[50] In the opera, which focused on the eponymous medieval Frenchman's rebellion against the monarchy, "the authors played up a transparent connection to the Paris Commune of 1871 in order to enhance the *aesthetic* experience of contemporary audiences.... Defeat by a foreign power; rebellion in Paris; a revolutionary vanguard in the face of weakened central authority; the quick collapse of demagogues: all this engaged recent memories."[51] Although *Étienne Marcel* was not classical in subject, other composers did draw allegorical material from antiquity. We might, for example, turn to the readings of the Prometheus myth found in cantatas by Saint-Saëns and Augusta Holmès, the latter work (unfinished) being a musical reflection on the Franco-Prussian War.[52]

If new works could be written with allegorical overtones in order to take advantage of the postwar culture of mourning, why not use older operas as well? Gluck's works present such a possibility; *Orphée, Alceste, Iphigénie en Auride,* and *Iphigénie en Tauride* each present stories of dramatic sacrifice in the face of senseless oppression, and, moreover, present a positive resolution to the conflict (a feature unavailable in classical tragedy). It would be overly simplistic for me to suggest that Gluck's works were read purely as allegories of the twentieth-century French cultural climate. Yet it is certainly plausible that the Greek subjects echoed the themes of sacrifice and tragic loss prevalent in the national mourning that typified the decades following the Franco-Prussian War, particularly as more right-wing nationalistic movements began to gain momentum in France after 1900.[53]

From a French perspective, perhaps the greatest tragedy of the Franco-Prussian War was the annexation of Alsace-Lorraine to the German Empire. This horrific loss continued to be a major rallying point for French nationalism in the decades following the war, until the eventual return of the "lost provinces" in 1919. Sentimental depictions of Alsace and Lorraine were a common theme in literature around the turn of the century—for instance, in the perennially popular short stories of Alphonse Daudet, including "Alsace! Alsace!" and "La Dernière Classe."[54] In the realm of nonfiction, in a study of fin-de-siècle guidebooks, Douglas Mackaman has demonstrated the consistently emotional and strongly nationalistic rhetoric surrounding the provinces, memorializing the traumatic defeat of 1870.[55] The main feature of historical and artistic representations of the lost provinces is the recurring image of ultimate sacrifice. In 1918, for example, Lucien Gallois (a professor at the Université de Paris) asked, "Is it necessary to recall the solemn and touching protest which the two sacrificed provinces made? Without a word of complaint, with thanks to those who had defended them, they voiced their infinite sorrow and their unshaken hope."[56]

The infamous letter to the French government from Alsatian Mgr. Freppel, quoted again and again in the following decades, sets the tone for this interpretation of the events of 1870: "And will France, Sire, France which can be defeated but not destroyed, accept in the future a situation to which it is forced to submit today? For her [France], to cede Alsace is equivalent to the sacrifice of a mother from whom one wrests a child who does not wish to be separated from her."[57] Édouard Schuré (also the author of *Le Drame musical* [1886]) similarly wrote in 1916 that "the result of the war of 1870 was a disaster for Alsace-Lorraine. Its annexation to Germany wrested from the mother country two provinces that had become French with every fiber of their beings."[58] In both these descriptions, the parental France is forced to sacrifice a child to the onslaught of the Prussians. Given the fact that the loss of Alsace-Lorraine weighed heavily on the national consciousness (and conscience) at the fin de siècle, it seems likely that seeing similar themes reflected on the operatic stage would strike a resonant chord.[59]

To return finally to opera, this same description of tragic sacrifice could almost without alteration refer to almost any of Gluck's five major works—excepting *Armide*, which perhaps not coincidentally was the only opera to appear at the less politically conservative Opéra—making them powerful instruments for striking politically resonant chords at the fin de siècle. These passages depict Alsace-Lorraine as a woman wrenched from her home and cruelly sacrificed, a subject evidently dear to Gluck's heart. Alceste, for example, nobly sacrifices her life to save her husband, King Admète. In acting out of both love and the good of the kingdom, she agrees to take his place in Hades—much as Alsace was ceded to the hellish Prussia in exchange for the well-being of the French nation. Even the names of the sacrificed—"Alceste" and "Alsace"—are almost homophones, not a point to be taken lightly in a culture as obsessed with the sounds of its language as fin-de-siècle France. Significantly, through the heroism of Admète and Hercule, Alceste is returned to her rightful place at her husband's side, an ending that Parisian audiences of the early twentieth century no doubt applied to their own political situation.

Orphée et Eurydice similarly centers on a beloved wife taken to Hades too soon, and the efforts of her beloved to win her back from the land of the dead. Through his music he does so, and although he loses her again by violating his commandment not to look back, his affection and dedication to his wife please the gods, and Eurydice is restored to life. The parallels between this familiar story and the loss of Alsace-Lorraine are again obvious. Orphée stands in for the French state, while Euridice, wrested by cruel fate from her beloved husband, evokes the loss of Alsace-Lorraine. The apparent senselessness of her demise becomes a crucial point; she dies through no fault of her own, and with no evident motivation. In the same way, the French rhetoric surrounding the Franco-Prussian War invariably depicted the French as blameless in the conflict, subjugated by the brutish Germans. One might also point out that the role of Orphée was taken by a woman, rendering the connection between Orphée and the "motherland" more apparent, as France (*la* France) was typically depicted iconographically as female.[60]

This theme of women being ripped from their homes was used more than once in reference to the loss of Alsace-Lorraine after the Franco-Prussian War. Perhaps the most prominent example (though lost today) is Frémiet's sculpture *Gorille emportant la Vénus de Milo* (ca. 1871), which depicts a gorilla abducting the famous sculpture. To quote Leoussi again, the sculpture may be read as "an account of the conquest of Alsace-Lorraine, with the Prussians represented by the gorilla as an indication of their animal-like barbarism and of their biological primitivism; Alsace-Lorraine is represented by the *Venus de Milo*, the representation of cities and countries in the shape of women being a traditional convention in western art."[61] Substituting Eurydice for the *Venus de Milo* is not so difficult to imagine, and in *Orphée* the menacing furies make an effective alternative to the barbaric gorilla of Frémier's sculpture.

Other reinterpretations of Gluck operas in light of the Franco-Prussian War are equally easy to envision. Both of the *Iphigénie* operas, for example, deal primarily with the sacrifice of a family member. In *Iphigénie en Aulide*, for the greater good of her homeland the eponymous heroine is destined for sacrifice to the goddess Diana at the hands of her father Agamemnon. Far from shirking her duty to her nation, Iphigénie demands to be sacrificed even in the midst of a battle waged to protect her. Only at the last moment does Diana change her mind, allowing Iphigénie to live and spare her father from having to make such an unthinkable sacrifice. Again, the gods are presented as fickle; the ultimate sacrifices demanded of both Agamemnon and Iphigénie are seemingly out of proportion to the trespass committed: Agamemnon unknowingly killed off one of Diana's favorite stags. The theme of sacrifice is prominent in *Iphigénie en Tauride*, as well, although this time we have a male victim: Iphigénie's brother Oreste, whom Iphigénie is required to sacrifice through unfortunate twists of fate. As in *Aulide*, this tragic conclusion is only narrowly avoided in the end by a battle to liberate the prisoners (both Oreste and Iphigénie). In both cases, a military action is required to retake the lost children from their foreign captors, suggestive of the revanchist furor in postwar Paris. And once again, Oreste and Iphigénie are presented as blameless in the whole ordeal, merely the pawns of a tragic fate.

Gluck's operas represented an opportunity for Parisian audiences to see works onstage that reflected their own national concerns. At the same time, however, the fact that all these operas were set in ancient Greece provided an appropriate historical and geographical distance between the subject material and its listeners—an emotional buffer. They thus allowed an artistic expression for the growing "revanchist" sentiment of the 1880s and beyond, without tainting the Opéra or Opéra-Comique with overtly political works. While critics never, to my knowledge, directly connected Gluck's works with political thought, it is certain that the idea of sacrifice was a major point in the reception of these works. And, moreover, sacrifice with which audiences could sympathize, as Rolland eloquently summarized in 1905:

> Gluck's art is profoundly human. In contrast to the mythological tragedies of Rameau, he remains on the earth: his heroes are men; their joys and their sorrows are sufficient for him. He has sung of the most pure passions: married love in *Orphée* and in *Alceste*, the love of a father and daughter in *Iphigénie en Aulide*, fraternal love and friendship in *Iphigénie en Tauride*, selfless love, sacrifice, the offering of the self for those one loves.[62]

Thus Gluck provided audiences with the best of both worlds. His mythological subject material remained distant enough from modern politics to avoid explicit connections, but the plot material and "humanness" of the characters allowed audiences to express national grief through the onstage tragedy.

We will return to the topic of Gluck's classicism and its relevance to French audiences in the following chapter. But while I have focused above on the inherent Frenchness of Gluck and his operas, I now turn to his complicated relationship with a decidedly un-French composer: Richard Wagner. These topics, of course, are not entirely unrelated. While making yet another comparison between Gluck and the ancient Greeks in his 1882 study of the composer, for example, Hippolyte Barbedette briefly shifts his focus to Wagner: "Like Gluck, Wagner turned to Greece after noting the debasement of theater in his time. It is there, in the land of Aeschylus, that he found, in his own words, 'the model and example of art.' Among the Greeks, all branches of art were assembled to collaborate toward the same ends."[63] For Barbedette and similarly minded critics, the same Greekness (and thus Frenchness) that enabled Gluck's music to speak so powerfully to modern audiences also applied to Wagner. Assessing the similarities and differences between the two composers and their approaches to opera occupied French critics and musicologists throughout the fin de siècle, and shaped the reception of both composers in profound, and often surprising, ways.

Chapter Seven

Symbols

As Wagner's controversial music-aesthetic theories began to appear in print in France, French critics quickly seized upon Gluck as an analogue. Comparisons between the two composers began to crop up as early as the 1850s, as many anti-Wagnerians sought evidence that the newer composer's supposedly groundbreaking theories were fundamentally derivative.[1] Gluck, like Wagner, was an operatic reformer (but a *successful* one, in the eyes of many French critics) with a "système" of musical composition, and the eighteenth-century operatic reforms Gluck had proposed in his well-known preface to *Alceste* clearly demonstrated French superiority.[2] On the other side of the fence, Wagner obviously viewed Gluck as a pivotal composer in opera history; in 1847 he had adapted *Iphigénie en Aulide* for a performance in Dresden, and he held the overture, in particular, in high esteem.[3] As early as 1841, Wagner showered the work with praise in the French press in an article titled "De L'Ouverture" in *La Revue et Gazette musicale de Paris* (January 10, 14, and 17, 1841), where it served as his primary example for the dramatic capabilities of the opera overture.[4]

In 1861, however, this somewhat tenuous connection between Gluck and Wagner escalated in the press into a large-scale debate that helped to shape both composers' fin-de-siècle reception in France.[5] Only a few months after Wagner's *Tannhäuser* failed so spectacularly at the Opéra, the same theater mounted a production of *Alceste*. The similarities between the two works were too much for critics to miss, particularly in terms of comparing Wagner's music-theoretical innovations with Gluck's much-lauded preface to *Alceste*. The critic Paul Smith succinctly summarized the situation in a review of the 1866 *Alceste*: "The last revival of *Alceste*, still quite recent, took place on October 21, 1861, the memorable year that began with the resounding downfall of *Tannhäuser*. The music of the future and that of the past confronted one another as if in a dueling arena, and the past readily triumphed over the future, which it well and truly buried."[6]

After that time, Wagner and Gluck became irrevocably linked in the minds of critics and, presumably, the operagoing public. Initially, the primary motivation for connecting Gluck and Wagner was to demonstrate that the latter composer's controversial musical "system"—as it was called in the press—was highly derivative of the well-known ideas that Gluck had set forth in his preface to *Alceste*, in which he rejected the excesses of Italian opera seria and set forth his principles of reform nearly a century before Wagner. As early as 1852, Paul Scudo acerbically remarked that "Mr. Wagner believes himself the inventor of a system as old as opera itself."[7] Less than a decade later, Ange-Henri Blaze (*dit* Henri Blaze de Bury) wrote in a review of *Alceste* at the Opéra in 1866:

> I imagine that one would not surprise the author of *Tannhäuser* and *Lohengrin* too much by telling him that he had invented nothing, and that all this theory that he lays out with such great uproar in his volumes was explained by Gluck in a few prefatory pages written in that simple and clear style that honest men use; but does Mr. Richard Wagner suspect that this method, which he has not invented, comes to him from France, and that it is French wine from our region that he drinks in his German glass? Silliness and contradiction, here is a man who, in order to reform the national art of a country that yesterday gave to the world Beethoven and Weber, addresses himself to the most obsolete traditions of the old *tragédie française*! This man, having nothing in view except the future, looks only to the past.[8]

According to Blaze, Wagner's musical contributions were nothing more than an overblown paraphrase of Gluck's compositional tenets. More insidiously, Blaze finds that Wagner co-opts, as German, elements of Gluck's essentially French style, corrupting the traditions of *tragédie française*. Barbedette, though less explicitly anti-Wagner, similarly compared the composer to Gluck, giving Gluck credit for most of Wagner's "developments," including the leitmotif: "Like Gluck, Wagner gives the librettist the larger role [in the collaboration with the composer] (he is his own librettist, so his self-esteem need not suffer). Like Gluck, he wishes for the musical language to truly and exactly reflect the states of the soul; like him, he exalts the power of the orchestra; like him, he likes to precede the entrance of a character with a symbolic phrase that characterizes and announces it."[9] In suggesting that Wagner's reforms echoed Gluck's, Barbedette again minimizes the importance of these "new" approaches to composition; Wagner was just late to the party that Gluck had brought to France a century before.

By the final decades of the nineteenth century, however, the tables had turned. Although Gluck remained tied to Wagner, the connection served more and more to create a music-historical narrative that led directly from one composer to the other, thus imbuing the author of *Tannhäuser* with an impeccably French artistic heritage that could facilitate his long-delayed triumphal march into Paris. Chief among those for whom Gluck served this pivotal role was Vincent d'Indy, who, in his capacity as director of the influential Schola Cantorum, wielded an enormous amount of power in shaping public perceptions of music history. As Katharine

Ellis has argued, for d'Indy and his group, the worth of "early" composers lay in "the proximity of their musical styles to that of the master of Bayreuth."[10] For d'Indy's teleological view of music history to work, Gluck had to point forward all the way to Wagner and beyond. D'Indy's conception of the history of opera involved the migration of French styles to Germany via a lineage that encompassed Rameau, Gluck, and Carl Maria von Weber en route to Wagner. From that point onward, true operatic greatness returned to France, where Wagnerians—implicitly d'Indy himself—took up the banner.

Although he may have been the most prominent, d'Indy was certainly not the only critic to place Gluck in line with Wagner. Julien Tiersot, who had played such a large role in the Pelletan Edition, seized upon the preface to *Alceste* as a means of connecting the two composers, just as numerous other critics had done before him, describing the document as a "déclaration des droits" for operatic composers.[11] This time, however, the focus of the argument shifted away from calling Wagner's reforms derivative, and toward situating Wagner comfortably in a French music-historical narrative. In response to the perennial issue of the relationship between music and poetry, for example, Julien Tiersot quotes Wagner directly and then embarks on an excursus defending him from detractors.[12] Although Tiersot connects Gluck to Wagner, he also points out that Gluck "never thought of breaking the molds used by Lully and Rameau, but on the contrary . . . his highest ambition was to continue their traditions."[13] Thus, Tiersot places Gluck in a historical narrative that begins with the origins of French opera in the *tragédie lyrique* and continues inexorably to the nineteenth-century music drama. In a review of the performance of the *Iphigénie en Aulide* overture d'Indy conducted in 1908, Michel Brenet (pseudonym of Marie Bobilier) also found in Gluck a forerunner to Wagner's dramatic capabilities: "Under the direction of a fiery baton, the overture to *Iphigénie en Aulide* stopped appearing to us as a majestic portico peopled with hieratic mannequins, and became, as Wagner has forseen, the living synthesis of all the passions, sadness, and conflicts of Greek drama."[14] This line of reasoning highlights the Operatic Museum's power to shape historical narratives. With Gluck and Wagner constantly juxtaposed, audience members and critics were strongly encouraged to draw parallels in a way they would not likely have done had Gluck's works been absent from the stage.

Although nearly all critics agreed that there was some sort of historical progression from Gluck to Wagner, some were less than pleased at the outcome of such progress. Chief among these was Claude Debussy, who saw Gluck as "a disaster for French music" for the same reasons that the Wagnerian Tiersot celebrated him.[15] From his vantage point of the postwar 1920s, Léon Vallas astutely pointed out that "Debussy systematically opposed to Rameau, the true Frenchman, the German musician, Gluck, who usurped his colleague's place. According to him, Gluck was the hereditary enemy who broke through our [French] national tradition and destroyed our music."[16] Debussy had earlier explicated Gluck's crimes in a sarcastic open letter addressed directly to Gluck: "From having known you, French music gained the unexpected bebefit of falling straight into the arms of Wagner; I like to think that, had it not been for you, it might not have happened. But then French music shouldn't have had to ask the way so often of people only too ready to lead her astray."[17]

For Debussy, Gluck—the German in French clothing—was positioned as the anti-Rameau, and as such served a useful purpose. The idea that Gluck derailed the natural progress of French music could effectively explain the reason for Rameau's decline in popularity during the nineteenth century, removing any possibility that the latter's music might be in any way deficient—a topic to which we will return in part 3. But however sharply Tiersot and Debussy may have diverged in their opinions of Wagnerian influence on French music, their opinions regarding Gluck's historical placement are not so dissimilar. Both figures saw the composer of *Alceste* as guiding French music down a teleological path that culminated in *Tristan*, whether for good or ill.

The musicologist Jean d'Udine, however, in his influential 1906 biography of Gluck, saw the relationship between the two composers in a different light. While Tiersot and Debussy found in Gluck a forerunner to Wagner, d'Udine joined with those who saw the later composer only as derivative. Gluck, he says, "imagined, well before Wagner, the 'unending melody,' with the advantage over the author of *Tristan* and the *Ring* that he did not fear to depart from either in the sense of the recitative or in that of the aria."[18] Even more damningly, d'Udine states explicitly that

> the colossus of Bayreuth, who believed himself to be a good Gluckist, was not.... The Wagnerian "unending melody" is a sophism; sophism defended genially by an incomparable orchestra, but sophism all the same.... The disciples of Wagner, for example, Humperdinck, Vincent d'Indy, and Alfred Bruneau, are outside of the Gluckist tradition every time they remain slaves to the aesthetic of the leitmotif and they systematically avoid the straightforward forms, the true lyric forms.[19]

In his positions, d'Udine echoes many critics of the 1850s and 1860s, protecting audience members from being duped by Wagner's claims of novelty. Once again we see the Operatic Museum's ability to educate audiences in their own musical history, and thereby refusing to allow Germanic composers to take credit for French musical ideas.

Given the lasting connection between Gluck and Wagner in the French press, we should hardly be surprised to find a distinct correlation between productions of the two composers' works in fin-de-siècle Paris. After the *Tannhäuser* debacle of 1861, Wagner's works only gradually began to return to the Parisian spotlight. Much as we have already seen with Gluck's music at the fin de siècle, Wagner's music first appeared (or reappeared) in Paris in concert series, with shorter pieces as well as entire acts of works beginning in the mid-1880s.[20] In 1887, Charles Lamoureux attempted to bring *Lohengrin* to the Eden Théâtre, but the timing of the production was poor: Paris was at that moment in an anti-German furor over the imprisonment of a French police commissioner by German authorities. The right-wing nationalist newspaper *La Revanche* successfully incited enormous demonstrations against Wagner's opera, and the whole enterprise ended in the failure of *Lohengrin* to reach a receptive French audience.[21] Only five years before *Orphée*, the 1891 production of *Lohengrin* at the Opéra had led to what Manuela Schwartz refers to as the "second *Lohengrin* scandal," in which (among other difficulties), a large crowd assembled to protest the work's performance.[22]

After this point, however, the popularity of Wagner's operas in France quickly began to soar. In 1893, *Die Walküre* made its Opéra debut, followed in 1895 by a production of *Tannhäuser*. This last work was a milestone in French Wagner reception, as it contrasted dramatically with the turmoil that had surrounded the work's first performance in Paris. The fact that *Orphée* followed a year later is noteworthy: it seems that Gluck was always to follow close on Wagner's heels into the Paris opera houses, just as *Alceste* had followed *Tannhäuser* to the stage in 1861. After the initially slow start in the early 1900s, Wagner's works somewhat ironically came to form the core of the Opéra's repertory; Steven Huebner has pointed out that no other composer's works were performed more frequently at the Opéra after 1890 (see table 7.1).[23] Not coincidentally, it is precisely during this time that all of Gluck's major operas were revived in Paris.

Many critics used the (entirely noncoincidental) simultaneous popularity of Gluck and Wagner to reopen debates from the 1850s and 1860s, calling renewed attention to the proximity of the two composers' aesthetic stances. In *La Nouvelle revue*, for example, the Wagnerian librettist and critic Louis Gallet wrote: "Regarding Gluck's *Orphée*, just performed at the Opéra-Comique, we are pleased to bring the famous theories of the illustrious composer into the spotlight again; we ourselves have brought them up here many times with regard to the definition of the true *drame lyrique*, the character of which was determined entirely by the preface to *Alceste*."[24]

Alfred Bruneau, reviewing *Orphée* for *Le Figaro*, devoted a substantial portion of his review to quoting extensively from this preface in order to praise Gluck's dramatic conceptions. Bruneau went a step farther, claiming that it "is impossible—one can see—to better express, to define more clearly, more neatly, the noble and lofty ambitions of today's musicians."[25] By

Table 7.1. Wagner opera productions in Paris, 1891–1914

Opera	Year	Theater
Lohengrin	1891	Opéra
L'Or du Rhin (*Das Rheingold*)	1893 (two-piano version)	Opéra
La Walkyrie (*Die Walküre*)	1893	Opéra
Tannhäuser	1895	Opéra
Le Vaisseau-Fantôme (*Der fliegende Holländer*)	1897	Opéra-Comique
Siegfried	1901	Opéra
Tristan et Isolde	1904	Opéra
Les Maîtres Chanteurs (*Die Meistersinger*)	1907	Opéra
Le Crepuscule des Dieux (*Götterdämmerung*)	1908	Opéra
L'Or du Rhin	1909	Opéra
L'Anneau du Nibelung (*Der Ring des Nibelungen*)	1911	Opéra
Parsifal	1914	Opéra

"today's musicians," Bruneau is surely referring to his own work as a composer and to that of his circle of colleagues and friends—a group whose compositional aims were heavily influenced by Wagner's theories. Indeed, in his *La Musique française* (1901) Bruneau would characterize his operas as being a combination of Wagnerian and Gluckian elements.[26] His review of *Orphée* essentially takes for granted a connection between the styles of these two composers, supporting the assertion that the Wagnerian (or perhaps post-Wagnerian) composers of the fin de siècle were recreating Gluck's eighteenth-century innovations in a contemporary musical language.

As we no doubt expect at this point, not all critics in the 1890s shared the notion that Gluck's and Wagner's theories were compatible. Camille Bellaigue wrote in *La Revue des deux mondes* that "Gluck's *Orphée* is singular in the sense that Gluck's dramatic conception, like Monteverdi's in another time, and contrary to Wagner's, is human and practical. Gluck had no philosophical pretensions. He was not at all seeking to solve the enigma of the world."[27] Gluck is portrayed as a practical musician, in contrast to Wagner's "philosophical pretensions." Bellaigue continued:

> We never miss a chance these days to compare, or assimilate, Wagner and Gluck from the point of view of declamation. We go around repeating that the one or the other were servants, worshippers of the language, to which they have sacrificed everything, even the music. Perhaps we should listen. If Gluck and Wagner meet and agree here in theory, in practice they diverge and oppose each other entirely. We could not find two styles more opposed than theirs to understand and to regulate the role of the words. While with Wagner it serves only to determine the subject, the situation, the sentiment that the orchestra is charged with creating, with Gluck the language itself—and it alone—is the method or the agent of the expression; in it lies the center or the summit of the work, and the seat of the beauty. In a word, the text is what could be with the least trouble omitted from the Wagnerian *drame lyrique*, but even a small betrayal or alteration of it would destroy Gluck's *drame lyrique* in a single blow.[28]

In praising Gluck and his techniques, Bellaigue delivered some stinging rebukes to Wagner. While the artistic credos of the two composers might superficially be very similar in terms of the respective roles of music and text, in the actual implementation of these techniques Bellaigue found Wagner's music to be profoundly lacking.

This tone, firmly established by the 1896 *Orphée*, continued over the following decade. The Wagnerian critic Henry Bauer even explicitly pointed to Wagner's success as the main impetus for the revival of Gluck's works:

> The music of the future has become the music of the present. We joyfully applaud this metamorphosis. But drinking each night from the cup of the same Titan, does one not experience a bit of satiation, or rather does one not dread the monotony of the grandeur and the power? Then it is necessary to muse on varying the pleasure of the listeners, offering a pure food to the taste that was refined at the table of the God. Such is the genesis of the classical renewal in these past years, the cause of the triumphal revivals of *Orphée, Iphigénie en Tauride, Alceste,* and finally *Armide*. The tragedy of Gluck has seemed young again in glory and immortality in the vicinity of the *drame lyrique*. Olympus is not at all a contemptible little mount from the view of the summits of Valhalla.[29]

While Bauer's analysis is essentially a partisan celebration of Wagnerism, he makes a good point. Certainly, given the preexisting connection between the two composers, Gluck's works would have appeared to fin-de-siècle audiences as a counterpart to Wagner's operas, tempting listeners to compare and contrast them.

While the Opéra had a near monopoly on Wagner operas (with the exception of the 1897 production of *Der Fliegende Holländer* at the

Opéra-Comique), as we have seen, Gluck's works appeared predominantly at the Opéra-Comique. It may be that the Opéra-Comique turned to Gluck's operas to create an alternative to Wagner's dominance at the Opéra, whether as a related but lighter option or as an antidote to the Wagnerian sound. On the one hand, Gluck presented a less expensive and less esoteric option for those interested in Wagner's music dramas (a sort of poor-man's Wagner). For those who saw Wagner as an interloper, on the other hand, Gluck's use of mythological themes represented a more conservative alternative to *Tristan*, and, perhaps more important, an alternative composed by a French (or "French") composer.[30] Saint-Saëns, for example, points out that the fin-de-siècle turn toward mythological subject material was rooted in Wagnerism: "Oceans of ink have been spilled in discussing the question of whether the subjects of operas should be taken from history or mythology, and the question is still moot.... The only worthwhile things are whether the music is good and the work interesting. But *Tannhäuser, Lohengrin, Tristan*, and *Siegfried* appeared and the question sprang up."[31]

Further emphasizing the connection between the two composers was the fact that the same few sopranos—undoubtedly the most popular singers in Paris—were performing the leads in both Wagner and Gluck operas, often with similar presentation of the roles in terms of details like costuming as well as in the rhetoric surrounding them in the press. After the turn of the century, three main sopranos took the lead in Gluck's works: Rose Caron, Félia Litvinne, and Lucienne Bréval (see table 7.2). Each of these popular singers was also widely known for her Wagnerian interpretations, and comparisons between their handling of Wagner and Gluck were fairly common in the press. In an article on Bréval in *Le Courrier musical*, for example, Georges Pioch placed her Wagnerian and Gluckian roles side by side, concluding by comparing her style for each: "[Bréval] found here [in Gluck] the benefits of her willingness to sacrifice, the willingness by which she diminished almost to a whisper the force of the voice that uttered with a heartrending violence the '*hoïotohos*' of Brünnhilde.... It is this willingness that is certainly going to make Lucienne Bréval a spot-on Iphigénie."[32] A review by d'Udine in the same journal described Félia Litvinne singing excerpts of *Armide* in the Concerts Colonne, lauding the singer and opining, "I am sure that if one asked Mme. Litvinne to confess her secret preference between the death of Armide and the death of Brünnhilde, she would not be able to choose between these two brilliant passages."[33]

Press photographs of these singers in their Wagner-Gluck roles also reveal such similarities. The costumes given to the main characters in Gluck's operas were often similar, in fact, to those given to some Wagner heroines—in particular, Elsa from *Lohengrin* and Isolde. Compare, for example, the portraits of Litvinne in the roles of Alceste and Isolde found

Table 7.2. Prima donnas in selected Parisian productions of Gluck operas, 1875–1918

Opera	Year	Prima donna
Orphée	1896	Marie Delna
Orphée	1899	Marie Bréma (substitution)
Iphigénie en Tauride	1900	Rose Caron
Iphigénie en Tauride	1903	Rose Caron
Alceste	1904	Félia Litvinne
Armide	1905	Lucienne Bréval
Orphée	1905	Rose Caron
Iphigénie en Aulide	1907	Lucienne Bréval
Orphée	1914	Claire Croiza

in figures 7.1 and 7.2 (both from 1904). In both representations, Litvinne is garbed in long flowing robes denoting the antiquity of the settings of *Alceste* and *Tristan*. Furthermore, both images capture the somber, essentially tragic nature of the roles, portraying their protagonists not sensually (as many contemporary depictions of prima donnas did) but rather as embodiments of the ideal of classical tragedy.

Wagner's pervasive influence on operatic composition in fin-de-siècle Paris is well documented. It is clear from the preceding section, however, that what Ernest Chausson once referred to as "the red specter of Wagner" affected the reception of earlier music, as well. As a result of the sustained comparisons between the two composers over more than a half century, Gluck's operas were seen in a Wagnerian light to a much greater extent than those by other historical composers. Throughout the turn of the century, Wagner played a major role in the way that French critics and audiences understood Gluck's musical achievements as well as his place in music history. But the relationship was certainly not one-sided. Even as Wagner became the dominant operatic force in Paris, Gluck's operas continued to offer audiences either an alternative to the fashionable master of Bayreuth or a glimpse at the French origins of his style. Both interpretations served to connect Gluck to Wagner, which—from both pro- and anti-Wagner perspectives—could not help but emphasize Gluck's prominent position in (French) music history. In the following section, we look at one particular instance of how Wagnerian thought—combined with the neoclassical elements we traced in chapter 6—might have colored fin-de-siècle

Figure 7.1. Félia Litvinne as Alceste. *Musica*, July 1904.

Figure 7.2. Félia Litvinne as Isolde. *Musica*, July 1904.

interpretations of the Gluck revival from the very beginning, with the 1896 production of *Orphée*.

Gluck the Symbolist: *Orphée* and Modernity

In the previous chapters, I have tried to pick apart some of the strands running throughout French Gluck reception over several decades. In this final portion I would like to weave several of these threads back together, examining the intersections of discussions of Frenchness, classicism, and Wagnerism in the reception of Gluck's *Orphée* in 1896. Doing so offers us a fuller picture of the early workings of the Operatic Museum, shedding some light on how audiences may have understood these chronologically displaced works in a modern setting. By 1896, Wagnerism had subtly infiltrated French society on a much deeper level than simple appreciation, or even adulation, of the composer's music and compositional concepts. Wagner's writings, in particular, exerted a strong influence over the visual and literary arts, and so it should come as no surprise that the fin-de-siècle understanding of *Orphée* was affected by another prominent artistic trend deeply rooted in his aesthetic ideals: symbolism. The aesthetic values promoted by the master of Bayreuth formed the cornerstone of the symbolist movement in France; the *Revue wagnerienne* (1885–88) was the leading symbolist journal of the fin de siècle, and nearly every major symbolist thinker in Paris at the time was a contributor.[34] In the words of literary theorist Eva Kushner, in this symbolist culture "Wagner reigned as a god."[35] By the end of the century, the constant juxtaposition of Gluck's ideology and works with Wagner's would doubtless have encouraged audiences to see *Orphée* through a Wagnerian-symbolist lens.

As we discussed in chapter 5, the ancient subject matter of Gluck's opera likely facilitated approaching it as a modern work. Fin-de-siècle Parisians were fascinated by Greek antiquity in general, and the Greek-Gallic "origins" of the French people in particular. This fascination played a major role in the way critics understood the revival Gluck's operas in general, and why their topics struck such a chord with opera audiences. Capitalizing on the popularity of classical themes was especially important for framing this first Gluck production of the fin de siècle. Other theaters were certainly doing so: recall that in 1893 the Comédie-Française's production of *Antigone* was hailed as "one of the most instructive and moving artistic events of these past years."[36]

These factors help explain why Greek mythological subject matter was well received by opera audiences at the fin de siècle. But the importance of the Orpheus myth went far beyond a general interest in antiquity; the legend of the poet-composer was laden with significance for symbolist artists, and thus appeared frequently in their works. Gustave Moreau's *Young Thracian Woman Carrying the Head of Orpheus* (1865) and *Orpheus at the Tomb of Eurydice* (ca. 1891; see fig. 7.3) are perhaps the most prominent examples, but other significant representations of the myth in painting would include Louis Français's *Orpheus* (1863), Émile Lévy's *Death of Orpheus* (1866), Jean Delville's two *Orpheus* paintings (1893, 1896), and Alexandre Séon's *Lamentations of Orpheus* (1896), among numerous other examples.[37] In literature, Paul Valéry's sonnet "Orphée" (1891–92) stands as a prominent example of the myth's resonance with symbolist thought, and Orpheus and Orphic thought were prominent in the works and ideology of Stéphane Mallarmé.[38] Although the myth appears in earlier nineteenth-century Parnassian works, it became central to symbolist art. Art historian Dorothy Kosinski provides some explanation: "For the Symbolists, Orpheus has a very specific meaning: he is priest, initiate, martyr, ideal artist whose work magically summons aspects of the Symbolist aesthetic—art as religion, the artist as priest, the art object as revelation."[39] This outlook was shaped to a large extent by Wagner's writings, and so, not surprisingly, music took a place of honor among the arts for its ability to communicate abstractly, without the limitations of language.[40]

Music essentially became for symbolists an ideal synthesis of all the arts, with Orpheus as its mythic personification. He represented the essence of the poet and musician, both saint and martyr in the symbolist religion of art. From a slightly different perspective, we can note the similarities between Orpheus and Wagner's ideal of the perfect musician; both demonstrate the possibilities of the poet-composer, and both exemplify the emotional powers of music.[41] The connection between Wagner and Orpheus was not lost on fin-de-siècle artists. Gustave Moreau's *Orpheus* (ca. 1891), for example, depicts the lamenting Orpheus standing over the body of Eurydice, with a dead swan lying next to her body, an apparent reference to Wagner's *Lohengrin* (1850), in which the swan is a recurring image of purity or loss.[42]

If we accept Orpheus as the embodiment of symbolist perfection, then why did no fin-de-siècle composers—even those that might be described as symbolist—treat the material? After all, as Édouard Schuré opined in 1886, the "myth of Orpheus can find its dramatic and poignant form only through the plenitude of musical expression."[43] Jacques Offenbach's operetta *Orphée aux Enfers* (1858), of course, stands as an exception, but that opera's farcical treatment of the material sets it apart from Gluck's work, and in any case it predates the symbolist meanings that permeated the myth at the fin de siècle. Debussy (no admirer of Gluck) did try his hand at creating a serious Orpheus opera—*Orphée-roi*—but two years of work on the project ended with not a single note on paper.[44] The cause of this lack of Orpheus-related works may simply be that at the turn of the century,

Figure 7.3. Gustave Moreau, *Orpheus at the Tomb of Eurydice* (ca. 1891). Reproduced with permission from CCI / The Art Archive at Art Resource, New York.

Gluck essentially owned the Orpheus myth in music. *Orphée* was simply too well known and too highly respected; the "anxiety of influence" the opera created may have been too great for composers to risk challenging Gluck's authority. Julien Tiersot certainly thought as much in 1896: "From the nineteenth century onward, the name of Gluck is so completely associated with the idea of Orpheus that no musician would dare to touch this legend, on the subject of which it seems that, from then on, everything has already been said."[45]

Because Gluck's treatment of the myth was the most prominent musical version known to Parisian audiences (and composers were unwilling to attempt a new operatic version), *Orphée et Eurydice* presented the only reasonable option for music theaters to exploit the popularity of the Orpheus legend.[46] Gluck's opera had the potential to be particularly relevant to modern audiences, as Raymond Bouyer pointed out in the literary journal *L'Artiste*:

> In the gloomy depths of the sacred protective Wood, does he himself not point out the path for us, the distraught white Poet who brandishes his lyre, confiding in his harmonious despair that he will create the song for regaining love? The eternal myth speaks in his gesture. Let us identify our soul with his, walk with him, live in him, in order to decorate the internal museum of our fugitive memories: his sorrowful beauty reveals us to ourselves; that he should be in our hopes, that he should return amid our regrets so as to beautify them in his image, with the rebirth of the first leaves.[47]

For Gluck's opera to be perceived in a modern fashion, it was crucial to align the work with the symbolist interpretation of the myth, essentially creating a live version of the symbolist artworks on the stage. The two primary ways in which this process was enacted—in terms of both the production and its critical reception—involved employing the symbolist tropes of Orpheus's gender ambiguity and focusing on the role of lamentation in *Orphée*.

A recurring theme in the symbolist Orpheus works was the depiction of him as a profoundly androgynous figure. As the allegorical manifestation of the symbolist (or Wagnerian) high priest of art, Orpheus transcends the limitations of specifically masculine or feminine beauty. Art historian Patricia Mathews has pointed out that for symbolist artists, androgyny—in males—"became a sign of creative force . . . incorporating the female principle without the taint of sexuality. . . . [It] asserted the notion of the feminine as creative while maintaining the exclusion of actual women from the ideology of creativity.[48]

The works of Alexandre Séon and Jean Delville (see figs. 7.4 and 7.5), depict the poet-musician with a kind of ideal nongendered beauty, and prominently feature the lyre—the tool of artistic creation—as an extension of the hero's body. Nineteenth-century performances of Gluck's *Orphée* contribute to the sense of androgyny by featuring a female mezzo-soprano in the role of the mythological hero.[49] The Opéra's 1859 revival may in fact have been a catalyzing factor in the androgynous portrayal of Orpheus in art, as Viardot's performance was patently the inspiration for François Louis Français's painting *Orpheus* (1863), in addition to works by other artists from the same period.[50] We can thus view the 1896 *Orphée* as part of a circular progression; Gluck's opera influenced visual artists, who in turn helped bring about the opera's return to popularity decades later. This androgyny also has a distinctly Wagnerian interpretation. Wagner's music and writings are saturated with the idea of combining male and female elements, and Wagner frequently turned in his writings to the analogy of the female Music being impregnated by the male Poetry, producing the fusion as an offspring.[51] Furthermore, as Jean-Jacques Nattiez points out: "As the poet of the future, Wagner himself is an androgynous being, bearing within him the active male principle, in the form of the poetic seed, and the passive female principle, embodied in music. And the work that results from this inner impregnation is itself an androgynous creation, since Wagner's musical drama bestows its blessing on the union of male poetry and female music."[52] Orpheus, as Wagnerian composer-poet, represents such an offspring; an androgynous Orphée had the potential to become a figurehead for the ideal Wagnerian artist, imbued with the masculine and feminine elements necessary for greatness.

Orphée was not the only gender-ambiguous character on the fin-de-siècle operatic stage, however. Although featuring a soprano *en travesti* as a major character was rare for the fin de siècle, French audiences would have been reasonably accustomed to such devices, from Mozart's Cherubino or Nicklausse in Offenbach's *Les Contes d'Hoffmann* (1881), for example.[53] Despite precedents, however, one must agree with literary theorist Wendy Bashant when she points out that the Berlioz version of *Orphée* "is one of the queerest operas I know," plagued by "gendered complexity" and "the ambiguity created by voices that refuse to rest on their prescribed staffs."[54]

Females *en travesti* might have been fairly common at the fin de siècle, but most often in secondary roles or as male youths. A heroic protagonist like Orpheus sung by a woman was far from typical, and audiences would certainly have noticed the character's inherent androgyny. The musicologist and critic Henri de Curzon noted in his review that "the most bizarre" thing in the production was "Orphée's feminine costume: without his lyre, he was indistinguishable from Eurydice. It seems that this is still another new idea of performance... alas!"[55] Curzon's observation seems to be on the mark. In contrast to the fairly masculine costume worn by Pauline Viardot in 1859, the 1896 production evidently saw Marie Delna in more

Figure 7.4. Alexandre Séon, *Lamentation of Orpheus* (1896). Reproduced with permission from Réunion des Musées Nationaux / Art Resource, New York.

Figure 7.5. Jean Delville, *Orpheus* (1893). © 2013 Artists Rights Society (ARS), New York / SABAM, Brussels. Reproduced with permission from Bridgeman-Giraudon / Art Resource, New York.

ambiguous clothing: a loose-fitting white robe much like what one would expect female characters to wear (see fig. 7.6). Furthermore, one may interpret the de facto same-sex relationship between Orpheus and Eurydice as appealing to the same turn-of-the-century fascination with lesbian behavior—and in particular "Greek" lesbian behavior—evident in works like Pierre Louÿs's extremely successful novel *Aphrodite* (1896) and his poetic cycle *Les Chansons de Bilitis* (1894).[56] Historian Lenard Berlanstein has also pointed out that "the fictions of the stage provided a cover for erotic pleasures that would otherwise have been suspect. Transvestite performance allowed audiences to enjoy the sight of attractive women embracing or exchanging longing glances."[57] Thus, *Orphée* would have allowed audiences to appreciate the production's lesbian overtones, while maintaining a suitably academic "Greek" aspect to the work.

Significantly, only at the conservative Schola Cantorum was the character of Orpheus sung by a tenor rather than a mezzo-soprano, in a move that some may well have been seen as rescuing the opera from the decadent implications of its casting. From Vincent d'Indy's *Cours de composition musicale*, it is clear that he found the tradition of having the role performed by a woman to be extremely distasteful:

> The French Orphée, like the Italian one, was written for a tenor voice, and the alteration of this role for a contralto, adopted for so long at the Opéra-Comique under the pretext that the effort demanded was too great for a tenor, changes both the character and the tone very unfavorably. In Italy, they very much cultivated a high-pitched tenor voice, to the point where they borrow, so to speak, a register more within the grasp of women's voices; but these high notes are very fierce, and replacing them with a feminine medium is a sweetening equivalent to murder.[58]

Although this passage leans on Gluck's original intentions for support, this explanation for d'Indy's antipathy toward casting a woman as Orphée falls flat. For one thing, d'Indy is either simply wrong about the original Italian version being written for a tenor (it was written for an alto castrato) or he is deliberately misleading his readers in order to lend his aesthetic judgment an air of historical authenticity. Such a call for "authenticity" is particularly ironic when one considers the extensive alterations that d'Indy was willing to make to Rameau's music, for example, in order to make it sound more "progressive" (see chapter 8). Instead, the composer's uneasiness with the Opéra-Comique's performance seems to run deeper. In a retrospective from the late 1920s, Eugène Borrel backed up d'Indy's version of events as an attempt at "authenticity":

Figure 7.6. Marie Delna as Orphée, ca. 1896. *Musica*, April 1909.

Gluck has been a preferred composer for the Schola: the *Iphigénies*, *Alceste,* and *Armide* have been given [in concert performances] successively; but the most striking is the performance of *Orphée* with the principal role restored to a tenor; this performance was the prelude and the determining reason for the revival at the Opéra-Comique [in 1912]; until then, in effect, it was customary since Mme Viardot to replace the tenor with an alto, which disrupted all the expressive effect of the role, written for a man by Gluck. Here again we must count the actions of the Schola as a small aesthetic police action.[59]

For d'Indy and his Schola compatriots, a female Orphée was not so much androgynous as emasculated, an unacceptable situation; only with a male voice could the character's heroic qualities be represented appropriately. D'Indy's example calls attention to the fact that at least some audience members did, in fact, feel that casting Orphée as a woman had a profound effect on the opera, not just in terms of the sound but also in terms of "the character" of Orphée.[60]

Related to Orphée's gender ambiguity was another aspect of the opera shared with symbolist thought: the work's focus on the traditionally feminine realm of lamentation. *Orphée* begins, unlike many other works on the subject, after the death of Eurydice. Never is the audience treated to a glimpse of a happily wed Orpheus; instead, Gluck's opera focuses from the beginning on the idea of the hero's suffering. To some extent, this lamentation may be read as a function of Orpheus's gender confusion. As classicist Charles Segal points out:

> A singer who makes his poetry of his passion and his passion of his poetry, Orpheus transforms grief into song. This is a song whose primary character is its intense, personal expressiveness rather than its ritual character as consolation for sorrow. In Greek culture particularly, the ritual lament is the special prerogative of women.... Orpheus, however, claims this lamentation for the male voice. His is a voice of total mourning and perpetual lament.[61]

In Gluck's opera, the idea that Orpheus exhibits typically female lamentation in the "male voice" is turned on its head; he may be a male character, but the voice is most certainly female.

A focus on Orpheus's lamentations is evident from the critical response to the 1896 production of *Orphée*. The critic E. de Trémon found even the orchestral music to reflect this quality, writing that at the performance "One was overwhelmed, in listening to these symphonic lamentations, by the intensity of insight from these notes, wherein the rending of the superhuman soul is combined with earthly thought."[62]

The opening scene at Eurydice's tomb and, most particularly, the lamentation of "J'ai perdu mon Eurydice" were the focus of the majority of the reviews, whereas the opera's happy ending was largely ignored, or glossed over. The text of the opera's first scene reflects the sense of overwhelming tragedy favored by the symbolists in their interpretation of the Orpheus myth:[63]

CHŒUR
Ah! dans ce bois tranquille et sombre,
Eurydice, si ton ombre
Nous entend, . . .

ORPHÉE
Eurydice!

CHŒUR
. . . Sois sensible à nos alarmes,
Vois nos peines, vois nos larmes
Que pour toi l'on répand.

ORPHÉE
Eurydice!

CHŒUR
Ah! prends pitié du malheureux Orphée,
Il soupire, il gémit,
Il plaint sa destinée.

ORPHÉE
Eurydice!

CHŒUR
L'amoureuse tourterelle,
Toujours tendre, toujours fidèle,
Ainsi soupire et meurt
De douleur.[64]

[CHOIR
Ah! in this tranquil and somber wood
Eurydice, if your shade
hears us, . . .

ORPHÉE
Eurydice!

CHOIR
... be aware of our alarms,
see our suffering, see our tears
that we shed for you.

ORPHÉE
Eurydice!

CHOIR
Ah! take pity on the unfortunate Orphée,
he sighs, he moans,
he laments his destiny.

ORPHÉE
Eurydice!

CHOIR
The turtledove in love,
always tender, always true,
sighs and dies like this
of grief.]

Critics likewise picked up on the hero's overwhelming pathos. In the review of the 1896 production found in *Le Guide musical*, for example, the description of this scene is as follows: "From the raising of the curtain we were admiring the tableau worthy of Poussin depicting Orphée prostrate before the tomb of Eurydice, responding to the beautiful lamentations of the choir with his harrowing cry of 'Eurydice.'"[65] Bruneau uses equally exalted language to describe the same scene: "The slow lamentation of the people before the tomb of Eurydice, the three heart-rending cries of Orphée that loom above it, the funereal pantomime that follows it are of a superb solemnity."[66]

Similarly, regarding Orphée's lament "J'ai perdu mon Eurydice," one of the most enduringly popular excerpts from the opera, the critic for the *Journal des débats* wrote: "What prodigious emotion comes from this cry of love: *J'ai perdu mon Eurydice* [I have lost my Eurydice]! And would you think to find a single person who is truly sensitive to the charms of music who would be able to remain unmoved in the face of this explosion of despair, even after all the dramatic changes made in music by Beethoven, Berlioz, or Wagner?"[67] This passage reveals again the critical emphasis on the suffering of the main character; the eventual cessation of that suffering (in Gluck's opera, if not the myth) is almost beside the point. Instead, it is the overwhelming loss that Orphée endures, combined with the lengths to which he goes to defy the gods, that captures the fin-de-siècle attention.

Emphasizing the lamentations of Orpheus also, as we have already seen, allowed audiences to tap into the shared French national sense of mourning, a focus that carried over into productions of Gluck's other operas.

However well Gluck's opera played into modern conceptions of the Orpheus myth, I do not mean to suggest that the sole impetus for the revival of *Orphée* at the Opéra-Comique was a desire to embrace symbolist aesthetic ideals. Nevertheless, the idea that fin-de-siècle audiences might interpret *Orphée* in new ways was not lost on critics. Bouyer, for example, found that a useful way to approach the 1896 production would be to examine

> the three different aspects concealed within the same work according to the various times [of its performance], to compare with sympathy the three *Orphées* and the three Glucks in how they appeared to Parisian listeners in 1774, in 1859, and in 1896: the mirror is the measure of all things, and the immortal image is deformed through its reflection. Each age has its pleasures—and its point of view. Would the philosopher not add that there are perhaps as many *Orphées* as there are listeners? . . . Which leaves nothing but to be worried.[68]

This remarkably modern perspective allowed the work itself to be unchanging and eternal (the "immortal image"), while the audience members would impose differing interpretations based on the vantage point provided by their particular time and place. Bouyer also suggests here that the 1896 *Orphée* was necessarily a reflection of the culture that created it, which was one deeply permeated by Wagnerian and symbolist rhetoric.

Certainly *Orphée* is not an inherently symbolist work in the manner of, for example, Debussy's *Pelléas et Mélisande* (1902). Rather, Gluck's opera may have been seen from a symbolist perspective, particularly for those who sought to tie the work to post-Wagnerian aesthetic sensibilities. *Orphée*, in other words, was a work that lent itself easily to the prevailing artistic image of Orpheus, but did not necessarily require audiences to hold that image. This flexibility not only allowed operatic traditionalists to appreciate that an eighteenth-century work was being revived but also encouraged audiences who were primarily interested in newer works to see the work in a modern light. The key to Gluck's fin-de-siècle success lay in the fact that his operas looked both forward and backward in time. They were old enough to serve as a critical part of the nationalist mission of the Operatic Museum; their constant presence at the Opéra-Comique, in particular, provided audiences with constant reminders of the greatness of French opera in the eighteenth century. Simultaneously, Gluck's works reflected the preoccupations of the early twentieth-century society on stage, proving again and again their relevance to modern audiences.

Part Three

Rameau

Chapter Eight

Monuments

If fin-de-siècle critics could agree on anything, it was that Jean-Philippe Rameau had a place among the greatest French composers. A shining paragon of French musical virtues, his music exuded clarity, grace, and elegance. And here, for once, was a composer for whom they did not have to construct elaborate rationales to claim as French, since Rameau was actually French by birth. As a result, he was the object of unanimous and continuous praise in musical circles, as this passage from the musicologist and critic Adolphe Jullien reveals:

> By a law of nature that is not in our power to alter, France has produced only a very small number of great musicians, by which I mean those superior geniuses who are like gods of music: almost all of them have seen the light of day in Italy or, above all, in Germany. We can pride ourselves for having as compatriots musicians of high quality, who have played a major role in the history of French music: Campra, Destouches, Monsigny, Philidor, Berton, Boïeldieu, Nicolo, Hérold, etc.; but I see none but Rameau, and perhaps Méhul and Berlioz, who can be placed among the leading figures of musical art.[1]

For Jullien, Rameau was the only French composer (with the *possible* exceptions of Méhul and Berlioz) who could be counted among the Great Composers—Bach, Handel, Mozart, Beethoven, and so on.

In his 1908 biography of the composer, the ardent Ramiste Louis Laloy even placed Rameau on a pedestal above all others, German and French alike:

> Rameau's dances and descriptive pieces shine with unchanged splendor. Time, which kills so many glories, seems to have even added to their beauty, erasing what contemporaries saw as brash, making it clearer and more harmonious. None of his compositions have aged, although Beethoven, Schubert, Berlioz, Liszt, Wagner, and César Franck show us so many outdated pages or phrases. Nothing loses its freshness so quickly as operatic effusions, be they the most touching in the world, because nothing changes faster than our manner of living. It

is by refraining from such display that Rameau has ensured his greatest chance of immortality.²

For Laloy and similar-minded critics, Rameau's music was "newer" and more modern than music by Wagner and Franck (the latter of whom had died fewer than twenty years before). Laudatory descriptions like these were common in fin-de-siècle Paris, as French critics and audiences seized on Rameau as the representation of a French musical Golden Age. He was destined to be the central exhibit in the Operatic Museum: a French composer whose music could be placed on the same level as that of any German or Italian.

Opinions to this effect, though seldom expressed quite so polemically, were endlessly repeated in French narratives of music history. Henri Lavoix, for example, situated Rameau among German musical luminaries in his 1877 *Histoire de la musique*:

> Rameau was the greatest French musician of the eighteenth century, covering with his name, like a triumphal banner, the period extending from Lully to Gluck.
>
> It was he who gave color and depth to harmony, who developed the expressive powers of the orchestra, who created the overture, which had before him been only a sort of more or less agreeable murmur. With Bach and Handel, Rameau completes the great musical trinity of the first half of the eighteenth century, and we can say that Gluck could not avoid succumbing to the strong and beneficial influence of the Burgundian master.³

Lavoix not only situates Rameau with Bach and Handel—no small praise in France during this time—but also suggests that Rameau's operas strongly influenced Gluck.⁴ As we saw in part 2, Gluck was widely regarded as the creator of the modern musical drama, a lineage culminating in Wagner. And so the nationalist goals of Lavoix's post–Franco-Prussian War text are clear: by suggesting that Rameau was a major influence on that historical trajectory, he insinuates that modern operatic styles originated with the archetypically French *tragédie lyrique*.

Rameau's incontrovertible historical importance and subsequent neglect during the nineteenth century made him the perfect candidate for fin-de-siècle restoration, returning him and his music to pristine condition for inclusion in the Operatic Museum. A number of critics found Rameau a useful figurehead for "early music" in the concert hall and on the stage. Recall from chapter 1 Félix Clément's chapter on Rameau in his *Histoire de la musique* (1885), in which he calls for a "retrospective theater . . . for the great geniuses of the musical art."

For Clément, the state of "ancient" music at the fin de siècle was reprehensible. If ever there was a case for the Operatic Museum, this was it: how could such a genius be allowed to languish in obscurity while representative works from the other arts were presented to the public on a regular basis? Unfashionable music was allowed to fade away into insignificance based on the fickle whims of the public, regardless of its historical or aesthetic merits.

Clément's museal goals for Rameau eventually caught on with other critics, as well. Gabriel Fauré—who had been an advocate for both Gluck and a more classical Mozart—made a similar plea to Parisian theaters after hearing *Hippolyte et Aricie* at the Opéra in 1908, suggesting that the state-run opera houses were not doing enough to preserve France's musical history. Turning again to the theaters for precedent, he sought a place for Rameau alongside modern works, "just as the works of Corneille, Racine, and Molière are permanently in the repertoire of the Comédie-Française and the Odéon." Fauré followed up with two rhetorical questions that essentially summarize the Operatic Museum concept in France: "Is equal treatment of our past glories not simple fairness? And would our sense of a unique national culture not have everything to gain?"[5] For Fauré, Rameau's operas in particular begged to be included in the Opéra's standard repertoire, not for economic reasons but for the much loftier goal of defining a sense of shared French music history.

Not surprisingly, both Clément and Fauré focused their efforts on preserving Rameau's music in his operas. Although Rameau was prolific in a number of genres—and, as fin-de-siècle critics never tired of pointing out, he only began composing dramatic works at age fifty—the operas took on a special significance. Clément dated Rameau's influence to the premiere of *Hippolyte et Aricie*, his first opera: "The history of music in France began a period of immense progress on October 1, 1733, brought about entirely by the works of a single composer: Rameau, the greatest French musician of the eighteenth century."[6] Rameau's earlier works were insignificant compared to the major musical "progress" his dramatic works created. This distinction between operas and nondramatic works was widespread throughout the fin de siècle. In 1901, shortly after the new edition of *Hippolyte et Aricie* was published (a subject to which we will return later), Paul Dukas succinctly noted in the *Revue hebdomadaire* that "the less important preceding volumes were devoted to his harpsichord music ... to his concert music, to his cantatas, and to his motets."[7] Once again, Rameau's nondramatic music was only a precursor to his later glory. Rameau's operas represented for many critics the pinnacle of French eighteenth-century French musical styles; their grandeur perfectly captured the spirit and the glory of the ancien régime, with all the overtones of French cultural and military superiority that implied.[8]

Or at least that was the theory. The problem with Rameau was that while his name carried vast cultural capital—symbolizing everything magnificent about French operatic history—most of his music was unknown to modern audiences.[9] The last full production of *Castor et Pollux* (1737), Rameau's most enduringly popular opera, took place in 1784. His dramatic works were tied too clearly to ancien régime French culture to be effectively resurrected after the Revolution. The closest any complete Rameau opera came to a full revival during the nineteenth century was a performance of *Castor et Pollux* in 1814, including Pierre-Joseph Candeille's significant musical alterations from 1791. In reality, this work included only a small amount of Rameau's music, and even that was heavily adapted to correspond to the style of the late eighteenth century. This performance coincided with a celebration of the Bourbon restoration, and the music itself was largely irrelevant—a symbolic resurrection of the ancien régime rather than an actual attempt to return Rameau's music to the operatic repertoire.[10]

Rameau was not entirely without his romantic advocates. In 1832, the first of François-Joseph Fétis's "Concerts historiques" included a chorus from *Zoroastre* (1749), and the late 1830s saw several articles on the composer (if not specifically his operas) in major music journals.[11] A few decades later, a few tuneful morceaux from Rameau's operas appeared on Jules Pasdeloup's "Concerts populaires," though these pieces never achieved anything approaching the popularity of the Mendelssohn, Mozart, Beethoven, and Weber works in the series.[12] Rameau's works were represented occasionally (though certainly not to the extent that Gluck's were) at the Société des Concerts, largely thanks to the influence of Charles Poisot and Adolphe Adam—the latter of whom also wrote a Rameau biography in 1852 to help return the composer to the public eye.[13] In a similar effort, Pauline Viardot included a Rameau aria in her collection of arias titled *Ecole de chant classique* (1863)—an endorsement of the composer by one of France's most revered advocates of eighteenth-century music.[14] But despite these gestures, the general musical public remained unaware of Rameau's music, and the composer himself was relegated to the list of historically important composers whose music was irrelevant to modern audiences.

These perceptions began to change over the fin de siècle, particularly in the years after 1900. Gluck's late nineteenth-century successes on stage, in the concert halls, and in the library with the Pelletan Edition revealed a path to repopularizing classical composers with modern audiences. For the remainder of this chapter I trace the similar—if even more grandiose—efforts that took place on Rameau's behalf. We begin in the concert halls, where audiences were gradually reintroduced to eighteenth-century French musical styles. We then turn to the monolithic Complete Edition of the composer's works—by far the most lavish and ambitious edition created in France up to that time, and a task that occupied many of the most notable composers and historians of the fin de siècle.

Repopularizing Rameau

Like the operas of Gluck, those of Rameau underwent an extended incubation period on Parisian concert series before reaching maturity on the operatic stage. Short morceaux from Rameau's works were not unheard of at the oldest of the Parisian series—the Société des Concerts du Conservatoire—as early as the 1840s, but they were treated as antiquated curiosities added for novelty's sake.[15] Excerpts became more common beginning in the 1880s, generally the most immediately "charming" (i.e., palatable to modern audiences) choruses and instrumental interludes from *Castor et Pollux* and *Hippolyte et Aricie*—not coincidentally, the two operas that were fully staged during the fin de siècle. The length of these excerpts gradually increased, expanding from isolated arias, choruses, or dances to complete acts around the turn of the century. The programs of the Société des Concerts du Conservatoire offer clear evidence of this trend (see table 8.1): a single chorus from *Castor et Pollux* (probably "En ces doux asiles") was performed in five concert seasons between 1877 and 1900, making up the vast majority of Rameau's music that appeared on the concert series during that time.[16] After 1900, lengthier excerpts began to appear; audiences in 1902, for example, were treated to both the extended Airs de Ballet from *Les Indes galantes* and a portion of act 3 of *Hippolyte et Aricie*. More excerpts from *Les Indes galantes* (this time including vocal music) appeared in 1904, portions of *Platée* in 1908, and so on.

Several factors enabled this progression in the length of excerpts. The first is also the simplest: availability of scores. It is probably no coincidence, for example, that the first significant Rameau excerpt to appear during the fin de siècle was from *Hippolyte et Aricie* in 1902—just two years after the score of that work was published in the *Œuvres complètes*. The Airs de Ballet from *Les Indes galantes* were performed in 1902, the same year the edition of that opera was published, and excerpts from *Platée* were given the year after that edition appeared (see table 8.2 for the order of the Rameau edition). Longer excerpts familiarized the audience with Rameau's music, with the ultimate goal of preparing listeners to see a complete opera— a process we have already seen with both Gluck and Wagner on Parisian concerts around this time. These concert programs shaped French musical taste in a "refining" process that encouraged a preference for "serious" music over the lighter fare that had dominated the concert scene before the 1890s.[17] Increasing awareness of French music history was

Table 8.1. Rameau at the Société des Concerts du Conservatoire, 1875–1918

Works	Dates
Chorus from *Castor et Pollux*	1877
"Trio et choeur des Parques" from *Hippolyte et Aricie*	1881
Chorus from *Castor et Pollux*	1883
Excerpts (Chorus, Rigodon, Trio and Chorus) from *Dardanus*	1887
Chorus from *Castor et Pollux*	1888
Chorus from *Castor et Pollux*	1889
Chorus from *Castor et Pollux*	1900
Excerpt from *Hippolyte et Aricie*, act 3	1902
Les Indes galantes, Airs de Ballet	1902
Excerpts from *Les Indes galantes*	1904
Excerpts from *Platée*	1908
Les Indes galantes, Airs de Ballet	1908
Overture to *Zaïs*	1914
Excerpts from *Hippolyte et Aricie*	1914

a major goal of several series during this time, and Rameau's works fulfilled a significant part of that educative mission. His name appears with regularity, for example, on a series at the popular Concerts Colonne from 1897 to 1901 that mixed *musique ancienne* with *musique moderne*.

Although Rameau's music became increasingly familiar fare on programs from a number of concert series around 1900, nowhere were his works featured more frequently than at the Schola Cantorum. Almost every year between 1900 and 1909 (except 1905) the Schola's concert series featured at least one work by Rameau, often extended excerpts (see table 8.3). During that time Vincent d'Indy, the Schola's director, also produced concert versions of several "complete" (i.e., probably with some significant cuts) versions of *Zoroastre* (1903), *La Guirlande* (1903), *Dardanus* (1907), and *Castor et Pollux* (1909). The last of these was performed five times in rapid succession—a rarity for Schola productions, which were typically onetime events. These concert performances served as an important transition between the excerpts seen on most concert series and a fully staged production. Surprisingly, given the focus on Rameau's operas seen at the Schola after 1900, after 1909, productions of Rameau's operas suddenly

Table 8.2. Operas published in the Rameau *Œuvres complètes*

Work	Date published	Editor
Hippolyte et Aricie	1900	Vincent d'Indy
Les Indes galantes	1902	Paul Dukas
Castor et Pollux	1903	Auguste Chapuis
Les Fêtes d'Hébé	1904	Alexandre Guilmant
Dardanus	1905	Vincent d'Indy
La Princesse de Navarre/ Les Fêtes de Ramire/ Nélée et Myrthis/Zephyre	1906	Paul Dukas (*La Princesse de Navarre*)/ Camille Saint-Saëns
Platée	1907	Georges Marty
Les Fêtes de Polymnie	1908	Claude Debussy
La Temple de la Gloire	1909	Alexandre Guilmant
Les Fêtes de l'Hymen et de l'Amour	1910	Reynaldo Hahn
Zaïs	1911	Vincent d'Indy
Pygmalion/Les Surprises de l'Amour	1913	Henri Büsser
Anacreon/Les Sybarites	1913	Henri Büsser
Naïs	1924	Reynaldo Hahn

ceased.[18] This change, however, seems to be less a reflection specifically on Rameau than a more general rethinking of the Schola's repertoire. Between 1909 and the start of World War I, the school simply stopped presenting complete operas of any kind, preferring instead longer religious works such as Handel's *Messiah* and Bach's *B-Minor Mass*, as well as sacred Renaissance works such as masses by Palestrina.

The critical response to fin-de-siècle Parisian concert performances of Rameau's works was mixed. Clément complained in 1885 about the quality of the performers: "Let no one say that we have any understanding of the old masters' music from the excerpts sung in some concerts or printed in some collections. The performances are generally pitiful, because they have not been prepared with the learnedness and the attention that it demands."[19] In other words, Clément warned audiences against judging Rameau based on the "generally pitiful" concert performances, which he thought demonstrated no concern for the music quality or any effort to understand eighteenth-century styles. This perceived inferiority frustrated

Table 8.3. Rameau's Operas at the Schola Cantorum

Work	Dates
Excerpts from *Castor et Pollux*	1894
Excerpts from *Castor et Pollux, Les Indes galantes,* and *Hippolyte et Aricie*	1894
Excerpts from *Dardanus* and *Hippolyte et Aricie*	1895
Excerpt from *Hippolyte et Aricie*	1900
Excerpt from *Dardanus,* act 2	1901
"Trio des songes" from *Dardanus,* Excerpt from *Hippolyte et Aricie,* act 4	1901
Excerpt from *Castor et Pollux*	1902
Unspecified arias	1902
Excerpts from *Hippolyte et Aricie* and *Castor et Pollux*	1903
Excerpts from *Castor et Pollux*	1903
Excerpt from *Dardanus,* act 2	1903
La Guirlande	1903
Excerpts from *La Guirlande*	1903
Zoroastre (complete?)	1903
Hippolyte et Aricie, act 4	1904
Excerpt from *Hippolyte et Aricie,* act 4	1904
Excerpts from *Castor et Pollux,* acts 1 and 2	1904
Excerpts from *Zoroastre*	1906
Dardanus (complete?)	1907
Excerpts from *L'Entretien des muses* and *Dardanus*	1908
Castor et Pollux (series of five performances)	1909
Dardanus (abridged)	1909
Unspecified works (possibly arias)	1910

a number of critics, some of whom believed that Rameau's newfound popularity stemmed more from a sense of popular fashion rather than from a deeper appreciation for his works.

Jullien is a prime example of this perspective: as we have seen, he was perfectly willing to place Rameau among the greatest figures of music history, but the proliferation of the composer's works on public concerts left Jullien cold. He accused Reynaldo Hahn, an advocate of early music (and the "authentic" performance thereof) of, in Catrina Flint de Médicis's words, "pandering to public whimsy."[20] In particular, Jullien suggested that Hahn had abandoned Mozart after his successful 1903 production of *Don Giovanni* (see part 1), turning instead to the trendier field of French early music: "Sensing that today's fashion turns toward the old masters of French opera, Reynaldo Hahn—made fashionable by the success of his scrupulously exact restoration of *Don Giovanni* last year—just offered ... two sessions where various portions of the most beautiful operas of Lully and Rameau were performed. This curious endeavor arrived at precisely the right time, and has been crowned with the most notable success."[21] Jullien rejected the commodification of early music, and Rameau's music in particular, for mass audiences. While Rameau's utter neglect was inexcusable, a purely superficial appreciation of his music—the type of appreciation that Jullien attributed to Hahn's concerts and similar endeavors—was equally dangerous. Until audiences could appreciate Rameau with the right education and reverent attitude, his music should remain a secret known only to the musically elite.

Rameau's operas could not have acquired their newfound cachet before 1900. Before then, the repertoire options were too limited for musical directors, with only a few excerpts from Rameau's operas published in orchestral score. The scores for most of the pre-1900 performances at the Société des Concerts, for example, were almost certainly taken from Ernest Deldevez's 1859 *Piéces diverses choisies dans les œuvres des célèbres compositeurs*, a collection of orchestrated excerpts from operas from seventeenth- and eighteenth-century operatic composers. Selections of this kind were heavily adapted from their original forms, particularly before 1900. The "Trio des Parques" from *Hippolyte et Aricie* as performed in 1881 at the Société des Concerts (which Deldevez conducted from 1872 to 1885), for example, would have been a mélange of music from two different acts of the opera, focusing on the choral writing at the expense of both instrumental and solo vocal music.[22] After about 1900, however, the Société des Concerts likely began using the new Rameau complete edition, as did d'Indy and the Schola. This editorial effort was crucial in shaping the way Rameau's music was performed and understood at the fin de siècle, and its creation was crucial in monumentalizing Rameau.

Editing History: The *Œuvres complètes*

In 1894, the composer Albéric Magnard issued a rallying cry for French musicians to support their historical predecessors, and Rameau in particular.[23] Thanks to family connections, Magnard's bold claims appeared in a major public forum, *Le Figaro*, where his father, François Magnard, was the editor. This appeal was couched in typical nationalist rhetoric, citing the numerous editions other nations had created for their own great composers, implying that the absence of similar French editions was symptomatic of a lack of patriotism.[24] After listing a number of Rameau's qualities, Magnard asked his compatriots:

> Why does Rameau almost never appear on the programs of our theaters or our concerts? Why is he only known to a few musicians and library rats? The reason, alas, is entirely to our shame.
>
> There is no complete and correct modern edition of Rameau.
>
> In Germany, Breitkopf is completing the publication of Bach's immense œuvre. In Belgium, Gervaert has restored Grétry's scores. In England, the complete edition of Handel has been finished for some time. Will we remain behind our neighbors? Will we leave the scores and manuscripts of our most glorious musician in the dust of the conservatories? . . .
>
> The task would be long and costly, but I presume there remains in us some sense of national pride, and we will not back down in the face of expenses that are covered by the government in England, and by the mass of subscribers in Germany. . . .
>
> Will anyone hear me ringing the bell in Rameau's memory? I doubt it. We are not very curious about music in France, and our musicians have little respect for the past.[25]

This clarion call, once sounded, was not easily ignored. Musicians and publishers who did not act quickly to rescue the French master from his unjust neglect opened themselves to charges of unpatriotic behavior, or, at the very least, they confirmed Magnard's allegation that French musicians had "little respect for the past."

Others were quick to take up Magnard's patriotic cause. Only a few months later, Paul Dukas seconded the need for a new Rameau edition. After pointing out the treatment Gluck had recently been given in the Pelletan/Saint-Saëns edition of his operatic works (see chapter 5), Dukas wondered why Rameau had not received similar attention:

> There is another master, this one completely French, who we would like to see treated in an equally generous manner. We dare not ask the Opéra to attempt the restoration of one of Rameau's masterworks, since it is already impossible to have Gluck in the repertoire of this theater—which should be, given its title and its sumptuous subvention, like the Louvre of music. But it would at least be desirable to prepare a serious edition of his works that would permit connoisseurs to familiarize themselves with them and concert orchestras to popularize some excerpts.[26]

Later that year, the music publishing house Durand acceded to these pleas, and agreed to take on the publication of the first complete edition of Rameau's works.[27] Saint-Saëns was chosen to be the general editor (as Magnard had suggested in his column), and Charles Malherbe, the Opéra archivist, was appointed to write extensive critical notes for each volume. The first volume in the *Œuvres complètes* appeared in 1895, and an additional volume followed each year until the outbreak of World War I in 1914 brought the enterprise to a halt. One additional volume appeared after the war (in 1924), but due to several factors (including Saint-Saëns's death in 1921), the edition never regained its prewar momentum and ultimately remained incomplete.

Critics were happy to accept at face value this dramatic narrative of a young composer sparking new interest in Rameau, and the famous publishing house and a number of influential composers and scholars rushing to the ancient master's defense. The timing of these events is suspicious, however, and the response a bit too convenient. In only a year, Magnard's highly public call to arms led to the publication of the first volume in the *Œuvres complètes*, an unusual feat of editorial alacrity.[28] Magnard was not without connections to those in charge of the new edition. He was a close friend and former student of d'Indy (who edited a number of volumes in the edition), and he later taught at the Schola Cantorum. Magnard was also well acquainted with Jacques Durand, having attended both lycée (high school) and classes at the Conservatoire with him.[29] It seems likely that Magnard had already made some arrangements with Durand before writing the letter in *Le Figaro*, and that work had already begun on the edition. Perhaps Magnard, with his connections at *Le Figaro*, was simply chosen by Durand (or d'Indy, who had been an advocate for Rameau for some time) to be the mouthpiece of this appeal. The purpose of Magnard's missive, then, was to elicit public support for the venture in the form of subscribers, or perhaps even a government subsidy. After all, Magnard pointed out specifically that the edition would be costly, but called on French nationalism to provide for "expenses that are covered by the government in England, and by the mass of subscribers in Germany." He then blatantly attempted to bully readers into buying subscriptions out of a sense of national duty, lamenting that probably no one would heed his pleas, and that "we are not very curious about music in France."

Whatever the exact circumstances of its origins, the new edition was perceived as a major contribution to French music history. Saint-Saëns certainly felt that the *Œuvres complètes* filled a major lacuna:

> Rameau, the greatest French composer of the eighteenth century, whose works held so important a place on the stage, had become almost forgotten in the twentieth. A few pieces for the harpsichord and the delightful

chorus, "En ces doux asiles" [from *Castor et Pollux*], were almost all that anyone knew of him, for practically the whole of his work had remained unpublished.

This injustice has now come to an end, thanks to Durand, who undertook the gigantic task of publishing the complete works of this marvelous genius, the contemporary and rival of Sebastian Bach.[30]

While still at work completing the Pelletan Edition of Gluck's operas, Saint-Saëns took to this new project with gusto. In his 1922 biography of the composer (also published by Durand), Jean Bonnerot emphasized the seriousness with which Saint-Saëns approached editing Rameau's music—and the editorial strategies he used in doing so:

> To establish a complete and correct text, he was aided by scholars who managed the work, made copies, and noted the variants. The new edition adopted modern notation, discarding "those of the ornaments that no longer have any reason to exist because of changes in the instruments for which they were imagined." It faithfully reproduces the thought of the author in suppressing "parasitic insertions, tempo indications, nuances, and fingerings" that obstruct without benefit. Saint-Saëns took care to inspect everything personally in the manuscripts, to weight everything, here interpreting with the respect owed to an old master, and there, transposing the voices.... Every year Saint-Saëns spent several weeks reviewing the text of the prepared volume. Under his care, seventeen volumes were published; this was not one of the least important services that he did for music, to have resurrected, after Gluck, Rameau—the glorious contemporary of Sébastien [J. S.] Bach.[31]

Bonnerot calls attention to the amount of time and effort that Saint-Saëns put into the edition, devoting "several weeks" per year to the project, and reviewing all editorial decisions personally. These choices likely had a significant effect on how audiences understood the music in performance—a topic to which we will return briefly in chapter 10.

Like Magnard's original appeal, it was understood that this luxurious new edition was an explicitly nationalist endeavor. The preface to the first volume (the keyboard works) begins with the following statement of purpose: "In publishing this first volume of Rameau's works, the editors have set themselves a double goal: first, to pay homage to the memory of one of the greatest composers France has produced; following that, to increase awareness of his works and contribute to popularizing them by placing within everyone's reach what previously the curious could only discover from antiquated editions or ancient manuscripts from our libraries."[32] The explicit primary goal of the edition was "to pay homage to the memory of one of the greatest composers that France has produced." By mentioning France directly, the editors cast their project in a nationalist light, suggesting that the edition was a necessary tribute to a composer too long neglected by his homeland. Furthermore, the invocation of memory here directly invests the edition with the quality of a memorial, as visible as any monument. Such ideology resonates with the idea of creating a *lieu de mémoire* for Rameau, a nexus of cultural memory by which the French could celebrate their artistic heritage. Rameau's music itself, although the subject of artistic and cultural reverence, was inherently intangible and invisible; the new edition provided a static physical object to represent the composer's—and France's—musical glories. Finally, this bold goal from the editors had a populist aspect. By providing these modern scores to "everyone" (or at least everyone who could afford them) rather than only to those who were willing to delve into musty libraries to find manuscripts and early prints, the editors sought to bring Rameau to a larger audience and to facilitate public performances of his works—a process that would culminate in Rameau's return to the Opéra.

Rameau's operas were without question the crowning jewel of this new edition. The preface to the first published *Hippolyte et Aricie* made it clear that this was a new and particularly significant stage of the project:

> The sixth volume of the complete works of Jean-Philippe Rameau, appearing in 1900, also constitutes the first of a new series. The preceding volumes were dedicated to instrumental or religious music; they contained the keyboard works, the cantatas, and the motets. However, it is to dramatic music that the old master dedicated the principal efforts of his genius; it alone must occupy us from now on. *Tragédies lyriques*, opera-ballets, comedies, pastorales, and divertissements will follow in chronological order; each year will see the rebirth of one of the past century's masterworks. We begin with *Hippolyte et Aricie*, the first link in a long and glorious chain.[33]

The editors, it would seem, viewed the operas as the major focus of the *Œuvres complètes*. It is not surprising, then, that many of the major figures in fin-de-siècle French musical culture contributed their editorial efforts to producing the editions. Although Saint-Saëns oversaw the entire project (and edited some earlier volumes), other musicians were responsible for many of the operas (see table 8.2 for a complete list). D'Indy, Dukas, Debussy, and Hahn—all of whom were outspoken advocates for Rameau—edited volumes, as did other noted musical figures including the organist-pedagogues Alexandre Guilmant and August Chapuis (both of whom were professors at the Conservatoire at the time they edited the Rameau volumes).

I am particularly interested here in the editorial approaches of d'Indy, Debussy, and Dukas; their strategies conveniently encapsulate both fin-de-siècle perceptions of Rameau and the concept of "authenticity" in general during this time. In his description of Saint-Saëns's involvement with the project, Bonnerot pointed out several aspects of his editorial policies that might seem questionable today, including the removal of ornaments (particularly in the keyboard works) and the transposition of vocal parts to accommodate modern vocal ranges to compensate for the lack of castrato singers. Yet overall, Bonnerot clearly felt that Saint-Saëns was being faithful to Rameau's intentions; the alterations were necessary for the modernization of the work.[34]

Interpretations of "musical fidelity" varied widely among the editors. Many were primarily concerned with preserving Rameau's music exactly as written; others, however, were much more cavalier with his scores in the name of creating a modern Rameau. Although he was not alone, d'Indy's editions exemplify this latter approach, to the point that the musicologist Graham Sadler—himself the editor of a number of Rameau's works in modern edition—suggested in a 1993 article that d'Indy's editions were outright forgeries.[35] D'Indy's major alterations consisted of adding inner voices to flesh out textures, and, on a number of occasions, composing independent musical lines—often in sections clearly marked "unison." The brief entrance of the Zephyrs near the end of the final act of *Hippolyte et Aricie* serves as a clear example. Scored for basso continuo and unison flutes and violins in Rameau's original (see ex. 8.1), the dance was evidently not complex enough for d'Indy. His alterations, visible in example 8.2, include the addition of two inner string parts (second violin and viola) that fundamentally change the character of the piece, creating "a jolly but anachronistic oom-pah effect."[36]

Dukas's alterations to *Les Indes galantes*, much less severe in nature, are equally revealing. In his efforts to restore Rameau's "original" version of the opera, he blatantly ignored the composer's later changes to instrumentation (especially the simplification of string passages) and even pitches.[37] Like d'Indy, Dukas focused on making Rameau's compositions appear as complex as possible, but he approached the goal from the opposite perspective. While d'Indy started from a modern perspective and worked backward, Dukas hid behind Rameau's "original intentions," selectively applying them when it was most convenient for his own ends. For both Dukas and d'Indy Rameau's modernity was crucial; as Anya Suschitzky succinctly puts it, "The more modern and impressive Rameau looked, the better France looked."[38]

The editors of the *Œuvres complètes* thought it necessary for Rameau to be able to withstand comparison to Bach and Handel, shielding France from accusations of musical inferiority to Germany. Several of the editors,

Example 8.1. *Hippolyte et Aricie*, act 5, Entrance of the Zephyrs, mm. 1–18, Jean-Philippe Rameau, *Œuvres complètes*, vol. 6, ed. Vincent d'Indy (Paris: Durand, 1900).

however, likely also had more personal goals in mind. D'Indy, Dukas, and Debussy each traced his compositional lineage to Rameau, albeit by different paths. As we saw in part 2, d'Indy perceived that the eighteenth-century *tragédie lyrique* essentially "migrated" to Germany after being perfected by Gluck, leading to Weber and eventually Wagner.[39] If Wagner's music was so indebted to French styles, then d'Indy was not being Germanic in style by emulating the Master of Bayreuth—on the contrary, he was returning a

Example 8.2. *Hippolyte et Aricie*, act 5, Entrance of the Zephyrs, mm. 1–21. Jean-Philippe Rameau, *Opera Omnia*, series 4, vol. 1, ed. Sylvie Bouisseau (Paris: Billaudot, 2002).

fundamentally French style to its homeland.[40] Read in this light, d'Indy's choices as an editor for the Rameau *Œuvres complètes* become more understandable. By making Rameau a more "progressive" composer, d'Indy strengthened his own claims to this French lineage. In other words, the more he made Rameau resemble his own style, the more modern audiences would assume he descended from Rameau.[41]

The connection between Dukas's and Debussy's editing and their musical agendas is less direct, but no less reflective of their own historical self-positioning. Rameau's cultural importance was a recurring theme in Dukas's music criticism from the late 1890s on, particularly in his perennial call for an Operatic Museum. The creation of the *Œuvres complètes*, not surprisingly, was a major musical coup from Dukas's perspective: "Rameau slept for a long time in the dust of our libraries. He would sleep there still, if his oeuvre were not, thanks to the initiative of A. Durand and Son, reappearing little by little in a luxurious and reconstructed edition, this time based on the original documents revised according to the most scrupulous critical methods."[42] By praising the Rameau edition for "awakening" Rameau from his slumber in the libraries, Dukas implicitly compliments himself and his role in the process. Dukas goes on to say that the quality of the edition does great honor to the editors, an observation that came only a year before his own contribution appeared as the seventh volume. Dukas's efforts set his own musical style in dialogue with Rameau's. His name was connected with a major work in the *Œuvres complètes*, and his advocacy of Rameau's musical aesthetic was well known by the early 1900s. These associations played into the way critics viewed Dukas's music. Some critics saw his opera, *Ariane et Barbe-Bleue* (1907), not only as a rejection of Wagnerism but as a return to the classical French methods of composition exemplified by Rameau.[43]

Debussy's association with Rameau was similar in nature to Dukas's. His music criticism is filled with references to the eighteenth-century composer, and in particular to the innate "Frenchness" of his musical style. As we saw in part 2, Debussy believed that Gluck led French music away from its true path, leaving Rameau as the last bastion of truly French music.[44] Gluck was a disruption in French music history; everything following him was to some extent Germanic, paving the way for Wagner's eventual domination of musical (particularly operatic) culture. Debussy made this point explicitly in his review of the 1908 production of *Hippolyte et Aricie* at the Opéra: "Marie Antoinette, an Austrian through and through (something for which she had to pay in the end), imposed Gluck upon the French taste; as a result our traditions were led astray, our desire for clarity drowned, and having gone through Meyerbeer, we ended up, naturally enough, with Richard Wagner."[45] This perspective is actually very similar to d'Indy's historical narrative, but while d'Indy believed that French musical styles transferred to Germany (leading to a "French" Wagner), Debussy viewed Rameau as the last French composer uncorrupted by Germanic influence. "We have a purely French tradition in the works of Rameau," Debussy reported in 1903: "They combine a charming and delicate tenderness with precise tones and strict declamation in the recitatives—none of that affected German pomp.... At the same time one is forced to admit that French music has, for too long, followed paths that definitely lead away from this clearness of expression, this conciseness and precision of form, both of which are the very qualities peculiar to French genius."[46] Debussy believed his own music returned to this lost "French" style, restoring the aesthetic values—clarity, concision, and formal precision—that Rameau represented.[47]

These associations between Rameau and fin-de-siècle composers were not lost on contemporary critics. After pointing out the efforts of both d'Indy and Debussy to bring Rameau's music to light, Jean Chantavoine sarcastically noted that

> under the combined authority of d'Indy and Debussy, *Scholistes* and *Pelléastes* communed in Rameau. Since D'Indy and Debussy collaborated on the new Rameau edition, admiration for Rameau became an article of faith for both *d'indyisme* and *Debussysme*. One could not fully admire either of these two artists without including Rameau in the same admiration. A strange solidarity has been created between *Castor et Pollux, Fervaal,* and

> *Pelléas*: some "informed" people maintain that *Fervaal* resulted directly from *Castor* or *Zoroastre*, and if you ask them what led to this opinion, they can only tell you: "I find . . ." which means "I heard someone say," even when it is pronounced with a tone that says, "It is obvious, and you are a brute for not having perceived it." Others, no less "informed," connect *Pelléas et Mélisande* with *Hippolyte et Aricie*.[48]

Although Chantavoine evidently found no evidence of Rameau's musical style in the operas of either d'Indy or Debussy (nor, presumably, in Dukas), it is clear that many critics and audience members did, and were keen to trace modern French music back to its eighteenth-century roots.

Central to the historical narratives created by d'Indy, Dukas, and Debussy (and their critics) was the concept of Rameau's innate "Frenchness." This inscription of national identity was the driving force behind the *Œuvres complètes*, for example, turning the project from a purely archival task into a nationalist enterprise. Rameau became a symbol of the French musical past, demonstrating the glories of ancien régime opera and culture as no other composer could.[49] Not surprisingly, then, reinforcing Rameau's French identity was a major focus of fin-de-siècle descriptions of the composer and his works. Nothing brought out this inherent Frenchness more than the so-called Querelle des Bouffons—the intense debate between partisans of the French *tragédie lyrique* and supporters of Italian operatic styles that raged through Paris in the 1750s. It is to this topic that we turn in the next chapter, which explores how issues of French music and national identity became tied up in revisiting the Querelle and its two most famous participants: Rameau and Jean-Jacques Rousseau.

Chapter Nine

Quarrels

The unifying factor of Rameau's fin-de-siècle reception was the composer's role as a nationalist figurehead for French music; any praise directed at the composer was also praise for the land that had produced his genius. In his brief 1876 Rameau biography, the critic and musicologist Arthur Pougin said as much unequivocally: "Outside of all comparison, and judging Rameau from an absolute point of view, it is only fair to say that such an artist gives eternal glory to his homeland."[1] The publication of Pougin's text coincided with a major event in Rameau reception: a festival in Dijon, the composer's birthplace.[2] In Paris, the festival sparked renewed interest in the composer, resulting in daily reports in musical periodicals and updates in both specialist and general newspapers. The central concept of this festival was not only the celebration of a great composer, but of a great *French* composer.[3]

Rameau's Frenchness continued to be a major focus for critics and audiences after the festival as well. Only a few years later, the preface to the Michaëlis piano-vocal score of *Castor et Pollux* (1878/79) urged readers not to forget that "Rameau's glory is eminently French."[4] In a 1905 article on Rameau's life, the critic Gustave Bret gave voice to the commonly held opinion that Rameau exemplified the best qualities of French music: "The deeper one delves into Rameau's art, the more one becomes convinced that one must return to him to recover, in all its grace, clarity, and truth, the very essence of French genius."[5] This pure French pedigree set Rameau apart from the composers who dominated Parisian opera houses before and after him—Lully and Gluck—and represented for some critics an age of French opera unsullied by foreign musical styles. This was certainly true for Adolphe Jullien, who wrote in 1894 that Rameau, an "outstanding musician, one of the greatest of any nation," was "readily neglected, perhaps because he is French, and gets crushed between the Italian Lully and the German Gluck."[6] Jullien went on to suggest that Gluck's music was in fact modeled entirely on Rameau's:

> Rameau . . . moved dramatic music after Lully so far forward, made such progress for the *tragédie lyrique* from the triple point of view of the accuracy of the expression, the rapidity of the declamation, and the variety of the orchestra, that Gluck could only study and imitate him in order to create his admirable masterworks. Rameau, in a word, was in every

respect the model and inspiration for Gluck, who replaced him too easily in the public's admiration—because without Rameau the author of *Alceste* would have perhaps remained the Italian composer that he was in the beginning, only the author of *Siface* and *Fedra*.[7]

Jullien positioned Rameau opposite Italian musical styles, suggesting that only the composer's French influence led to Gluck's success. Rameau thus became for many critics a symbol of French music's struggle against Italian and German influence. Yet as important as Rameau's status as French by birth was for fin-de-siècle critics, the extent of his immanent "Frenchness" went much further. Being born in France was clearly a virtue, but it was by nature passive—Rameau did not choose this fate for himself. Almost more important was the fact that Rameau had taken a strong stand for French musical values in one of the most heated debates in music history: the "Querelle des bouffons."[8]

Although this "quarrel" was fairly complex, involving a number of competing philosophical perspectives, for fin-de-siècle French critics and audiences it boiled down to a conflict between French and foreign musical styles. On one side of the debate was Rameau, who epitomized the values of the classical French *tragédie lyrique*. On the other side were Jean-Jacques Rousseau and (to a lesser extent) the rest of the Encyclopedists, who advocated embracing the "natural" styles of the Italians. This battle initially took place in a series of pamphlets and open letters published from 1752 to 1754, the most famous of which was Rousseau's *Lettre sur la musique*—a document that vindicated Rousseau's own compositional style, best illustrated in his one-act "intermède" *Le Devin du Village* (1752). The Querelle was well remembered by early twentieth-century critics, a touchstone of French operatic history in the manner of Gluck's *Alceste* preface.[9] For the most part, until the early twentieth century, the Querelle remained only a historical footnote to French history, with little impact on modern concerns—after all, no one was listening to either Rameau or Rousseau during the nineteenth century. These cooled embers sparked again, however, in the years around 1900, as Rameau's rediscovered cachet rekindled old debates about French versus foreign musical styles. The tension only escalated around 1912, as the celebration of Rousseau's bicentennial generated virtually innumerable new articles and books about the philosopher. As critics and scholars simultaneously attempted to set up both Rameau and Rousseau as exemplars of French music history, the Querelle inevitably resurfaced as a key (if sometimes unspoken) point of discussion—putting fin-de-siècle critics in an awkward position. Rameau and Rousseau were both French cultural treasures (despite Rousseau's Swiss origins), and revisiting the Querelle always had the end result of tarnishing the reputation of one or the other. And those French historians, critics, and musicologists who were unwilling to choose a side tied themselves in rhetorical knots writing and revising French musical history to accommodate both Rameau and Rousseau in favorable positions.

Jean-Jacques Rousseau, *Musicien?*

Before comparing his aesthetic stance to Rameau's, critics first had to establish Rousseau's musical pedigree and influence. Many articles, in fact, stopped at that point, minimizing the Querelle's importance or simply ignoring it altogether. This approach was common with historians and literary critics, for whom the musical aspects of Rousseau's life generally held less interest than his philosophical and literary achievements. The critic and playwright Jules Lemaître's 1907 biography of Rousseau, for example, omits the Querelle from discussion entirely, and avoids any mention of the name "Rameau."[10] Likewise, the Querelle and Rameau play very little role in Émile Faguet's successful Rousseau series—five books the scholar and author published to coincide with the Rousseau bicentennial. The summary of the Querelle in the first volume, *La Vie de Rousseau*, is typical in its understatement: "Rousseau had returned to Paris in early October [1754]. He resumed his work. He wrote, perhaps on a bet, a nice enough story called *la Reine fantasque* and some polemical music articles against Rameau."[11] Few fin-de-siècle scholars were willing to paint either Rousseau or Rameau in a negative light, so they let the Querelle remain the elephant in the room. The historian Arthur Chuquet's 1893 Rousseau biography— one of the few to discuss it at all, albeit briefly—was deeply ambivalent:

> His *Lettre sur la musique*, inspired by hatred of Rameau, who called him an untalented thief, stirred up all of Paris; Jean-Jacques was accused of offending the nation because he denied its music; he was insulted; he withdrew his entries to the Opéra; he was burned in effigy at that theater. His anger was aggravated by unjust suspicions. He imagined that his friends envied the success of *Le Devin* and could not forgive him for adding compositional genius to his genius as a writer.[12]

Chuquet wisely chose to remain above the fray, resisting the temptation to give his own opinions on the relative merits of the two composers, if indeed he had any such opinions at all. In his description of the events we see Paris turning against its beloved Rousseau, insulting him and burning him in effigy at the Opéra (metaphorically, one hopes). Chuquet seems to paint a sympathetic picture of Rousseau, cruelly rejected by his adopted homeland. Yet the qualities he ascribed to Rousseau are anything but complimentary: the *Lettre sur la musique*—the centerpiece of the Querelle—was the product of a fit of pique, and megalomaniacal paranoia led him to erroneously believe his critics were motivated entirely by jealousy of his achievements.

Upon closer look, however, we can read this seemingly unsympathetic portrayal in another way. If Rousseau's polemical *Lettre* was written solely out of desire to wound Rameau, then it likely did not accurately reflect his actual aesthetic views; his distaste for French music may have been overstated, if not entirely fictitious. Similarly, Rousseau's sustained support for this anti-French position could be an aspect of his paranoia, a reaction against his friends' perceived treachery. The personality foibles of geniuses (musical and otherwise) were old hat to fin-de-siècle audiences, and were entirely forgivable sins. Chuquet's position thus rescues Rousseau by making his role in the Querelle the result of personal grudges and intellectual vanity rather than a well-reasoned diatribe against French national musical style—something much less understandable to modern audiences, particularly given Rameau's heroic position in music history by the fin de siècle.

Minimizing the Querelle's importance let literary critics keep Rousseau on his pedestal without denigrating Rameau's historical contributions. As long as they kept away from Rameau, in fact, some critics felt free to exaggerate Rousseau's musical accomplishments. Of these critics, Faguet is perhaps the most revealing in another of his bicentennial books, *Rousseau artiste*:

> Rameau is very fashionable today. As for me—limited to trying to understand—I will simply say: they are two powerful gods. I do not compare them; I acknowledge that they both have the right to exist and I believe I understand the beauty of that very simple and unaffected art that is Jean-Jacques's *and which certainly survived in the creators of opéra comique.* Monsigny, Grétry, "natural men" like him who followed his example very well.[13]

Pleading ignorance, Faguet simply refused to compare Rousseau and Rameau. But what he does say is just as interesting, and quite ingenious: by setting up Rousseau as the progenitor of opéra comique, he allows the two to coexist more or less happily. Rameau maintained his reputation as the continuation of the *tragédie lyrique*, while Rousseau went on to found the "eminently French" genre of opera comique: a win-win solution to a thorny problem.

Not content to leave the issue there, however, Faguet expanded Rousseau's musical sphere of influence even further:

> There is no doubt that Rousseau was considered a truly great musician of his time, as a man with the highest degree of musical sense by the following century and this one.

In any case, he thought deeply about music. We should not dwell too much on his famous *Lettre sur la musique*, which is a polemical work—and one that he returned to over and over—that contains some things that are very fair, and others that are singularly subjective. But if one reads his "opera" article (in the *Dictionnaire de musique*)—in my opinion entirely extraordinary—one will see that Rousseau is the precursor of all the great modern ideas in music.[14]

Rousseau not only founded an entire genre but apparently presaged "all the great modern ideas" that followed. Faguet, notably, does not enumerate precisely what these great ideas might be, but it seems likely that to a literary critic modern ideas implied Wagnerism, undoubtedly the most visible musical trend of the fin de siècle—a revealing observation to which we will return shortly.

While literary scholars and historians by and large avoided delving too deeply into the implications of Rousseau's musical tendencies, music critics and musicologists had no such compunctions. In particular, two early twentieth-century monographs with nearly antithetical conclusions shed light on the complexities of the situation: Arthur Pougin's *Jean-Jacques Rousseau, musicien* (1901) and Julien Tiersot's *Jean-Jacques Rousseau* (1920) from the well-known "Maîtres de la musique" series.[15] By this point, these names should both be familiar. Among his other scholarly contributions, Pougin was the author of the influential 1876 biography of Rameau that I discussed in chapter 8, and the near ubiquitous Tiersot was a major figure in the Gluck revival. These distinguished scholars' diverse positions on Rousseau expose how vestiges of the Querelle overlapped with issues in modern music. To an extent, these discussions raise the inherent issues of the Operatic Museum, placing eighteenth-century debates and works alongside modern musical issues. They also mirror to a striking extent the music-historical debates we have already seen with regard to the Rameau edition, typified by Debussy and d'Indy.

Pougin's study first appeared as a twenty-five-part series of articles in the music journal *Le Ménestrel*, occupying a prominent portion of the text from September 24, 1899, until March 15, 1900 (with a few brief interruptions), and was quickly published as a monograph in 1901. Because it appeared in such a prominent venue, Pougin's work likely had a significant impact on Rousseau's musical reception during the fin de siècle. Although he acknowledged Rousseau's contributions to eighteenth-century French music, Pougin dismissed the philosopher's musical talents. *Le Devin du village*, for example, remained a topic of discussion "above all because of the glorious personality of its author," rather than for its musical merits.[16] Pougin discusses the Querelle at length (as I discuss below), but saves his most damning critique for the volume's conclusion:

> Rousseau had a lifelong passion for music, the desire to pass for a musician, and the urge to become one—but he did not have the time, courage, or energy necessary to learn the principles of an art that requires the special technique of those who engage in long and serious study. In hopes of making this study quicker and less laborious, he tried to reform the way this art was written, not realizing that this reform—had it been possible—could not change these basic requirements. Moreover, he had the presumption to become a composer without wanting to learn the language of musical composition, and so he wrote the music without knowing how to coordinate, develop, or accompany his ideas.... Finally, he mistakenly believed that with only superficial study he could become familiar with the rules and regulate the precepts of an art that one can master only by constant practice, long experience, and the help of reasoning applied to sensitivity....
>
> Despite his pride in the success of *Le Devin du village*, it must be declared: no, Rousseau was not a musician in the serious sense of the word.[17]

Rousseau's celebrity clearly did not compel Pougin to pull any punches. Despite his status as one of the great luminaries of eighteenth-century France, the critic paints him as an egomaniacal dilettante, tragically unaware of his own mediocrity, too lazy or afraid to learn how to compose "real" music. His works (which, in fairness, Pougin rarely if ever heard performed) displayed nothing of musical art and craft, and his efforts to "reform" opera were poorly masked excuses for his own ignorance. In short, Pougin seems to say, Rousseau had no understanding of harmony and music theory—elements that were, coincidentally enough, Rameau's strong suit. In a sense, Pougin's entire book leads to this point. He called it *Jean-Jacques Rousseau, musicien* only to reveal in its final pages the bitter irony of the title: despite all his self-important grandstanding, Rousseau was no musician at all. His music might reveal new insights into the philosopher's mind, but it had no real place in music history.

Tiersot's *Jean-Jacques Rousseau*, a project that occupied the scholar for years (Faguet refers to it as a work in progress a decade earlier) stands in stark contrast to Pougin's clearly pro-Rameau stance. In part 2, we saw Tiersot's efforts to link Gluck to Wagner, creating an unbroken historical lineage; here the musicologist's teleological inclinations come into play again. In his conclusion, Tiersot invokes Rousseau's entry on "imitation" in the *Dictionnaire*—devoted to music's ability to reflect the natural (and supernatural) world—includes a list of some possibilities for evoking various scenes in a picturesque fashion. Tiersot found Rameau's definition striking, and in discussing it reveals his entire historical timeline:

These examples appear to us very clearly in compositions that flourished after him, among which we find some of our truest masterpieces. The divine calm of the Champs-Élysées and the horror of the underworld when Alceste sacrifices herself; the alternately penetrating and sublime poetry of the Scene at the Brook, the Storm, and the Hymn of Thanksgiving in Beethoven's symphony; the oppression of the Scene in the Fields and the dread of the Marche to the Scaffold by Berlioz; the searing intensity of the fires at Valhalla; the powerful image of the Flood in Saint-Saëns's *Le Déluge*; all the way to the radiance and clarity of Debussy's *La Mer*; Rousseau seems to have foretold and defined all this with a singular precision.[18]

Tiersot's examples are not chosen at random, though they are perhaps a bit surprising toward the end. Although important enough in their own time, Rousseau's musical ideals took on a much grander significance for later generations; they appeared (in conveniently chronological order) in the works of Gluck, Beethoven, Berlioz, Wagner, Saint-Saëns, and Debussy. This teleology, which would have infuriated both Debussy and d'Indy, nonetheless resembles the historical narrative that Wagnerians like Tiersot had established around Gluck beginning in the late nineteenth century—Rousseau simply added another link to the beginning of the chain.

But such narratives created an issue of influence: even if Rousseau had foreseen the direction of music history, it does not necessarily follow that he affected it. His works were seldom performed, and his writings on music were overshadowed by his numerous other accomplishments. Tiersot provided a convenient solution for this problem as well:

If we went further, what new analogies would we find? We would compare the sense of nature in Beethoven, his aspirations toward the Divine, with the ideal of the Savoyard Vicar and the Solitary Walker. We would see Wagner, haunted by philosophical and humanitarian ideas, proposing to the people during a revolution a constitution with a base not unrelated to the *Social Contract*, leading to the creation of an immense work—*The Ring*—that proclaims the necessity of returning to primitive nature and, like the *First Discourse*, condemns gold as fatal to human happiness. . . .

From a musical point of view, he heralded the evolution of modern art, divining its spirit, supplying its justification in advance, and perhaps effectively encouraging its formation.[19]

Not only did Rousseau foresee the musical developments of the nineteenth and early twentieth centuries, he actively contributed to them through his writings (though Tiersot moderates his speculation with a carefully placed "perhaps"). Beethoven and Wagner almost certainly did not know Rousseau's music, but his philosophical writings were another matter entirely. Tiersot went to great lengths to situate Rameau not as the historical dead end Pougin saw, but as a major influence on the greatest composers since his time. The music of Beethoven and Wagner—threateningly Germanic, despite Tiersot's postwar vantage point—was rescued by French philosophy, situated as the logical outcome of Rousseau's writings.

Quarrels, Old and New

Once Rousseau's musical abilities and historical influence—or lack thereof—had been established, critics could turn to the Querelle des Bouffons and its effects. Naturally, the dichotomous historical narratives Pougin and Tiersot wove around Rousseau reflected their thoughts about this matter, as well, and they were not alone. Camps formed around each of the two eighteenth-century thinkers, with Pougin and Tiersot as more or less terminal points on the continuum. For many musicologists and critics, Rameau came out ahead, the French classical style triumphing over the Italianate invasion. Pougin, of course, never lost an opportunity to compare the philosopher unfavorably to Rameau. After citing a passage in which Rousseau praises his own skills as a composer, for example, Pougin writes:

> We see what a lofty idea Rousseau had of his talents as a composer. It is like this every time he finds a reason to discuss his music, and he found them often.... But what is truly strange ... is the jealousy that he so naively and sincerely attributes to Rameau. Does one see the author of *Castor et Pollux* afraid of a rivalry with the author of *Les Muses galantes*? ...
>
> Rousseau claims to give us new proof of Rameau's terrible jealousy—jealousy that Rousseau did not grasp was nothing but the natural distain of a great artist for his truly presumptuous musical pretentions.[20]

Here again we see Rousseau possessed by delusions of grandeur, blinded to both Rameau's genius and his own incompetence. If Pougin's message were not clear enough, the critic succinctly summed up a few pages later: "Rousseau the equal of Rameau—it is enough to make one smile."[21] Pougin was no kinder regarding Rousseau's role in the Querelle. After a description of Rousseau's pamphlet *Examen de deux principes avancés par M. Rameau dans sa brochure intitulée: Erreurs sur la musique dans l'Encyclopedie,* Pougin opined that "Rousseau sufficiently proved in this writing that he understood nothing of the admirable genius of the author of *Castor et Pollux,* and that he did not know how to do him justice."[22] All the philosopher's arguments are summarily dismissed, unworthy of serious contemplation.

Other critics shared Pougin's harsh assessments of Rousseau. Louis Laloy, for example, referred to the Querelle repeatedly in his 1908 Rameau biography, continually extolling the merits of Rameau's French style. In response to a typical complaint about the lack of melody in Rameau's works (as opposed to Italian opera), for example, Laloy indignantly wrote that "no Italian of any era ever drew out a melody with such a firm hand, carried it out with this assurance, or foregrounded it with this decisiveness."[23] A bit later, Laloy continued: "With the Italians, [melody] seeks only to please, to astonish, or to divert. With Rameau, there is always a reason: it is an image, not a game."[24] Like his close friend Debussy, Laloy felt that Rameau represented the apex of France's musical history. French music was too readily misled by the efforts of Rousseau and composers like Gluck, who bastardized the *tragédie lyrique* with elements of foreign musical styles.

The fundamental complaint against Rousseau, of course, was that he had traitorously turned his back on the music of nation that had so graciously adopted him. Henri Lavoix began his 1891 book *La Musique française* with the following:

> If some cultured person had the peculiar idea to defend the paradox that there was no French literature, poetry, painting, or sculpture, the idea would be laughable, and no one would agree. But if music were added, it would be entirely different: without looking too ridiculous, and all evidence to the contrary, anyone could maintain that French music does not exist, never has existed, and never will exist. J.-J. Rousseau, with all the authority of genius, simply stated the axiom that the French had no music and could not have it. A good number of disciples have religiously taken in the master's words, and it is still an article of faith for many dilettantes.[25]

Lavoix blamed Rousseau for the persistent and erroneous belief that France had no national music. As we have seen time and again, fin-de-siècle critics, composers, and scholars went to great lengths to create historical narratives that stressed French musical achievements. Rousseau's dismissal of French music must have been infuriating, and the fact that his opinion still carried such weight—at least according to Lavoix—even more so. Lavoix spent the remainder of his book attempting to make Rousseau into a fool, disproving at every turn French music's inferiority to foreign styles, either in the eighteenth century or in more modern times.

The Querelle offered a convenient opportunity to simultaneously demonstrate Rousseau's absurdity and Rameau's greatness. Pougin, of course, found Rousseau's rejection of French music utterly ridiculous: "If we want to examine this famous *Lettre* [*sur la musique*], we will see that Rousseau goes to great lengths to try to prove that French music is and always will be detestable because the French language is extremely hostile to music. . . . He gathers on this subject a group of supposed examples, the most bizarre reasons, and poses as axioms a number of unfounded statements that . . . can do nothing today but make us smile."[26]

Pougin, who evidently found himself smiling quite a lot at Rousseau, was not alone in this indictment of the *Lettre.* Lionel de la Laurencie—founder of the Société Française de Musicologie and author of a monograph on Lully—expressed similar sentiments in his 1905 monograph *Le Goût musical en France*:

> For Rousseau, the French, whose language is flat and deprived of accents, proved their most pitiable taste in their "ariettas" and in their recitative, full of "noisy and shrill intonations." "There is," he writes, "neither meter nor melody in French music, because the language is not sensitive to them; French singing is nothing but a continual barking, unbearable to any unprepared ear; the harmony is crude and without expression . . .; French arias are not arias; French recitative is not recitative. Thus I conclude that the French have no music, and cannot have it—or if they ever do have any, it will be too bad for them." Rousseau dared utter such blasphemies twenty years after *Castor et Pollux*! He treated Rameau cavalierly.[27]

De la Laurencie painted Rousseau as a villain—a blasphemer against both Rameau and French musical taste. The critic felt he only needed to offer up *Castor et Pollux* as a counterexample to disprove Rousseau's scandalous claims; Rameau's opera was beyond any possible reproach. Despite his importance to cultural history, Rousseau was the enemy of all French musical values, and his insults cut no less deep a century and a half later. This attitude, in line with Pougin (and Debussy), was the dominant one with music scholars in the 1890s and early 1900s. By the 1910s and 1920s, however, the balance of power had shifted, and Tiersot's view of eighteenth-century music history became more prevalent.

De la Laurencie is a case in point. The same critic who had so brazenly accused Rousseau of blasphemy in 1905 backpedaled considerably in his 1926 Rameau biography, presenting a much more favorable view of the Encyclodpedists and their aesthetic achievements. Where once they had rejected all things good and French in music, they now "set out with great foresight the aesthetic foundations of the future *drame lyrique.* They herald Grétry, Gluck, and even Richard Wagner; they express the new requirements of dramatic art that were subtly at work on the eighteenth-century spirit—needs that the Italian works of the *bouffons* partially satisfied."[28] It seems de la Laurencie could not deny the teleological progression that connected Rousseau and his cadre to Gluck and Wagner (and Grétry, linking Rousseau again to early opéra comique). The critic explained away the Encyclopedists' antipathy for Rameau by suggesting that Rousseau, Grimm, and the rest did not really understand instrumental music, negatively disposing them toward Rameau's works: "They all find too much music in French opera."[29]

None of this is to say that de la Laurencie had lost his allegiances to Rameau. In fact, he spent a significant amount of time defending Rameau from the Encyclopedists, and saving them from themselves—or at least some of them. In an inspired nationalist move, de la Laurencie shifted nearly all blame for the Querelle onto Melchior Grimm, mitigating any anti-French sentiment that Rousseau or the others might have expressed: "So great was his hatred of everything typical of the French spirit that Grimm, that German disguised as a Parisian, attacked [Rameau] without measure, scoffing at him even after his death—whereas the excessive and passionate Rousseau combined the worst errors with comments of rare insight, and [Denis] Diderot and [Jean le Rond] d'Alembert are in general more evenhanded and moderate in their criticism."[30] The vitriol de la Laurencie had previously reserved for Rousseau was redirected to Grimm, that "German disguised as a Parisian," who was no doubt motivated by his "hatred for everything that characterizes the French spirit." Such a blind loathing required no further explanation—he was German and hated France, hence the Querelle. Rousseau, while not blameless, was a misguided eccentric rather than an actual opponent of French music. He committed "errors" (presumably accidental), but at the same time contributed moments of real insight. Diderot and d'Alembert were moderates who had sought some operatic reforms but nonetheless appreciated and understood Rameau's eminently French style.

Clearly, something changed de la Laurencie's perceptions of Rousseau and the Querelle between 1905 and 1926. Tiersot's fierce defense in 1920 likely played a part, as did the furor that surrounded the 1912 Rousseau bicentennial. This momentous event prompted two issues of the *La Revue musicale S.I.M.* (June and July) mostly dedicated to the music and aesthetics of the philosopher, featuring articles by de la Laurencie, Tiersot, the Rameau scholar Paul-Marie Masson, and other notable musicologists. On June 23, the Opéra-Comique even presented Rousseau's *Le Devin du village* under Tiersot's direction as part of a Rousseau festival. Despite this newfound cultural celebration of Rousseau, however, critics could not embrace his musical judgments without some caveats. Masson eloquently summarized the nationalist and aesthetic issues at play:

> It is said that [Rousseau] was not French, and that we should withhold the label "French" to everyone who enthusiastically followed him in his adventurous dream. Is it really to understand France, or even to love it,

> to claim to define it once and for all? . . . [Rousseau's passion] separated him cleanly from Rameau to turn in an entirely new direction where he encounters Gluck, and where Berlioz would appear. Whatever one might think of his attitude and his inclinations, and one has the right to treat his errors harshly, it would be unjust not to see in him—in the realm of music as in many others—one of the most fruitful *remueurs d'idées* who ever existed.[31]

Again we find Rousseau positioned as the precursor to Gluck and Berlioz (and presumably Wagner), and with a nationalist defense to back it up. With a subtle take on nationalism that was uncommon in music criticism of the time, Masson suggested that opposing the dominant musical style (i.e., Rameau) did not make Rousseau or his music any less French—and that whatever one might think of the philosopher's aesthetics, he nonetheless deserved admiration as an "idea shaker" (*remueur d'idées*).

Even as early as 1908 some critics claimed that the nationalist aspects of the Querelle played a large role in Rameau's fin-de-siècle success. The critic Jean Chantavoine, for example, clearly felt that a desire to cast off the Querelle's long-term effects was a major catalyst for Rameau's revival: "There is certainly a share of artistic chauvinism in this new Rameau cult, and also a share of anti-Encyclopedist spirit. One admires Jean-Philippe Rameau for being a 'hometown' musician; one also admires him for having been little appreciated by Rousseau and the Encyclopedists, who many people have not forgiven for their influence on the modern spirit."[32] Rameau's reputation as a champion of French taste against Rousseau was a major point in the composer's favor, at least according to Chantavoine. The critic—who in this article actually expressed a preference for Gluck over Rameau—argued (perceptively) that audiences appreciated Rameau for his French identity rather than for his music. We also see yet another hint at Rousseau's long-lasting influence: Gluck—irrevocably tied to Wagnerism, the Encyclopedists, or both—was positioned in opposition to Rameau's music.

Such had not always been the case: Saint-Saëns, for example, compellingly argued that Rameau and Gluck should be viewed as part of a continuous French historical narrative. His position is not particularly surprising. He had, after all, written extensively in favor of both composers, and had a major role in both the Rameau *Œuvres complètes* and the Pelletan Edition of Gluck's operas. Rather than casting one composer as more representative of French musical values than the other, in his *Harmonie et mélodie* (1885) Saint-Saëns united them under the same banner:

> Let us note in passing that France is the chosen land of opera. It has not been easy to persuade her that realistic stage action, good declamation, and fine verses were nothing when compared to a graceful tune,

decked out with a pedal point like an ostrich feather on a hat; it has not been easy to succeed in destroying the work begun by Rameau and completed by Gluck, in the midst of a fierce struggle; because the struggle was already going on and, essentially, it was the same struggle we are seeing now. Pergolesi was set against Rameau and Piccini against Gluck. The enemies of these great men were using the weapon that is still being wielded by their descendants: "melody." When faced with the highest levels of reasoning or with the most self-evident beauties, they always countered with "melody." . . . For a hundred and fifty years, "melody" has been the touchstone of musical criticism.[33]

Rameau and Gluck both represent the struggle of dramatic verity against partisans of pure "melody" (i.e., Italian opera). Saint-Saëns then goes on—shockingly—to compare Rameau's and Gluck's historic struggles against partisans of Italianate melody to those faced by Richard Wagner at the fin de siècle.[34] Whereas more xenophobic critics were content with separating music into two categories—French and "foreign"—Saint-Saëns allied French and German musical traditions against Italian music, allying Rameau and Gluck rather than setting them in opposition. Such an optimistic, reconciliatory tone would have been unthinkable a few decades later, as partisan politics came to a head regarding the two composers.

This tension between Gluck and Rameau became an idée fixe in criticism after 1900, particularly in discussions of the latter composer. Comparisons abound in the Rameau biographies of de la Laurencie and Laloy, for example, and we have already seen examples from Tiersot's Rousseau biography. Since the late nineteenth century, Gluck was lauded as a reformer, the messianic figure foretold by the Encyclopedists who would unite the best aspects of French and Italian musical styles. For some, Gluck had altered the natural progression of French music history, while for others he had modernized the antiquated *tragédie lyrqiue*, thereby ensuring the continued influence of French musical styles. In either case, Gluck could be set up as a surrogate for Rousseau, and one with impeccable musical credentials. Rousseau's lack of musical training and (arguably) compositional ability could be set aside, and his ideas could be attached to Gluck's music. An argument against Rousseau became an argument against Gluck—and by extension, against Berlioz and Wagner.

Or, from a slightly different perspective, to favor Rameau over Rousseau was to challenge the "progress" of history. For decades, critics had been working to create narratives that stressed French contributions to music history. We have seen many of these already: Mozart was French in spirit and musical style; Gluck was French, and his music led directly to Wagner; and so on. Placing Rousseau into this narrative—as most critics were willing to do by the 1910s—suggested that Germanic music from Beethoven to Wagner was the evolution of French styles, thereby strengthening the French contributions to European music history. Rameau, by contrast, was an interrupted tradition, the last specimen of a beautiful but extinct species. Suggesting that he had been "right" all along was to reject these carefully crafted narratives and pick up where Rameau left off. And so the conflict became about Rameau against Gluck, Rousseau's mouthpiece.

Consequently, many *Ramistes* felt compelled to denigrate Gluck's operas. During a 1903 performance of Rameau's *La Guirlande* at the Schola Cantorum, Debussy was supposedly moved to shout: "Vive Rameau! A bas Gluck!" Charles Malherbe expressed much the same idea in 1908 regarding *Hippolyte et Aricie* at the Opéra: "Once again the giant Gluck is set in opposition to someone: no longer to Piccini *le petit*, as in the past, but to Rameau *le grand*. Everyone must declare themselves either a *Gluckiste* or a *Ramiste*, and the ink flows anew for or against the god of your choice."[35] The argument essentially became a fin-de-siècle reenactment of the Querelle, with each side fighting for a different historical narrative. Although both groups sought to put French musical achievements on display in the Operatic Museum, they sought vastly different sets of exhibits. Many of Rameau's partisans sought a pure French history, unsullied by foreign influences. On the other hand, showing French influence on Germanic music was another, subtler, form of nationalism.

Balancing Rameau and Rousseau was a matter of the utmost importance for fin-de-siècle scholars and critics, and for good reason. This resurgence of the Querelle was in many ways a microcosm of modern French musical debates: Wagnerism versus anti-Wagnerism, Debussy versus d'Indy, classical versus romantic, "pure" French music versus musical cosmopolitanism— or, on a deeper level, even a challenge to teleological perceptions of history. How these two titans of eighteenth-century thought were positioned shaped which historical narratives were emphasized and which were omitted, affecting the way modern French music was understood as much as it affected Rameau or Rousseau. But however much it may have shaped public opinion, the reawakened Querelle that raged anew through the Parisian musical press principally concerned scholars and more musically educated critics. During the same stretch of time, however, French audiences were able to make their own judgments about Rameau's merits as a theater composer for the first time in over a century. In the course of the previous two chapters, we have examined Rameau's role in debates about music history and national identity in several locations: the concert hall, the library, in scholarly discourse, and in press debates about aesthetics. We now turn finally to the most publically visible site of Rameau reception, and where the French people would make a final judgment regarding his artistic and historical worth: the stage of the Opéra.

Chapter Ten

Archaeologies

"It is beyond hope that we shall ever hear *Castor et Pollux, Dardanus,* or *Zoroastre* at the Opéra," Félix Clément lamented in his 1885 *Histoire de la musique*.[1] Not without good reason he believed that despite the unquestionable musical quality of Rameau's operas, they were too antiquated for modern audiences. After all, for most of the nineteenth century, Rameau had routinely been "cited as an archetype of musicians judged too antiquated to ever again be played."[2] The *tragédie lyrique* (before Gluck, at least) was entirely disconnected from fin-de-siècle expectations of opera, shaped by nineteenth-century French musical styles such as *grand opéra* to (post-)Wagnerian music dramas. The years between 1885 and 1908, however, convinced many critics, producers, and audiences that such a revival might be possible. For one thing, the Opéra-Comique (and occasionally the Opéra) had successfully produced Gluck's works since 1896—a feat that critics had initially thought impossible. And, of course, the theaters had more or less run out of Gluck operas to stage—the 1907 *Iphigénie en Aulide* had exhausted the supply of his French "masterwork" operas. By that time, the groundwork—most prominently concert performances and the *Œuvres complètes*—had been laid for a Rameau revival.

Critics and audiences knew that eighteenth-century works had the potential to appeal to modern audiences, on an aesthetic as well as intellectual level; in other works, they knew audiences could respond favorably to the Operatic Museum mindset. But would they respond well to Rameau? Producers had some reason to think so. The frequent appearances of his music on concert series garnered some positive accolades, culminating in some fairly successful productions of Rameau's operas (in whole or in part) in concerts. Vincent d'Indy conducted a production of *Dardanus* in Dijon in 1907, and Charles Bordes (founder of the Schola Cantorum) had directed a production of *Castor et Pollux* in Montpellier in early 1908—events noted with interest in the Parisian press.[3]

Hippolyte et Aricie was a deeply symbolic choice for the Opéra's production, a testament to the Operatic Museum as an institution. The work had a long history at the Opéra; fin-de-siècle critics and scholars viewed its 1733 premiere there as one of the most significant moments in French music history.[4] Returning to the same work in 1908 suggested a triumphal return for Rameau to his rightful place, a long-delayed homecoming that simultaneously reaffirmed the composer's historical importance and called attention to the lengthy and distinguished history of the Opéra. Critics were well aware of this production's symbolic importance; the musicologist Henri Quittard even referred to it as an "apotheosis of the old master."[5] It was also supposed to be a grand entrance for the Opéra's new directors, André Messager and Leimistin Broussan, who selected *Hippolyte et Aricie* for their first production. This choice strongly suggested that their directorship would coincide with the ultimate opening of the Operatic Museum—the fulfillment of an ideal that critics, scholars, and connoisseurs had pursued since the 1860s. Despite the successful precedents and all the groundwork laid for a Rameau revival, the 1908 production remained a daring move. As the critic Georges Pioch pointed out, because of the specific pitfalls of presenting classical operas to a modern audience, "Messager and Broussan risked much more by reviving *Hippolyte et Aricie* than by staging a new work."[6] It was a wholly different kind of work for the Opéra, one that neither the theater nor its audience might be able to accept.

Because staging *Hippolyte* was such a risk—for both economic and nationalistic reasons—the producers at the Opéra had to be very careful in their choices. How should the work be staged? How, if at all, should the music be adapted for the enormous performance space at the Palais Garnier, or to conform to audience preferences? Part of what had made Gluck's operas so successful was their ability to appear modern to fin-de-siècle audiences, both visually and in subject matter. This approach was more difficult with *Hippolyte*, chiefly because of how Rameau was perceived. Gluck and Mozart occupied a liminal space between the classical and the modern—Gluck's operas were associated with Wagner and (in two cases) adapted by Berlioz, and Mozart's had a Parisian performance history unbroken since the early nineteenth century. Their works were recognizable enough that audiences could generally look past their age, even when issues of historical fidelity arose.

Rameau's operas, on the other hand, were unfamiliar and fragile objects, museum pieces that encouraged a different kind of approach from many critics—one more oriented around archaeology than modernization.[7] An article by the Opéra-Comique singer and Conservatoire professor Georges Imbart de la Tour, for example, carefully presented details of Rameau's original staging and costumes—as well as his thoughts on why a historical kind of staging was necessary with *Hippolyte*, but not with Gluck's works.[8] This imperative was something wholly new; not only must the music be Rameau's original (or be perceived as such), but the staging—and by extension, the entire experience—had to follow suit. As Rémy Campos puts it in his recent study of the 1908 production: "By refining until he [Imbart de la Tour] distinguished the ancient conceptions of stage machinery (those of Rameau's time) from the modern notion of 'antiquity,' which was based on a later Neoclassical aesthetic (dating from 1770 to 1810), the archaeologist laid the foundation for an aesthetic revolution. What remained was to lead the artists, the public, and most important, the leadership of the Académie nationale de musique."[9]

In other words, whereas with the Gluck production at the Opéra-Comique the two definitions of classical had become conflated—simultaneously evocative of the classicism of the eighteenth century and Greek antiquity—with Rameau these two concepts were becoming divorced. The Operatic Museum ideal was shifting, at least in implementation. Initially the idea had been that old masterworks could be placed into dialogue with newer works, creating a historical narrative. By 1908, at least some critics were becoming adamant that the museum exhibits be presented in precisely their original state, approximating as closely as possible what eighteenth-century audiences would have seen and heard.

The Opéra management, not surprisingly, was hesitant to go along with such radical ideas. A totally "faithful" spectacle complete with eighteenth-century costumes, sets, and elaborate stage machinery was more likely to end in alienated audiences and financial disaster than in a successful Rameau revival; audiences were unprepared for that kind of musical archaeology. It might have been possible to stage *Hippolyte* similarly to the fin-de-siècle Gluck productions, playing up the Frenchness and perceived modernity of ancient Greece while creating an impression of Rameau that looked both forward and backward in time. Yet this approach had been taken before, and did not allow the theater to easily connect to the work's eighteenth-century heritage. The Opéra managers chose a third option: compromise. Their vision of *Hippolyte* was by turn evocative of the Opéra's original eighteenth-century production, and modern in the manner of the Gluck productions.[10] It was immanently classical (*antique* or *ancien*, as French critics would say) in both senses of the word. As figures 10.1 and 10.2 demonstrate, the costumes that were the most similar between the eighteenth- and twentieth-century productions were those that aimed at "realistic" antiquity, rather than the clearly ancien régime costumes that some characters wore in Rameau's time. By choosing this hybrid staging, the Opéra directors tried to have it both ways: they could point out clear examples of the production's faithfulness to Rameau's original, yet avoided the aspects that might be most objectionable or confusing to modern audiences, such as goddesses of antiquity wearing elaborate eighteenth-century dresses (see fig. 10.3).

As important as the sets and costumes may have been for audience experiences, however, they were seldom the topic of significant critical discussion. Periodicals did not routinely reproduce images, for example, as they often did when the staging was considered particularly remarkable. The music, however, was much more noteworthy to the press. In its musical choices, the Opéra adopted a strategy similar to what we have seen

Figure 10.1. Costume from Rameau's production (1742?), reprinted in Imbart de la Tour, "La Mise en scène d'*Hippolyte et Aricie*," fig. 11.

M. DELMAS DANS LE RÔLE DE THÉSÉE.

Figure 10.2. Jean-François Delmas as Thésée in *Hippolyte et Aricie*, 1908. *Musica*, July 1908.

Figure 10.3. Costume from Rameau's production (1742?), reprinted in Imbart de la Tour, "La Mise en scène d'*Hippolyte et Aricie*," fig. 12.

already in the décor: it created a hybrid of historical fidelity and modernization presumably designed to win over both the general operagoing population and the more musically educated Rameau aficionados. Naturally enough, the Opéra turned to the *Œuvres complètes* for a reliable edition of *Hippolyte*, which d'Indy had prepared in 1900. As we have already seen, the score is itself a modernization, full of d'Indy's "improvements"—extra contrapuntal lines, filled-out orchestrations, and so on. The performance also proved a mélange of historical and modern practices: recitatives, for example, were accompanied by harpsichord—an instrument that was still very much a historical curiosity in 1908—but it was supplemented with strings.[11] This decision was probably practical as much as aesthetic; it may have been difficult for the audience, the singers, or both to hear the instrument in such a large space. Nevertheless, the *accompagnato* recitative brought Rameau's music much more into line with what audiences might expect from Gluck. The Opéra orchestra and singers evidently also trimmed back the ornamentation in their performances, probably on the grounds that the French classical penchant for embellishment would sound overly antiquated to modern listeners.

These decisions reveal a great deal about the complexities of including Rameau in the Operatic Museum. There was simply no way to please everyone: if the production had been as historically faithful as some critics and scholars wanted, the general public would likely have been left confused—a result that could have tarnished Rameau's (and thus France's) musical reputation and damaged the still tenuous future of the Operatic Musuem, or at least the possibility of any future forays into territory earlier than Gluck. On the other hand, a thoroughly modernized production (as, for example, *Don Giovanni/Don Juan* before 1912) would have been lambasted in the press, accomplishing the same end result. The Opéra directors walked a fine line between these two outcomes, with mixed results. What does seem clear, however, is that the directors and nearly all critics shared a common goal: for Rameau's operas to be a successful part of the Operatic Museum, objects of veneration that put France's glories on display to the world.

This acknowledgment of Rameau's place at the Opéra was long overdue in the eyes of many critics. One of the greatest proponents of the Opéra's decision to stage a Rameau work was Adolphe Jullien. The critic was overjoyed to see *Hippolyte* restored finally to the Parisian stages, something he had anticipated since the 1870s:

> I have waited thirty-four years: but luckier than many others, my hope since February 1874 has been realized: "If I could only hear my preferences," I said then, "I would ask to go back as far as Rameau, the greatest French musician, and that one should produce anew one of his masterworks: *Castor et Pollux, Hippolyte et Aricie*, or *Dardanus*..." Must I wait as long again to see *Dardanus* or *Castor et Pollux* played once more in Paris?[12]

A number of critics joined Jullien in his hope that *Hippolyte* would be only the first of many Rameau operas to reappear in the twentieth century. He was the "greatest French musician," and as such it was necessary that his works be prominently displayed to the public. As we saw in chapter 1, several critics seized on the 1908 production as both an example of the Operatic Museum's possibilities and a call to action regarding its continued existence. The critic Robert Mondor noted that the Opéra should maintain works that illustrate music history to the audience in its repertoire constantly, and "above all the history of French music. The musical education of a people should take place in the state-subsidized theaters, just as their artistic education takes place in museums."[13] Another opined, "On the stage that must be like the museum of our national music, it would be shocking if Rameau did not have a place."[14] Henri Quittard had a more tempered take on the rising popularity of the Operatic Museum: "It might be said that the Opéra, a largely subsidized national theater, has the responsibility to be a sort of museum of music, and that, heedless of material considerations, it should add every interesting and significant work of an era to its repertoire. In practice . . . this theater cannot be indifferent to its prosperity."[15] Quittard understood the idealistic lure of an Operatic Museum unburdened by monetary concerns; the repertoire could expand immensely, perhaps including interesting but unknown works by Lully, Campra, and others. The scholar was not blind to reality, however, and astutely noted that the Operatic Museum was and must remain built on compromise between historical importance and financial viability. Luckily, Quittard believed Rameau's reentry to the Opéra had shown the benefits of such a compromise, and that it would likely be a commercial success:

> It would appear *Hippolyte et Aricie* has nothing to fear. . . . Although it has encountered a lot of half-avowed hostility and been preemptively declared incapable of holding the interest of today's musical public, the work seems to have established itself from the first performance. The experiment that both enemies and friends of the French master wanted is over. The results are reassuring. I will not hide that they might very well not have been. That is true at the Opéra more than anywhere, and no one deserves more praise for having taken the chance on the undertaking.[16]

Quittard could breathe a sigh of relief that the audiences of the Opéra were willing to leave their expectations aside (at least to an extent) and embrace the unfamiliar eighteenth-century musical styles.

Other critics reaffirmed Quittard's assessment of the audience reaction. Although he detected a "manifest suspicion" from the audience initially, Gabriel Fauré found that they came around: "I add quickly that this suspicion did not take too long to dissipate; that, gradually, the opera worked its charm; that—despite the genre, a style forgotten for so long that it seemed new again—little by little the beauties of the music, the grandeur of its character, the variety, and the movement that animated it appeared; and that the night's performance ended as a triumph."[17] Fauré believed that the greatness of Rameau's music eventually won listeners over to its style, "forgotten so long that it seemed new again." Like Debussy and others, Fauré connected Rameau's music with the aesthetics of French modernity, much as the classical interpretation of Mozart's operas was more in line with early twentieth-century concepts of musical style (see part 1).

Unfortunately for Rameau's fin-de-siècle supporters, not all critics shared Fauré's and Quittard's unbridled enthusiasm for the 1908 *Hippolyte et Aricie* production. Many were deeply ambivalent, appreciating Rameau's music on intellectual and nationalist levels yet finding themselves emotionally detached from the radically different dramatic style he represented. Pierre Lalo, the influential music critic for *Le Temps*, encapsulated many of the production's more problematic aspects in his review. He began, as most critics, did, by praising the production:

> Paris is finally giving Rameau the homage he is due. It is the decisive test, the happy success of which revives the greatest of the masters of our art. One cannot overstress the importance of such an event.... French music had lost its titles of nobility: the production of *Hippolyte et Aricie* has just given them back.
>
> Because the success surpassed our hopes. It is not that the public was not surprised when faced with an art so different in both spirit and style from the types it is accustomed to. But their surprise is natural, and it would have been impossible for them not to experience it. For almost the entire public, music is an art without origins, without evolution, without development, the history of which is lost, and only the most recent music escapes obscurity.[18]

On one hand, the 1908 production was a success—one that gave French music back its "titles of nobility"—and the public's surprise was only to be expected given the masterwork's age. Yet Lalo continued by delving into the fundamental issues of Rameau's music that isolated it—perhaps irrevocably—from modern expectations of opera:

> Almost everything in [Rameau's] art is tailor-made to shock and disturb today's audiences. First, even his concept of musical theater has nothing in common with ours. Our idea of musical theater is entirely Romantic: since Gluck, Romanticism has had a hold on us. An opera is for us a drama, where the point is to seize, shake, and move the soul of the listener. Art is entirely directed, straining toward this goal; everything is sacrificed in searching for effect, according to Gluck's own words.... With

> Rameau, the pure and supreme representative of our Classical tradition, the principle of art is entirely different. Emotion, as powerful as it may be, is subjugated to intelligence; reason imposes order on feelings. This music brings clarity with it; it exudes certainty; it is governed by a general sense of equilibrium and harmony. Rameau's opera is not a drama, but a *tragédie lyrique* in the widest meaning of the term: a spectacle of beauty and celebration, where the pathos of the great movements of the soul mix with the peace and grace of divertissements; where moments of passion and sadness alternate effortlessly with moments of joy and repose; where art, taste, and superior reason can unite diverse musical forces without sacrificing any element, producing an impression of noble exaltation and beneficent serenity.[19]

Lalo lauded the Opéra's willingness to display Rameau's music in the Operatic Museum, stressing the historical importance of the production. But even in his lavish praise, the critic could not ignore his uneasiness regarding the wide gap between classical and modern notions of music dramas. Rameau's works were products of a different time and culture that emphasized "reason" and "intelligence" over "emotion." We also find the contrast between Rameau and Gluck begin to creep into the discourse, as we have already seen with the fin-de-siècle resurgence of the Querelle des Bouffons. In both cases, Gluck represents the modern direction in opera, culminating in the modern (Wagnerian) music drama. Rameau, by contrast, is the "pure and supreme representative of our [French] Classical tradition," an aesthetic totally separate from post-Gluckian ideas about music drama. In other words, Gluck looks forward in time while Rameau looks backward. All his concerns aside, however, Lalo remained hopeful for the Operatic Museum, and ended his review with an exhortation: "Go to Rameau's work. I hope you will like it. I even hope that if necessary you will make a bit of an effort to like and understand it; be assured that you will be rewarded for your trouble."[20]

Other critics were unwilling even to advise their readers to work harder at understand the opera. Like Lalo, the traditionalist Louis de Fourcaud was caught between appreciating Rameau's music and finding it too "distant," but he suggested a different solution:

> Rameau's music is admirable. This score, almost two hundred years old, demonstrates a solidity, frankness, and sincerity of expression that cannot be praised too highly.... It is only that at the Opéra, in its current [i.e., modern] state, we are uncomfortable with performing archaeology. These continual juxtapositions of tragic forms, cantata forms, and choreographed divertissements; the orchestra—very sonorous for its time, and infinitely ingenious in its detail, but thin and entirely primitive to

our ears; the plucked or jagged notes from the sour harpsichord, all this comes to us from too far away, with too much wear and tear, and above all exhibited in too large a space.

Suppose these five acts were given in a small hall, with an educational focus.... I believe we would better understand the historic grandeur, and we would enjoy the charm and the grace of his episodes in a more intimate setting.[21]

Despite the excellence of the music, in Fourcaud's estimation, Rameau's operas were inappropriate for the Opéra and its audience. Productions of this kind should be limited to smaller halls with productions explicitly labeled as educational. The critic couched his criticism of the "admirable" music in terms of praise—Rameau was still a historically important composer for France, after all—but his distaste for the production is nonetheless clear. He dismisses the modest attempts at eighteenth-century performance practice as "primitive," and the style coming from "too far away, with too much wear and tear." Putting such a shabby show on at the Opéra was in no one's best interest, Fourcaud seems to suggest—it would be much better to relegate such performances to smaller, more intimate spaces, and more musically educated audiences.

Even Saint-Saëns, a tireless advocate of bringing Rameau's music to modern audiences, was eventually willing to admit that the 1908 *Hippolyte* had been in some ways a failed experiment. He remained confident that a successful production was possible, however: "Some years ago an attempt was made to restore [Rameau's] works to the stage; the result has not been what was anticipated. It must, however, be acknowledged at once that this was not the fault of the composer, the interpreter, or the public. This does not prove that the resurrection is impossible, failure being due to difficulties that had not been suspected."[22] According to Saint-Saëns, the real impediments to modern Rameau productions were not apathetic audiences or unskilled performers, but the technical issues of historical performance practice. For one, the historically lower pitch meant that vocal parts were awkward for modern ranges, and produced odd tone colors from the singers. Further problems stemmed from the difficulty of correctly reading period notation (particularly ornaments, which were largely omitted from the 1908 performances). Rectifying these issues, required recitatives accompanied by orchestra rather than harpsichord, and orchestration altered with "a very respectful and light pen" to reflect modern tastes.[23] "The difficulties are great, though not insurmountable," Saint-Saëns concluded, "and we may hope that the day will come when the music of Rameau, regarded in its true light, will no longer be confined to the erudite, but will be acclaimed by the masses."[24] In other words, the 1908 Opéra production had not compromised enough, and—despite what

Fauré and other optimistic critics had hoped—audiences had left the theater feeling alienated rather than educated.

Other critics agreed with Saint-Saëns that the fundamental issue was the Opéra's allegedly overzealous approach to historical fidelity in performance. Victor Debay, for example, revealed that

> the first impression at the beginning of the evening, without being completely disenchanting, did not entirely live up to the pleasure expected from this overdue rehabilitation of a genius that has been disregarded for too long. The ear, accustomed to the splendors of modern orchestration, finds only meager pleasure in the more discreet charms of a continual [string] quartet, with some woodwinds added occasionally. The harpsichord accompanying the recitatives seemed quite thin, with its fragile sonorities, and moreover it had the drawback of uncovering voices that—without the envelope of sound that normally protects them—showed defects in their pronunciation, softness in their attacks, and a lack of rhythm in the accentuation of the musical phrase.[25]

Debay added that the instrumental music and dance in the opera were much superior to the vocal element, but the underlying insinuation of his review is that *Hippolyte et Aricie* was somehow unsuited to the Opéra, and perhaps to modern audiences at all.

Debay also gives us another clue to explaining the public's ambivalent reaction to *Hippolyte*: audience expectations were simply too high. By 1908, musicologists and critics had been extolling Rameau as the paradigm of French musical excellence for more than a decade, constantly reinforcing both the beauty and historical importance of his operas. That enthusiasm alone may have made it difficult for *Hippolyte* to live up to expectations, but there was more: nearly all the Parisian concert series that featured excerpts from Rameau's operas had (in accordance with standard practice) played the most beloved morceaux, the moments of these lengthy dramatic works considered the most palatable to fin-de-siècle audiences. Pleasant trios, tuneful arias, and elegant dances had not adequately prepared French audiences for the amount of recitative accompanied by the harpsichord they would hear, for example. More important, they were unprepared for the fundamentally different aesthetic of Rameau's *tragédies lyriques*: as music they were fine, as drama they were lacking. Even the performances of large excerpts or complete operas at the Schola Cantorum could not circumvent this issue entirely. Audiences at the Schola expected (and wanted) musical "archaeology," but Opéra audiences were accustomed to modern works. Additionally, the comparably intimate environment and lack of staging at d'Indy's productions created much different expectations regarding the acoustic and visual surroundings for Rameau's works.

Ultimately, despite the unquestionable historical importance of *Hippolyte et Aricie* and its composer, the 1908 production failed to spark the Rameau revival that critics sought. Celebrating the accomplishments of the eighteenth-century master was clearly a high priority in the fiercely nationalistic climate of early twentieth-century France, yet audiences were unwilling or unable to accept the purely French aesthetics of the pre-Gluckian *tragédie lyrique*—which were, ironically, too foreign for them to understand. Producers, likewise, were unwilling to sacrifice profit to the extent that would have been necessary to maintain Rameau in the Operatic Museum; that task would have to fall to organizations like the concert series or the Schola, much as Forcaud had suggested.

Only in 1918, in the patriotic fervor that accompanied the closing months of World War I, did Rameau appear again on the stage of the Opéra. Since the war's beginning, the Opéra's repertoire had relied on popular favorite operas in already existing productions, minimizing the cost while maximizing the audience attendance. Only one new production appeared in the entirety of the war: Rameau's *Castor et Pollux*. Because the war disrupted the publication of most Parisian music periodicals, reviews of the 1918 *Castor et Pollux* are less plentiful than reviews of most other fin-de-siècle productions—the longer, more scholarly assessments are particularly lacking. The narrative that emerges, however, is that the production was in general much better received than the 1908 *Hippolyte et Aricie*. This shift in reception seems linked to a surge of nationalist pride that went beyond even the chauvinist histories of the first decade of the twentieth century—this production was "a bold, expensive gesture of defiance."[26]

The press lauded the decision of the Opéra's director, Jacques Rouché, to stage a work by Rameau—a choice understood in nationalist terms, as many of Rouché's repertoire selections were.[27] Henri Quittard, for example, wrote:

> It is impossible to envision a spectacle simultaneously more artistic and more magnificent than the one to which the Opéra invited Paris last Thursday. In returning *Castor et Pollux*—forgotten since 1784—to the stage, Mr. Jacques Rouché intended to . . . render a just homage to Rameau and one of his masterworks. With *Hippolyte et Aricie*, some years ago now, the redress of such a great injustice against our national art began. The performances of *Castor et Pollux* will do still more. And it is truly about time—after preaching for a number of years about French music and what must be done to help it—to decide that the best method for defending it is to familiarize the public with the great classics it has produced.[28]

For Quittard, the production was directly aimed at eliminating Rameau's unjust neglect, which the critic viewed as an "injustice" to the French "national art." Furthermore, Quittard suggested that finally Parisian audiences were getting the opportunity to see the merits of French classical music for themselves, rather than merely hearing about its virtues secondhand via critics and musicologists—with the implication being that surely this time around the French would appreciate this great music. For giving them that chance, and for restoring Rameau to his rightful place, Rouché was depicted as a musical patriot.

The critic Edmond Epardaud even more explicitly supported the Rameau production as a nationalist endeavor: "Rouché's production is a sumptuous and charming celebration. It feels as though he wanted to create a dazzling demonstration of our greatest Classical musician, and he has fully succeeded in this laudable endeavor of national glorification."[29] The critic's comments are insightful; critics and audiences alike undoubtedly saw the production as an "endeavor of national glorification," a triumph of French musical styles analogous to its long-awaited military triumph, finally visible on the horizon as German forces began to weaken.

This wartime setting was not without historical precedent, and as with *Hippolyte*, *Castor* was a symbolic choice for the Opéra. As did several of Rameau's operas, the original 1737 version (significantly rewritten in 1754) included a prologue unrelated to the main plot, in which Venus (with the Charities, or Graces) and Minerva (with the Arts) pacify Mars, bringing peace to the world. The allegorical aspects of this prologue would have been immediately obvious to its original listeners: it celebrated the conclusion of the War of the Polish Succession, a political quagmire that—among other conflicts—pitted France against Austria, Prussia, and Saxony.[30] Audiences in 1918 found themselves in a similar situation, once again slowly emerging from a lengthy war against (among others) German-speaking lands. Witnessing the spectacle of these classical deities delivering the earth from warfare—combined with both the emotional weight of French history and the music of the greatest French ancien régime composer—must have been a powerful event indeed.[31]

Whereas the 1908 *Hippolyte* had to some extent buried the work's eighteenth-century origins in favor of a modern antiquity, the 1918 *Castor* reveled in its ancien régime origins—a fact not lost on critics. In a brief note in *Le Matin*, the composer Alfred Bruneau tied the production back to the artistic golden age of the ancien régime, noting that the production "magnificently evoked the glorious era of the French Opéra in the eighteenth century."[32] By making this comparison, Bruneau connects modern France with its historical achievements—which was, of course, always meant to be one of the chief goals of the Operatic Museum. Another critic wrote that the costumes instantly brought to mind the eighteenth century:

Perhaps at first the preference for recreating the anachronistic style of costumes that the actors wore in 1737 was a bit bothersome to audience members in 1918. We could not help being slightly baffled when in front of Castor's tombstone we saw the Spartan women of the mythological era bedecked in ample farthingales, with their hair styled like coquettes out of [the eighteenth-century playwright] Marivaux. . . . This period setting wittily brought out the quaint charms of some pages of the score, and I hasten to add that after the surprise passed, our only thoughts were of admiration.[33]

A quick look at the artist's designs for *Castor* (see fig. 10.4) confirms the eighteenth-century style of the costuming, bombarding the audience with reminders of where and when the work was created. An unnamed critic in the Écho de Paris similarly noted the eighteenth-century styles with relish, opining, "this reconstruction of a spectacle from the time of Louis XV—with hoopskirts, feathers, and plumes—is of an incomparable beauty."[34]

The reviewer identified a similarly historical approach to the music, singling out the conductor for special attention: "We must unreservedly praise Alfred Bachelet for the tact with which he restored the score of *Castor et Pollux*. This conductor of the first order scrupulously respected the original text. He made not a single sacrilegious addition. Bachelet contented himself with discreetly realizing the figured bass recitatives with the strings."[35] Far from the general complaints about the Opéra's modest efforts at historical performance, this critic suggested that any alterations to the score would be "sacrilegious." Clearly, the mindset regarding historical fidelity had shifted somewhat between *Hippolyte* and *Castor*—perhaps not terribly surprising, given the successful "restorations" of Mozart's *Magic Flute* and *Don Giovanni* at the Opéra-Comique during the intervening years.

Despite the strong ancien régime overtones of the 1918 *Castor et Pollux*, critics did not find the work outdated or stylistically incomprehensible, as they had *Hippolyte et Aricie* only a decade before. Louis Schneider's review in *Le Gaulois*, for example, took a nationalistic view of every aspect of the production, including the costumes and sets:

> [*Castor et Pollux*]—which one hundred and thirty-four years of silence has slowly entombed in the dust of oblivion, forgotten—reappears to us full of youth, grace, and beauty. It is to Jacques Rouché, the highly artistic director of the Opéra, that we owe the miracle of this score's rebirth. He has presented it to us not as an object in a museum, or as an archaeological knickknack, but as a living thing, as the triumph of immutable French taste. Let us loudly proclaim from the rooftops this victory of our national arts of music, decor, and costuming; it has been won in full war, in the least favorable conditions that it could have produced; it is all the more brilliant for that.[36]

Figure 10.4. Jacques Drésa's designs for the 1918 *Castor et Pollux* at the Opéra. Courtesy of the Bibliothèque Nationale de France.

In unbridled nationalist rhetoric, Schneider situated Rameau's opera in a historical tradition of great French works. It was a "triumph of immutable French taste," suggesting that Rameau's music contained within it something inherently French that spoke to the nation's people on a fundamental level. Moreover, Schneider implied that the production was a victory over Germany and its musical styles—and one that should be "loudly proclaimed," at that—both because it demonstrated their incomparable skill in their "national arts of music, decor, and costuming" and because it was a wartime triumph, an aesthetic conflict won in the midst of a military one.

Schneider's review also illustrates the differences between the 1918 *Castor et Pollux* and the 1908 *Hippolyte et Aricie* in terms of how *Castor* was perceived as classic. It was not understood as "an object in a museum, or as an archaeological knickknack"—it was a "living" work of art that resonated with modern audiences rather than a dusty relic of a bygone era. The same aspects of the production that had been perceived as hopelessly outdated in 1908 were almost too modernized in 1918. Regarding the changes to the music (adding strings to harpsichord, etc.), for example, Epardaud noted: "Perhaps the scale of the means used led a bit to the distortion of its intimate and quaint graces. And the opera's orchestra definitely neglects the crisp sound of the original harpsichord a bit too much. But in this test of modernization—useful enough, in fact—we must praise the skill and excellent taste of the conductor, Bachelet."[37] For Epardaud, like Schneider, this new production was less a perfectly preserved museum piece than a modernization of a classical work. Though he acknowledged the downside of departing from the original score, the critic found the overall effect of the modernization "useful" and in "excellent taste." Even Jullien, usually a difficult critic to please, was satisfied with the production, which he found a "very skillful sort of compromise between the new art of our time and that of the eighteenth century."[38]

This change in Rameau's presentation is revealing. The 1908 production had aimed at a compromise between historical fidelity and modernization, yet audiences (and many critics) judged it too antiquated. The 1918 *Castor*, on the other hand, was presented much more as a product of the eighteenth century. It had just as few musical capitulations to modern taste—probably fewer, given the questionable editorial practices d'Indy had employed with *Hippolyte*—and yet the critical response was much more positive. Some, like Epardaud, even suggested the Opéra could have gone farther in terms of musical fidelity. Any lingering skepticism of a "historically accurate" performance was outweighed by the political necessity for modern Parisian audiences to enjoy and respond to Rameau's operas as a symbol of French artistic triumph. Critics finally grasped the full potential of the Operatic Museum to shape issues of historical understanding and national identity. *Castor et Pollux* allowed Parisian audiences—broad audiences, not only the select elites who attended the historical performances at smaller venues—to connect France's musical history to its present, creating a much-needed sense of national heritage and pride in the achievements of the eighteenth-century French composer.

The critic Théodore Lindenlaub found the audience for *Castor et Pollux* affected in an atypically personal manner, much more so than any critics reported for previous attempts at reviving Rameau's operas on the fin-de-siècle stage:

> For the diverse crowd of the vast Opéra yesterday, this music was something at once famous and unknown. And, once the curtain fell, when it [the crowd] returned to the street after leaving this sung tragedy, it was the street, and the city, and everything tangible that seemed to them artificial and fragile. A rare victory of order and harmony over that pell-mell of passersby, a sudden and profound revelation of the only reality that exists: the interior life. That is what an old master created in a gathering of people today. Those are the effects and the marks of genius, and this is how they manifested themselves the other day, in the middle of circumstances that were surely the most adverse to such a kind of metamorphosis of the soul. But it is the distinctiveness of genius to position its universe in opposition to the other, and to delight the living.[39]

Rameau reached across the chronological divide and spoke directly to his modern audience, creating a (hyper)reality so profound that it made their own seem drab by comparison. The performance reified the potential of the Operatic Museum—demonstrating both the educative and nationalist aspects of eighteenth-century opera as well as providing concrete evidence that modern audiences could connect with premodern masterworks of French music history. By presenting operagoers with the greatest triumphs of France's musical past, narrating its musical history, the Operatic Museum instilled in listeners a sense of national artistic accomplishment and self-worth in the fiercely patriotic atmosphere of World War I.

Even more than that of Mozart or Gluck, Rameau's French reception from 1875 to 1918 illustrates the remarkable capabilities of the Operatic Museum. Rameau's operas were central in creating and supporting nationalist narratives that affected how Parisian operagoers understood their own history, musical and otherwise. Before 1900, the idea of resurrecting his works on the stage of the Paris Opéra—certainly the most prestigious dramatic venue in France, and arguably in all of Europe—was unthinkable, an idealistic dream espoused by a few naive critics and scholars. Less than two decades later, the second lavish Rameau revival of the twentieth century was widely hailed as a triumph of French musical taste and refinement, and was perceived as one of the greatest musical events of the early twentieth century. The Operatic Museum had not only taken hold in fin-de-siècle France but also had changed the musical culture in profound ways. It nurtured a new concept of the opera house as a space in which works from a variety of historical eras and aesthetic models could coexist comfortably, providing both education and entertainment. Furthermore, the opera house became a place where audiences had to make at least some effort to understand these historical works as a product of their time, rather than having them completely altered to fit modern expectations.

Notes

Introduction

1. Dans le calme logis qu'habite la grand'tante
   Tout rappelle les jours défunts de l'ancien temps,
   La cour au puits sonore et la vieille servante,
   Et les miroirs ternis qui datent de cent ans.

   Le salon a gardé ses tentures de Flandre,
   Où nymphes et bergers dansent au fond des bois;
   Aux heures du soleil couchant, on croit surprendre
   Dans leurs yeux un éclair de l'amour d'autrefois.

   Du coin sombre où sommeille une antique épinette,
   Parfois un long soupir monte et fuit au hasard,
   Comme un écho des jours où, pimpante et jeunette
   La grand'tante y jouait Rameau, Gluck et Mozart.

   Un meuble en bois de rose est au fond de la chambre.
   Ses tiroirs odorants cachent plus d'un trésor:
   Bonbonnières, flacons, sachets d'iris et d'ambre,
   D'où le souffle d'un siècle éteint s'exhale encore.

   Un livre est seul parmi ces reliques fanées,
   Et sous le papier mince et noirci d'un feuillet,
   Une fleur sèche y dort depuis soixante années:
   Le livre, c'est *Zaïre*, et la fleur, un œillet.

   L'été, près de la vitre, avec le vieux volume,
   La grand'tante se fait rouler dans son fauteuil . . .
   Est-ce le clair soleil ou l'air chaud qui rallume
   La couleur de sa joue et l'éclat de son œil?

   Elle penche son front jauni comme un ivoire
   Vers l'œillet, qu'elle a peur de briser dans ses doigts:
   Un souvenir d'amour chante dans sa mémoire,
   Tandis que les pinsons gazouillent sur les toits.

   Elle songe au matin où la fleur fut posée
   Dans le vieux livre noir par la main d'un ami,
   Et ses pleurs vont mouiller ainsi qu'une rosée
   La page où soixante ans l'œillet rouge a dormi.

2. "La Grand'tante" was published in Theuriet's 1874 collection *Le Bleu et le Noir*. This text is taken from André Theuriet, *Poésie de André Theuriet, 1860–1874* (Paris: Lemerre, 1879), 137–38.

3. Robert Gildea, *The Past in French History* (New Haven: Yale University Press, 1994), 119.

4. Pierre Nora, ed. *Les Lieux de mémoire*, 3 vols. (Paris: Gallimard, 1992).

5. For a brief but insightful overview of the relationship between cultural memory and the creation of identity, see John R. Gillis, "Memory and Identity: The History of a Relationship," in *Commemorations: The Politics of National Identity*, ed. John R. Gillis (Princeton: Princeton University Press, 1994), 1–24.

6. As musicologist Anselm Gerhard tells us (with a touch of dramatic hyperbole), after 1871 "all universalist trends in Parisian cultural life came to an abrupt halt, and the 'capital city of the nineteenth century' began its slow decline toward a poorly disguised provincialism." Anselm Gerhard, *The Urbanization of Opera: Music Theater in Paris in the Nineteenth Century*, trans. Mary Whittall (Chicago: University of Chicago Press, 1998), 394.

7. Christophe Charle, "Opera in France, 1870–1914: Between Nationalism and Foreign Imports," trans. Jennifer Boittin, in *Opera and Society in Italy and France from Monteverdi to Bourdieu*, ed. Victoria Johnson, Jane F. Fulcher, and Thomas Ertman (Cambridge: Cambridge University Press, 2007), 243.

8. For an overview of the development of museum culture in France, see Daniel J. Sherman, *Worthy Monuments: Art Museums and the Politics of Culture in Nineteenth-Century France* (Cambridge, MA: Harvard University Press, 1989).

9. David Carrier, "Remembering the Past: Art Museums as Memory Theaters," *Journal of Aesthetics and Art Criticism* 61 (2003): 61. The art historian and museum scholar Donald Preziosi makes a similar point regarding the spectators' self-directed journey through history—we might substitute the process of selecting which operas to attend for the idea of physical motion: "Walking (through) a museum appears to resemble walking through history: we move in and among a succession of objects, pantomiming not only the passage of time but also appearing to exemplify evolutionary changes or even the progressive developments in form, style, invention, value, or mentality. This extraordinary interactive machinery is designed to engage and be operated by its users, who literally (re)enact history and chronology *choreographically*." Donald Preziosi, "Art History and Museology: Rendering the Visible Legible," in *A Companion to Museum Studies*, ed. Sharon Macdonald (Malden, MA: Blackwell, 2006), 50.

Chapter One

1. *La France musicale*, October 27, 1861. "Notre première scène doit être un Louvre lyrique, où les ouvrages classiques, alternant avec nos grandes productions contemporaines, soient la sève fortifiante propre à former une nouvelle génération de compositeurs et d'artistes."

2. After Louis XIV moved the court to Versailles in the 1680s, the Louvre palace became primarily a gallery for displaying the royal art collection. It became a public museum after the Revolution, opening in 1793. Louis XIV founded the Opéra in 1669, making it the oldest permanent opera company in Europe. For more on the history of the Louvre, see Andrew McClellan, *Inventing the Louvre: Art, Politics, and the Origins of*

NOTES TO PP. 8–10   199

the Modern Museum in Eighteenth-Century Paris (Berkeley: University of California Press, 1994).

3. Jean-Pierre Babelon, "The Louvre: Royal Residence and Temple of the Arts," in *Symbols*, ed. Lawrence D. Kritzman, trans. Arthur Goldhammer, vol. 3 of *Realms of Memory: The Construction of the French Past* (New York: Columbia University Press, 1998), 254.

4. Carol Duncan and Alan Wallach, "The University Survey Museum," in *Museum Studies: An Anthology of Contexts*, ed. Bettina Messias Carbonell (Malden, MA: Blackwell, 2004), 64.

5. For an overview of the major theaters in nineteenth-century Paris, see Alicia Levin, "Musical Theaters in Paris, 1830–1900: A Documentary Overview," in *Music, Theater, and Cultural Transfer: Paris, 1830–1914*, ed. Annegret Fauser and Mark Everist (Chicago: University of Chicago Press, 2009), 379–402; and Nicole Wild, *Dictionnaire des théâtres parisiens au XIXe siècle: les théâtres et la musique* (Paris: Aux Amateurs de Livres, 1989). More detailed information about the specific major theaters in this time period may be found in the following: for Opéra and Opéra-Comique, see Patrick Barbier, "Opera in Paris, 1800–1850: A Lively History," trans. Robert Luoma (Portland, OR: Amadeus Press, 1995); for Théâtre Italien, see Janet Lynn Johnson, "The Théâtre Italien and Opera and Theatrical Life in Restoration Paris, 1818–1827," 3 vols. (PhD diss., University of Chicago, 1988); for Théâtre Lyrique, see T. J. Walsh, *Second Empire Opera: The Théâtre Lyrique, Paris, 1851–1870* (New York: Riverrun Press, 1981).

6. Lucien Augé de Lassus, *Saint-Saëns* (Paris: Delgrave, 1914), 132. Quoted (in English) in Hervé Lacombe, *The Keys to French Opera in the Nineteenth Century*, trans. Edward Schneider (Berkeley: University of California Press, 2001), 215.

7. For an overview of the artistic hierarchy of nineteenth-century French opera houses, see Lacombe, *The Keys to French Opera*, particularly chapter 7, "The Parisian Operatic World."

8. *L'Univers musical*, October 31, 1861. "C'est en s'appuyant sur le passé qu'on prend possession de l'avenir. . . .

"Les formes de l'art sont et doivent être sans limites; mais il est nécessaire d'avoir la connaissance parfaite de ce qui a été fait pour arriver à faire autre chose.

"Donc, ouvrez à l'étude les portes du sanctuaire où dorment les vielles gloires dans leur auguste immortalité, et vous donnerez l'essor au génie qui s'ignorait lui-même."

9. Preziosi, "Art History and Museology, 52. Note also Rosalind Krauss's comment that in a traditional museum "One proceeds . . . from space to space along a processional path that ties each of these spaces together, a sort of narrative trajectory with each room the place of a separate chapter, but all of them articulating the unfolding of the master plot." Rosalind E. Krauss, "Postmodernism's Museum Without Walls," in *Thinking about Exhibitions*, ed. Resa Greenberg, Bruce W. Reguson, and Sandy Nairne (London: Routledge, 1996), 242.

10. For an overview of "early music" in France, see Katharine Ellis, *Interpreting the Musical Past: Early Music in Nineteenth-Century France* (Oxford: Oxford University Press, 2005).

11. Concert series that featured "early music" include the Société des Concerts de Chant Classique (founded 1860), the Société Académique de Musique Sacrée (founded 1861), and the Société Sainte-Cécile (founded 1865), to name only three.

12. On early music at the 1889 Exposition Universelle, see Annegret Fauser, *Musical Encounters at the 1889 Paris World's Fair* (Rochester, NY: University of Rochester Press, 2005), 27–42.

13. Lydia Goehr, *The Imaginary Museum of Musical Works* (Oxford: Oxford University Press, 1992).

14. Flora Willson, "Classic Staging: Pauline Viardot and the 1859 *Orphée* Revival," *Cambridge Opera Journal* 22 (2010), 304. On the Théâtre-Lyrique's role, see also Katharine Ellis, "Systems Failure in Operatic Paris: The Acid Test of the Théâtre-Lyrique," in Fauser and Everist, *Music, Theater and Cultural Transfer*, 49–71.

15. *L'Europe artiste*, November 27, 1859. Quoted in Willson, "Classic Staging," 305.

16. The concept of cultural capital permeates many of Bourdieu's works, but perhaps the most straightforward exploration of the idea is in Pierre Bourdieu, *La Distinction: critique sociale du jugement* (Paris: Éditions de Minuit, 1979).

17. Donald Preziosi, "The Art of Art History," in *The Art of Art History: A Critical Anthology* (Oxford: Oxford University Press, 1998), 508. Preziosi returns to this point in a later book chapter: "The museum's function was to provide a space within that of the nation or community whose unity and autonomy both prefigured and was paradigmatic of the projected unity of the nation. At the same time, in juxtaposing subjects vis-à-vis artifacts, the museum provided its citizen-subjects with *exemplary* objects, "object-lessons" of aesthetic, ethical, political, and historical worth: no museum object is mute, but is already entailed with a legend and an address in cultural and historical space-time." Preziosi, "Art History and Museology," 50.

18. Preziosi, "The Art of Art History," 509.

19. For a detailed and insightful contemporary look at the structure of the Palais Garnier, see Charles Nuitter, *Le Nouvel Opéra* (Paris: Hachette, 1875). For a more modern examination of the Opéra's fin-de-siècle importance, see Frederique Patureau, *Le Palais Garnier dans la société parisienne, 1875–1914* (Liège: Mardaga, 1991).

20. Duncan and Wallach, "The University Survey Museum," 53. The authors also point out that "by performing the ritual of walking through the museum, the visitor is prompted to enact and thereby to internalize the values and beliefs written into the architectural script" (48).

21. "L'Opéra n'est pas un théâtre d'essai: il doit être considéré comme le musée de la musique." The *cahiers des charges* are held in the Archives Nationales in Paris, but these alterations were widely commented upon in the press. See, for example, the commentary found in *Le Ménéstrel*, June 29, 1879. The phrase (along with a number of other directives) was removed in 1884 when Jean Ritt and Pedro Gailhard assumed the directorship, much to the dismay of Henri Huegel, publisher of *Le Ménéstrel*, who lambasted the change in the journal in the July 29, 1888, issue (under the pseudonym H. Moreno).

22. Félix Clément, *Histoire de la musique depuis les temps anciens jusqu'à nos jours* (Paris: Hachette, 1885), 520–21. "Combien il est regrettable que l'art de la musique ne soit pas considéré comme les autres arts dont on conserve les chefs-d'œuvre dans les musées et les palais avec tant de soin, de dépense, de prévoyance! Les moindres fragments des statues antiques, les sculptures de Michel-Ange, les tableaux de Raphaël et du Titien ... sont offerts à l'étude, à l'admiration, au jugement du public, des amateurs et des artistes. Les ouvrages de musique qui ont été l'objet de l'enthousiasme de deux ou trois générations, dans lesquels des compositeurs aussi grands que les grands peintres, que les plus parfaits statuaires, ont fait preuve de génie, sont laissés dans l'oubli le plus profond, et disparaissent sous la poudre des bibliothèques ou moisissent sur les quais, sans qu'on se soucie d'en signaler les beautés. On tire des objections de la mobilité du goût du public qui ne supporterait plus un opéra démodé et des formes surannées. Qu'en sait-on? Et d'ailleurs ce n'est pas pour égayer ou distraire la foule qu'un gouvernement maintient les grands établissements consacrés aux beaux-arts, les musées du Louvre, de Cluny,

les manufactures de Sèvres et des Gobelins.... Je demande depuis tant d'années une sorte de théâtre rétrospectif qui soit pour les grands génies de l'art musical ce qu'est le Louvre pour les artistes anciens. Il se formerait un auditoire beaucoup plus nombreux qu'on ne le pense, composé d'une élite d'amateurs, de gens au goût délicat et exercé."

23. *Le Gaulois*, March 24, 1918. "notre art national de la musique, du décor, et du costume."

24. These opera ticket prices are taken from Eugen Weber, *France: Fin de Siècle* (Cambridge, MA: Belknap Press, 1986), 167; the statistic of French population income is taken from Steven Huebner, *French Opera at the Fin de Siècle: Wagnerism, Nationalism, and Style* (Oxford: Oxford University Press, 1999), 2. For an examination of the social makeup of opera audiences in the decades leading up to the fin de siècle, see Huebner's "Opera Audiences in Paris, 1830–1870," *Music and Letters* 70 (1989): 206–25.

25. On the change in the Opéra audience, see Elisabeth Bernard, "L'Évolution du public d'Opéra de 1860 à 1880," in *Regards sur l'opéra: du ballet comique de la reine à l'opéra de Pékin*, ed. Joseph-Marc Bailbé (Paris: Presses Universitaires de France, 1976): 33–46.

26. Jann Pasler, "Material Culture and Postmodern Positivism: Rethinking the 'Popular' in Late Nineteenth-Century French Music," in Jann Pasler, *Writing through Music: Essays on Music, Culture, and Politics* (Oxford: Oxford University Press, 2008), 417–49.

27. Of course, although many French museums were financially accessible to the working classes, that does not mean they were culturally accessible. In the end, most museum attendees were (and are) members of the upper classes regardless of the cost of attendance. See Pierre Bourdieu and Alain Darbel, with Dominique Schnapper, *The Love of Art: European Art Museums and Their Public*, trans. Caroline Beattie and Nick Merriman (Stanford: Stanford University Press, 1990).

28. For details on the extensive exportation of French opera during this time period, see Charle, "Opera in France," 252–58.

29. Daniel J. Sherman, "Objects of Memory: History and Narrative in French War Museums," *French Historical Studies* 19, no. 1 (Spring 1995), 52–53.

30. For specifics of the Opéra's programming, see Charles Dupêchez, *Histoire de l'Opéra de Paris: Un siècle au Palais Garnier* (Paris: Librairie Académique Perrin, 1984).

31. Ellis, *Interpreting the Musical Past*, 120.

32. Ibid., 168. For a discussion of the *Jeu* in nineteenth-century France, see pages 164–70.

33. *Revue hebdomadaire*, August 1894. Reprinted in Paul Dukas, *Les écrits de Paul Dukas sur la musique* (Paris: Société d'éditions françaises et internationales, 1948), 192. "Nous n'osons pas demander que l'Opéra tente la reconstitution d'un des chefs-d'œuvre de Rameau puisqu'il est déjà impossible d'obtenir que Gluck soit représenté au répertoire de ce théâtre qui devrait être, cependant, de par son titre et sa fastueuse subvention, comme le Louvre de la musique."

34. *Revue hebdomadaire*, September 1896. Reprinted in Dukas, *Les Écrits de Paul Dukas sur la musique*, 343. "Voici déjà plusieurs années que nous n'avions eu *Don Juan*. Il n'y a peut-être qu'en France qu'on voit de ces longues éclipses des chefs-d'œuvre de la musique dont personne ne songe à se formaliser. Supposez que demain on remise dans les greniers du Louvre certaines toiles de Rembrandt ou de Velasquez. Le beau tapage! Mais qu'on ait proscrit du répertoire de nos scènes lyriques *Freischütz, Fidelio, Alceste, Armide, Iphigénie*, les *Troyens*, etc., etc., qui donc y prend garde?"

35. *Le Figaro*, February 1, 1898. "L'Opéra-Comique devrait être une sorte de musée du répertoire lyrique, comme la Comédie-Française l'est du répertoire dramatique;

il serait même convenable de l'augmenter en puisant plus qu'on ne l'a fait dans les œuvres de Lulli, Rameau, Gluck, Mozart, Méhul, Grétry." Philippe Blay examines these articles as well as the role of the Opéra-Comique in fin-de-siècle Paris in his "'Un théâtre français, tout à fait français,' ou un débat fin-de-siècle sur l'Opéra-Comique," *Revue de musicologie* 87 (2001): 105–44.

36. *Chronique des Arts et de la Curiosité*, November 1896. Reprinted in Dukas, *Les Écrits de Paul Dukas sur la musique*, 353. "Ne devraient-elles par alterner, d'une façon courante, avec les ouvrages modernes et former le fond du répertoire de l'Opéra et de l'Opéra-Comique, comme on voit à la Comédie Française Racine, Corneille et Molière faire les lendemains de Dumas, d'Augier et de M. Pailleron?"

37. *Le Figaro*, May 14, 1908. "Les théâtres subventionnés inscrivent les œuvres à leur répertoire, comme sont inscrites au répertoire de la Comédie-Française et de l'Odéon les œuvres de Corneille, de Racine, de Molière. Cette égalité de traitement envers nos gloires passées, ne serait-ce pas l'équité même? Et la culture de notre individualité nationale n'aurait-elle pas tout à y gagner?"

38. Benedict Anderson, *Imagined Communities: Reflections on the Origin and Spread of Nationalism*, rev. ed. (London: Verso, 1991), 6, 178.

39. Pierre Bourdieu, "The Historical Genesis of a Pure Aesthetic," trans. Charles Newman, in *The Field of Cultural Production: Essays on Art and Literature*, ed. Randal Johnson (New York: Columbia University Press, 1993), 260.

Chapter Two

1. *La Revue et gazette musicale de Paris*, December 5, 1875. "A présent que l'admiration pour *Don Juan* est devenue un article de foi de la religion musicale, et que celui-là se ferait généralement honnir qui méconnaîtrait dans ces ouvrage l'une des plus éclatantes manifestations du génie, il est curieux de se reporter au temps de l'apparition des ouvrages de Mozart en France et de voir quel triste accueil ils reçurent."

2. *Les Arts de la vie*, January 1904. "Jusqu'au dernier quart du XIXe siècle, Mozart passa, dans l'opinion des dilettantes, pour le génie souverain de la musique, et, comme celui de Raphaël en peinture, son nom devint presque dogmatiquement synonyme de perfection, de grâce et d'idéal inégalables. . . . Le culte de Beethoven, suivi du culte de Wagner, allait bientôt ébranler cet article de foi. Devant les mondes formidables que ces deux génies, tardivement reconnus, découvrirent aux amateurs de grand art, on oublia le musicien de Salzbourg."

3. Such changes were typical and were expected of any updated or imported operatic works through most of the nineteenth century. One example analogous to the alterations to Mozart's operas is the French reception of Weber's *Der Freischütz*, which was heavily altered and retitled *Robin des Bois* in Paris. A discussion of the origins and circumstances surround this version may be found in Annegret Fauser, "Phantasmagorie im deutschen Wald? Zur 'Freischütz'-Rezeption in London und Paris 1824," in *Deutsche Meister-böse Geister? Nationale Selbstfindung in der Musik*, ed. Hermann Danuser and Herfried Münkler (Schleigen: Argus, 2001), 245–73.

4. For a thorough discussion of the alterations to Mozart's score that took place in early Parisian performances of *Le Nozze di Figaro*, see Sherwood Dudley, "Les Premières versions françaises du *Mariage de Figaro* de Mozart," *Revue de musicologie* 69 (1983): 55–83.

5. *Journal de Paris*, March 22, 1793. "La pièce a été trouvée excessivement longue, et... dans les derniers actes les plus beaux morceaux de musique ne produisoient plus d'effet." Reprinted in Belinda Cannone, *La Réception des opéras de Mozart dans la presse parisienne (1793–1829)* (Paris: Klincksieck, 1991), 145.

6. For a detailed look at this production, see Rudolph Angermüller, "*Les mystères d'Isis* (1801) und *Don Juan* (1805, 1834) auf der Bühne der Pariser Oper," *Mozart-Jahrbuch* (1980–83): 32–97.

7. For a plot summary of *Les mystères*, see Cannone, *La Réception des opéras de Mozart dans la presse parisienne*, 56–58. See also Jean Mongrédien, "*Les Mystères d'Isis* (1801) and Reflections on Mozart from the Parisian Press at the Beginning of the Nineteenth Century," in *Music in the Classic Period: Essays in Honor of Barry S. Brook*, ed. Allan W. Atlas (New York: Pendragon Press, 1985), 202.

8. Jullien, *Paris dilettante*, 124. "et franchement, ce n'était pas trop tôt."

9. Jean Mongrédien has demonstrated the existence of a French published version of the overture to *Don Giovanni* dating from 1795, but there is no evidence regarding its public performance. Jean Mongrédien, *French Music from the Enlightenment to Romanticism, 1789–1830*, trans. Sylvain Frémaux (Portland, OR: Amadeus Press, 1996), 324. This production has recently been the subject of an edifying and detailed study: Laurent Marty, *1805, La création de Don Juan à l'Opéra de Paris* (Paris: Harmattan, 2005). In addition to his meticulously documented analysis of this seminal staging, Marty helpfully includes the entire text of the French libretto as an appendix.

10. For details on the adaptation of Mozart's score, see Marty, *1805, La création de Don Juan*, 115–80.

11. Adolphe Jullien, *Paris dilettante au commencement du siècle* (Paris: Firmin-Didot, 1884), 131. "Un seul morceau était resté en sa place, un seul, et ce morceau, c'était l'ouverture."

12. *Journal de l'Empire*, September 19–20, 1805. One of the more damning passages—penned by Julien-Louis Geoffroy—is: "Il y a trop de musique dans *Don Juan*; c'est un festin ou l'extrême abondance rassasie promptement: les morceaux d'ensemble sont tellement multipliés, ils sont se pleins et si forts, que les auditeurs se trouvent pour ainsi dire écrasés sous le poids de l'harmonie... Les Allemands ont un plus grand appétit et un estomac plus robuste que les Français; ils sont insatiables de musique et d'harmonie... L'enthousiasme des Allemands pour le *Don Juan* de Mozart n'était donc pas un sûr garant qu'il devait produire en France."

13. *Courrier de l'Europe et des spectacles*, December 25, 1807. Reprinted in Cannone, *La réception des opéras de Mozart*, 274. "comment ce même ouvrage, donné il y a quelques années à l'Opéra, a obtenu si peu de succès?"

14. *Journal de l'Empire*, January 27, 1808. Reprinted in Cannone, *La réception des opéras de Mozart*, 271. "Un grand nombre d'opéras comiques de Grétry, *la Colonie* de Sacchini, *la Bonne Fille* de Piccini, plusieurs même des opéras bouffons joués sur le théâtre de l'Impératrice, sont supérieurs au *Figaro* de Mozart; mais les disciples de l'école allemande n'admettent pas même de comparaison."

15. Jullien, *Paris dilettante*, 107. "Cette représentation des *Nozze* à l'Opéra-Italien établit définitivement chez nous la réputation du grand musicien."

16. *Journal de l'Empire*, January 27, 1809. Reprinted in Cannone, *La Réception des opéras de Mozart*, 291. "Tout ce qu'a fait Mozart est sûr de plaire à Paris: c'est le musicien à la mode"; *Courrier de l'Europe et des spectacles*, February 3, 1809. Reprinted in Cannone, *La Réception des opéras de Mozart*, 296. "Quant on nomme Mozart, on a aussitôt l'idée de tout ce que la musique a de plus parfait."

17. Pauline Girard, "*Don Giovanni* au Théâtre-Italien, 1811–1877," in *Don Juan*, exhibition catalogue (Paris: Bibliothèque Nationale, April 25–July 5, 1991), 193.

18. *Journal de l'Empire*, October 15, 1811. "Il y a plusieurs années que ce Don Juan, traduit en Français, fut joué au grand Opéra; malgré la vogue de Mozart, l'effet fut médiocre: le chef-d'œuvre fut admiré en bâillant, et bientôt abandonné. Les enthousiastes ne manquèrent pas de rejeter toute la faute sur l'exécution; ils prétendirent qu'on avoit massacré Mozart; ils crièrent au sacrilège. Voici le même Don Juan représenté en italien à l'Opéra-Buffa [Théâtre-Italien] par une troupe excellente; et l'ennui, fidèle compagnon de ce chef-d'œuvre, s'obstine encore à le suivre jusque sur le théâtre où l'on devait lui rendre la plus éclatante justice." Reprinted in Cannone, *La Réception des opéras de Mozart*, 306. For more on Geoffroy's views of Mozart, see Katharine Ellis, "A Dilettante at the Opera: Issues in the Criticism of Julien-Louis Geoffroy, 1800–1814," in *Reading Critics Reading: Opera and Ballet Criticism in France from the Revolution to 1848*, ed. Roger Parker and Mary Ann Smart (Oxford: Oxford University Press, 2001), 46–68.

19. *Journal de Paris*, October 13, 1811. "Le poème de cet opéra est, comme la plupart des productions italiennes de ce genre, un tissu d'invraisemblances bizarres: c'est le *Festin de Pierre*, non pas traduit, mais travesti." Reprinted in Cannone, *La Réception des opéras de Mozart*, 309.

20. Mark Everist, *Music Drama at the Paris Odéon, 1824–1828* (Berkeley: University of California Press, 2002), 160. For a plot summary of the fascinating pasticcio, see pp. 159–60.

21. Letter to Louise Colet, October 3, 1846. Quoted in Girard, "*Don Giovanni* au Théâtre-Italien," 197. "Les trois plus belles choses que Dieu a faites, c'est la mer, l'*Hamlet* et le *Don Juan* de Mozart."

22. Girard, "*Don Giovanni* au Théâtre-Italien," 194.

23. *Revue musicale* 2 (1828): 151. Quoted in Girard, "*Don Giovanni* au Théâtre-Italien," 194. "Garcia donna au rôle principal une physionomie dont le souvenir restera longtemps dans la mémoire des musiciens comme le type de la perfection."

24. Katharine Ellis, "Rewriting *Don Giovanni*, or 'The Thieving Magpies,'" *Journal of the Royal Musical Association* 119 (1994), 213. This article also contains an analysis of the changes to the opera's characters as well as a fascinating look at the critical reception of the production.

25. Ibid., 232.

26. Martine Kahane, "Don Juan à l'Opéra," in *Don Juan*, exhibition catalogue (Paris: Bibliothèque Nationale, April 25–July 5, 1991), 212.

27. Walsh, *Second Empire Opera*, 91.

28. Ibid., 191.

29. Jullien, *Paris dilettante*, 138.

30. Girard, "Don Giovanni au Théâtre-Italien," 197.

31. *Le Ménestrel*, May 13, 1866. "Puisque c'est une lutte, puisque c'est un duel, à qui est resté l'avantage? Si tout est bien qui finit bien, c'est l'Opéra qui la emporté avec l'admirable scène finale; mais pendant tout la première moitié de la soirée, et même au-delà, on s'accordait généralement à donner la victoire au Théâtre-Lyrique."

32. Ibid. "Faure, qui chant *Don Juan* comme personne, qui tient le rôle avec autorité, distinction, élégance."

33. Hoffmann's romantic ideas about music, and in particularly his Mozart criticism became known in France in the 1820s and 1830s, at least partially as a result of the success there of Weber's *Der Freischütz* (known in France as *Robin des Bois*). Castil-Blaze was an early proponent of Hoffmann in France, adopting many of Hoffmann's perspectives

on Mozart's music. Annegret Fauser has pointed out that "*Robin des Bois* scheint 1824 in Paris eine Katalysator-Funktion angenommen und den Weg für eine Französische Rezeption der deutschen Romantik und gerade auch von E. T. A. Hoffmann geebnet zu haben, die sich langsam anzubahnen begann und erst in den 1830er Jahren gänzlich entfaltete. Castil-Blaze gehörte schon früh zu jenen französischen Intellektuellen, die Hoffmanns Werk rezipierten, und seine Hoffmann-Verehrung kam schließlich zehn Jahre später in einer anderen Bearbeitung, nämlich der von Mozarts *Don Giovanni* voll zum tragen." Fauser, "Phantasmagorie im deutschen Wald?" 268.

34. For a more thorough discussion of Mozart's place in literary romanticism, see Gernot Gruber, *Mozart and Posterity*, trans. R. S. Furness (Boston: Northeastern University Press, 1994), particularly ch. 2.

35. Mark Everist, "Enshrining Mozart: *Don Giovanni* and the Viardot Circle," *19th-Century Music* 25 (2001–2): 165–89. Interestingly, Viardot was the daughter of Manuel Garcia, whose memorable performances of the lead role in *Don Giovanni* in the 1820s may have made his daughter an even more suitable choice to be Mozart's Parisian champion.

36. Gerhard, *The Urbanization of Opera*, 394.

37. Katharine Ellis, "Rewriting *Don Giovanni*," 214.

38. *Le Ménestrel*, March 24, 1861. "nos chefs-d'œuvres... notre *Guillame Tell*, notre *Don Juan*, notre *Lucie*, notre *Juive*, nos *Huguenots*."

39. Jullien, *Paris dilettante*, 380–82.

40. Quoted in Kahane, "Don Juan à l'Opéra," 215. "Quant à la fête chez don Juan, avec ses quadrilles masqués, ses costumes renouvelés de l'ancienne Comédie Italienne, ses ballets défilant et se trémoussant sur le rythme entraînant da la marche turque au milieu d'un torrent de lumière et dans la profondeur immense du théâtre, on n'imagine pas un pareil spectacle, éblouissant ne suffit pas; c'est surtout très amusant par le miroitement des étoffes, le pittoresque et la variété des groupes."

41. *Le Ménestrel*, December 5, 1875.

42. Ibid., September 25, 1887. "Mon Dieu, l'Opéra l'avait délaissé depuis quelques années, cet incomparable chef-d'œuvre.... On l'aimait sans doute, mais d'un amour purement platonique.... C'était un ancêtre respecté, auquel on donnait la meilleure place... dans la bibliothèque, mais pour lequel on ne se souciait pas d'allumer les quinquets."

43. Ibid., October 30, 1887. "La célébration du centenaire de *Don Juan* à Paris a été ce qu'elle devait être avec les ressources actuelles de notre Académie nationale de musique, rien autre qu'une aimable parodie du chef-d'œuvre de Mozart. Il faut avouer que les directeurs de l'Opéra ont une façon singulière de *célébrer* les gens; heureusement que les morts ne sortent pas de leur tombeau!"

44. *Le Temps*, October 31, 1887. "On peut prévoir ce que je suis obligé de dire de l'exécution."

45. Charles Gounod, *Mozart's* Don Giovanni: *A Commentary*, trans. Windeyer Clark and J. T. Hutchinson (New York: Da Capo, 1970), vi. Translation amended.

46. Ibid., 60.

47. Reprinted in Adolphe Jullien, *Musique: mélanges d'histoire et de critique musical et dramatique* (Paris: Librairie de l'Art, 1896), 281–82. "M. Gounod, désespéré de voir les journaux ne rien dire de lui tandis qu'on parle encore et toujours de Richard Wagner, appelle Mozart à la rescousse."

48. Ibid., 295. "Conclusion: ce livre de rhétorique enfantine et rempli de prétendue explications contre les quelles Mozart se révolterait ne peut être d'aucune utilité,

ni pour ceux que admirent *Don Juan* et qui s'en font une idée beaucoup plus juste à [l'œuvre], ni pour ceux qui ne le goûtent guère et que cette exégèse interminable éloignerait plutôt du maître."

49. For more on Gounod's quasi-religious idolization of Mozart's music, as well as an insightful deconstruction of several passages from Gounod's *Don Juan* text, see Gérard Condé, "Mozart et Gounod," in *Présence du XVIIIe siècle dans l'opéra français du XIXe siècle d'Adam à Massenet*, ed. Jean-Christophe Branger and Vincent Giroud (Saint Étienne: Université de Saint-Étienne, 2011), 121–36.

50. Huebner, *French Opera at the Fin de Siècle*, 202.

51. *Revue hebdomadaire*, September 1896. Reprinted in Dukas, *Les Écrits de Paul Dukas sur la musique*, 343. "Voici déjà plusieurs années que nous n'avions eu *Don Juan*. Il n'y a peut-être qu'en France qu'on voit de ces longues éclipses des chefs-d'œuvre de la musique dont personne ne songe à se formaliser. Supposez que demain on remise dans les greniers du Louvre certaines toiles de Rembrandt ou de Velasquez. Le beau tapage! Mais qu'on ait proscrit du répertoire de nos scènes lyriques *Freischütz*, *Fidelio*, *Alceste*, *Armide*, *Iphigénie*, les *Troyens*, etc., etc., qui donc y prend garde? *Don Juan* était au nombre de ces partitions frappées d'ostracisme. Il sera remis à son rang, et nul ne s'en plaindra. Et nous aurons même deux *Don Juan* au lieu d'un, l'Opéra et l'Opéra-Comique se disputant à présent la gloire de nous rendre le chef-d'œuvre de Mozart, lequel doit sans doute être bien ébahi de ce regain d'enthousiasme. Ainsi va le monde: vieux ou jeunes, morts ou vifs, on ne vous jouera point, à moins qu'on ne vous joue trop."

52. *L'Europe artiste*, November 22, 1896. "Mozart est joué, chanté, louangé à Paris en cette fin d'année 1896: l'Académie de Musique reprenait *Don Juan* il y a quelques jours, l'Opéra-Comique le donne cette semaine, et l'Exposition du Théâtre et de la Musique offrait à ses spectateurs de mardi dernier une Conférence sur Mozart enfant, suivie d'un acte en vers: *Mozart enfant*. Mozart est donc en relief, et nous en profitons pour lui décerner nous-même un hommage dans nos colonnes."

53. *Chronique des Arts et de la Curiosité*, November 1896. Reprinted in Dukas, *Les Écrits de Paul Dukas sur la musique*, 353. "On sait que les plus authentiques chefs-d'œuvre de l'art musical ne sont pas, dans nos théâtres, exécutés aussi couramment qu'on le pourrait supposer: ils subissent des éclipses dont il est permis de déplorer la fréquence. La reprise de l'*Orphée* de Gluck a été l'an dernier un événement retentissant et la représentation presque simultanée de *Don Juan*, de Mozart, à l'Opéra et à l'Opéra-Comique, au début de la présente saison, a pris une importance qui doit appeler l'attention sur la désinvolture avec laquelle on traite les maîtres classiques; leurs œuvres essentielles devaient-elles jamais quitter, pour un si long temps, la scène? Est-il admissible qu'elles y reprennent rang tous les dix ans environ, pour une série de quelques exécutions, après lesquelles on n'en entend plus parler? Ne devraient-elles par alterner, d'une façon courante, avec les ouvrages modernes et former le fond du répertoire de l'Opéra et de l'Opéra-Comique, comme on voit à la Comédie Française Racine, Corneille et Molière faire les lendemains de Dumas, d'Augier et de M. Pailleron?"

54. Anya Suschitzky has pointed out the ways in which, because of its "clarity" and "lightness"—two terms that Dukas and others found in abundance in Mozart's operas—Dukas's opera *Ariane et Barbe-Bleue* (1907) was received as a continuation of French classicism and Rameau's music in particular (see chapter 4 for more on Dukas's connection to Rameau). Anya Suschitzky, "*Ariane et Barbe-Bleue*: Dukas, the Light, and the Well," *Cambridge Opera Journal* 9 (1997): 133–61.

55. Kahane, "Don Juan à l'Opéra," 215.

56. Quoted in ibid. "Sauf l'air *Ah! fuggi traditore*, remplacé par un autre, écrit pour l'Elvire de Vienne, sauf l'air de don Juan (*Metà di voi*), coupé comme inutile, sauf celui de Leporello (*Ah! pietà, Signori*), biffé comme faisant longueur, sauf un grand ballet, construit de pièces et de morceaux, introduit, de force, dans le premier finale, sauf un air de ténor (*Dalla sua pace*), transformé en air de clarinette pour servir le lever de rideau, sauf le dénouement qui a été changé, sauf les récitatifs originaux remplacé par ceux de Castil-Blaze, sauf enfin quelques autres modifications, de tout aussi peu d'importance, la partition est maintenant absolument intacte."

57. As Katharine Ellis reminds us, this conflict between "authentic" and "inauthentic" version of *Don Giovanni* was nothing new; similar arguments took place in the 1830s, as the Blaze-Deschamps version struggled to gain acceptance. Eventually, however, it (or some variation thereof) became the standard version and by the 1870s was well established as the "authentic" French *Don Juan*. Ellis, "Rewriting *Don Giovanni*."

58. *Le Ménestrel*, December 5, 1875. "Quelques esprits chagrins persistent pourtant à ne pas retrouver à l'Opéra français leur *Don Juan* italien. Ils ajoutent que l'œuvre y est devenue trop grande, trop importante, trop prétentieuse, que les mouvements en sont trop larges, trop lents, et que la gaieté, l'esprit et la verve disparaissent finalement du chef-d'œuvre de Mozart,—tel qu'on le représente à notre grand Opéra.

"Il est évident qu'en changeant le cadre de la sublime partition de Mozart, on a dû en élargir le dessin, mais est-on bien sûr que le style de *Don Juan* ne soit pas au contraire plus à l'aise dans le grand cadre de l'Opéra? Je parierais volontiers pour l'affirmative. Ce n'est pas que j'approuve, en principe, les tendances regrettables de l'Opéra à ralentir indéfiniment les récits et la plupart des morceaux de tous nos chefs-d'œuvre lyriques, mais j'incline à croire qu'à part ce juste reproche,—applicable à tout le répertoire de l'Opéra,—la partition de *Don Juan* perdrait à être interprétée dans les conditions italiennes sur notre première scène lyrique française. C'est du moins mon humble opinion."

59. Camille Saint-Saëns, *Outspoken Essays on Music*, trans. Fred Rothwell (London: Paul, Trench, and Trubner; New York: Dutton, 1922), 159.

60. Kahane, "*Don Juan* à l'Opéra," 217. "une demande pressante des amateurs pour un autre type de production, conforme à la version originale."

61. *Le Figaro*, December 18, 1903. "l'interpretation [était] alerte, légère, tendre, pathétique ou dramatique, totalement exempte de l'insupportable accent de solennité dont on aloudit, d'ordinaire, ce chef-d'œuvre, sous prétexte de le mieux honorer." This passage is also briefly discussed in relationship to Fauré's thoughts on German music in Nicole Labelle, "Gabriel Fauré: Music Critic for *Le Figaro*," in *Regarding Fauré*, ed. and trans. Tom Gordon (Amsterdam: Gordon and Breach, 1999), 24.

62. *Musica*, November 1904.

63. *Le Figaro*, October 29, 1904. "L'Opéra reprenait hier soir *Don Juan*, c'est-à-dire un *Don Juan* spécial à l'Académie national de musique et qui diffère, hélas, de *Don Giovanni* . . . sur bien d'autre points que le remplacement d'un texte italien par un texte français, un *Don Juan* amplifié, parce qu'il était nécessaire qu'il occupât la soirée entière, et solennisé parce que, de tout temps, nous avons marqué une propension à entourer les chefs-d'œuvre d'une pompe qu'ils ne réclament point.

"Énumérer les travestissements qu'a subis le *Don Giovanni* de Mozart serait trop long. Rechercher les causes multiples de ces travestissements aboutirait à des conclusions peu flatteuses pour notre goût."

64. *Le Figaro*, November 6, 1904. Fauré complained: "Neither is this *Don Juan* [at the Opéra-Comique] the *Don Giovanni* that only perfect Italian singers can restore to us.

However, thanks to a stage with limited proportions that permits one to impress on the action a less solemn allure, thanks to a hall where the music can spread out without losing its charm or emotion, the Opéra-Comique's *Don Juan* comes appreciably closer to Mozart's original work than the Opéra's *Don Juan*." [Ce *Don Juan* n'est pas non plus le *Don Giovanni* que, seuls, de parfaits chanteurs italiens pourraient nous restituer. Cependant, à la faveur d'une scène de proportions restreintes et qui permet d'imprimer à l'action une allure moins solennelle, à la faveur d'une salle où la musique se répand sans rien perdre de son charme ne de son émotion, le *Don Juan* de l'Opéra-Comique se rapproche plus sensiblement de l'œuvre primitive de Mozart que le *Don Juan* de l'Opéra.]

65. For a brief discussion of the influence of Fauré's education at the École Niedermeyer and his musical dependence on musical traditions, see Carlo Caballero, *Fauré and French Musical Aesthetics* (Cambridge: Cambridge University Press, 2001), 71–75. On Fauré's reforms as director of the Conservatoire, see Gail Hilson Woldu, "Gabriel Fauré as Director of the Conservatoire National de Musique et de Declamation, 1905–1920" (PhD diss., Yale University, 1983).

66. Fauré was certainly not the only fin-de-siècle composer to be influenced by eighteenth-century dance forms, which came into vogue during this time. Debussy, Ravel, Chausson, Saint-Saëns, and d'Indy, among a myriad of others, composed works in genres such as minuets, gavottes, passepieds, and so on. On this topic, see Jann Pasler, *Composing the Citizen: Music and Public Utility in Third Republic France* (Berkeley: University of California Press, 2009), 501–7. See also Scott Messing, *Neoclassicism in Music: From the Genesis of the Concept through the Schoenberg/Stravinsky Polemic* (Rochester, NY: University of Rochester Press, 1996), ch. 1. Fauré's reference is in a letter to his wife Marie Fauré, dated April 14, 1919. Reprinted in Gabriel Fauré, *Gabriel Fauré: A Life in Letters*, trans. and ed. J. Barrie Jones (London: B. T. Batsford, 1988), 181.

67. Fauré, Letter to Marie Fauré, April 14, 1919. Reprinted in *Gabriel Fauré: A Life in Letters*, 181.

68. *Le Courier musical*, April 15, 1906. "Je souhaite surtout que cette démonstration pique le zèle de M. Albert Carré qui, dans son répertoire, remplacerait avec avantage le *Domino Noir* par *Don Juan*, *Mignon* par les *Noces*, *Mireille* par la *Flûte enchantée*, les *Dragons de Villars* par la *Flûte enchantée*, et *Fra Diavolo* par *Così fan tutti*." It seems likely that Chantavoine intended this passage to replace *Les Dragons de Villars* with *The Abduction from the Seraglio* rather than listing *The Magic Flute* twice.

69. Albert Carré, *Souvenirs de théâtre* (Paris: Plon, 1950), 325–26. "avec un orchestre réduit aux proportions de celui que dirigeait Mozart à Prague, le 29 octobre 1787." A fairly detailed list of Hahn's alterations to the score appeared in the *nouvelles* of *Le Ménestrel*, April 13, 1912. A brief notice in the *Journal des débats* (May 1, 1912) reveals the novelty of Hahn's conception: "Last night the Opéra-Comique held the dress rehearsal of Mozart's *Don Juan* as the composer wrote it. M. Reynaldo Hahn directed the orchestra; the recitatives were accompanied at the piano. Finally, the work ended after the disappearance of Don Juan; all the characters appeared on stage, searching for Don Juan and expressing their joy at the punishment that he received." [Le théâtre de l'Opéra-Comique a donné hier la répétition générale du *Don Juan* de Mozart tel que le compositeur l'avait écrit. M. Reynaldo Hahn a dirigé l'orchestre; les récitatifs ont été accompagnés au piano. Enfin la pièce se termine plus sur la disparition de Don Juan; tous les personnages apparaissent sur la scène, cherchant Don Juan et exprimant leur joie du châtiment qu'il a reçu.]

70. Carré, *Souvenirs de théâtre*, 325–26. "*Don Juan*, trois ans plus tard, fut présenté pour la première fois à Paris dans sa forme originale et intégrale. . . .

"L'Opéra, en 1934, représenta à nouveau *Don Juan* sous cette forme, mais l'auteur de cette nouvelle version, M. Adolphe Boschot, ayant proclamé que c'était la première restitution intégrale de l'œuvre en France, je fus bien obligé de le démentir, d'autant plus qu'en 1928 j'avais remonté au Conservatoire, avec M. Henri Rabaud qui conduisait l'orchestre, le *Don Juan* donné à l'Opéra-Comique avec un retentissant succès."

71. *Le Ménestrel*, May 4, 1912. "parmi les innovations—ou les restitutions, comme on voudra—il en est une dont je ne suis nullement partisan: c'est celle qui consiste, après la foudroiement de Don Juan, à faire revenir sur la scène tous les personnages du drame, qui depuis longtemps ont disparu, et à leur faire entonner un ensemble final qui n'a que faire avec une action dûment terminée. Cela rappelle le "couplet au public" qui, jadis, servait en quelque sorte de moralité dans les anciens vaudevilles, et, n'en déplaise à la mémoire de D'Aponte [*sic*] et de Mozart, cela est parfaitement ridicule au point de vue scénique. Jamais Molière n'aurait eu une idée aussi burlesque."

72. *La Revue musicale S.I.M.*, May 15, 1912. "Mais que sont ces menues imperfections en regard de la masse énorme de choses nouvelles,—ou plutôt heureusement renouvelées d'après la partition originale,—dont nous voici redevable à la providentielle collaboration "mozartienne" de MM. R. Hahn et Albert Carré? Un orchestre réduit à ses proportions naturelles, les dernières scènes du second finale rappelées à la vie après plus d'un siècle de complet abandon . . . la division primitive en deux actes scrupuleusement conservée (tout au moins sur le programme et en théorie), et l'installation de trois petits orchestres "reels" au au milieu des danseurs, dans le premier finale: autant de véritables victoires remportées désormais sur une tradition le plus souvent imbécile, sans compter vingt autres victoires moins apparentes, peut-être, mais mieux faites encore pour émouvoir délicieusement toute âme qui se soucie de goûter le pur et subtil parfum du génie de Mozart. A quoi j'ajouterai que, pour ne rien dire de l'excellente tenue de l'orchestre sous la direction personnelle de M. Hahn, l'interprétation des rôles atteste un progrès considérable sur celles où le même théâtre nous avait naguère habitués."

73. Ibid. "Que si maintenant l'on me demandait mon opinion sur les résultats pratiques et les probabilités d'avenir de cette admirable reprise de *Don Juan*, j'aurais à émettre le pronostic le plus pessimiste. Car je suis à peu près certain que, cette fois encore, le chef-d'œuvre de Mozart disparaîtra bientôt de la scène de l'Opéra-Comique,—tout de même qu'en a disparu, l'année dernière, la *Flûte enchantée*. De nouveau, le public ne tardera pas à se lasser de *Don Juan*, ce qui achèvera de confirmer les directeurs dans la croyance,—absolument erronée,—qu'il n'y a plus de vie possible, chez nous, pour la génie dramatique de Mozart. Et pourquoi? Parce que *Don Juan*, avec toute sa beauté immortelle, est une pièce vieille de plus d'un siècle, et qui, cela étant, ne saurait nous être présentée de la même façon qu'une pièce écrite aujourd'hui pour nous. . . .

"Voilà ce que nos directeurs de théâtres musicaux semblent ne pas vouloir comprendre, au grand détriment de leurs propres efforts et de la gloire des maîtres anciens! C'est ainsi que *Don Juan*, sur l'affiche, ne comporte que deux actes: en réalité, il nous condamne à subir, en plus du grand entracte régulier, une demi-douzaine d'entractes un peu plus courts, mais, tout de même, bien ennuyeux pour des auditeurs qui ne sont pas encouragés à la patience par la curiosité de découvrir ce qui va ensuite leur être montré sur la scène. Le premier finale, par exemple se trouve coupé, après le *trio des masques*, d'une façon qui en altère l'unité musicale. Au second acte, nous devons attendre dix minutes le petit *duo du cimetière*, puis de nouveau dix minutes l'air,—si fâcheux au point de vue dramatique, il faut bien l'avouer!—de Dona Anna; et, après cet air, dix minutes encore d'attente avant d'être admis à la jouissance du second finale. Et que l'on n'allègue pas que ces petits arrêts ne sont pas de véritables 'entractes,' parce que l'on est invité à ne pas bouger de sa place! J'affirme, au contraire, que cet obligation d'attendre sur place est pour nous, inconsciemment, plus agaçante encore qu'un entracte où nous pouvons échanger nos impressions avec des amis. Je l'ai bien vu à la répétition générale: tout autour de moi, à partir du milieu du second acte, des auditeurs commençaient par relire leurs programmes,—durant l'un ou l'autre de ces désastreux arrêts,—et puis, machinalement, fatigués d'attendre, ils prenaient leur chapeau et s'en allaient chez soi."

Chapter Three

1. Letter to A. W. Schlegel, July 23, 1796. This translation from the German is (ironically) taken from Wolfram Wilss, *The Science of Translation: Problems and Methods* (Tubingen: Gunter Narr, 1982), 35.

2. *Le Ménestrel*, February 26, 1865. "fidèle et dévoué restaurateur de Glück, de Weber et de Mozart."

3. Ibid. "L'appropriation nouvelle est aussi convenable et agreeable que possible; nous voudrions seulement que MM. Nuitter et Beaumont resserrassent encore davantage leur dialogue."

4. David J. Levin, *Unsettling Opera: Staging Mozart, Verdi, Wagner, and Zemlinsky* (Chicago: University of Chicago Press, 2007), 75.

5. Lawrence Venuti, "Translation, Community, Utopia," in *The Translation Studies Reader*, ed. Lawrence Venuti (London: Routledge, 2000), 468.

6. Victor Debay, writing in *Le Courrier musical* (June 15, 1909), was one of the few who challenged the production on musical grounds, and his complaints had more to do with the performers than with the score itself: "With the exception of M. Fugère, who has the style, all the performers of this reprise have lost, if they ever had it, their sense of classical music in general, and of Mozart in particular. They do not know how to draw out a harmonious and flexible line, they do not understand the nobility and simplicity of form, they feel neither the touching grace nor the delicate joy, and finally, they do not love that pure melody that pours out of the most sensible of hearts, in that style of melancholy tenderness of which *La Flûte enchantée* was the final sigh." [A l'exception de M. Fugère, qui a du style, tous les artistes de cette reprise, s'ils l'eurent quelquefois, on à jamais perdu le sens de la musique classique en général et de celle de Mozart en particulier. Ils n'en savent pas dessiner la ligne harmonieuse et souple, ils n'en comprennent pas la noblesse et la simplicité de forme, ils n'en sentent ni la grâce émue ni la joie délicate, ils n'aiment pas enfin cette mélodie pure où s'est épanché le plus sensible des cœurs, en des accents d'une mélancolique tendresse dont la *Flûte enchantée* fut le dernier soupir.]

7. *Le Figaro*, June 1, 1909. "Existe-t-il une musique que puisse faire ressentir des impressions à la fois si immédiates et si profondes, une musique qui, sans exiger le moindre effort, maintienne l'esprit en une telle joie, en une telle quiétude, et d'où découle, en même temps que les émotions les plus fortes, ou les plus exquises, ou les plus sereines, tant de grands enseignements?"

8. *Le Courrier musical*, July 1, 1909. "Jamais sûrement, le chef-d'œuvre de Mozart n'avait connu une telle splendeur et un pareil éclat."

9. As the critic Louis Weill put it in an article on the history of *The Magic Flute's* libretto in Paris: "The [1865] libretto by Nuitter and Beaumont ... is less an adaptation

than a complete rewrite of the German text." Weill continued, "The authors cared nothing for Schikaneder's intentions; still less about the origins of the fable. They cut scenes out of the original without respect to their model. They even distorted the plot to the point of rendering it incomprehensible." [Le livret de Nuitter et Beaumont... est moins une adaptation qu'une refonte du texte allemand. Les auteurs ne sont guère souciés des intentions de Schikaneder; encore moins des origines de la fable. Ils ont taillé dans la donnée originale des scènes sans rapport avec le modèle. Ils ont même dénaturé l'intrigue, au point de la rendre incompréhensible.] Weill, "Le livret de *la Flûte enchantée*," pt. 2, *Revue musicale* (August 1909): 391.

Paul Ferrier (1843–1928) was a playwright and librettist, whose best known efforts in the latter category are Offenbach's *La Marocaine* (1879) and Messager's *Le Chevalier d'Harmental* (1896). Evidently his skills as a translator of libretti were in high demand. In the same month as the premiere of his *The Magic Flute* translation, for example, his translation of *Tosca* appeared at the Théâtre Sarah Bernhardt. Alexandre Bisson (1848–1912) was a playwright chiefly successful for his sensational *Madame X* (1908), which became a hit in France and the United States (and has subsequently been made into a film at least ten times).

10. In the piano-vocal score (Paris: Choudens, 1909) this line reads "Et mon amour se détournera de toi!" [And my love will turn away from you!], which is likely a misprint. The spirit of the text does not seem to support such a reading, and the parallel effect two lines later is lost.

11. Reprinted in Gabriel Fauré, *Lettres intimes*, ed. Philippe Fauré-Fremiet (Paris: Grasset, 1951), 166. "Le directeur de l'Opéra-Comique, qui pense peut-être que je flâne pendant les vacances, m'a envoyé une traduction nouvelle de la *Flûte Enchantée*, de Mozart, avec prière de la revoir au point de vue des accents. Hélas! elles sont nombreuses les erreurs à relever! Enfin, j'essaierai."

12. Carré, *Souvenirs de théâtre*, 325. "Et puis, il y avait les œuvres classiques.... Depuis longtemps, je remettais sans cesse le projet qui me tenait le plus à cœur: la remise à la scène des œuvres de Mozart. Je réussis tout de même à le réaliser en sollicitant le concours de deux de nos plus grands musiciens: Gabriel Fauré pour *la Flûte enchantée* et Reyaldo Hahn pour *Don Juan*.... Gabriel Fauré apporta à ces études un soin passionné."

13. *Le Figaro*, June 1, 1909. "une pièce rétablie dans sa sévérité première, grâce à une nouvelle et fidèle version ... qui va nous éloigner enfin et pour toujours des fantaisies extraordinairement arbitraires de MM. Niutter et Beaumont."

14. *Le Guide musical*, June 6, and 13, 1909. "l'interêt principal de cette reprise est de nous donner *pour la première fois* en France l'état authentique du radieux chef-d'œuvre" (emphasis in the original).

15. Ibid. "Il appartenait à M. Albert Carré ... de ne pas laisser subsister plus longtemps le malentendu que pouvait en concevoir un public insuffisamment averti. Rejetant la version précédente, il a demandé à la collaboration de MM. Paul Ferrier et Alexandre Bisson, la traduction intégrale du texte allemand simplement éclairci, par endroits ou allégé.... *La Flûte enchantée* nous est rendue dans toute sa poésie, dans tout son caractère original. Nous ne saurions trop en remercier le directeur de l'Opéra-Comique."

16. *Le Journal des débats*, June 13, 1909. "Qu'elles étaient loin, hélas!"

17. *Le Courrier musical*, June 15, 1909. "La première est l'insanité du livret de Schikaneder, qu'ont remanié sans esprit MM. Paul Ferrier et Alexandre Bisson. On était en droit d'attendre d'eux autre chose que de plates facéties qui ne feraient même pas sourire des collégiens aux matinées du dimanche. Mais ils avaient à lécher un ours dont ils n'étaient pas le père, et il convient d'être indulgent pour des adaptateurs qui ont

cherché, par un respect qu'elle ne méritait pas, à se rapprocher de la version primitive. Qui peut s'intéresser à la querelle de Monsieur le Soleil et de Madame la Lune se disputant leur fille Pamina, aux épreuves imposées à l'amoureux Tamino pour conquérir la gracieuse enfant du Jour et de la Nuit? . . . Mais il n'est plus aujourd'hui qu'un fastidieux verbiage qui nuit à la musique dont il sépare les pages exquises. Entre des minutes divines il nous impose des quarts d'heure de bâillement. L'intervention suprême de MM. Ferrier et Bisson aurait été plus utilement remplacée par d'énergiques coups de ciseau supprimant dans le dialogue de Schikaneder tout ce qui n'est pas nécessaire ou n'a pas de sens, et, comme l'action est à peu près nulle, il ne serait resté que la partie chanté, qui elle, a la délicate et idéale signification que le génie de Mozart ajoutait aux vaines paroles."

18. *Le Journal des débats,* June 13, 1909. "dans *la Flûte enchantée* il ne se rencontre pas une seule scène intéressante."

19. *Le Courrier musical,* July 1, 1909. "Celle-ci est réduite trop facilement à l'accompagnement quelconque des épaisses drôleries sorties de l'imagination de Schikaneder . . . Mozart avait pourtant réussi à leur donner, avec son génie incomparable, de la finesse quelquefois, un peu d'originalité, presque de l'intérêt, à défaut d'esprit impossible à y introduire. Malheureusement le génie est étouffé et la musique disparaît. Point n'était besoin, pour ce résultat, de la collaboration d'un aussi grand musicien."

20. *Musica,* July 1909. "Les adaptateurs français se sont toujours refusés à discerner la véritable volonté dont témoigna Mozart. MM. Bisson et Ferrier ont voulu surtout faire amusant, 'moderniser.' . . . Sans doute, l'adaptation de MM. Bisson et Ferrier constitue, quant à la clarté de l'affabulation, un progrès sur l'ouvrage de Nuitter et Beaumont. Mais il est, ce progrès, cruellement compensé par l'ahurissant langage que parle Tamino, Pamina, et tous les habitants de la poétique féerie. N'existe-t-il donc pas d'adaptation 'sérieuse' de *la Flûte enchantée?*"

Paradoxically, in the same article Pioch also ascribed a kind of moral sublimity to *The Magic Flute,* pointing out that in the opera, Mozart "seemed driven by that emotion of thought that raises all the arts to the highest summit of human consciousness. . . . The libretto of *La Flûte enchantée,* by its dual nature as both magical and religious, was perfect for evoking his effusions, which are at once thoughtful and enjoyable." [Il y apparaît animé de cette émotion de pensée qui élève tous les arts au plus haut faîte de la conscience humaine. . . . Le livret de *la Flûte enchantée,* par son double aspect féerique et religieux, était bien propre à susciter ses effusions à la fois pensives et agréables.]

21. *Le Guide musical,* September 26, and October 3, 1909. "Pour avoir tenu à donner une impression *fidèle* du texte original parlé de l'œuvre allemande,—car, pour fidèle, elle l'était, beaucoup plus que certains critiques 'avertis,' mais qui n'avaient certainement pas lu l'allemand, ont affecté de le croire; elle l'était jusque dans ses défauts, ses lourdeurs et ses inutiles longueurs,—M. Albert Carré avait un peu trop demandé à l'attention, facilement lassée, du public courant."

22. Carré, *Souvenirs de théâtre,* 325. "Pour *la Flûte enchantée,* j'avais demandé à Alexandre Bisson et Paul Ferrier de refaire the livret de cette œuvre, la dernière—et la plus belle peut-être—du maître qui allait mourir à trente-six ans mais dont le poème il faut bien le dire, est inepte autant qu'incohérent."

23. We may find echoes here of Richard Taruskin's insights regarding the "performance practice" movement of the 1980s, such as when he points out that "I am convinced that 'historical' performance today [that is, in 1988] is not really historical; that a thin veneer of historicism clothes a performance style that is completely of our own time, and is in fact the most modern style around." Richard Taruskin, "The Pastness of

the Present and the Presence of the Past," in *Authenticity and Early Music: A Symposium*, ed. Nicholas Kenyon (Oxford: Oxford University Press, 1988), 152. See also Taruskin, *Text and Act: Essays on Music and Performance* (Oxford: Oxford University Press, 1995), which contains a version of the previously cited article.

24. A fairly detailed list of Hahn's changes to Mozart appeared in the *nouvelles* section of *Le Ménestrel*, April 13, 1912. A brief notice in the *Journal des débats* (May 1, 1912) reveals the novelty of Hahn's conception: "Last night the Opéra-Comique held the dress rehearsal of Mozart's *Don Juan* as the composer wrote it. M. Reynaldo Hahn directed the orchestra; the recitatives were accompanied at the piano. Finally, the work ended after the disappearance of Don Juan; all the characters appeared onstage, searching for Don Juan and expressing their joy at the punishment that he received." [Le théâtre de l'Opéra-Comique a donné hier la répétition générale du *Don Juan* de Mozart tel que le compositeur l'avait écrit. M. Reynaldo Hahn a dirigé l'orchestre; les récitatifs ont été accompagnés au piano. Enfin la pièce se termine plus sur la disparition de Don Juan; tous les personnages apparaissent sur la scène, cherchant Don Juan et exprimant leur joie du châtiment qu'il a reçu.]

Chapter Four

1. Katharine Ellis, *Music Criticism in Nineteenth-Century France: "La Revue et Gazette musicale de Paris," 1834–1880* (Cambridge: Cambridge University Press, 1995), 90.

2. Charles Forster, *Quinze ans à Paris (1832–1848): Paris et les Parisiens*, 2 vols. (Paris: 1848), 1:9–10. Quoted (in English) in Lloyd S. Kramer, *Threshold of a New World: Intellectuals and the Exile Experience in Paris, 1830–1848* (Ithaca, NY: Cornell University Press, 1988), 49.

3. On the popularity and importance of Italian opera in nineteenth-century Paris see, for example: Benjamin Walton, *Rossini in Restoration Paris: The Sound of Modern Life* (Cambridge: Cambridge University Press, 2007); James Johnson, *Listening in Paris: A Cultural History* (Berkeley: University of California Press, 1996); Gerhard, *The Urbanization of Opera*; and Andreas Giger, *Verdi and the French Aesthetic: Verse, Stanza, and Melody in Nineteenth-Century Opera* (Cambridge: Cambridge University Press, 2008).

4. On Weber's reception in the midcentury, see Ellis, *Music Criticism in Nineteenth-Century France*, 127–30.

5. On the Parisian *Tannhäuser* scandal, see Carolyn Abbate, "The Parisian 'Vénus' and the 'Paris' *Tannhäuser*," *Journal of the American Musicological Society* 36 (1983): 73–123; and Annegret Fauser, "'Cette musique sans tradition': Wagner's *Tannhäuser* and Its French Critics," in Fauser and Everist, *Music, Theater, and Cultural Transfer*, 228–55.

6. Anselm Gerhard has pointed out that "the cosmopolitan character of the Paris Opéra, and grand opéra as a genre, was already threatened in the 1850s and '60s; then, with Prussia's defeat of France in 1871, all universalist trends in Parisian cultural life came to an abrupt halt, and the 'capital city of the nineteenth century' began its slow decline toward a poorly disguised provincialism." Gerhard, *The Urbanization of Opera*, 394.

7. Blay, "Un Théâtre français, tout à fait français."

8. Huebner, *French Opera at the Fin de Siècle*, 12.

9. Clément, *Histoire de la musique*, 767–68. "Gluck s'est naturalisé compositeur français. Il s'est séparé des symphonistes allemands et des mélodistes italiens. Mozart n'a

jamais fait aucune concession à notre goût. Nous l'avons admiré et aimé néanmoins, à cause des qualités françaises de son cœur, de sa nature expansive, de la clarté limpide de son style et de ses idées, et enfin à cause de la beauté souveraine de son génie. A une telle hauteur, les frontières s'effacent. Je dirai plus: le divin Mozart, détrôné par les sectaires de la nouvelle école allemand, conservera chez nous ses autels."

10. *Le Figaro*, February 1, 1898. "L'Opéra-Comique devrait être une sorte de musée du répertoire lyrique, . . . il serait même convenable de l'augmenter en puisant plus qu'on ne l'a fait dans les œuvres de Lulli, Rameau, Gluck, Mozart, Méhul, Grétry."

11. *Musica*, April 1906. "Il est des types de *faux bonshommes* qu'on ne saurait trop démasquer: Melchior Grimm, en dépit de ce qu'on imagine d'habitude, a joué sur la carrière de Mozart, à notre point de vue tout au moins, le rôle le plus néfaste. C'est grâce à lui que Mozart n'est pas devenu, comme Gluck, un *compositeur français*. . . .

"Grimm, exaspéré par le succès de Gluck, aigri de voir son autorité musicale battue en brèche, était dans une excitation d'esprit sans bornes, au moment où Mozart lui tomba sur les bras. Et il irait soutenir un autre compositeur allemand? A d'autres! . . .

"Il avait bien eu le talent d'inculquer au jeune homme sa haine ou son dédain du goût français, du public français, de la musique française,—et la défiance, ou la sottise, dont Mozart fait preuve à ce sujet dans ses lettres, sont encore imputables à ce méchant esprit de Grimm. . . .

"C'est pour nous qu'il aurait écrit ces partitions dont le sujet déjà nous appartient: *Les Noces de Figaro* et *Don Juan*, et il en eût ajouté bien d'autres, avec nos livrets français si bien 'selon son esprit.'"

12. *La Revue musicale S.I.M.*, February 15, 1913. Reprinted in Claude Debussy, *Debussy on Music: The Critical Writings of the Great French Composer Claude Debussy*, ed. François Lesure and Richard Langham Smith, trans. Richard Langham Smith (Ithaca, NY: Cornell University Press, 1977), 276–80.

13. *La Revue musicale S.I.M.*, November 1, 1913. Reprinted in Debussy, *Debussy on Music*, 295–98. Quotation from 298.

14. On Raphael's adoption as a French figure, see Martin Rosenberg, *Raphael and France: The Artist as Paradigm and Symbol* (University Park: Pennsylvania State University Press, 1995).

15. Ibid., 149.

16. Thomas Tolley, *Painting the Cannon's Roar: Music, the Visual Arts, and the Rise of an Attentive Public in the Age of Haydn, c. 1750–1810* (Aldershot, UK: Ashgate, 2001), 36. Tolley discusses Mozart's association with Raphael on pages 36–37, briefly tracing the history of the association before focusing more squarely on Haydn.

17. Blaze de Bury was reviewing the 1855 production of *La Flûte enchantée* at the Théâtre Lyrique. The passage is reprinted in *Musiciens du passé, du présent et de l'avenir* (Paris: Michel Lévy, 1880), 64.

18. Alfred Tonnellé, *Fragments sur l'art et la philosophie, suivi de notes et pensées diverses*, 2nd ed. (Paris: Douinol and Reinwald, 1860), 271. "Mozart est un de ces rares génies de la même famille que Raphaël, à qui il a été donné à la fois et dans une égale mesure d'émouvoir le cœur, de charmer l'imagination, de satisfaire le goût et l'esprit, et de répandre sur toutes choses une certaine fleur de beauté et de grâce idéal."

19. This poem was originally published in Marquis Anatole-Henri-Philippe de Ségur, *La Maison: stances et sonnets* (Paris: Tolra et Haton, 1869). I have taken the text from its fin-de-siècle reprint in Marquis de Ségur, Œuvres poétiques (Paris: Retaux, 1899), 196–97.

20. *Les Arts de la vie*, January 1904. "Mozart passa, dans l'opinion des dilettantes, pour le génie souverain de la musique, et, comme celui de Raphaël en peinture, son

nom devint presque dogmatiquement synonyme de perfection, de grâce et d'idéal inégalables."

21. Gustave Choquet, *Histoire de la musique dramatique en France depuis ses origines jusqu'à nos jours* (Paris: Didot, 1873), 173. "Mozart a conduit la comédie musicale à son plus haut degré de perfection dans *le Nozze de Figaro*; en écrivant *la Flûte enchantée*, il a créé le drame fantastique, et en composant *Don Giovanni* il a sondé les profondeurs du monde surnaturel et ouvert au romanticisme la porte de l'opéra.

"Ces trois dernières partitions sont celle où le Raphaël de la musique nous a livré les secrets de son âme pieuse, mélancolique et tendre."

22. Camille Bellaigue, *Mozart* (Paris: Laurens, 1906), 104. "C'est le secret des grands idéalistes, celui du musicien de *Don Juan* aussi bien que du peintre de l'*Héliodore* et de la *Messe de Bolsène* [both by Raphael], de réserver ainsi jusque dans les pages grandioses, un asile et comme un coin familier à la vie intime, à la plus modeste, à la plus humble réalité."

23. Ibid., 94.

24. *La Revue des deux mondes*, October 1, 1896. "Bien des fois déjà on l'a comparé à Raphaël, et si, à raison des similitudes évidentes de leur génie et de leur destinée, la comparaison se présentait d'elle-même à l'esprit, les travaux récents de la critique sur l'un et sur l'autre n'ont fait que confirmer les nombreuses analogies qu'on avait remarquées en eux. Non seulement, en effet, leur vocation a été marquée par des indices aussi manifestes, mais, fils d'artistes tous deux, ils ont trouvé, dès leur berceau, une direction intelligente dont des facultés d'assimilation semblable leur ont permis de profiter sans relâche. A travers les influences les plus diverses et les plus heureusement combinées, ils ont conservé l'un et l'autre toute leur originalité, ce goût, ce sens de la beauté et des proportions, cette fécondité d'invention inépuisable, ce rare mélange d'élégance et de force, de savoir et d'inspiration, cette souplesse et cette universalité d'aptitudes que nous admirons en eux et qui leur ont permis d'exceller dans toutes les branches de leur art."

25. *La Revue de Paris*, 1830. Quoted in Rosenberg, *Raphael and France*, 179.

26. Katharine Ellis, "Female Pianists and Their Male Critics in Nineteenth-Century Paris," *Journal of the American Musicological Society* 50 (1997): 353–85.

27. I take the term "crisis of masculinity" from Annelise Maugue, *L'Identité masculine en crise au tournant du siècle: 1871–1914* (Paris: Rivages, 1987), which remains a central work on the topic. For another take on the significance of masculinity in France at this time, see Robert A. Nye, *Masculinity and Male Codes of Honor in Modern France* (Oxford: Oxford University Press, 1993).

28. Edward Berenson, for example, has pointed out that "improvements in the status and condition of women, achieved in large part through the efforts of a growing feminist movement, created intense feelings of fear, hostility, and vulnerability among France's male commentators of the era. Exacerbating these feelings was a lingering sense of impotence stemming from France's disastrous defeat at the hands of Prussia in September 1870. . . . French males—defeated in war, vulnerable to a potent working class—feared deep down that foreigners saw them as lacking in the honor and warriorlike virility still widely believed to embody masculinity itself." Edward Berenson, *The Trial of Madame Caillaux* (Berkeley: University of California Press, 1992), 113–14.

29. Annegret Fauser, "Gendering the Nations: The Ideologies of French Discourse on Music (1870–1914)," in *Musical Constructions of Nationalism: Essays on the History and Ideology of European Music, 1800–1945*, ed. Harry White and Michael Murphy (Cork, IR: Cork University Press, 2001), 91.

30. Gruber, *Mozart and Posterity*, 163–64.

31. Choquet, *Histoire*, 176. "Poëte fantaisiste, poëte élégiaque et poëte chrétien, Mozart brille plus encore par la grâce et par la sensibilité que par le don de la gaieté communicative: il a tant aimé, il a tant souffert! . . . L'artiste demeure fidèle à son style particulier, dont on ne se lasse pas d'admirer l'élégance et la perfection. Ce style se fait remarquer par son évidente spontanéité, et néanmoins il porte en même temps l'empreinte d'une mûre réflexion."

32. Henri Lavoix's description of Mozart in his *Histoire de la musique*, written a decade after Choquet's volume, is much the same: "Mozart's genius is in his *grace*, in the ineffable *tenderness* that nothing can surpass; it is also in the miraculous balance of all the parts of the work, in the clarity, in the perfect purity of the musical language. But Mozart, *gentle, tender*, and classical *par excellence*, possesses at the same time the spirit of finesse, as in *les Noces de Figaro* and *Così fan tutte*, and *boldness of force*, as in *Don Juan*" (emphasis added). [Le génie de Mozart est dans son grâce, la tendresse ineffable, que nul n'a pu surpasser; il est aussi dans la merveilleuse pondération de toutes les parties de l'œuvre, dans la clarté, dans la parfaite pureté de la langue musicale. Mais ce doux, ce tendre, ce classique par excellence, possède en même temps l'esprit de la finesse, comme dans les Noces de Figaro et Cosi fan tutte, la hardiesse et la force, comme dans Don Juan.] Henri Lavoix, *Histoire de la musique* (Paris: Quantin, 1884), 211–12.

33. Téodor de Wyzewa and Georges de Saint-Foix, *Wolfgang Amédée Mozart: Sa vie musicale et son œuvre*, 5 vols. (Paris: Desclée de Brouwer, 1936–46), 1: iv–v. "Toujours, avec sa nature essentiellement 'féminine,' ce génie poétique a eu besoin de recevoir d'ailleurs l'élan nécessaire pour engager son art dans des voies nouvelles,—sauf pour lui à transfigurer tout de suite, en les animant d'une signification et d'une beauté à la fois bien plus hautes et tout originales, les idées ou les procédés que lui révélait l'œuvre de tel ou tel musicien rencontré au passage."

34. Though the character of Mozart is played by a female soprano, he does spend much of the operetta pursuing various female love interests, making Mozart into something of a Cherubino figure. This element of his character, however, does not mitigate the overall feminine portrayal of the composer.

35. Reprinted in Romain Rolland, *Romain Rolland's Essays on Music*, ed. David Ewen (New York: Dover, 1959), 255.

36. Richard Wagner, "Das Publikum in Zeit und Raum." Quoted in Gruber, *Mozart and Posterity*, 166.

37. Katharine Ellis, "Berlioz, the Sublime, and the *Broderie* Problem," in *Hector Berlioz: Miscellaneous Studies*, ed. Fulvia Morabito and Michela Niccolai (Bologna: Ut Orpheus Edizioni, 2005), 29–59.

38. Bellaigue, *Mozart*, 101. "Le génie de Mozart est à la fois idéal et familier, supérieur et prochain, sans que jamais un choc, ou même un froissement, résulte de cette rencontre. Il arrive au sublime tantôt par la grandeur, tantôt—plus souvent même—par la grâce. Et je ne sais que les Grecs, et Raphaël après eux, qui sachent y atteindre par ce dernier chemin."

39. Ellis, "Berlioz, the Sublime, and the *Broderie* Problem," 41. Caballero argues that praise of the sublime became "exceedingly rare" in later French criticism, suggesting that "in refusing the grand the superiority of the sublime to the perfect, many French musicians, while absorbing so many other tendencies from across the Rhine, put up an isolated but fundamental resistance to German idealism." While evocations of sublimity may have been less common in France than in Germany, however, many fin-de-siècle critics were certainly willing to use the term in a positive sense, and the term is often used to denote

either a particularly moving performance or any musical passage or piece with transcendent qualities. Saint-Saëns, like Berlioz, seems to have used the term to indicate the highest levels of human emotion. For instance, in a discussion of Wagner's operas, he noted that "Womankind in Wagnerian drama, initially loving and tender like Elsa or passionate like Isolde, becomes sublime with Brünnhilde who, in her love and sorrow, progresses from divinity to humanity—a bold idea, indeed a truly modern and philosophical one." Thus, the sublimity attained through the work is by the heights and purity of Brünhilde's emotion. Michael Puri has also recently speculated as to the influence of the concept of sublimity in Ravel's oeuvre around 1910, influenced by the archetype of the dandy, one who, in Baudelaire's words, "aspires to be sublime without interruption." Caballero, *Fauré and French Musical Aesthetics*, 296–97 (n. 79); Saint-Saëns's description of Brünnhilde is found in the Introduction to *Harmonie et mélodie* (Paris: Calmann Lévy, 1885). Reprinted in Camille Saint-Saëns, *Camille Saint-Saëns on Music and Musicians*, trans. and ed. Roger Nichols (Oxford: Oxford University Press, 2008), 7; Michael J. Puri, "Dandy, Interrupted: Sublimation, Repression, and Self-Portraiture in Maurice Ravel's *Daphnis et Chloé* (1909–1912)," *Journal of the American Musicological Society* 60 (2007): 317–72.

40. Blaze de Bury, *Musiciens du passé, du présent et de l'avenir*, 93–94. The original review appeared on March 15, 1855. "De tous les sentiments que l'homme éprouve, le plus pur, le plus divin est celui que la femme fait naître. Seulement cet amour dont parle Tamino n'est point la passion comme dans *Don Juan* ou *les Noces de Figaro*, c'est quelque chose de plus moral, de plus sublime, un but auquel on n'atteint que par la vertu de l'initiation."

41. *Le Figaro*, June 1, 1909. Reprinted in Gabriel Fauré, *Opinions musicales* (Paris: Reider, 1930), 93. "Existe-t-il une musique que puisse faire ressentir des impressions à la fois si immédiates et si profondes, une musique qui, sans exiger le moindre effort, maintienne l'esprit en une telle joie, en une telle quiétude, et d'où découle, en même temps que les émotions les plus fortes, ou les plus exquises, ou les plus sereines, tant de grands enseignements?"

42. These maxims and their interpretation have occupied a number of Mozart scholars, who have at various times cited them as everything from proof of the opera's Freemasonic agenda to examples of Mozart's use of musical irony. Though the French critics in 1909 did not comment significantly on these maxims, it seems almost certain that they were interpreted seriously rather than tongue-in-cheek. For a thorough recent analysis of the both these maxims and the historiography surrounding them, see Martin Nedbal, "Morals Across the Footlights: German Opera, National Identity, and the Aesthetics of Morality" (PhD diss., Eastman School of Music, 2009); and Nedbal, "Mozart as Viennese Moralist: *Die Zauberflöte* and Its Maxims," *Acta Musicologica* 81 (2009): 123–57.

43. *Musica*, July 1909. "Il est certain que les sublimes phrases de Sarastro, les scènes religieuses qui confèrent à *la Flûte enchantée* une valeur sacrée passent les beautés où le clair génie de Mozart s'était jusqu'alors (1791) épanoui. On sait que *la Flûte enchantée* est sa dernière œuvre dramatique. Il y apparaît animé de cette émotion de pensée qui élève tous les arts au plus haut faîte de la conscience humaine. . . . Le livret de *la Flûte enchantée*, par son double aspect féerique et religieux, était bien propre à susciter ses effusions à la fois pensives et agréables."

44. On *Fervaal* and d'Indy's moral agenda, see Huebner, *French Opera at the Fin de Siècle*, 301–7 and 317–50. Anya Suschitzky has also persuasively argued that the Catholicism in *Fervaal* represents a fundamental aspect of the work's French identity. Anya Suschizky, "*Fervaal, Parsifal*, and French National Identity," *19th-Century Music* 25 (2002): 237–65.

45. See Carlo Caballero, *Fauré and French Musical Aesthetics* (Cambridge: Cambridge University Press, 2001), ch. 5. Louis Laloy, for example, opined that the *Requiem* was "the music of the Elysian field; the tender gravity and soft sadness of [it] remind me more of Athenian tombs than of the edifying sculptures of the portals of our churches.... And this conception of Paradise is not so far removed as one might believe from orthodox Catholicism; certainly it is more Catholic than Protestant since it is somewhat pagan in character." Quoted in Caballero, *Fauré and French Musical Aesthetics*, 188.

46. For a thorough discussion of *La Chanson d'Ève* and religion, see Caballero, *Fauré and French Musical Aesthetics*, 198–207.

47. *La Revue des deux mondes*, July 1, 1909. "Mais qui niera que leurs sublimes cantiques respirent l'essence même ou l'idéal du sentiment religieux!"

48. On the "New Woman," see Mary Louise Roberts, *Disruptive Acts: The New Woman in Fin-de-Siècle France* (Chicago: University of Chicago Press, 2002), esp. ch. 1; Debora L. Silverman, *Art Nouveau in Fin-de-Siècle France: Politics, Psychology, and Style* (Berkeley: University of California Press, 1989), ch. 4; and James F. McMillan, *France and Women, 1789–1914: Gender, Society and Politics* (New York: Routledge, 1999), ch. 10.

49. Silverman, *Art Nouveau in Fin-de-Siècle France*, 67.

50. *La Revue des deux mondes*, August 1, 1897. Quoted in Roberts, *Disruptive Acts*, 28. Roberts describes the increasing number of plays that depicted the New Woman (often in a favorable light), much to the dismay of more conservative critics and audience members.

51. Berenson, *The Trial of Madame Caillaux*, 92.

52. These efforts to present positive bourgeois female role models were not limited to onstage characters. Leonard Berlanstein has similarly traced a strong critical trend in the Third Republic to "clean up" theatrical women—actresses, dancers, and the like—at least in terms of public perception. The alluringly decadent women prized for most of the nineteenth century gave way to a new, politically convenient image. In Berlanstein's words: "Rather than accepting the erotic culture of the stage, public opinion under the Third Republic found the theater increasingly moralized. The prevailing political myths after 1880 admitted that while France had had an elitist ruling class, the theater had been a threat to domestic virtue; but now that the regime of the people was in power and the aristocracy was irrelevant, the theater world had lost its wickedness and become more or less chaste." Leonard Berlanstein, *Daughters of Eve: A Cultural History of French Theater Women from the Old Regime to the Fin de Siècle* (Cambridge, MA: Harvard University Press, 2001), 162.

53. There was no shortage of redemptive women on the fin-de-siècle stage. Wagner's operas provide notable examples, including Elizabeth in *Tannhäuser*, who dies purely to save the hero's soul. Similarly, in d'Indy's *Fervaal*, the hero's soul is saved (indirectly) by the loving sacrifice of the heroine Guilhen. Examples of "real women" who demonstrate their faithfulness and are rewarded include the eponymous heroines of Massenet's *Griséldis* and Fauré's *Pénélope*. Fin-de-siècle women punished for their transgressive actions include, most notably, Carmen, whose "misdeeds" lead inexorably to her death at Don José's hands. Isolde, in Wagner's Isolde also dies for her forbidden love for Tristan, as does the adulterous Guenièvre (by suicide) in Ernest Chausson's *Le Roi Arthus*, to name only a few examples.

54. Again, Wagner's perennially popular operas contain no shortage of valiant heroes, most prominently Lohengrin and Parsifal. Other examples include Ulysse in Fauré's *Pénélope*, the title character in d'Indy's *Fervaal*, Ernest Reyer's eponymous Sigurd, the young Dominique in Bruneau's *L'Attaque du Moulin*, and so on.

55. Mary Hunter, *Mozart's Operas: A Companion* (New Haven: Yale University Press, 2008), 141.

56. David J. Levin, *Unsettling Opera: Staging Mozart, Verdi, Wagner, and Zemlinsky* (Chicago: University of Chicago Press, 2007), 78.

57. Charles Ford, *Così? Sexual Politics in Mozart's Operas* (Manchester, UK: Manchester University Press, 1991), 152.

58. Kristi Brown-Montesano has argued that the negative musicological (and performative) reception of Donna Anna's character—Edward Dent referred to her as a "thoroughly unpleasant lady," for example—is a reflection of her usurpation of the traditionally masculine realm of revenge and her refusal to conform to traditional opera buffa ideas of domesticity. Kristi Brown-Montesano, *Understanding the Women of Mozart's Operas* (Berkeley: University of California Press, 2007), ch. 1.

59. Paul Dukas, normally one to celebrate any production of Mozart's operas, reported that "apart from some charming pieces, *L'Enlèvement au Sérail* is, at present, a historically interesting work more than a creation likely to spark a truly unprovoked admiration." [à part quelques morceaux charmants, l'*Enlèvement au Sérail* est, à présent, une œuvre historiquement intéressante plutôt qu'une création propre à susciter une admiration vraiment spontanée.] *Chronique des Arts et de la Curiosité*, December 1903. Reprinted in Dukas, *Les Écrits de Paul Dukas sur la musique*, 601.

60. For a historiographic summary of gender in the interpretation of *The Magic Flute*, see Brown-Montesano, *Understanding the Women of Mozart's Operas*, ch. 4 and 5.

61. Jacques Chailley, The Magic Flute *Unveiled: Esoteric Symbolism in Mozart's Masonic Opera*, trans. Herbert Weinstock (Rochester, VT: Inner Traditions International, 1992), 93. For Chailley, this conflict is resolved by the essential union of Tamino and Pamina, effectively creating a "whole" entity.

62. Brown-Montesano, *Understanding the Women of Mozart's Operas*, 115.

63. David M. Pomfret, "'A Muse for the Masses': Gender, Age and Nation in France, Fin de Siècle," *American Historical Review* 109 (2004): 1439–75.

64. The Coronation was not, in fact, a conservative event, but was embraced by the left-leaning portions of French society as well. Central to the event was the idea of elevating the masses to a higher level, eroding class boundaries and uniting the people in the wake of the divisive Dreyfus affair. Nonetheless, these progressive tendencies did not extend to the depiction of women.

65. Pomfret, "'A Muse for the Masses,'" 1456.

66. Brown-Montesano, *Understanding the Women of Mozart's Operas*, 81.

67. Quoted in Roberts, *Disruptive Acts*, 33.

68. Carolyn Abbate, *In Search of Opera* (Princeton: Princeton University Press, 2001), 71. Abbate's analysis of *The Magic Flute* touches on a number of issues related to the Queen and her struggles for power and against masculine domination. See chapter 2, "Magic Flute, Nocturnal Sun."

Chapter Five

1. Mark Everist, "Gluck, Berlioz and Castil-Blaze: The Poetics and Reception of French Opera," in Everist, *Giacomo Meyerbeer and Music Drama in Nineteenth-Century Paris* (Aldershot, UK: Ashgate, 2005), 65.

2. Jean Monrédien, for example, reveals that at the Opéra around 1800, "it was as though French opera had begun with Gluck in the 1780s." Mongrédien, *French Music from the Enlightenment to Romanticism*, 72.

3. As Katharine Ellis points out in her study of the prominent journal *La Revue et gazette musicale de Paris*, "It would be difficult to argue that [Gluck] was ever canonic in the nineteenth century." Ellis, *Music Criticism in Nineteenth-Century France*, 80.

4. *Empire*, January 16, 1810. Quoted in Ellis, "A Dilettante at the Opera," 57. "Il est probable que le musicien allemand n'entendait pas assez bien le français pour être sensible à la mélodie du plus harmonieux de nos poètes." Above, I use Ellis's translation of the French. The underlying purpose of Geoffroy's interest in Gluck's German-ness, according to Ellis, was to enable the critic to establish Sacchini as the ultimate example of classical French opera.

5. *Journal de l'empire*, February 21, 1811. Quoted in Johnson, *Listening in Paris*, 175.

6. This dichotomous critical view of the composer is the focus of Everist, "Gluck, Berlioz and Castil-Blaze."

7. *Journal des débats*, December 10, 1825. Quoted in Everist, "Gluck, Berlioz and Castil-Blaze," 71. "*Armide* est dans une contradiction continuelle avec le goût du jour, et les tournures gothiques et surannées qui s'y montrent à chaque page ne disposent pas les amateurs à l'écouter sans impatience." Here I use Everist's translation.

8. *Journal des spectacles*, 4 Frimaire X (November 25, 1801). Quoted in Mongrédien, *French Music from the Enlightenment to Romanticism*, 73.

9. Joël-Marie Fauquet, "Berlioz and Gluck," trans. Peter Bloom, in *The Cambridge Companion to Berlioz*, ed. Peter Bloom (Cambridge: Cambridge University Press, 2000), 200.

10. The complete programs for the Société des Concerts may be found online at http://hector.ucdavis.edu/SdC/. This useful repository was created by D. Kern Holoman as a companion to his book *The Société des Concerts du Conservatoire, 1828–1967* (Berkeley: University of California Press, 2004).

11. For a fascinating look at the historical significance of the 1859 production and its role in the evolving French awareness of music-historical narratives, see Willson, "Classic Staging." I agree with Willson that the production was a particularly significant historical moment, but I do think that most French critics (and audience members) viewed it as an isolated event on a more experimental stage—a magnificent novelty rather than a sustainable model for operatic theaters, particularly the Opéra or Opéra-Comique. Furthermore, it eschews the Operatic Museum model a bit by virtue of being heavily adapted by Berlioz (though the adaptations were nowhere near as severe as those seen in Mozart operas during the nineteenth century, for example).

12. Fauquet lists one performance in 1829, two in 1830–31, and an incomplete performance in 1833. Joël-Marie Fauquet, "Berlioz's Version of Gluck's *Orphée*," trans. Peter Bloom, in *Berlioz Studies*, ed. Peter Bloom (Cambridge: Cambridge University Press, 1992), 191.

13. Interestingly, Viardot was initially skeptical of performing the role of Orphée, citing a distaste for Gluck's operas as well as an unwillingness to perform *en travesti*. Fauquet, "Berlioz's Version of Gluck's *Orphée*," 198.

14. *L'Univers musical*, November 20, 1859. "*Orphée*, l'un des immortels chefs-d'oeuvre de Glück, était chanté devant une salle remplie d'illustrations musicales et artistiques, écoutant avec un religieux silence ces récitatifs admirables, où la tendresse, la douleur, la passion la plus exaltée se trouvent exprimées avec une éloquence indescriptible, sans bruit, simplement, naturellement."

15. *La France musicale*, November 20, 1859. "la simplicité la plus touchante enchaîne le drame musical. Là, rien de heurté, rien de faux, rien de banal; c'est l'inspiration dramatique dans toute sa grâce et dans toute sa puissance; c'est la pureté de la ligne mélodique; c'est le charme de Raphaël, uni à la grandeur et à l'énergie de Corneille! Tout est

divin dans cet éternel chef-d'oeuvre, éclairé des rayons de l'immortalité, et le chant et l'orchestre. Les années passeront, les siècles aussi. . . . Gluck ne passera pas; il restera sur son socle d'airain, debout, comme les dieux antiques."

16. For more detail on the 1861 struggles around Gluck and Wagner, see William Gibbons, "Music of the Future, Music of the Past: *Tannhäuser* and *Alceste* at the Paris Opéra," *19th-Century Music* 33, no. 3 (Spring 2010): 232–46.

17. *La France musicale*, October 13–27, 1861; *Le Journal des débats*, October 12–24, 1861.

18. *La Revue et gazette musicale*, November 10, 1861. Here Fétis is writing in response to Paul Smith's highly laudatory review of *Alceste* in the issue of October 27. Perhaps not surprisingly, the idea that this repertoire should be presented only in concert version represents a direct (and perhaps intentional) contrast to Wagner's opinions. In an article in the *Neue Zeitschrift für Musik*, for example (July 1, 1854), Wagner opines that he "can imagine no more hideous travesty of a dramatic, and especially a tragic piece of music, than to have Orestes and Iphigenia, for instance,—in tail-coat and ball-dress . . .—proclaiming their death-agonies in front of a concert-orchestra." Translation taken from Richard Wagner, *Judaism in Music and Other Essays*, trans. William Ashton Ellis (Lincoln: University of Nebraska Press, 1995), 156.

19. For more on concert life in Paris, see, for example, Holoman's detailed *The Société des Concerts du Conservatoire*; Élisabeth Bernard, "Jules Pasdeloup et les concerts populaires," *Revue de musicologie* 57 (1971): 150–78; and Jann Pasler, "Building a Public for Orchestral Music: Les Concerts Colonne," in *Concert et public: Mutation de la vie musicale en Europe de 1780 à 1914*, ed. Hans-Erich Bödeker, Patrice Veit, and Michael Werner (Paris: Editions de la Maison des sciences de l'homme, 2002), 209–40.

20. Pasler addresses the educational aims of these concert series in her "Concert Programs and Their Narratives as Emblems of Ideology," in Pasler, *Writing through Music*, 365–416. See also her discussion of *musique ancienne* on concert programs and as a model for modern composers in *Composing the Citizen: Music as Public Utility in Third Republic France* (Berkeley: University of California Press, 2009), 629–42.

21. Jane Fulcher, "The Concert as Political Propaganda in France and the Control of 'Performative Context,'" *Musical Quarterly* 82 (1998), 43, 57.

22. Edme-Marie-Ernest Deldevez, *La Société des Concerts, 1860 à 1885*, ed. Gérard Streletski (Heilbronn: Edition Lucie Galland, 1998), 22–23. "On regrette, ne cesse-t-on de répéter, que l'Opéra ne s'occupe pas de reprendre *Armide*, la *Vestale*, *Fernand Cortez*, ainsi que d'autres chefs-d'œuvre. Mais au moins, pour ce qui concerne nos concerts, on avait lieu d'espérer que l'exécution de quelques fragments de ces mêmes ouvrages tant attendus seraient accueillis [sic] favorablement par ce même public-amateur qui voudrait voir au théâtre la reprise de ces opéras. Eh bien! non, le public reste froid à ces avances."

23. For a useful table of the performances of Gluck's works (as well as those of other "early music" composers) on Parisian concert series, see Jann Pasler, "Deconstructing d'Indy, or the Problem of a Composer's Reputation," in Pasler, *Writing through Music*, 135–36.

24. Pasler, "Building a Public for Orchestral Music," 228.

25. On music in the salon of the Princesse de Polignac, including a list of concerts, see Sylvia Kahan, *Music's Modern Muse: A Life of Winnaretta Singer, Princesse de Polignac* (Rochester, NY: University of Rochester Press, 2003). On the Société des Grandes Auditions, see Jann Pasler, "Countess Greffulhe as Entrepreneur: Negotiating Class, Gender, and Nation," in Pasler, *Writing through Music*, 285–317.

26. *Le Ménestrel*, March 8, 1896. "Si ceux de ma génération n'avaient encore pu voir les œuvres de Gluck sur aucun théâtre de Paris, du moins avons-nous été élevés dans le

culte du vieux maître, et sa musique nous est devenue familière, grâce aux auditions fréquentes qu'en ont données les concerts symphoniques."

27. For a thorough examination of the Schola and its early music practices, see Catrina Flint de Médicis, "The Schola Cantroum, Early Music and French Political Culture, from 1894–1914," PhD diss., McGill University, 2006. See also Gail Hilson Woldu, "Debussy, Fauré, and d'Indy and the Conceptions of the Artist: The Institutions, the Dialogues, the Conflicts," in *Debussy and His World*, ed. Jane Fulcher (Princeton: Princeton University Press, 2001), 235–53.

28. For some details on the Pelletan family's odd history with this heart (and the political issues involved), see Christian Régnier, "The Heart of the King of France: 'Cordial Immortality,'" *Medicographia* 31 (2009): 430–39.

29. *Le Ménestrel*, July 7, 1906. Berlioz "en [the excerpts] a offert en souvenir le manuscript original, auquel est joint le poème de l'acte du *Cri de guerre*, à Mlle Fanny Pelletan, son admiratrice autorisée ... ; celle-ci, ayant aussi reçu des mains du maître les fragments également incomplets d'un autre opera, *la Nonne sanglante*, et l'autographe de deux parties de *l'Enfance du Christ*, a remis à son tour la totalité de ce précieux depot à la Bibliothèque Nationale."

30. Hector Berlioz, *The Musical Madhouse: An English Translation of Berlioz's "Les Grotesques de la musique,"* trans. and ed. Alastair Bruce (Rochester, NY: University of Rochester Press, 2003), 124.

31. The best resource on Damcke's life and music remains Prince Alexandre Bibesco, *Berthold Damcke: Étude biographique et musicale* (Paris: Lemerre, 1894). The salon of Bibesco's wife, Princess Hélène, hosted luminaries including Debussy, Saint-Saëns, Anatole France, and Proust.

32. Camille Doucet, letter to Charles Nuitter, July 5, 1870, Charles Nuitter Papers, Bibliotheque Nationale de France, Bibliothèque-musée de l'Opéra (Paris). "de réaliser ce beau projet."

33. Fanny Pelletan, letter to Charles Nuitter, December 20, 1874, Charles Nuitter Papers, Bibliotheque Nationale de France, Bibliothèque-musée de l'Opéra (Paris).

34. Bibesco, *Berthold Damcke*, 83. "Cette mort porta d'abord un coup cruel aux projets artistique de Mlle Fanny Pelletan. Heureusement elle avait pratiqué Damcke assez longtemps, pour ne pas perdre courage."

35. Ibid. "Les principaux matériaux sont amassés pour les trois tragédies qui restent: *Paris et Hélène*, *Armide*, *Orphée*, les principes critiques du grand éditeur défunt resteront gravés dans la mémoire de son successeur, qui les avait appris par cœur."

36. Camille Saint-Saëns, *Musical Memories*, trans. Edwin Gile Rich (Boston: Small, Maynard, 1919), 156.

37. Ibid.

38. Ibid., 154.

39. Ibid., 155–56.

40. *La Revue et gazette musicale de Paris*, June 28, 1874: "Bach, Handel, Beethoven ont le leur sous forme de splendides éditions, publiées par la *Bachgesellschaft* de Leipzig, par Chrysander, par Breitkopf et Härtel. Voici Gluck en leur compagnie, recevant enfin l'hommage qui lui était dû depuis longtemps."

41. Jean Bonnerot, *C. Saint-Saëns (1835–1921): sa vie et son oeuvre* (Paris: Durand, 1922), 75. "Il avait suffit de trente années de labeur pour mener à bien cette édition de Gluck, un des plus riches monuments que la France ait élevés à la musique, digne pendant des grandes éditions de Bach et de Handel publiées en Allemagne."

42. Several of Lully's works did appear on the series *Les chefs d'oeuvres classiques de l'opéra français*, ed. T. de Lajarte (Paris, 1878–83). Despite its similarly nationalist focus, however, that edition was not dedicated to a single composer and was less ambitious, containing only piano-vocal scores.

43. Although reviews do not specifically mention the use of the Berlioz adaptations in concert excerpts, the use of a period orchestra or any specific attempt at "authenticity" in the performances usually merited special attention.

44. *Le Guide musical*, March 8, 1896. "Puis, se servant du travail de reconstitution fait avec tant de soin et d'intelligence par Mlle Pelletan, dans le but d'enlever les fautes de rédaction, de copie et aussi (il faut bien le dire) les négligences de Gluck, M. Tiersot, le savant sous-bibliothécaire du Conservatoire, a quelque peu modifié l'orchestration, qui laissait encore à désirer."

45. *La Revue hebdomadaire*, July 1895, reprinted in Dukas, *Les écrits de Paul Dukas sur la musique*, 256–57. "Les œuvres signées de noms glorieux qui, dans leur temps, furent l'objet de discussions qu'elles ne soulèveraient plus à coup sûr aujourd'hui, sont de la sorte classées d'avance dans la catégorie des opéras qui ne peuvent faire recette, c'est-à-dire condamnées à l'oubli; l'Opéra, en effet, ne peut rien tenter de volontairement aléatoire en ces matières, son existence dépendant étroitement de sa prospérité commerciale et ses traditions lui ayant créé des exigences de luxe auxquelles, sous peine de déchoir, il ne peut se dérober. Il faut donc renoncer à l'espoir de voir se former à l'Opéra un répertoire véritablement classique, comprenant les œuvres les plus importantes des grands maîtres français et étrangers. D'ailleurs, il est probable que l'intérêt porté par le public à ses œuvres serait platonique; on l'a bien vu lors des représentations de *Don Juan* et du *Freischütz*, auxquelles l'Opéra dut finalement renoncer."

46. Ibid., 257. "En ce qui concerne Gluck, il est revenu à la mode depuis quelque temps, et, le vent soufflant de son côté, il ne serait pas étonnant que la promesse, formulée par trois générations de directeurs, de remettre à la scène un de ses ouvrages, fût enfin réalisée."

47. I am not considering here the isolated few productions of *Orphée* by a visiting opera troupe in 1889, performed at the Théâtre de la Gaîté. The production does not seem to have been particularly successful, and critics almost universally ignored it when writing about the 1896 *Orphée*. Popular opinion about the 1889 production is perhaps best summed up by the critic for *Le Temps*: "It was truly a massacre to play Gluck's music like this" [C'était un massacre, en vérité, que de jouer ainsi du Gluck]. *Le Temps*, March 15, 1896. Garnier's comment appeared in *L'Europe artiste*, March 15, 1896. "le plus grand et le plus puissant effort dramatique des temps modernes."

48. The 1866 revival of *Alceste*, which featured Marie Battu in the title role, was largely a recreation of the 1861 Berlioz-Viardot production and made little impression on critics or audiences.

49. Raphaëlle Legrand and Nicole Wild, *Regards sur l'opéra-comique: Trois siècles de vie théâtrale* (Paris: CNRS, 2002), 149, 168.

50. *Le Temps*, March 15, 1896. "L'*Orphée* que nous a donné M. Carvalho n'est pas tout à fait l'*Orphée* qu'il a donné, lui-même, en 1859. Il y a des différences de texte, de mise en scène; et l'interprétation ne se ressemble pas. En 1859, Mme Pauline Viardot—qui était l'Orphée d'alors, un Orphée inimitable,—chantait à la fin du premier acte, un air que Nourrit autrefois, et Mlle Delna aujourd'hui ont remplacé par un air tiré d'*Echo et Narcisse*."

51. *Le Guide musical*, March 8, 1896. "Cette représentation nous remémorait également la superbe interprétation qu'avait donnée Mme Viardot du rôle d'Orphée en l'année 1859."

52. *Le Ménestrel,* October 4, 1896. "Enfin, dans l'année même où ces lignes sont écrites, une nouvelle reprise de l'œuvre a eu lieu, également sous la direction de M. Carvalho, à l'Opéra-Comique, conformément aux traditions précédemment établies au Théâtre-Lyrique. Le succès n'en a pas été moins complet, et sans doute n'est pas encore épuisé.

"Cette continuité de l'admiration publique est, certes, le plus bel hommage qui ait été rendu au génie de Gluck et aux principes de son art. Et cet hommage est d'autant plus significatif que, par le fait, il est unique, *Orphée* étant la seule œuvre de musique dramatique de cette époque à qui soit échue une telle fortune."

53. *Le Temps,* March 15, 1896. "*Orphée,* ce n'est pourtant ni *Alceste,* ni *Iphigénie en Tauride.* Mais sans être le chef-d'œuvre de Gluck, c'est déjà un chef-d'œuvre.... Donnez un verre d'eau à l'homme qui meurt de soif: cet homme songera-t-il à vous demander si vous avez d'abord . . . orné votre réservoir d'un filtre perfectionné? Non, le malheureux à qui vous rendes la vie ne fera pas trop le difficile. Il vous remerciera, même si vous ne le méritez guère, même si votre recours est tardif ou incomplet; et il boira, avidement."

54. *Revue hebdomadaire,* March 1896. Reprinted in Dukas, *Les Écrits de Paul Dukas sur la musique,* 295–96. "Combien de fois n'avions-nous pas prédit le triomphe de ces sublimes créations le jour où elles nous seraient rendues, et en combien d'occasions n'avons-nous pas insisté sur l'opportunité de remettre au répertoire au répertoire de nos théâtres les chefs-d'œuvre les plus authentiques dont ils puissent s'enorgueillir! Gluck a vaincu cette fois comme il vaincra toujours pas sa seule force et sans le secours de réclames préalables. Est-il permis d'espérer qu'on ne s'arrêtera pas en si beau chemin, et qu'après la représentation d'*Orphée* à l'Opéra-Comique, nous sommes en droit d'attendre de l'Opéra qu'il nous donne *Alceste, Armide* ou l'une des deux *Iphigénie?*"

55. The Schola Cantorum, for example, produced *Orphée* in 1910 and again in 1911 (in single performances), with the title role sung by a tenor.

56. On the "eminémment français" quality of the opéra-comique (both the genre and the institution), see, for example, Lesley Wright, "Carvalho and the Opéra-Comique: L'Art de se hâter lentement," in Fauser and Everist, *Music, Theater, and Cultural Transfer,* 99–126. Wright demonstrates that the resurrection and maintenance of a repertoire of opéras comiques was a central feature of Carvalho's plan to revitalize the Opéra-Comique around the turn of the century.

57. These columns in *Le Figaro* are treated extensively in Blay, "'Un théâtre français.'"

58. *Le Figaro,* February 4, 1898. Quoted in Blay "'Un théâtre français,'" 105. "Un théâtre français, tout à fait français. Et, par là, j'entends non pas réservé à nos seuls compositeurs, qu'il importe cependant de placer au premier rang, mais mené par un esprit de large et fière générosité française, c'est-à-dire respectueux au même degré de nos vielles gloires authentiques et des indiscutables gloires universelles; conservateur du génie national tel que nous le transmettent nos vrais maîtres d'aujourd'hui."

59. *Le Temps,* May 7, 1898. Quoted in Blay, "'Un théâtre français,'" 124. "Le vrai genre national, on l'a oubliée, c'est le grand opéra français créé par Quinault . . . la tragédie lyrique dont la qualité première était la belle déclamation, tradition fidèlement gardée jusqu'à l'invasion italienne du commencement de ce siècle. En se retournant vers le chant déclamé, vers le drame lyrique, la France ne ferait donc autre chose que de reprendre son bien, sous des apparences plus moderne."

60. *Musica,* November 1905. "Tandis que les générations passent, et avec elles les éphémères répertoires, *Alceste, Orphée, Armide,* les deux *Iphigénies* figurent encore aujourd'hui sur l'affiche de presque tous les théâtres lyriques. Si jamais compositeur défunt fut constamment d'actualité, et mérita d'éternels hommages, c'est bien celui-ci."

61. *La Revue hebdomadaire*, August 1900. Reprinted in Dukas, *Les écrits de Paul Dukas*, 497–504.

62. Léon Vallas, *Vincent d'Indy* (Paris: Albin Michel, 1950), 2:71.

63. *Le Guide Musical*, January 5, 1908. "rien n'est au point dans cette interpretation: ni les récits, trop solennels; ne les airs, manquant totalement de vie et d'expression; ne l'orchestre, parfait au point de vue de la note, absolument à côté au point de vue de l'accent et du style; ni même le ballet." D'Indy also referred to the performance in a letter as the "*massacre d'Iphigénie* au profit d'une affaire accessoire dans laquelle l'outrecuidance ne le cède qu'à la mauvaise foi." Letter to Octave Maus, January 3, 1908. Printed in Vincent d'Indy, *Ma Vie: Journal de Jeunesse, Correspondance Familiale et Intime, 1851–1931*, ed. Marie d'Indy (Paris: Séguier, 2001), 693.

64. Andrew Thomson, *Vincent d'Indy and His World* (Oxford: Clarendon Press, 1996), 162.

65. For a more in-depth examination of this particular instance, see William Gibbons, "*Iphigénie à Paris*: Positioning Gluck Historically in Early Twentieth-Century France." *Intersections: Canadian Journal of Music* 27 (2006): 3–15.

66. *Le Courrier musical*, January 1, 1908. "Malgré notre admiration pour l'oeuvre de Gluck ... ce nous est un devoir, par souci de la vérité et par scrupule surtout, de confesser ici l'impression de froideur, nous n'oserons pas dire d'ennui, que nous avons rapportée de la reprise de cet opéra qui n'avait pas été à Paris depuis 1824. Nous en accuserons à la fois la conception dramatique de l'œuvre et sa moderne interprétation."

67. *Le Mercure de France*, January 16, 1908. "On éprouve, à l'entendre, un amas d'impressions confusément hétérogènes dont la pire est une impossibilité parfaite de prendre un instant au sérieux l'action qu'on voit se dérouler sur les planches."

Chapter Six

1. Hippolyte Barbedette, *Gluck, sa vie, son système et ses oeuvres* (Paris: Heugel, 1882), iii, n. 1. "Ne peut-on dire aussi qu'en matière d'art, la nationalité ne dépend pas d'un acte de naissance?—Gluck est et restera le fondateur du drame lyrique français; à ce titre, il est Français comme Meyerbeer et la France aurait le droit de le revendiquer. Les Allemands, lorsqu'ils sont de bonne foi, la reconnaissent eux-mêmes."

2. Clément, *Histoire de la musique*, 529. "La théorie de Glück ... combattait exclusivement les tendances et les écarts de l'art dramatique italien. ... Les idées publiées par le célèbre compositeur bohème dans ses lettres et développées par ses partisans étaient essentiellement françaises et avaient été mise en pratique par Lulli, par Campra et même par Rameau, surtout dans *Castor et Pollux*."

3. Romain Rolland, *Musiciens d'autrefois* (Paris: Librairie Hachette, 1908), 207. "La révolution de Gluck ... ne fut pas l'œuvre du seul génie de Gluck, mais de tout un siècle de pensée. Elle était préparée, annoncée, attendue depuis vingt ans par les Encyclopédistes."

4. Rolland's position here is a somewhat ironic reversal of Julien Louis Geoffroy's 1810 damnation of Gluck for ruining Racine's drama, which I briefly discussed in the previous chapter. Geoffroy writes: "It is likely that the German musician did not understand French well enough to be sensitive to the melody of the most harmonious of our poets." *Empire*, January 16, 1810. [Il est probable que le musicien allemand n'entendait pas assez bien le français pour être sensible à la mélodie du plus harmonieux de nos poètes.]

5. In response to one of Clytemnestra's passages, for example, Diderot writes: "I do not know, either in Quinault or in any other poet, more lyrical verses, nor a situation more appropriate for musical imitation." [Je ne connais, ni dans Quinault, ni dans aucune poète, des vers plus lyriques, ni de situation plus propre à l'imitation musicale.] He goes on to rhapsodize about the suitability of Racine's play for operatic setting for several pages.

6. Rolland, *Musiciens d'autrefois*, 225.

7. Ibid., 213n2. "Si . . . les Encyclopédistes ne tardèrent pas à prendre violemment parti pour Rousseau et pour l'opéra italien, c'est qu'ils furent exaspérés par la brutalité scandaleuse avec laquelle les partisans de l'opéra français les combattirent."

8. *Le Figaro*, December 19, 1907. "Lulli et Rameau avaient tracé la route; Gluck, avec son génie ardent, passionné, profondément humain, devait l'élargir."

9. Henri Quittard, "Publications et œuvres récentes: *Iphigénie en Aulide*, de Gluck," *Revue musicale* (January 1908): 17. "L'art de Lulli, de Campra, de Rameau, c'est déjà l'art de Gluck. . . . *Iphigénie en Aulide* est le premier hommage du génie de Gluck au génie des maîtres français, en que il reconnaissait ses véritables précurseurs et qu'il allait faire oublier en réalisant plus complètement ce qu'ils avaient conçu."

10. "le chef-d'oeuvre de l'ancien opéra français." This positioning of Gluck is not surprising given Quittard's primary focus on music of the seventeenth century. Connecting Gluck with the French musical past, then, would require connecting him with those traditions. As Catrina Flint de Médicis has pointed out, all "early music" was not created equal in fin-de-siècle Paris. There was a significant distinction between the treatments of seventeenth- and eighteenth-century music in French scholarship (and performance) of this time, with one often being privileged over the other depending on the historical and political value systems of the author (or performer). See Médicis, "The Schola Cantroum," esp. 26–27.

11. Lavoix, *Histoire de la musique*, 232. "[Gluck's operas] marquent le point culminant de l'ancien drame lyrique, qui commence en France avec Lulli pour arriver à son apogée avec Glück."

12. *La France musicale*, November 20, 1859. "c'est le charme de Raphaël, uni à la grandeur et à l'énergie de Corneille!"

13. Chouquet, *Histoire de la musique dramatique en France*, 163. "Comme Pierre Corneille, il [Gluck] a doté notre scène de tragédies sublimes. . . . Entre ces deux mâles génies, plus réfléchis que spontanés, nous trouvons encore ce point de ressemblance: leurs tragédies ont toutes un type de grandeur commun, mais elles différent les unes des autres par la physionomie, par les formes et par les caractères. Leur théâtre enfin n'amollit pas; tout au contraire, il élève, il fortifie les cœurs."

14. For an analysis of attempts to masculinize French music history during the fin de siècle, see Fauser, "Gendering the Nations."

15. On the musical ramifications of Racine's turn-of-the-century feminization, see Ellis, *Interpreting the Musical Past*, 145–46.

16. M.-D. Calvocoressi even compared Gluck directly to Racine rather than Corneille in his article on the composer in the November 1905 issue of *Musica*, though the comparison is superficial rather than substantive (in the same passage, at the head of the article, Calvocoressi compares Gluck to Michelangelo).

17. Lavoix, *Histoire de la musique*, 234. "Glück est le plus fidèle traducteur musical de la grand tragédie de Racine et de Corneille."

18. *Le Ménestrel*, April 6, 1907.

19. For a contemporary discussion of Corneille's prominence at the fin de siècle, see Roger Le Brun, *Corneille devant trois siècles* (Paris: Sansot, 1906), lxxi–lxxxvii.

20. This passage is reprinted in ibid., 91. "Eschyle, Sophocle, et Euripide ensemble ne balancent point le seul Corneille. . . . Corneille est le créateur d'un pathétique nouveau, inconnu à l'antiquité et à tous les modernes avant lui."

21. This passage from *Essais de critique idéaliste* is reprinted in ibid., 92. "Si la France était forcée, dans quelque naufrage, à sacrifier tous ses poètes hormis un seul, celui qu'elle devrait sauver, c'est Corneille."

22. Gustave Lanson, *Corneille*, 3rd ed. (Paris: Librairie Hachette, 1909), 187. "Avant [Corneille], la tragédie classique n'existait pas. Par lui elle a existé."

23. The performance of sections of *Idomeneo* at the Schola Cantorum in 1902 and 1903 might have been aimed at demonstrating Mozart's more tragic side. These performances, however, failed to draw much attention to the opera, which remained unpopular with Parisian audiences.

24. *Musica*, June 1914. "Rameau n'est plus que le reflet aimable d'une époque; il le faut ouïr avec des oreilles d'historien; Gluck est éternel."

25. Simon Goldhill, *Victorian Culture and Classical Antiquity* (Princeton: Princeton University Press, 2011), 92.

26. Goldhill provides a series of references to Greece from French critics, of which this one is typical: "Every time I listen, I feel myself cast back to the days of ancient Athens, and I believe that I am sitting at productions of the tragedies of Sophocles and Euripides." Goldhill, *Victorian Culture and Classical Antiquity*, 92–93.

27. Hector Berlioz, *Gluck and His Operas*, trans. Edwin Evans (London: Reeves, 1915), 81.

28. Édouard Schuré, *Le Drame musical*, rev. ed., 2 vols. (Paris: Didier, 1886), 1:261–62. "Si Beethoven a trouvé la langue universelle de l'humanité modern, Gluck a retrouvé dans le langage des sons l'essence immortelle de l'âme grecque et a recréé la tragédie classique à travers le monde le l'harmonie." Though Schuré avoids directly connecting Wagner to Gluck in this teleological position, he posits Wagner as the modern incarnation of Greek ideals of musical drama, thus creating an oblique connection to Gluck, who was an eighteenth-century incarnation of the same underlying ideals.

29. Barbedette, *Gluck*, 81. "Gluck entreprit à quarante ans d'apprendre les langues anciennes. . . . Il se pénétra du sentiment de l'antique; il connut la sainte majesté des temples hellènes; il entrevit la suavité des champs Élyséens et l'horreur du Tartare."

30. *La Revue des deux mondes*, March 15, 1896. "[Par] cette magnificence et cette économie, l'auteur d'*Orphée* est antique. Enfin par la recherche et par la réalisation constante d'une beauté que la passion, même au paroxysme, ne déforme jamais, en un mot par tout son génie et toute son âme, ce fut bien un Grec—le dernier—que Willibald le Bohémien."

31. *La Revue des deux mondes*, March 15, 1896. "De cet Allemand, ou de ce Bohémien, trois chefs-d'œuvre—les derniers—furent écrits en français et pour la France."

32. The fin de siècle was not the first time that a vogue for all things Greek had swept through France. The Greek struggle for independence in the 1820s had caused a wave of sympathetic philhellenism to briefly unite the divided French society in favor of Greece, a fact that musicians were keen to take advantage of. See Walton, *Rossini in Restoration Paris*, ch. 3.

33. On France's turn to an ancient Greek history in the late nineteenth century, see Athena S. Leoussi, *Nationalism and Classicism: The Classical Body as National Symbol in Nineteenth-Century England and France* (New York: St. Martin's Press, 1998).

34. Leoussi, *Nationalism and Classicism*, 180–81.

35. For two analyses of the role of Greek themes in turn-of-the-century French music, see Kerstin Mira Schneider-Seidel, *Antike Sujets und moderne Musik: Untersuchungen zur französischen Musik um 1900* (Stuttgart: Verlag J. B. Metzler, 2002); and Samuel Dorf, "Listening between the Classical and the Sensual: Neoclassicism in Parisian Music and Dance Culture, 1870–1935" (PhD diss., Northwestern University, 2009).

36. Schneider-Seidel, *Antike Sujets und modern Musik*, 74. Laloy's dissertation concerned Greek music theory and Emmanuel wrote on Greek dance. For a brief biographical look at Laloy, see the introduction to Louis Laloy, *Louis Laloy (1874–1944) on Debussy, Ravel, and Stravinsky*, trans. and ed. Deborah Priest (Aldershot, UK: Ashgate, 1999). For more on Emmanuel and his theories on Greek music, see Samuel Baud-Bovy, "Maurice Emmanuel et la Grèce," *Revue musicale* 410/411 (1988): 109–15; and Dorf, "Listening between the Classical and the Sensual," ch. 4.

37. On Debussy and the pastoral mode, see David J. Code, "A Song Not Purely His Own: Modernism and the Pastoral Mode in Mallarmé, Debussy and Matisse" (PhD diss., University of California at Berkeley, 1999).

38. Weber, *France: Fin de Siècle*, 11–12. Weber treats the idea of the decadence of Parisian society extensively in chapter 1.

39. As I discuss in the following chapter, other critics focused on the lamentations of Orpheus rather than on his eventual reunion with Eurydice. On the supposed decline of the family in fin-de-siècle Paris, see Nicholas White, *The Family in Crisis in Late Nineteenth-Century French Fiction* (Cambridge: Cambridge University Press, 1999); and Roddey Reid, *Families in Jeopardy: Regulating the Social Body in France, 1750–1910* (Stanford: Stanford University Press, 1993).

40. Huebner, *French Opera at the Fin de Siècle*, 416–17.

41. Visual artists turned to the same allegorical techniques. Leoussi has pointed out the dramatic number of works on Greek subject material after the Franco-Prussian War, as these safely distanced themes could stand in for French ones, for example, when the siege of Athens could evoke the siege of Paris in 1870. Leoussi, *Nationalism and Classicism*, 180–85.

42. For a discussion of the allegorical content of these paintings, see Hollis Clayson, *Paris in Despair: Art and Everyday Life under Siege (1870–1871)* (Chicago: University of Chicago Press, 2002), ch. 5.

43. Brian Petrie, *Puvis de Chavanne*, ed. Simon Lee (Aldershot, UK: Ashgate, 1997), 82.

44. Jennifer H. Shaw, *Dream States: Puvis de Chavannes, Modernism, and the Fantasy of France* (New Haven: Yale University Press, 2002), 161.

45. Ibid., 162–63.

46. *Le Figaro*, November 22, 1893. "l'une des plus instructives et des plus émouvantes manifestations d'art de ces dernières années." For an analysis of this production, see Sylvie Humbert-Mougin, *Dionysos revisité: Les tragiques grecs en France de Leconte de Lisle à Claudel* (Paris: Belin, 2003), 182–88. Interestingly, the critic René Doumic found that Saint-Saëns pushed the music "close to the eminently French genre of the opéra comique," suggesting a growing connection at the fin de siècle between Greek drama and opera. *Le Moniteur universel*, November 27, 1893. "vers le genre éminemment français de l'opéra-comique."

47. Declaration from André Antoine and Paul Ginistry, codirectors of the Odéon. Archives nationales. "*Répertoire classique*. Nous considérons que c'est là un point important de notre mission, et ce répertoire sera l'objet de tous nos soins.... Nous ferons, si nous pouvons nous exprimer ainsi, une sorte d'exposition permanente du théâtre." Quoted in Humbert-Mougin, *Dionysos revisité*, 188–89.

48. Ibid., 77. "les années 1890–1910 voient fleurir des pieces symboliques ou allégoriques, où le mythe antique est librement retravaillé en vue d'un message édifiaent, moral ou politique."

49. Ibid., 79–80.

50. Huebner, *French Opera at the Fin de Siècle*, 214–16. In typically eloquent fashion, Saint-Saëns himself calls into question the distinction between mythological and historical subject material for operas at the fin de siècle: "It is a question whether there is any essential difference between history and mythology. History is made up of what probably happened; mythology of what probably did not happen. There are myths in history and history in myths. Mythology is merely the old form of history." Saint-Saëns, *Musical Memories*, 62.

51. Huebner, *French Opera at the Fin de Siècle*, 214.

52. Paul A. Bertagnolli, *Prometheus in Music: Representations of the Myth in the Romantic Era* (Aldershot, UK: Ashgate, 2007), 204–31.

53. On the rise of nationalistic movements in France during the early twentieth century, see Eugen Weber, *The Nationalist Revival in France, 1905–1914* (Berkeley: University of California Press, 1968). On the right-wing uses of concert music, see Fulcher, "The Concert as Political Propaganda."

54. On the impact of the Franco-Prussian War on French nationalist literature, see Catharine Savage Brosman, *Visions of War in France: Fiction, Art, Ideology* (Baton Rouge: Louisiana State University Press, 1999), 108–27.

55. Douglas Mackaman, "Regaining the 'Lost Provinces': Textual Battles for Alsace-Lorraine and the First World War," in *World War I and the Cultures of Modernity*, ed. Douglas Mackaman and Michael Mays (Jackson: University of Mississippi Press, 2000), 125–34.

56. Lucien Gallois, "Alsace-Lorraine and Europe," *Geographical Review* 6 (1918): 103.

57. Reprinted in Stéphen Coubé, *Alsace, Lorraine et France rhénane* (Paris: Lethielleux, 1915), 111–12: "Et la France, Sire, la France qui peut être vaincue mais non anéantie, acceptera-t-elle dans l'avenir une situation qu'on la forcerait de subir aujourd'hui? Pour elle, céder l'Alsace équivaut au sacrifice d'une mère à laquelle on arrache l'enfant qui ne veut pas se séparer d'elle."

58. Édouard Schuré, *L'Alsace française: Rêves et combats* (Paris: Perrin, 1916), 123: "Le résultat de la guerre de 1870 fut un désastre pour l'Alsace-Lorraine. Son annexation à l'Allemagne arrachait à la mère patrie deux provinces devenues françaises par toutes leurs fibres."

59. On the prominence of Alsace-Lorraine in fin-de-siècle Paris, see, for example, Jules Duhem, *La Question d'Alsace-Lorraine, de 1871 à 1914* (Paris: Alcan, 1917), in which the author points out that "two points above all have captured the attention of the major players in the drama [of Alsace-Lorraine]: the territorial cession, and consequently the lamentable situation of the annexed populations" (4). [Deux points surtout ont fixé l'attention des grands personnages du drame: la cession territoriale, et, par voie de conséquence, la situation lamentable des populations annexées.]

60. For a brief overview of the female iconographic representation of France, see Brosman, *Visions of War in France*, 44–48.

61. Leoussi, *Nationalism and Classicism*, 195.

62. Rolland, *Musiciens d'autrefois*, 246. "L'art de Gluck est profondément humain. Par opposition aux tragédies mythologiques de Rameau, il reste sur la terre: ses héros sont des hommes; leurs joies et leurs douleurs lui suffisent. Il a chanté des passions les plus pures: l'amour conjugal dans *Orphée* et dans *Alceste*, l'amour paternel et l'amour filial

dans *Iphigénie en Aulide*, l'amour fraternel et l'amitié dans *Iphigénie en Tauride*, l'amour désintéressé, le sacrifice, le don de soi-même à ceux qu'on aime."

63. Barbedette, *Gluck*, 88. "Comme Gluck, Wagner, après avoir constaté l'abaissement du théâtre à son époque, se tourne du côté de la Grèce. C'est là, dans la patrie d'Eschyle qu'il trouve, suivant ses propres paroles,—'le modèle et le type de l'art.' Chez les Grecs, toutes les branches de l'art étaient réunies pour coopérer à un même résultat."

Chapter Seven

1. Gerald D. Turbow, "Art and Politics: Wagnerism in France," in *Wagnerism in European Culture and Politics*, ed. David C. Large and William Weber, in collaboration with Anne Dzamba Sessa (Ithaca, NY: Cornell University Press, 1984), 148. Katharine Ellis has also explored the extent to which Fétis's anti-Wagnerism shaped critical perceptions of the composer, including his derivation from earlier French sources. See Katharine Ellis, "Wagner and Anti-Wagnerism in the Paris Periodical Press, 1852–1870," in *Von Wagner zum Wagnérisme: Musik, Literatur, Kunst, Politik*, ed. Annegret Fauser and Manuela Schwartz (Leipzig: Leipziger Universitätsverlag, 1999), 51–83.

2. For a thorough (if idiosyncratic) analysis of the preface to *Alceste* as well as the complete text (in translation), see Alfred Einstein, *Gluck*, trans. Eric Blom (London: Dent, 1964). For details of the 1861 *Tannhäuser*, see Fauser, "'Cette musique sans tradition.'"

3. Barry Millington has succinctly summarized Wagner's changes: "His arrangement was, according to the lights of his time, a sincere and sensitive attempt to present the opera in an acceptable form. Finding the arias and choruses 'disconnected,' he linked them by means of preludes, postludes and transitions.... The orchestration was also revised but with restraint and always with the aim of highlighting features of Gluck's own score. His major alteration was to eliminate what he regarded as the predictable and sentimental marriage of Achilles and Iphigenia at the end; in order to effect this return to the spirit of Euripides it was necessary to introduce a new character (Artemis) as well as some recitatives." Barry Millington, *Wagner*, rev. ed. (Princeton: Princeton University Press, 1984), 31. For Wagner's own comments on adapting the work, see Richard Wagner, *My Life*, trans. Andrew Gray, ed. Mary Whitall (New York: Da Capo Press, 1992), 337–40.

4. Wagner also published an article in 1854 in the *Neue Zeitschrift für Musik* (July 1, 1854) focusing on his adaptation of the overture to *Iphigénie*.

5. For a fuller analysis of the 1861 production and its long-term ramifications for Gluck and Wagner reception in France, see Gibbons, "Music of the Future, Music of the Past."

6. *La Revue et gazette musicale de Paris*, October 14, 1866. "La dernière reprise d'*Alceste*, encore toute récente, eut lieu le 21 octobre 1861, année mémorable qui avait commencé par la chute éclatante de *Tannhäuser*. La musique de l'avenir et celle du passé s'y mesurèrent comme en champs clos, et le passé eut facilement raison de l'avenir, qu'il enterra bel et bien."

7. *Revue des deux mondes*, August 15, 1852. "M. Wagner se croit l'inventeur d'un système qui est aussi vieux que la musique même."

8. Ibid., November 1, 1866. "On n'étonnerait point beaucoup, j'imagine, l'auteur de *Tannhäuser* et de *Lohengrin* en lui disant qu'il n'a rien inventé et que toute cette théorie, qu'il étale à si grands fracas dans ses volumes, se trouve exposée par Gluck en

quelques pages de préface écrites de ce style simple et clair que pratiquent les honnêtes gens; mais M. Richard Wagner se doute-t-il que cette méthode, qu'il na pas inventée, lui vient en France, et que c'est du vin de notre cru qu'il boit dans son verre allemand? Inconséquence et contradiction, voilà un homme qui, pour réformer l'art national d'un pays qui donnait hier au monde Beethoven et Weber, s'adresse aux plus caduques traditions de la vielle tragédie française! Cette homme, n'ayant en vue que l'avenir, ne regarde que le passé."

9. Barbedette, *Gluck*, 89. "Comme Gluck, Wagner donne au poète la plus large part (il est poète lui-même, son amour-propre ne saurait en souffrir). Comme Gluck, il veut que le langage musical se fasse l'interprète fidèle et exact de tous les états de l'âme; comme lui il exalte la puissance de l'orchestre; comme lui, il aime à faire précéder l'entrée du personnage d'une sorte de phrase symbolique qui le caractérise et l'annonce."

10. Katharine Ellis, "En Route to Wagner: Explaining d'Indy's Early Music Pantheon," in *Vincent d'Indy et son temps*, ed. Manuela Schwartz (Sprimont, Belgium: Mardaga, 2006), 112. Here Ellis is specifically referring to the value given to composers in d'Indy's *Cours de composition musicale*.

11. Julien Tiersot, *Gluck*, 4th ed. (Paris: Alcan, 1919), 231.

12. Ibid., 235–37.

13. Ibid., 234. "[Gluck] n'a jamais eu la pensée de briser les formes utilisées par Lulli et Rameau, mais, au contraire . . . sa plus haute ambition fut de continuer leurs traditions."

14. *Le Guide musical*, January 26, 1908. "Au signe d'une baguette de feu, l'ouverture d'*Iphigénie en Aulide*, cessant de nous apparaître comme un majestueux portique, peuplé de mannequins hiératisés, est devenue, comme le devinait Wagner, la synthèse vivante de toutes les passions, de toutes les douleurs, de tous les conflits du drame grec."

15. Roger Nichols, *The Life of Debussy* (Cambridge: Cambridge University Press, 1998), 109.

16. Léon Vallas, *The Theories of Claude Debussy, Musicien Français*, trans. Marie O'Brien (London: Oxford University Press, 1929), 69.

17. *Gil blas*, February 23, 1903. This letter was eventually published in *Monsieur Croche, antidilettante*. Reprinted in Debussy, *Debussy on Music*, 123–26. Quotation at 125.

18. Jean d'Udine, *Gluck* (Paris: Librairie Renouard, 1906), 63. "il imagina, bien avant Wagner, la *mélodie continue*, avec cet avantage sur l'auteur de *Tristan* et de la *Tétralogie*, qu'il ne craignait de s'en écarter ni dans le sens du récitatif, ni dans celui de l'air."

19. Ibid., 121. "le colosse de Bayreuth, qui se croyait un bon gluckiste, ne l'était point. . . . La 'mélodie continue' wagnérienne est un sophisme; sophisme défendu génialement par un orchestre incomparable, mais sophisme tout de même. . . . Les disciples de Wagner, MM. Humperdinck, Vincent d'Indy et Alfred Bruneau, par exemple, sont hors de la tradition gluckiste, chaque fois qu'ils demeurent esclaves de l'esthétique du leitmotiv et qu'ils fuient systématiquement les formes carrées, les vraies formes lyriques."

20. Summaries of the rise of Wagner's music in France at the turn of the century may be found in Huebner, *French Opera at the Fin de Siècle*, 11–21; and Messing, *Neoclassicism in Music*, 1–7.

21. For more on *Lohengrin* in Paris during this time period, see Manuela Schwartz, "'La question de *Lohengrin*' zwischen 1869 und 1891," in Fauser and Schwartz, *Von Wagner zum Wagnérisme*, 107–36. A brief summary may also be found in Elaine Brody, *Paris: The Musical Kaleidoscope, 1870–1925* (New York: George Braziller, 1987), 51.

22. Schwartz, "'La question de *Lohengrin*' zwischen 1869 und 1891," 131.

23. Huebner, *French Opera at the Fin de Siècle*, 21.

24. *La Nouvelle revue*, March/April 1896. "A propos de l'*Orphée* de Gluck, que vient de nous donner l'Opéra-Comique, on s'est plu à remettre en lumière les théories fameuses de l'illustre compositeur; nous-mêmes les avons maintes fois rappelées ici, à propos de la définition du véritable drame lyrique, dont la préface d'*Alceste* a très purement déterminé le caractère."

25. *Le Figaro*, March 7, 1896. "Il est impossible—on le voit—d'exprimer mieux, de définir plus clairement, plus nettement les nobles et hautes ambitions des musiciens d'aujourd'hui."

26. Huebner, *French Opera at the Fin de Siècle*, 401.

27. *La Revue des deux mondes*, March 15, 1896. "L'*Orphée* de Gluck est individuel en ce sens, que la conception dramatique de Gluck, ainsi qu'autrefois celle de Monteverde, et contrairement à celle de Wagner, est humaine et concrète. Gluck n'a pas de prétentions philosophiques. Il ne cherche point à résoudre l'énigme du monde."

28. *La Revue des deux mondes*, March 15, 1896. "C'est à la point de vue de la déclamation qu'on ne manque jamais aujourd'hui de comparer, d'assimiler Wagner et Gluck. On s'en va répétant que l'un et l'autre ont été les serviteurs, les adorateurs du verbe ils ont tout sacrifié même la musique. Peut-être faudrait-il s'entendre. Si Gluck et Wagner se rencontrent et s'accordent ici en théorie, dans la pratique ils se séparent et s'opposent jusqu'à la contradiction. On ne saurait trouver deux manières plus opposées que les leurs de comprendre et de régler le rôle de la parole. Tandis que chez Wagner elle ne sert qu'à la détermination du sujet, de la situation, du sentiment que l'orchestre est chargé de rendre, chez Gluck elle est elle-même—elle seule parfois—le mode ou l'agent de l'expression; en elle est le centre ou le sommet de l'œuvre, et comme le siège de la beauté. En un mot la parole est ce qu'on pourrait avec le moins de dommage enlever au drame lyrique wagnérien; mais si peu qu'on la trahisse ou qu'on l'altère, voilà d'un seul coup le drame lyrique de Gluck anéanti."

29. *Musica*, December 1905. "La musique de l'avenir était devenue la musique du présent. Nous applaudissions, joyeux, à cette métamorphose. Depuis, à boire chaque soir à la coupe du même Titan, n'éprouve-t-on pas un peu de satiété, ou plutôt n'a-t-on pas redouté la monotonie de la grandeur et de la puissance? Lors il fallut songer à varier le plaisir des auditeurs, tout en offrant un pur aliment au goût qui s'était épuré et affiné à la table du Dieu. Telle est la genèse du renouveau classique en ces dernières années, la cause des triomphales reprises d'*Orphée*, d'*Iphigénie en Tauride*, d'*Alceste* et, enfin, d'*Armide*. La tragédie de Gluck a paru jeune encore de gloire et d'immortalité au voisinage du drame lyrique: l'Olympe n'est point un petit mont méprisable à la vue des sommets du Walhalla."

30. In discussing the frequent appearance of "musique ancienne" and "musique moderne" on the same concerts—that is, concerts that featured both "old" and "new" music, but generally not canonical nineteenth-century works—Jann Pasler has noted Wagner's historicizing effect on some audience members, noting that "the attraction to Wagner helped motivate this look backward and forward in French music. Wagner challenged French listeners' perceptions of their musical needs and desires." Pasler, *Composing the Citizen*, 630.

31. Saint-Saëns, *Musical Memories*, 61.

32. *Le Courrier musical*, December 15, 1907. "Elle [Bréval] trouva ici [dans Gluck] le bénéfice de sa volonté du sacrifice, de cette volonté selon laquelle elle atténue parfois jusqu'au soufflé la voix qui proféra avec une déchirante violence les *hoïotoho* de Brunnhilde.... C'est cette volonté ... qui va faire certainement de Lucienne Bréval une très exacte Iphigénie."

33. Ibid., April 15, 1906. "Je suis sûr que si l'on demandait à Mme Litvinne d'avouer ses secrètes préférences entre la mort d'Armide et la mort de Brunnhild, elle ne se résoudrait pas à faire un choix entre ces deux pages géniales." Litvinne herself would have likely agreed with this assessment of Gluck's dramatic soprano roles; she wrote rapturously of *Alceste* in her autobiography, and included the work in the "Étude des grands rôles" (Study of the great roles) portion of her text. See Félia Litvinne, *Mon vie et mon art* (Paris: Plon, 1933), 139–42, 233–37.

34. For more on the importance of the *Revue wagnerienne* in symbolist culture, see Pamela A. Genova, *Symbolist Journals: A Culture of Correspondence* (Aldershot, UK: Ashgate, 2002) and Kelly Jo Maynard, "The Enemy Within: Encountering Wagner in Third-Republic France" (PhD diss., University of California at Los Angeles, 2007).

35. Eva Kushner, *Le Mythe d'Orphée dans la littérature française contemporaine* (Paris: A. G. Nizet, 1961), 100–101. "Wagner régnait en dieu." Kushner goes on to say: "He embodied for all these fervent disciples 'the complete artwork,' at the heart of which fine art and music are called to support literature. These symbolists followed Wagner all the way to his philosophical conceptions, speaking like him of the true essence of things, which oppose their appearances." [Il incarnait pour tous ces disciples fervents "l'art complet," au sein duquel art plastique et musique sont appelés à appuyer la littérature. Ces symbolistes suivaient Wagner jusque ses conceptions philosophiques, parlant comme lui de la véritable essence des choses, qui opposée à leurs apparences.]

36. *Le Journal des débats*, November 22, 1893. "l'une des plus instructive et des plus émouvantes manifestations d'art de ces dernières années." Quoted in Humbert-Mougin, *Dionysos revisité*, 184.

37. For a thorough look at the Orpheus myth in symbolist art, see Dorothy M. Kosinski, *Orpheus in Nineteenth-Century Symbolism* (Ann Arbor, MI: UMI Research Press, 1989).

38. On the importance of Orphic thought to Mallarmé, see Walter A. Strauss, *Descent and Return: The Orphic Theme in Modern Literature* (Cambridge, MA: Harvard University Press, 1971), ch. 4. See also Robert McGahey, *The Orphic Moment: Shaman to Poet-Thinker in Plato, Nietzsche, and Mallarmé* (Albany: State University of New York Press, 1994).

39. Kosinski, *Orpheus in Nineteenth-Century Symbolism*, 49.

40. Certainly, not all symbolists agreed with Wagner that music stood at the pinnacle of the arts. René Ghil, for example, argued strongly that poetry was the true synthesis of the arts. In the symbolist discourse, as Joseph Acquisto points out, "What begins as a sort of competition among the arts for pride of place, a conflict incited by Wagner's published claims about poetry's eventual disappearance and replacement by music, eventually becomes a site of aporia, a space for critical discourse about poetry and the limits which both poetry and the critical metadiscourse can or should transcend." Joseph Acquisto, *French Symbolist Poetry and the Idea of Music* (Aldershot, UK: Ashgate, 2006), 4. This book provides an insightful look at the role of Wagner's writings in the development of symbolist thought. For a different perspective on the subject, see Louis Marvick, *Waking the Face That No One Is: A Study in the Musical Context of Symbolist Poetics* (Amsterdam: Rodopi, 2004).

41. Albert Lavignac, for example, ascribed enormous power to Wagner's music in 1898: "We look at the sun and watch it in its course, but we never think of congratulating it in its power, nor of thinking that its glory would in any way be augmented by the addition of our mite of personal appreciation." Albert Lavignac, *The Music Dramas of Richard Wagner and His Festival Theatre in Bayreuth*, trans. Esther Singleton (New York: Dodd, Mead, 1914), 69.

42. Kosinski points out this Wagnerian connection, as well. Furthermore, she observes that the type of "psychological landscape" depicted in this painting was understood at the time as being inherently Wagnerian, a fact noted by, among other critics, Edouard Schuré and Téodor de Wyzewa. Kosinski, *Orpheus in Nineteenth-Century Symbolism*, 121, and ch. 5.

43. Schuré, *Le Drame musical*, 1:268. "Le mythe d'Orphée ne pouvait trouver sa forme dramatique et poignante que part la plenitude de l'expression musicale." The historical importance of the Orpheus myth in music is addressed from a number of perspectives in Danièle Pistone and Pierre Brunel, eds., *Musiques d'Orphée* (Paris: Presses Universitaires de France, 1999). A list of significant musical works on the subject from the sixteenth to twentieth centuries may be found on pages 185–90.

44. For more on Debussy's work, see Rollo Myers, "The Opera that Never Was: Debussy's Collaboration with Victor Segalen in the Preparation of *Orphée*," *Musical Quarterly* 64 (1978): 495–506.

45. *Le Ménestrel*, August 30, 1896. "A partir du XIXe siècle, le nom de Gluck est si complètement associé à l'idée d'Orphée qu'aucun musicien n'oserait plus toucher à cette légende, au sujet de laquelle il semble que, désormais, tout soit dit."

46. Monteverdi's *Orfeo* was certainly known to musicologists at this time (many of them wrote of the work in opera histories), but was undoubtedly considered to be unperformable in modern times. In 1904 it was performed in a concert version at the Schola Cantorum, but onstage Gluck's version remained essentially unchallenged.

47. *L'Artiste*, March 1896: 215. "Dans les profondeurs funèbres du Bois sacré tutélaire, ne nous indique-t-il pas lui-même le sentier, le blanc Poète éperdu qui brandit sa Lyre, confiant dans son désespoir harmonieux qui va créer le chant pour reconquérir l'amour? Le mythe éternel parle en son geste. Identifions notre âme à la sienne, marchons avec lui, vivons en lui, pour orner le musée intérieur de nos fugitifs souvenirs: sa beauté douloureuse nous relève à nous-mêmes; qu'il soit dans nos espérances, qu'il revienne parmi nos regrets pour les embellir à son image, avec la renaissance des premières feuillées."

48. Patricia Mathews, *Passionate Discontent: Creativity, Gender, and French Symbolist Art* (Chicago: University of Chicago Press, 1999), 113.

49. Gluck's original Italian version of the opera (1762) called for a castrato contralto. In the French version (1774), the part was rewritten for a tenor voice. In Berlioz's 1859 version, which was used (with minor alterations) in the 1896 production, the role was restored to the contralto/mezzo-soprano range, performed by a female singer.

50. Kosinski, *Orpheus in Nineteenth-Century Symbolism*, 153. For a contemporary critic who connected these paintings to Gluck's opera, see Paul Mantz, "Salon de 1863," *Gazette des beaux-arts* 4 (1863): 40.

51. This is a central concept of Jean-Jacques Nattiez, *Wagner Androgyne*, trans. Stewart Spencer (Princeton: Princeton University Press, 1993).

52. Ibid., 40.

53. For an examination of the development and continuation of the *travesti* character in nineteenth-century opera, see Naomi André, *Voicing Gender: Castrati, Travesti, and the Second Woman in Early-Nineteenth-Century Italian Opera* (Bloomington: Indiana University Press, 2006). On Nicklausse in *Les Contes d'Hoffmann*, see Heather Hadlock, "The Career of Cherubino, or the Trouser Role Grows Up," in *Siren Songs: Representations of Gender and Sexuality in Opera*, ed. Mary Ann Smart (Princeton: Princeton University Press, 2000), 74. Hadlock also points to the gender issues inherent in the soprano title character in Massenet's *Chérubin* (1905), another example of the fin-de-siècle French trouser role.

54. Wendy Bashant, "Singing in Greek Drag: Gluck, Berlioz, George Eliot," in *En Travesti: Women, Gender Subversion, Opera*, ed. Corinne E. Blackmer and Patricia Juliana Smith (New York: Columbia University Press, 1995), 216, 221.

55. *La Gazette de France*, March 8, 1896. "le plus bizarre [chose], c'est le costume feminine d'Orphée: sans sa lyre, on ne le distinguerait pas d'Eurydice. Il paraît que c'est encore une idée nouvelle de l'interprète . . . hélas!"

56. On the widespread depictions of lesbianism in the French arts during this time, see Dorothy M. Kosinski, "Gustave Courbet's *The Sleepers*. The Lesbian Image in Nineteenth-Century French Art and Literature," *Artibus et historiae* 9 (1988): 187–99. Kosinski points out that often mythological themes (or allusion to them) were a common way of providing a veneer of "respectability" to depictions of lesbian behavior, avoiding the criticism that these works appealed to prurient interests. For a musicological perspective on these issues, see also Hadlock, "The Career of Cherubino," 75–76.

57. Lenard A. Berlanstein, "Breeches and Breaches: Cross-Dress Theater and the Culture of Gender Ambiguity in Modern France," *Comparative Studies in Society and History* 38 (1996), 339.

58. Vincent d'Indy, *Cours de composition musicale*, vol. 3, ed. Guy de Lioncourt (Paris: Durand, 1950), 62. "L'Orphée français, comme l'italien, était écrit pour une voix de ténor, et la transformation de ce rôle en contralto, adoptée longtemps à l'Opéra-Comique sous le prétexte que l'effort demandé au ténor était trop grand, en change très défavorablement le caractère et l'accent. En Italie, on cultivait beaucoup à l'aigu les voix de ténor, jusqu'à leur faire pour ainsi dire emprunter un registre mieux à la portée des voix des femmes; mais ces notes aiguës étaient très violentes, et leur remplacement par un medium féminin est une édulcoration qui équivaut à un assassinat." While this passage was not published until the mid-twentieth century (compiled from Lioncourt's notes from the Schola Cantorum), it presumably reflects d'Indy's earlier views as well. He expressed similar annoyance with the notion of a female Orphée in some program notes he wrote—and subsequently published in the April 1909 issue of the *Tablettes de la Schola*—for a concert that included portions of *Orphée* with a female soprano in the title role. See Vincent d'Indy, *Ma vie*, 703–4.

59. Eugène Borrel, "La Schola et la restauration de la musique ancienne," in Vincent d'Indy et al., *La Schola Cantorum en 1925* (Paris: Bloud et Gay, 1927), 136–37. "Gluck a été aussi un auteur de prédilection pour la Schola: les *Iphigénies*, *Alceste*, *Armide*, ont été données successivement; mais l'exécution la plus marquante est celle d'*Orphée* avec le rôle principal restitué à une haute-contre (ténor); elle a été le prélude et la raison déterminante de la reprise à l'Opéra-Comique; jusque-là en effet, on avait l'habitude, depuis Mme Viardot, de remplacer le ténor par un contralto, ce qui bouleversait tout l'effet expressif de ce rôle écrit pour un homme par Gluck. Ici encore il faut compter à l'actif de la Schola cette petite opération de police esthétique."

60. In seeking a definitely masculine version of Orpheus, d'Indy might also have sought to eliminate the lingering aspects of queer identity that have been associated with Orpheus since Ovid, including homosexuality and pederasty. According to the *Metamorphoses*, after the death of Eurydice, Orpheus rejected the company of women, preferring instead the sexual company of the men and young boys of Thrace. For a discussion of this aspect of Orpheus's character, see John F. Makowski, "Bisexual Orpheus: Pederasty and Parody in Ovid," *Classical Journal* 92 (1996): 25–38. Recently, Judith Peraino has explored Orpheus's queer identity in more musicological terms in *Listening to the Sirens: Musical Technologies of Queer Identity from Homer to Hedwig* (Berkeley: University of California Press, 2006), 24–26.

61. Charles Segal, *Orpheus: The Myth of the Poet* (Baltimore: Johns Hopkins University Press, 1989), 164. For one look at the lament as peculiarly feminine in opera, see Leofranc Holford-Strevens, "'Her Eyes Became Two Spouts': Classical Antecedents of Renaissance Laments," *Early Music* 27 (1999): 379–93.

62. *L'Orchestre*, March 17, 1896. "On est envahi, en écoutant ces lamentations symphoniques, par l'intensité de pénétration de ces accents où les déchirements de l'âme surhumaine s'allient à la pensée terrestre."

63. While Orpheus's lamenting was a trope of romanticism as well, the importance of his suffering was magnified at the fin de siècle. As Kosinski points out, "For the Symbolists . . . the contorted, solitary figure of Orpheus is the embodiment of spiritual torment, an expression of [their] own personal emotional or aesthetic struggles." Kosinski, *Orpheus in Nineteenth-Century Symbolism*, 152.

64. This French text is taken from the Stanford University online libretto collection, available at http://opera.stanford.edu/iu/libretti/orphee.html.

65. *Le Guide musical*, March 8, 1896. "Lorsqu'au lever du rideau, nous admirions ce tableau digne du Poussin, représentant Orphée prosterné devant le tombeau d'Eurydice, répondant par ce cri douloureux "Eurydice" aux belles lamentations du chœur."

66. *Le Figaro*, March 7, 1896. "La lente lamentation du peuple devant le tombeau d'Eurydice, les trois cris déchirants d'Orphée qui la dominent, la pantomime funèbre qui la suit sont d'une solennité superbe."

67. *Le Journal des débats*, March 15, 1896. "Quelle prodigieuse émotion se dégage de ce cri d'amour: *J'ai perdu mon Eurydice!* Et penseriez-vous trouver un seul homme véritablement sensible au charme de la musique qui pût rester froid devant cette explosion de désespoir, même après tous les bouleversements opérés dans l'art musical par Beethoven, Berlioz, ou Wagner?"

68. *L'Artiste*, March 1896: 198. "les trois aspects différents revêtus par un même ouvrage selon des époques diverses, de confronter avec sympathie les trois *Orphées* et les trois Gluck tels qu'ils apparurent successivement aux auditeurs parisiens de 1774, de 1859 et de 1896: le miroir est la mesure de toutes choses, et l'image immortelle se déforme en s'y réfléchissant. Chaque âge a ses plaisirs—et son point de vue. Le philosophe n'ajouterait-il pas qu'il y a peut-être autant d'*Orphées* que d'auditeurs? . . . Ce qui ne laisse pas que d'être inquiétant."

Chapter Eight

1. Jullien, *Paris dilettante au commencement du siècle*, 372. "Par une loi de nature, qu'il n'est pas en notre pouvoir de modifier, la France n'a vu naître qu'un nombre très restreint de grands musiciens, j'entends de ces génies supérieurs qui sont comme les dieux de la musique: presque tous out vu le jour en Italie et surtout en Allemagne. Nous pouvons bien nous honorer d'avoir pour compatriotes des musiciens de haute valeur, et qui ont joué un beau rôle dans l'histoire de la musique française: Campra, Destouches, Monsigny, Philidor, Berton, Boïeldieu, Nicolo, Hérold, etc.; mais je ne vois guère que Rameau, et peut-être Méhul et Berlioz, qui puissent être rangés parmi les sommités de l'art musical."

2. Lois Laloy, *Rameau* (Paris: Alcan, 1908), 181–82. "Les airs de danse et les morceaux descriptifs de Rameau brillent d'une splendeur inaltérée. Le temps, qui a fait tort à tant de gloires, semble avoir ajouté encore à leur beauté, y effaçant ce que les contemporains y voyaient de hardi, la rendant plus claire et plus harmonieuse. De toutes ces

compositions, rien n'a vieilli, alors que Beethoven, Schubert, Berlioz, Liszt, Wagner et César Franck nous montrent tant de pages ou de phrases surannées. Rien ne perd aussi tôt sa fraîcheur qu'une effusion lyrique, fût-elle la plus touchant du monde, parce que rien ne change plus rapidement que nos manières de vivre. C'est en s'abstenant de paraitre en son œuvre que Rameau lui a assuré les plus grandes chances d'immortalité."

3. Lavoix, *Histoire de la musique*, 226. "Organiste, claveciniste, théoricien, compositeur dramatique, Rameau fut le plus grand musicien français du XVIIIe siècle, couvrant de son nom, comme d'un pavillon triomphant, la période qui s'étend de Lulli à Gluck.

"Ce fut lui donna à l'harmonie la couleur et la profondeur, développa les forces expressives de l'orchestre, créa l'ouverture, qui n'était avant lui qu'une sorte de murmure plus ou moins agréable. Avec Bach et Haendel, Rameau complète la grande trinité musicale de la première moitié du XVIIIe siècle, et nous pouvons dire que Gluck ne fut pas sans subir la forte et salutaire influence du maître bourguignon."

4. On the nineteenth-century French reception of Bach and Handel, see Ellis, *Interpreting the Musical Past.*

5. *Le Figaro*, May 14, 1908. "les théâtres subventionnés inscrivent les œuvres à leur répertoire, comme sont inscrites au répertoire de la Comédie-Française et de l'Odéon les œuvres de Corneille, de Racine, de Molière. Cette égalité de traitement envers nos gloires passées, ne serait-ce pas l'équité même? Et la culture de notre individualité nationale n'aurait-elle pas tout à y gagner?"

6. Clément, *Histoire de la musique*, 517. "À la date du 1er octobre 1733 commence pour l'histoire de la musique en France une période d'immenses progrès, remplie tout entière par les œuvres d'un seul compositeur, de Rameau, le plus grand des musiciens français au dix-huitième siècle."

7. *Revue hebdomadaire*, May 1901. Reprinted in Dukas, *Les Écrits de Paul Dukas sur la musique*, 545. "Les volumes précédents, moins importants, étaient consacrés à sa musique de clavecin . . . à sa musique concertante, à ses cantates et à ses motets."

8. Ancien régime music, culture, and fashion underwent something of a revival in the late nineteenth century, at least among some segments of the Parisian population. Jann Pasler, for example, has noted the ancien régime overtones of Emmaneul Chabrier's *Le Roi malgré lui* (1887), as well as the trend of resurrecting Louis XIV-era dance styles—both in terms of neoclassical compositions based on these styles and, bizarrely, fin-de-siècle aristocrats dressing in costumes and performing period dances. See Pasler, *Composing the Citizen*, 498–507.

9. Composers and connoisseurs, however, were certainly more familiar with Rameau's work throughout the nineteenth century, as Jean-Claire Vançon has made clear in his dissertation, which is by far the most detailed study of Rameau's reception to date. Given the thoroughness of Vançon's treatment of the topic, I am limiting the amount of background I provide here. Jean-Claire Vançon, "Le Temple de la Gloire: Visage et usages de Jean-Philippe Rameau en France entre 1764 et 1895" (PhD diss., Université de Paris-Sorbonne, 2009), especially volume 3. See also Danièle Pistone, "Rameau à Paris au XIXe siècle," in *Jean-Philippe Rameau: Colloque international, organisé par la Société Rameau*, ed. Jérôme de la Gorce (Paris: Champion-Slatkine, 1987): 131–40.

10. The unsigned review in the *Journal des débats*, for example, highlights the relationship of *Castor et Pollux* to the *ancien régime*, pointing out that the work was "first performed in 1737 with music by Rameau, revived in 1753, then in 1770 for the Dauphin's marriage"—demonstrating a direct connection to the royal family. *Journal des débats*, December 30, 1814. [Cet opéra, donné d'abord en 1737 avec la musique de Rameau, repris en 1753, puis en 1770 pour le mariage du Dauphin.] The critic also suggested a

connection between the composer and France's monarchy: although other composers may have dethroned Rameau from his lofty perch as the greatest operatic composer, they had "perished in defeat: Rameau, as their king, has been held in reserve to embellish the triumph of the victors." [Les autres musiciens avaient péri dans la défaite: Rameau, comme leur roi, avait été réservé pour orner le triomphe des vainqueurs.]

11. Pistone, "Rameau à Paris," 133.

12. For background on the concert series, see Bernard, "Jules Pasdeloup et les Concerts populaires." Popular morceaux from Rameau's operas during the midcentury included the "Trio des songes" and Rigaudon from *Dardanus*, and the "Choeur de l'enfer" and "Choeur des Champs-Elysées" from *Castor et Pollux*.

13. Ellis, *Interpreting the Musical Past*, 76.

14. Pistone, "Rameau à Paris," 136.

15. Vançon, "La Temple de la gloire," 3:284–86.

16. Several of Rameau's sacred works also appeared on programs at the Société des Concerts, including his motets *Quam dilecta* (1898 and 1903) and *In convertendo* (1902).

17. See Pasler, "Concert Programs and Their Narratives."

18. It is possible that one performance, on December 22, 1910, may have contained some Rameau arias.

19. Clément, *Histoire de la musique*, 521. "Qu'on ne dise pas qu'on a une idée de la musique des maîtres anciens par les fragments chantés dans quelques concerts ou gravés dans quelques recueils. L'exécution en est généralement pitoyable, parce qu'elle n'a pas été préparée avec la science et l'attention qu'elle exige."

20. Médicis, "The Schola Cantorum, Early Music, and French Political Culture," 326. De Médicis covers in some detail Jullien's reception of Rameau during this time (see pp. 325–30); the critic, she points out, "addresses almost every major issue affecting the reception of Rameau's works" (325) in his writings in the *Journal des débats* during this time period. This material may also be found in Catrina Flint de Médicis, "Nationalism and Early Music at the French *Fin de Siècle*: Three Case Studies," *Nineteenth-Century Music Review* 1/2 (2004): 43–66.

21. *Le Journal des débats*, June 4, 1905. "M. Reynaldo Hahn, mis en goût par le succès que sa restitution minutieusement exacte de Don Giovanni eut l'année dernière et sentant que la mode aujourd'hui tourne du côté des vieux maîtres de l'opéra français, vient de donner . . . deux séances où il faisait entendre diverses pages empruntées aux plus beaux opéras de Lulli et Rameau, et cette curieuse tentative, qui arrivait bien à son heure, a été couronné du plus vif succès."

22. Ellis, *Interpreting the Musical Past*, 75–76.

23. For a study of the influence of classical French music, and particularly Rameau and Gluck, on Magnard's own music, see Jens Malte Fischer, "Klassizistischer Wagnérisme? Albéric Magnard und seine 'tragédies en musique,'" in *Von Wagner zum Wagnérisme: Musik, Literatur, Kunst, Politik*, ed. Annegret Fauser and Maneula Schwartz (Leipzig: Leipziger Universitätsverlag, 1999), 229–63.

24. Ellis briefly touches on Magnard and the subsequent Rameau edition in *Interpreting the Musical Past*, 141.

25. *Le Figaro*, March 29, 1894. "Pourquoi donc Rameau ne figure-t-il presque jamais au programme de nos théâtres et de nos concerts, n'est-il connu que de quelques musiciens et rats de bibliothèque? La raison, hélas! est tout à notre honte.

"Il n'existe pas une seule édition moderne complète et correcte de Rameau.

"En Allemagne, la maison Breitkopf termine la publication de l'œuvre immense de Bach. En Belgique, M. Gervaert a rétabli les partitions de Grétry. En Angleterre, l'édition intégrale de Haendel est achevée depuis longtemps. Resterons-nous en arrière de nos voisins? Laisserons-nous dans la poussière des Conservatoires les partitions et les manuscrits de notre plus glorieux musicien? . . .

"La tâche serait longue, coûteuse, mais il nous reste, je présume, quelque amour-propre national et nous ne reculerions pas devant des dépenses qui sont couvertes en Angleterre par le gouvernement, en Allemagne par la masse des souscripteurs.

"Mon coup de cloche en mémoire de Rameau sera-t-il [sic] entendu? J'en doute. Nous sommes peu curieux de musique en France et nos musiciens sont peu respectueux du passé."

26. *Revue hebdomadaire*, August 1894. Reprinted in Dukas, *Les écrits de Paul Dukas sur la musique*, 192. "Il est un autre maître, complètement français celui-là, envers lequel nous voudrions qu'on en usât d'une manière aussi généreuse. Nous n'osons pas demander que l'Opéra tente la reconstitution d'un des chefs-d'œuvre de Rameau puisqu'il est déjà impossible d'obtenir que Gluck soit représenté au répertoire de ce théâtre qui devrait être, cependant, de par son titre et sa fastueuse subvention, comme le Louvre de la musique. Mais au moins serait-il désirable qu'une édition sérieusement établie de ses œuvres permît aux amateurs de ses les rendre familières et aux orchestres de concert d'en populariser quelques fragments."

27. Brian Rees points out that Jacques Durand in particular was a driving force in the Rameau edition. Brian Rees, *Camille Saint-Saëns: A Life* (London: Chatto and Windus, 1999), 317. While this edition was to be the first *complete* Rameau edition, several piano-vocal scores of Rameau's stage works had already appeared in the *Chefs-d'œuvre de l'opéra français* series, begun in 1880 by the Michaëlis publishing house. These editions were, however, deemed too unscholarly (at least by the standard of the Durand edition), and unworthy of Rameau; in addition, they did not have orchestral parts and so did not encourage the performance of his works either onstage on in the concert hall.

28. In an article titled "Le Ramisme" in *Le Courrier musical*, Malherbe reported that Magnard received a letter from Durand only a few days after his original appeal in *Le Figaro* agreeing to undertake the edition, suggesting a near-instantaneous response from the publisher. *Le Courier musical*, May 15, 1908.

29. Durand mentions these connections with Magnard in his memoires, Jacques Durand, *Quelques souvenirs d'un éditeur de musique* (Paris: Durand, 1924), 57. Durand (pp. 99–104) supports the dramatic narrative that he and his father read Magnard's article in *Le Figaro* and immediately leapt into action, focusing all their energies on creating the Rameau edition.

30. Camille Saint-Saëns, "A Note on Rameau," in Saint-Saëns, *Outspoken Essays on Music*, 89.

31. Bonnerot, *C. Saint-Saëns (1835–1921)*, 160–61. "Pour établir un texte complet et correct, il fut aidé par des érudits qui débrouillèrent le travail, firent des copies, notèrent les variantes. On adopta la notation moderne, en écartant 'ceux des ornements qui n'avaient plus leur raison d'être par suite des transformations de l'instrument en vue duquel on les avait imaginés.' On reproduisit fidèlement la pensée de l'auteur en supprimant 'les interpolations parasites, indications de mouvements, de nuances, de doigté,' qui encombrent sans profit. Saint-Saëns prit soin de tout contrôler lui-même sur les manuscrits, de tout peser, ici interprétant avec le respect dû au maître ancien, et là, transposant les voix. . . . Chaque année Saint-Saëns passait quelques semaines à revoir le texte du volume préparé. Par ses soins dix-sept volumes ont été publiés et ce ne sera pas l'un des moindres services qu'il aura rendus à la musique que d'avoir ressuscité, après Gluck, Rameau, le glorieux contemporain de Sébastien Bach."

32. Preface to Jean-Philippe Rameau, *Pièces de Clavecin*, ed. Camille Saint-Saëns, vol. 1 of *Œuvres complètes* (Paris: Durand, 1895), i. "En publiant ce premier volume des œuvres de Rameau, les éditeurs se sont proposé un double but: d'abord rendre hommage à la mémoire d'un des plus grands compositeurs que la France ait produits; ensuite faciliter la connaissance de ses ouvrages et contribuer à les populariser en mettant à la portée de tous ce que les curieux ont été trop longtemps seuls à découvrir parmi les anciennes éditions ou les vieux manuscrits de nos bibliothèques."

33. Preface to Jean-Philippe Rameau, *Hippolyte et Aricie*, ed. Vincent d'Indy, vol. 6 of *Œuvres Complètes* (Paris: Durand, 1900), i. "Le sixième volume des œuvres complètes de Jean-Philippe Rameau, qui paraît en 1900, forme aussi le premier d'une série nouvelle. Les précédents étaient consacrés à la musique instrumentale et à la musique religieuse; ils contenaient des pièces de clavecin, des cantates, des motets. Or, c'est à la musique dramatique que le vieux maître a consacré le principal effort de son génie; elle seule doit nous occuper désormais. Tragédies lyriques, opéras-ballets, comédies, pastorales, divertissements vont se suivre dans l'ordre chronologique; chaque année verra renaître un des chefs-d'œuvre du siècle dernier. Nous commençons avec *Hippolyte et Aricie*, premier anneau d'une chaîne longue et glorieuse."

34. Omitting problematic ornamentation—that is, ornamentation that seemed overly complex, or "distracted" from the melody—was commonplace in publications of Rameau's music (particularly keyboard works, which were the most often published) throughout the nineteenth century and into the fin de siècle. Typical editorial explanations involved differences between the harpsichord and the modern piano, and the not entirely ridiculous suggestion that the abundance of ornamentation in eighteenth-century French works stemmed from the inability of the instrument to sustain for long periods of time. Other musical aspects—such as articulation, rhythm, phrasing, and occasionally transposition—were typically adjusted to modern tastes in a similar fashion. For a thorough look at the adaptions of Rameau editions before the Complete Edition, see Vançon, "La Temple de la gloire," 3:201–20.

35. Graham Sadler, "Vincent d'Indy and the Rameau *Oeuvres complètes*: A Case of Forgery?" *Early Music* 21 (1993): 415–22. Sadler points out (p. 416) that "the volumes edited by Dukas, Chapuis, and, above all, d'Indy are seriously flawed. They are specially misleading in two respects: the orchestration has often been distorted and the part-writing 'improved.'"

36. Ibid., 416.

37. On Dukas's role, see Anya Suschitzky, "The Nation on Stage: Wagner and French Opera at the End of the Nineteenth Century" (PhD diss, University of California at Berkeley, 1999), 124–39.

38. Ibid., 136.

39. Ellis has briefly examined the Rameau's role in d'Indy's *Cours de composition musical*, noting the fact that d'Indy begins the "flowering" of French opera in 1733, when *Hippolyte et Aricie* was premiered at the Opéra. Ellis, "En Route to Wagner," 114.

40. Such an approach also allowed d'Indy to minimize the importance of midcentury grand opera, which he considered to be unsavory and dominated by "Jewish" music, particularly Meyerbeer. If Rameau, a Catholic composer, founded this dramatic style, d'Indy could trace his way through Wagner and back to its fundamentally Catholic roots.

41. The cyclical nature of this narrative (France–Germany–France) would likely have appealed to d'Indy, as well. Jann Pasler has argued that d'Indy conceived of history not linearly but in a spiral, returning to the past in order to go forward. Jann Pasler, "Paris: Conflicting Notions of Progress," in *The Late Romantic Era*, ed. Jim Samson (London: Macmillan, 1991): 389–416, particularly 401–6.

42. *Revue hebdomadaire*, May 1901. Reprinted in Dukas, *Les Écrits de Paul Dukas sur la musique*, 544–45. "Depuis longtemps, Rameau dormait dans la poussière de nos bibliothèques. Il y dormirait encore si, grâce à l'initiative de la maison A Durand et fils, son œuvre ne reparaissait, peu à peu, dans une édition luxueuse et reconstituée, cette fois, d'après les documents originaux révisés selon la méthode critique la plus scrupuleuse."

43. See, for example, Henri de Busne, who compared Dukas's opera to Rameau's works in *Le Mercure musical*, May 15, 1907: 465–71.

44. Debussy's interest in Rameau's music has been explored by a number of scholars, most recently, Anya Suschitzky, in "Debussy's Rameau: French Music and Its Others," *Musical Quarterly* 86 (2002): 398–448. Suschitzky includes in this article a brief historiographical survey of previous scholarship on the material (402–3). For another take on this subject, see Dieter Winzer, *Claude Debussy und die französische musikalische Tradition* (Wiesbaden: Breitkopf and Härtel, 1981).

45. *Le Figaro*, May 8, 1908. Reprinted in Debussy, *Debussy on Music*, 229.

46. *Gil blas*, February 2, 1903. Reprinted in Debussy, *Debussy on Music*, 112.

47. Suschitzky argues persuasively that Debussy viewed Rameau as a "panacea against Wagnerism," a musical solution to the problem of mitigating Wagner's influence on his music. Suschitzky, "Debussy's Rameau," 403. Vançon makes a similar point in a more general sense, suggesting that one aspect of the Rameau revival was based on lingering (or reawakened) anti-Wagnerism in France. Vançon, "La Temple de la gloire," 3:308–13.

48. *Le Courrier musical*, May 15, 1908. "sous l'autorité convergente de MM. d'Indy et Debussy, *Scholistes* et *Pelléastes* communièrent en Rameau. MM. d'Indy et Debussy ayant collaboré à l'édition nouvelle de Rameau, l'admiration de Rameau devint un collaire [*sic*] de la foi dans le *d'indyisme* et dans le *Debussysme*. On ne pouvait admirer intégralement l'on ou l'autre de ces deux artistes sans englober Rameau dans la même admiration. Une solidarité étrange s'établissait entre *Castor et Pollux*, *Fervaal* et *Pelléas*: des gens 'avertis' vous soutenaient que *Fervaal* est issu directement de *Castor* ou de *Zoroastre*, et si vous leur demandiez de motiver cette opinion, ils se bornaient à vous dire: 'Je trouve . . .' ce qui signifie: 'Je l'ai entendu dire,' même quand on le prononce avec l'air de dire: 'C'est évident, et il faut que vous soyez une brute pour ne pas vous en apercevoir.' D'autres gens, non moins 'avertis' assimilaient avec la même assurance *Pelléas et Mélisande* à *Hippolyte et Aricie*."

49. A number of scholars have noted the importance of Rameau's French identity to fin-de-siècle narratives of music history. Charles B. Paul, for example, noted Rameau's importance to d'Indy's ideas of music history, pointing out that after the French loss in the Franco-Prussian war, Rameau "was flung into the enemy's face to bolster one's courage and one's faith in the national destiny of France." Paul also provides some historical information on this perspective, tracing the idea back to Cuthbert Girdlestone's 1957 biography of the composer. Charles B. Paul, "Rameau, d'Indy, and French Nationalism," *Musical Quarterly* 58 (1972): 46. This topic is also addressed in Ellis, *Interpreting the Musical Past*.

Chapter Nine

1. Arthur Pougin, *Rameau: Essai sur sa vie et ses œuvres* (Paris: Decaux, 1876), 118. "En dehors de toute comparaison, et pour juger Rameau à un point de vue absolu, il n'est que juste de déclarer qu'un tel artiste fait la gloire éternelle de sa patrie."

2. On the 1876 Dijon festivities, see Katharine Ellis, "Rameau in Late Nineteenth-Century Dijon: Memorial, Festival, Fiasco," in *French Music, Culture, and National Identity*,

1870–1939, ed. Barbara L. Kelly (Rochester, NY: University of Rochester Press, 2008): 197–214.

3. As Ellis points out, Rameau was "ammunition with which to argue that the widely perceived gap between the musical richness of Germany and that of France was overstated." Ibid., 198.

4. Quoted in Ellis, *Interpreting the Musical Past*, 131–32. (The translation is mine, however.) "N'oublions pas que la gloire de Rameau est une gloire éminemment française."

5. *Musica*, March 1905. "Plus l'on se pénètre de l'art de Rameau, et plus l'on arrive à se convaincre qu'il faut remonter jusqu'à lui pour retrouver, dans toute sa grâce, dans toute sa clarté, dans toute sa vérité, l'essence même du génie français."

6. Jullien, *Musique*, 122. "à ce musicien hors ligne, l'un des plus grands de tous les pays"; "qu'on néglige volontiers, peut-être parce qu'il est Français, et qu'on écrase entre l'Italien Lulli et l'Allemand Gluck." Jullien reprinted the latter statement wholesale in his 1908 review of *Hippolyte et Aricie* in the *Journal des débats* (May 17, 1908).

7. Jullien, *Musique*, 122. "Rameau . . . a fait faire un tel pas à la musique dramatique après Lulli, a tellement fait progresser la tragédie lyrique au triple point de vue de la justesse de l'expression, de la rapidité de la déclamation et de la variété de l'orchestre, que Gluck n'eut qu'à l'étudier et à l'imiter pour créer ses admirables chefs-d'œuvre. Rameau, en un mot, fut sur tous les points le modèle et l'inspirateur de Gluck, qui l'a trop facilement supplanté dans l'admiration de la foule, car sans Rameau l'auteur d'*Alceste* serait peut-être resté le compositeur italien du début, et simplement l'auteur de *Siface* et de *la Fedra*." Jullien reprinted this entire paragraph in his 1908 review of *Hippolyte et Aricie* in the *Journal des débats* (May 17, 1908).

8. For general sources on the Querelle, see Noël Boyer, *La Guerre des Bouffons et la musique française* (Paris: Éditions de la Nouvelle France, 1945); and Arnold M. Whittall, "La Querelle des Bouffons" (PhD diss., Cambridge University, 1964).

9. Henri de Curzon, for example, included a chapter on the Querelle—including texts from Rameau, Grimm, and Rousseau—in his collection of source readings, *La Musique: textes choisis et commentés* (Paris: Plon, 1914).

10. Jules Lemaître, *Jean-Jacques Rousseau* (Paris: Calmann-Lévy, 1907).

11. Émile Faguet, *Vie de Rousseau* (Paris: Société française d'imprimerie et de librairie, 1911), 177. "Rousseau était de retour à Paris au commencement d'octobre. Il reprit ses travaux. Il écrivit, peut-être par gageure, le conte assez joli qui s'appelle *la Reine fantasque* et quelques articles de polémique musicale contre Rameau."

12. Arthur Chuquet, *J.-J. Rousseau* (Paris: Hachette, 1893), 34. "Sa *Lettre sur la musique*, inspirée par la haine de Rameau qui le qualifiait de pillard sans talent, souleva tout Paris; on accusa Jean-Jacques d'offenser la nation parce qu'il niait sa musique; on l'insulta; on lui ôta ses entrées à l'Opéra; on le brûla en effigie sur ce théâtre. La colère qu'il ressentit, s'aggravait de soupçons injustes. Il s'imagina que ses amis enviaient le triomphe du *Devin* et ne lui pardonnaient pas de joindre au génie de l'écrivain celui du compositeur."

13. Émile Faguet, *Rousseau artiste* (Paris: Société française d'imprimerie et de librairie, 1912), 190. "Rameau est fort à la mode aujourd'hui. Moi, qui me borne à tâcher de comprendre, je vous dirai simplement: ce sont deux puissants dieux. Je ne les compare pas; je leur reconnais à tous le droit à l'existence et je crois comprendre la beauté d'un art très simple et sans apprêt qui est celui de Jean-Jacques *et dont on pourrait certainement retrouver la survivance chez les créateurs de l'opéra comique*. Monsigny, Grétry, 'hommes de la nature' comme lui et qui ont très bien suivi son exemple.'" (italics and ellipses in original).

14. Faguet, *Rousseau artiste*, 192. "Nul doute sur ceci que Rousseau a été considéré comme un très grand musicien de son temps; et, par des musiciens très savants du siècle suivant et de celui-ci, comme un homme ayant au plus haut degré le sens musical.

"En tout cas, il avait profondément réfléchi sur la musique. Il ne faut pas trop s'arrêter à sa fameuse *Lettre sur la musique*, qui est un ouvrage de polémique et sur lequel l'auteur est revenu et dont il est revenu, et qui contient, du reste, des choses très justes, ou singulièrement subjectives; mais si on lit avec attention son article *Opera* (*Dictionnaire de musique*), à mon avis tout à fait extraordinaire, on verra que Rousseau est comme le précurseur de toutes les grandes idées modernes sur l'art musical."

15. As both Pougin and Tiersot note, their work was anticipated by Albert Jansen's *Jean-Jacques Rousseau als Musiker* (Berlin: Reimer, 1884), a detailed monograph that Pougin describes as "a large volume with no fewer than 500 pages in octavo. That is excessive, and out of all proportions." Arthur Pougin, *Jean-Jacques Rousseau, musicien* (Paris: Fischbacher, 1901), 11. [un gros volume qui ne compte pas moins de 500 pages in-octavo. Ceci est excessif, et hors de toutes proportions.] I am omitting Jansen's significant contributions here, since I am concerned with the way French sociopolitical concerns shaped the Rousseau-Rameau debate.

16. Pougin, *Jean-Jacques Rousseau, musicien*, 59.

17. Ibid., 136–37. "Rousseau a eu toute sa vie la passion de la musique, le désir de se faire passer pour musicien et l'envie de le devenir; mais il n'a pas eu le temps, ou le courage, ou l'énergie nécessaire pour apprendre les principes d'un art dont la technique toute spéciale exige de ceux qui s'y livrent une étude sévère et longue. Dans le but et avec l'espoir de rendre cette étude plus rapide et moins laborieuse, il a tenté de réformer l'écriture de cet art, sans se rendre compte que cette réforme, eût-elle été possible, n'en pouvait d'ailleurs changer les conditions fondamentales. D'autre part, il a eu la prétention de devenir compositeur sans vouloir apprendre la langue de la composition musicale, de telle sorte qu'il a écrit de la musique sans savoir coordonner ses idées, sans savoir en tirer les développements qu'elles pouvaient comporter, sans savoir enfin les accompagner. . . . Enfin il a cru à tort qu'il pourrait, avec la seule aide d'une étude toute superficielle, faire connaître les règles et fixer les préceptes d'un art dont on ne peut se rendre maître que par une pratique constante, une longue expérience et le secours du raisonnement appliqué à la sensibilité. . . .

". . . Malgré l'orgueil que lui causait le succès du *Devin du village*, il faut bien le déclarer: non, Rousseau n'était pas musicien, au sens sérieux que nous attachons à ce mot."

18. Julien Tiersot, *Jean-Jacques Rousseau* (Paris: Alcan, 1920), 251–52. "ces exemples nous apparaissent très distinctement dans les compositions qui se multiplièrent après lui, et parmi lesquelles nous distinguons quelques-uns de nos plus authentiques chefs-d'œuvre. Le calme divin des Champs-Élysées et l'horreur des Enfers où va se dévouer Alceste, la poésie tour à tour pénétrante et sublime de la Scène au bord du ruisseau, de l'orage et de l'hymne de reconnaissance, dans la Symphonie beethovénienne, l'oppression de la scène aux champs et la hantise de la Marche au supplice de Berlioz, les fulgurances de l'incendie du Walhalla, le tableau puissant du Déluge dans l'œuvre de M. Saint-Saëns, jusqu'aux rayonnements et aux transparences de la Mer de M. Debussy, tout cela semble annoncé et défini avec une précision singulière par Jean-Jacques Rousseau." Here Tiersot refers to Gluck's *Alceste*, Beethoven's Pastoral Symphony, Berlioz's *Symphonie fantastique*, and Wagner's *Ring*, in addition to the listed Saint-Saëns and Debussy works.

19. Tiersot, *Jean-Jacques Rousseau*, 252–53. "Et s'il fallait aller plus loin encore, que de nouvelles analogies ne constaterions-nous pas? Nous comparerions le sentiment de

la nature de Beethoven, ses aspirations vers le Divin, avec l'idéal du Vicaire savoyard et du Promeneur solitaire. Nous verrions Wagner, hanté par des idées philosophiques et humanitaires, proposant au peuple, dans une révolution, une constitution dont la base n'est pas sans rapports avec celle du *Contrat social*, et aboutissant à la création d'une œuvre immense—*l'Anneau du Nibelung*—qui proclame la nécessité du retour à la nature primitive et, comme le premier *Discours*, maudit l'or funeste au bonheur de l'humanité. . . .

". . . Au point de vue musical, il a annoncé l'évolution de l'art moderne, en a deviné l'esprit, apporté la justification par avance, et peut-être efficacement favorisé l'éclosion." Tiersot refers to the following works by Rousseau: "La Profession de foi du vicaire Savoyard" (1765); "Les Rêveries du Promeneur solitaire" (unfinished, 1776–78); *Du Contrat social, ou Principes du droit politique* (1762); and *Discours sur les sciences et les arts* (1750).

20. Pougin, *Jean-Jacques Rousseau, musicien*, 36. "On voit quelle haute idée Rousseau avait de ses talents de compositeur. Il en est ainsi toutes les fois qu'il trouve l'occasion de parler de sa musique, et il la trouve souvent. . . . Mais ce qui est vraiment curieux . . . c'est la jalousie qu'il attribue si naïvement et si sincèrement à Rameau. Voit-on l'auteur de *Castor et Pollux* redoutant la rivalité de l'auteur des *Muses galantes*? . . .

"Rousseau prétend nous donner une nouvelle preuve de la terrible jalousie de Rameau, jalousie qui, Rousseau ne le comprend pas, n'est autre chose que le dédain naturel d'un tel artiste pour ses prétentions musicales vraiment outrecuidantes."

21. Ibid., 39. "Rousseau l'égal de Rameau, cela peut faire sourire."

22. Ibid., 114. "Rousseau prouvait suffisamment, dans cet écrit, qu'il ne comprenait rien à l'admirable génie de l'auteur de *Castor et Pollux* et qu'il ne savait pas lui rendre justice."

23. Louis Laloy, *Rameau* (Paris: Alcan, 1908), 183. "Aucun Italien, à aucun époque, n'a tracé la mélodie d'une main aussi ferme, ne l'a conduite avec cette assurance, ne l'a mise au premier plan avec cette décision."

24. Ibid., 184. "Chez les Italiens, elle [melody] ne cherche qu'à plaire, à étonner ou à divertir; chez Rameau, elle a toujours un sens: c'est une image, non un jeu."

25. Henri Lavoix, *La Musique français* (Paris: Quantin, 1891), 5. "S'il prenait à quelque homme d'esprit la pensée singulière de soutenir ce paradoxe qu'il n'existe ni littérature, ni poésie, ni peinture, ni sculpture françaises, l'idée ferait sourire et ne trouverait pas un adepte; mais s'il agit de musique, il en est tout autrement: chacun peut, malgré les démentis de l'histoire et sans paraître trop ridicule, soutenir que la musique française n'existe pas, qu'elle n'a jamais existé et qu'elle n'existera jamais. J.-J. Rousseau, avec toute l'autorité du génie, a posé simplement cet axiome que les Français n'avaient pas de musique et n'en pouvaient avoir; bon nombre de disciples ont recueilli religieusement la parole du maître et elle est encore article de foi pour bien des dilettantes."

26. *Le Ménestrel*, January 21, 1900. "Si nous voulons examiner cette fameuse *Lettre*, nous y voyons que Rousseau se donne beaucoup de peine pour essayer prouver que la musique française est détestable et qu'elle ne peut et ne pourra jamais être telle, parce que la lange française est radicalement hostile à la musique. . . . Il accumule à ce sujet une foule de prétendus exemples, de raisons des plus bizarres, et pose en axiomes quantité de sentences qui . . . ne reposent sur aucun fondement et ne peuvent aujourd'hui que nous faire sourire."

27. Lionel de la Laurencie, *Le Goût musical en France* (Paris: Joanin, 1905), 173. "Pour Rousseau, les Français, dont la langue est plate et dépourvue d'accents, font preuve du goût le plus pitoyable dans leurs 'ariettes' et dans leur récitatif, plein de 'bruyantes et criardes intonations.' 'Il n'y a, écrit-il, ni mesure, ni mélodie dans la musique française,

parce que la langue n'en est pas susceptible; le chant français n'est qu'un aboiement continuel, insupportable à toutes oreille non prévenue; l'harmonie en est brute, sans expression . . . ; les airs français ne sont pas des airs; le récitatif français n'est point du récitatif. D'où je conclus que les Français n'ont point de musique et n'en peuvent avoir, ou que, si jamais ils en ont une, ce sera tant pis pour eux.' Rousseau osait proférer de tels blasphèmes vingt ans après *Castor et Pollux*! Il traitait Rameau cavalièrement."

28. Lionel de la Laurencie, *Rameau: Biographie critique* (Pairs: Laurens, 1926), 35. "ils jettent, avec une grande clairvoyance, les bases de l'esthétique du futur drame lyrique. Ils annoncent Grétry, Gluck et même Richard Wagner; ils expriment les besoins nouveaux d'art dramatique qui sourdement travaillaient les esprits au XVIIIe siècle, besoins auxquels les pièces italiennes des bouffons apportaient une satisfaction partielle."

29. Ibid., 36. "Tous trouvent qu'il y a trop de musique dans l'opéra français."

30. Ibid. "Grimm, cet Allemand déguisé en Parisien, l'attaque sans mesure, et le bafoue après sa mort, tant est grande sa haine pour tout ce qui caractérise l'esprit français, alors que Rousseau, excessif et passionné, associe les pires erreurs à des remarques d'une rare pénétration, Diderot et d'Alembert mettent en général plus d'équité et de modération dans leur critiques."

31. *La Revue musical S.I.M.*, July 1912: 32. "On l'accuse de n'être pas Français: qu'on refuse donc le nom de Français à tous ceux qui l'ont suivi avec enthousiasme dans sa rêverie aventureuse. Est-ce bien comprendre la France, ou même bien l'aimer, que de prétendre la définir tout entière une fois pour toutes? . . . [By his passion] il se sépare nettement de Rameau pour s'orienter dans une direction tout autre, où il rencontre Gluck, et où apparaîtra Berlioz. Quoi qu'on puisse penser de son attitude et de ses tendances, bien qu'on ait le droit d'être sévère pour ses erreurs, il serait injuste de ne pas voir en lui, dans le domaine de la musique comme dans beaucoup d'autres, un des plus féconds remueurs d'idées qui aient jamais existé."

32. *Le Courrier musical*, May 15, 1908. "il entra certainement dans ce culte nouveau de Rameau une part de chauvinisme artistique, et une part aussi d'esprit antiencyclopédiste. On admira Jean-Philippe Rameau d'être un musicien de 'chez nous'; on l'admira aussi d'avoir été peu apprécié par Rousseau et les Encyclopédistes, à qui beaucoup de gens ne pardonnent par leur influence sur l'esprit moderne."

33. Reprinted in Camille Saint-Saëns, *Camille Saint-Saëns on Music and Musicians*, ed. and trans. Roger Nichols (Oxford: Oxford University Press, 2008), 104.

34. Pierre Lasserre also linked Rameau's operas to Wagner's on several occasions in his provocatively titled *L'Esprit de la musique française, de Rameau à l'invasion wagnérienne* (Paris: Payot, 1917), the second chapter of which is dedicated to Rameau.

35. *Le Courrier musical*, May 15, 1908. "On opposera de nouveau le géant Gluck non plus à Piccini le petit, comme autrefois, mais à Rameau le grand; il faudra se déclarer Gluckiste ou Ramiste, et les flots d'encre recommenceront à couler pour ou contre le dieu de son choix."

Chapter Ten

1. Clément, *Histoire de la musique*, 521. "Il ne faut pas espérer qu'on entende jamais à l'Opéra *Castor et Pollux*, *Dardanus* ou *Zoroastre*."

2. Vançon, "La Temple de la Gloire, 3:278. "[Rameau was] cité comme archétype des musiciens jugés trop anciens pour être jamais rejoués."

3. See, for example, the reviews of both productions in *Le Courrier musical*, January 1, 1908 (*Dardanus*) and February 1, 1908 (*Castor et Pollux*).

4. See, for example, Clément's comments, cited earlier in chapter 8.

5. Henri Quittard, "Exécutions et publications récentes: *Hippolyte et Aricie* à L'Opéra," *Revue musicale* (June 1908): 319. "cette apothéose du vieux maître."

6. *Musica*, June 1908. "MM. Messager et Broussan risquaient beaucoup en remontant *Hippolyte et Aricie*, beaucoup plus qu'en montant une œuvre nouvelle."

7. My thoughts on the staging of the 1908 production are indebted to Rémy Campos's study, "La reprise d'*Hippolyte et Aricie* de Rameau en 1908, ou l'impossible archéologie d'un chef-d'œuvre," in *Présence du XVIIIe siècle dans l'opéra français du XIX siècle d'Adam à Massenet*, ed. Jean-Christophe Branger and Vincent Giroud (Saint-Étienne, France: Publications de l'Univeristé de Saint-Étienne, 2011): 447–75. Campos does address the larger issues of nationalism and the archaeological-museal impulse at the fin de siècle, viewing these issues through the lens of the staging choices.

8. Georges Imbart de la Tour, "La Mise en scène d'*Hippolyte et Aricie*," *Bulletin français de la SIM* 4, no. 3 (March 15, 1908): 247–71.

9. Campos, "La reprise d'*Hippolyte et Aricie*," 451. "En raffinant jusqu'à distinguer les anciennes conceptions de l'appareil scénique (celles de l'époque de Rameau) de la notion moderne du style 'à l'antique' qui se fonderait sur une esthétique néo-classique tardive (datant des années 1770–1810), l'archéologue jetait les bases d'une révolution esthétique. Restait à entraîner les artistes, le public et en premier lieu les responsables de l'Académie nationale de musique."

10. See ibid., for details on the sets and costumes. As Campos points out (454n16), several of the critics who did comment on the costumes simply assumed they were all replicas of the eighteenth-century originals, and lauded both the costumes themselves and the Opéra's efforts at historical fidelity. On the other hand, Adolphe Jullien actually noted in the *Journal des débats* (May 17, 1908) that sets revealed "a very sophisticated antiquity—sophisticated to the point of being somewhat affected by modernism—which truly clashed a bit with the simple lines of the old master's music." [des décors d'une antiquité très raffinée, raffinée au point d'être entachée de quelque modernisme, jurent bien un peu avec la musique aux lignes si simples du vieux maître.]

11. Ibid., 457.

12. *Journal des débats*, May 17, 1908. "J'aurai donc attendu trente-quatre ans; mais, plus heureux que bien d'autres, j'aurais vu se réaliser le souhait que je formais dès février 1874 . . . : 'Si je n'écoutais que mes préférences, disais-je alors, je demanderais qu'on remontât jusqu'à Rameau, le plus grand musicien français, et qu'on reprît l'un de ces chefs-d'œuvre: *Castor et Pollux, Hippolyte et Aricie* ou *Dardanus* . . .' Me faudra-t-il attendre encore autant pour voir rejouer à Paris *Dardanus* ou *Castor et Pollux*?"

13. *La Presse*, May 15, 1908. "surtout l'histoire de la musique française. L'éducation musicale d'un peuple doit se faire dans les théâtres subventionnés, comme son éducation artistique se fait dans les musées."

14. *Le Jockey*, May 15, 1908. "Sur la scène qui doit être comme le musée de notre musique nationale, il serait choquant que Rameau n'eût pas sa place." Quoted in Campos, "La Reprise d'*Hippolyte et Aricie*," 465.

15. Quittard, "Exécutions et publications récentes," 319–20. "On dira peut-être que l'Opéra, théâtre national, largement subventionné, a le devoir d'être un sorte de musée de la musique et que, insensible aux considérations matérielles, il se doit d'annexer au répertoire toute œuvre intéressante et significative d'une époque. En pratique . . . ce théâtre ne saurait montrer indifférent à sa prospérité."

16. Ibid., 320. "Il semble bien que, pour *Hippolyte et Aricie*, il n'ait maintenant plus rien à craindre.... L'œuvre, encore qu'elle se soit heurtée a beaucoup d'hostilités à demi avouées, et qu'elle ait été proclamée d'avance incapable d'intéresser encore le public musical de nos jours, l'œuvre paraît s'être imposée dès la première représentation. L'expérience est donc fait, que souhaitaient à la fois ennemis et amis du maître français. Les résultats en sont rassurants. Ne nous dissimulons pas qu'ils eussent pu fort bien ne pas l'être. On le savait à l'Opéra mieux que nulle part ailleurs, et l'on n'en mérite que plus de louanges d'avoir couru la chance de l'entreprise."

17. *Le Figaro*, May 18, 1908. "J'ajoute bien vite que cette méfiance n'a pas tardé à se dissiper; que, graduellement, le charme la opéré et qu'en dépit d'un genre, d'un style qu'un si long oubli fait paraître nouveaux, les beautés de la musique, la grandeur de son caractère, la variété, le mouvement qui l'animent sont peu à peu apparus, et que la soirée s'est terminée un triomphe."

18. *Le Temps*, May 19, 1908. "Paris enfin rend à Rameau l'hommage qui lui est dû. C'est l'épreuve décisive, dont l'heureux succès fait revivre le plus grand des maîtres de notre art. On ne peut estimer trop haut l'importance d'un tel événement.... La musique française avait perdu ses titres: la reprise d'*Hippolyte et Aricie* vient de les lui rendre.

"Car le succès a passé notre espérance. Ce n'est pas que le public n'ait ressenti quelque surprise devant un art si différent, par l'esprit et par le style, des sortes d'art auxquelles il est accoutumé. Mais sa surprise est naturelle, et il était impossible qu'il ne l'éprouvât point.... Pour le public presque tout entier, la musique est un art sans origines, sans évolution, sans développement, dont toute l'histoire a été perdue, et dont la période la plus récente échappe seule à l'oubli."

19. Ibid. "Presque tout pourtant dans son art est fait pour étonner et troubler le spectateur d'aujourd'hui. D'abord, la conception même qu'il se fait du théâtre musical n'a rien de commun avec la nôtre. Notre idée du théâtre musical est toute romantique: depuis que Gluck est venu, le romantisme nous possède; un opéra est pour nous un drame, dont l'objet est de saisir, d'ébranler, de bouleverses, l'âme de l'auditeur; l'art est tout entier dirigé, tendu vers ce dessin; on y sacrifie tout à la recherche de l'effet, selon les propres paroles de Gluck.... Chez Rameau, pur et suprême représentant de notre tradition classique, le principe de l'art est tout autre. L'émotion, si puissante qu'elle soit, demeure soumise à l'intelligence; la raison impose une ordonnance à la sensibilité. Cette musique porte la clarté avec elle; elle répand la certitude; une idée générale d'équilibre et d'harmonie la gouverne. L'opéra de Rameau n'est pas un drame, mais une tragédie lyrique, au sens le plus ample de ces mots, un spectacle de beauté et de fête où le pathétique des grands mouvements de l'âme mêle à la paix et à la grâce des divertissements, où les moments de passion et de douleur alternent sans effort avec les moments d'allégresse et de repos, où un art, un goût, une raison supérieurs savent unir les forces diverses de la musique, sans sacrifier celles-ci à celles-là, pour produire une impression de noble exaltation et de sérénité bienfaisante."

20. Ibid., May 19, 1908. "Allez donc à l'œuvre de Rameau. Je souhaite que vous l'aimiez; je souhaite même, s'il est nécessaire, que vous fassiez pour l'aimer et la comprendre un peu d'effort; soyez assurés que vous serez payés de votre peine."

21. *Le Gaulois*, May 14, 1908. "Oh! la musique de Rameau est admirable. Cette partition, presque deux fois centenaire, se révèle d'une solidité, d'une franchise, d'une sincérité d'expression qu'on ne peut trop louer.... Seulement, à l'Opéra, dans les conditions actuelles, nous sommes mal à l'aise pour faire de l'archéologie. Ces juxtapositions continuelles de formes tragiques, de formes de cantates et de formes de

divertissements chorégraphiques; cet orchestre, très sonore pour son temps, infiniment ingénieux en son détail, mais grêle à nos oreilles et tout primitif; ces sons plaqués ou égrenés du clavecin aigrelet, tout cela nous vient de trop loin, avec trop d'usure matérielle et, surtout, exposé trop en grand.

"Supposez ces cinq actes donnés dans une petite salle, en des vues d'enseignement . . . j'estime que nous en saisirions mieux la grandeur historique, que nous goûterons plus intimement le charme et la grâce de ses épisodes."

22. Saint-Saëns, "A Note on Rameau," in *Outspoken Essays on Music*, 90.

23. Ibid., 95.

24. Ibid., 96.

25. *Le Courrier musical*, May 15, 1908. "Devons-nous avouer que la première impression au début de la soirée, sans être une désillusion toutefois, ne répondit pas entièrement au plaisir qu'on attendait de cette tardive réhabilitation d'un génie trop longtemps dédaigné. Notre oreille, accoutumée aux splendeurs de l'orchestration moderne, ne trouvait qu'un maigre régal aux charmes plus discrets d'un continuel quatuor auquel quelques instruments de bois venaient parfois s'ajouter. Le clavecin accompagnant les récitatifs semblait bien grêle avec ses sonorités fragiles, et de plus il avait l'inconvénient de mettre à découvert des voix qui, sans l'enveloppe sonore qui les pare habituellement, laissaient voir la défectuosité de leur prononciation, la mollesse de leurs attaques et leur manque de rythme dans l'accentuation de la phrase musicale."

26. Suschitzky, "Debussy's Rameau," 398.

27. Jane Fulcher notes Rouché's nationalist tendencies as the director, pointing out that he "knew that the Opéra should not only appeal to the public it sought to attract, but that it must serve current national interests as well. . . . The integrity of the state opera was a serious matter . . . it was to serve an educational role, [one that was] politically conservative and nationalist." Jane Fulcher, *The Composer as Intellectual: Music and Ideology in France, 1914–1940* (Oxford: Oxford University Press, 2005), 96–97.

28. *Le Figaro*, March 23, 1918. "Il est impossible d'imaginer un spectacle plus artistique et plus magnifique à la fois que celui auquel l'Opéra, jeudi dernier, avait convié Paris. En remettant à la scène *Castor et Pollux*, oublié depuis 1784, M. Jacques Rouché se proposait . . . de rendre un juste hommage à Rameau et à l'un de ses chefs-d'œuvre. Avec *Hippolyte et Aricie*, voici quelques années, avait déjà commencé la réparation d'une si grande injustice envers notre art national. Les présentations de *Castor et Pollux* feront davantage encore. Et vraiment il n'est que temps, après avoir disserté depuis tant d'années sur la musique française et ce qu'il faut faire eu sa faveur, de s'aviser que le meilleur moyen de la défendre est de familiariser le public avec les grands classiques qu'elle a produits."

29. *La Presse*, March 23, 1918. "La réalisation de M. Rouché est une fête somptueuse et charmante. On sent qu'il a voulu faire sur le nom de notre plus grand musicien classique une manifestation éclatante et il a pleinement réussi dans cette louable tentative de glorification nationale."

30. On the opera's association with the War of Polish Succession, see, for example, Cuthbert Girdlestone, *Jean-Philippe Rameau: His Life and Work*, rev. ed. (New York: Dover, 1969), 199.

31. The appropriateness of the 1737 prologue to the political situation in the early twentieth century was not lost on contemporaries. Two quick examples: the prologue and a few other morceaux from *Castor* appeared on the 1928 concert at which Debussy's final piece, the unfinished *Ode à la France*, was premiered. As for the relevance of the prologue to audiences at the close of World War I, it is interesting to note that the so-called peace prologue transcended purely nationalist rhetoric, joining works by Dvořak

and Elgar on a 1918 celebratory concert at the Royal Manchester College of Music. See Marianne Wheeldon, "Debussy's Legacy: The Controversy over the *Ode à la France*," *Journal of Musicology* 27 (2010): 304–41; and Michael Kennedy, *The History of the Royal Manchester College of Music* (Manchester, UK: Manchester University Press, 1971), 62.

32. *Le Matin*, March 23, 1918. "magnifiquement évoquée la glorieuse époque de l'Opéra français du dix-huitième siècle."

33. *Journal des débats*, March 23, 1918. "Peut-être, au premier abord, le parti pris de reconstituer le style anachronique des costumes que portaient les acteurs en 1737 a-t-il un peu gêné les spectateurs de 1918. On ne peut se défendre d'être légèrement déconcerté en apercevant, devant le monument funéraire de Castor, des femmes spartiates des temps mythologiques affublées d'amples vertugadins et coiffées comme des coquettes de Marivaux. . . . Ce cadre d'époque fait spirituellement ressortir les grâces surannés de quelques pages de la partition et j'ai hâte d'ajouter que, passée la surprise, on ne songe plus qu'à admirer."

34. *L'Écho de Paris*, March 23, 1918. "Cette reconstitution d'un spectacle Louis XV, avec robes à crinoline, plumes et panaches, est d'une beauté incomparable."

35. Ibid. "Il faut louer sans réserve M. Alfred Bachelet du tact avec lequel il a restitué la partition de *Castor et Pollux*. Le texte original a été scrupuleusement respecté par ce chef d'orchestre de premier ordre. Aucune adjonction sacrilège n'y fût apportée. M. Bachelet s'est contenté de réaliser discrètement, au quatuor, les basses chiffrées des récitatifs."

36. *Le Gaulois*, March 24, 1918. "[*Castor et Pollux*], que cent trente-quatre années de silence ont lentement ensevelie dans la poussière de l'oubli, nous est réapparue forte de jeunesse, de grâce, de beauté. C'est à M. Jacques Rouché, très artiste directeur de l'Opéra, que nous devons le miracle de la renaissance de cette partition. Il nous à présentée, non pas comme un objet de musée, ou comme un bibelot archéologique, mais comme une chose vivante, comme le triomphe de l'inaltérable goût français. Claironnons bien haut cette victoire de notre art national de la musique, du décor, et du costume; elle a été gagnée en peine guerre, dans les conditions les moins favorables où elle pouvait se produire; elle n'en est que plus éclatante."

37. *La Presse*, March 23, 1918. "La musique de Rameau nous parut donc à son aise parmi ces subtilités de tons, de formes et d'attitudes qu'elle inspira. Peut-être l'ampleur des moyens utilisés contribua-t-elle un peu à en dénaturer les grâces intimes et surannées. Et l'orchestre de l'opéra faisait sans doute un peu trop oublier l'aigre clavecin originel.

"Mais dans cet essai de modernisation, assez utile, d'ailleurs, il faut louer l'habileté de l'adaptateur et le goût excellent du chef, M. Bachelet."

38. *Le Journal des débats*, April 3, 1918. "une sorte de compromis très habile entre l'art nouveau de notre époque et celui du dix-huitième siècle."

39. *Le Temps*, April 1, 1918. "Hier, pour la foule diverse du vaste Opéra, cette musique était à la fois quelque chose d'illustre et d'inconnu. Et, le rideau baissé, quand elle rentre dans la rue, au sortir de cette tragédie chantée, c'est la rue et la ville et tout le palpable qui lui semble factice et comme fragile. Victoire rare de l'ordre et de l'harmonie sur le pêle-mêle de ce qui passe, soudaine et profonde révélation sur la seule réalité qui soit, celle de la vie intérieure. Voilà ce qu'a crée un maître d'autrefois dans un rassemblement d'hommes d'aujourd'hui. Ce sont là les effets et les marques du génie, et tels ils se sont manifestés, l'autre jour, au milieu des circonstances les plus contraires assurément à cette sorte de métamorphose des âmes. Mais c'est le propre du génie de poser son univers vis-à-vis de l'autre et d'y ravir les vivants."

Bibliography

Abbate, Carolyn. *In Search of Opera.* Princeton: Princeton University Press, 2001.
———. "The Parisian 'Vénus' and the 'Paris' *Tannhäuser.*" *Journal of the American Musicological Society* 36 (1983): 73–123.
Acquisto, Joseph. *French Symbolist Poetry and the Idea of Music.* Aldershot, UK, and Burlington, VT: Ashgate, 2006.
Anderson, Benedict. *Imagined Communities: Reflections on the Origin and Spread of Nationalism.* Rev. ed. London: Verso, 1991.
André, Naomi. *Voicing Gender: Castrati, Travesti, and the Second Woman in Early-Nineteenth-Century Italian Opera.* Bloomington: Indiana University Press, 2006.
Angermüller, Rudolph. "*Les mystères d'Isis* (1801) und *Don Juan* (1805, 1834) auf der Bühne der Pariser Oper." *Mozart-Jahrbuch* (1980–83): 32–97.
Babelon, Jean-Pierre. "The Louvre: Royal Residence and Temple of the Arts." In *Symbols*, edited by Lawrence D. Kritzman, 253–88. Translated by Arthur Goldhammer. Vol. 3 of *Realms of Memory: The Construction of the French Past.* New York: Columbia University Press, 1998.
Bailbé, Joseph-Marc, ed. *Regards sur l'opéra: du ballet comique de la reine à l'opéra de Pékin.* Paris: Presses Universitaires de France, 1976.
Barbedette, H. *Gluck, sa vie, son système et ses œuvres.* Paris: Heugel, 1882.
Barbier, Patrick. "Opera in Paris, 1800–1850: A Lively History." Translated by Robert Luoma. Portland, OR: Amadeus Press, 1995.
Bashant, Wendy. "Singing in Greek Drag: Gluck, Berlioz, George Eliot." In *En Travesti: Women, Gender Subversion, Opera.* In Blackmer and Smith, *En Travesti*, 216–41.
Baud-Bovy, Samuel. "Maurice Emmanuel et la Grèce." *Revue musicale* 410/411 (1988): 109–15.
Bellaigue, Camille. *Mozart.* Paris: Laurens, 1906.
Berenson, Edward. *The Trial of Madame Caillaux.* Berkeley: University of California Press, 1992.
Berlanstein, Lenard A. "Breeches and Breaches: Cross-Dress Theater and the Culture of Gender Ambiguity in Modern France." *Comparative Studies in Society and History* 38 (1996): 338–69.
Berlioz, Hector. *Gluck and His Operas.* Translated by Edwin Evans. London: Reeves, 1915.
———. *The Musical Madhouse: An English Translation of Berlioz's "Les Grotesques de la musique."* Translated and edited by Alastair Bruce. Rochester, NY: University of Rochester Press, 2003.
Bernard, Elisabeth. "Jules Pasdeloup et les concerts populaires." *Revue de musicologie* 57 (1971): 150–78.

———. "L'Évolution du public d'Opéra de 1860 à 1880." In Bailbé, *Regards sur l'opéra*, 33–46.

Bertagnolli, Paul A. *Prometheus in Music: Representations of the Myth in the Romantic Era*. Aldershot, UK: Ashgate, 2007.

Bibesco, Prince Alexandre. *Berthold Damcke: Étude biographique et musicale*. Paris: Lemerre, 1894.

Blackmer, Corinne E., and Patricia Juliana Smith, eds. *En Travesti: Women, Gender Subversion, Opera*. New York: Columbia University Press, 1995.

Blay, Philippe. "Un Théâtre français, tout à fait français, ou un débat fin-de-siècle sur l'Opéra-Comique." *Revue de musicologie* 81 (2001): 105–44.

Blaze de Bury, Henri. *Musiciens du passé, du present et de l'avenir*. Paris: Michel Lévy, 1880.

Bonnerot, Jean. *C. Saint-Saëns (1835–1921): sa vie et son œuvre*. Paris: Durand, 1922.

Borrel, Eugène. "La Schola et la restauration de la musique ancienne." In d'Indy et al., *La Schola Cantorum*, 133–38.

Bourdieu, Pierre. *La Distinction: critique sociale du jugement*. Paris: Éditions de Minuit, 1979.

———. "The Historical Genesis of a Pure Aesthetic." Translated by Charles Newman. In *The Field of Cultural Production: Essays on Art and Literature*, edited by Randal Johnson, 254–66. New York: Columbia University Press, 1993.

Bourdieu, Pierre, and Alain Darbel, with Dominique Schnapper. *The Love of Art: European Art Museums and Their Public*. Translated by Caroline Beattie and Nick Merriman. Stanford: Stanford University Press, 1990.

Boyer, Noël. *La Guerre des Bouffons et la musique française*. Paris: Éditions de la Nouvelle France, 1945.

Branger, Jean-Christophe, and Vincent Giroud. *Présence du XVIIIe siècle dans l'opéra français du XIX siècle d'Adam à Massenet*. Saint-Étienne, France: Publications de l'Univeristé de Saint-Étienne, 2011.

Brody, Elaine. *Paris: The Musical Kaleidoscope, 1870–1925*. New York: George Braziller, 1987.

Brosman, Catharine Savage. *Visions of War in France: Fiction, Art, Ideology*. Baton Rouge: Louisiana State University Press, 1999.

Brown-Montesano, Kristi. *Understanding the Women of Mozart's Operas*. Berkeley: University of California Press, 2007.

Caballero, Carlo. *Fauré and French Musical Aesthetics*. Cambridge: Cambridge University Press, 2001.

Campos, Rémy. "La reprise d'*Hippolyte et Aricie* de Rameau en 1908, ou l'impossible archéologie d'un chef-d'œuvre." In Branger and Giroud, *Présence du XVIIIe siècle dans l'opéra français du XIX siècle d'Adam à Massenet*, 447–75.

Cannone, Belinda. *La Réception des opéras de Mozart dans la presse parisienne (1793–1829)*. Paris: Klincksieck, 1991.

Carbonell, Bettina Messias, ed. *Museum Studies: An Anthology of Contexts*. Malden, MA: Blackwell, 2004.

Carré, Albert. *Souvenirs de théâtre*. Paris: Plon, 1950.

Carrier, David. "Remembering the Past: Art Museums as Memory Theaters." *Journal of Aesthetics and Art Criticism* 61 (2003): 61–65.

Chailley, Jacques. The Magic Flute *Unveiled: Esoteric Symbolism in Mozart's Masonic Opera*. Translated by Herbert Weinstock. Rochester, VT: Inner Traditions International, 1992.

Charle, Christophe. "Opera in France, 1870–1914: Between Nationalism and Foreign Imports." Translated by Jennifer Boittin. In *Opera and Society in Italy and France from Monteverdi to Bourdieu*, edited by Victoria Johnson, Jane F. Fulcher, and Thomas Ertman, 243–66. Cambridge: Cambridge University Press, 2007.

Choquet, Gustave. *Histoire de la musique dramatique en France depuis ses origines jusqu'à nos jours*. Paris: Didot, 1873.

Chuquet, Arthur. *J.-J. Rousseau*. Paris: Hachette, 1893.

Clayson, Hollis. *Paris in Despair: Art and Everyday Life under Siege (1870–1871)*. Chicago: University of Chicago Press, 2002.

Clément, Félix. *Histoire de la musique depuis les temps anciens jusqu'à nos jours*. Paris: Hachette, 1885.

Code, David J. "A Song Not Purely His Own: Modernism and the Pastoral Mode in Mallarmé, Debussy and Matisse." PhD diss., University of California at Berkeley, 1999.

Condé, Gérard. "Mozart et Gounod." In Branger and Giroud, *Présence du XVIIIe siècle dans l'opéra français du XIXe siècle d'Adam à Massenet*, 121–36.

Coubé, Stéphen. *Alsace, Lorraine et France rhénane*. Paris: Lethielleux, 1915.

Curzon, Henri de, ed. *La Musique: textes choisis et commentés*. Paris: Plon, 1914.

Danuser, Hermann, and Herfried Münkler, eds. *Deutsche Meister-böse Geister? Nationale Selbstfindung in der Musik*. Schliengen: Edition Argus, 2001.

Debussy, Claude. *Debussy on Music: The Critical Writings of the Great French Composer Claude Debussy*. Edited by François Lesure and Richard Langham Smith. Translated by Richard Langham Smith. Ithaca, NY: Cornell University Press, 1977.

Deldevez, Edme-Marie-Ernest. *La Société des Concerts, 1860 à 1885*. Edited by Gérard Streletski. Heilbronn: Lucie Galland, 1998.

d'Indy, Vincent. *Cours de composition musicale*. 3 vols. Paris: Durand, 1912–50.

———. *Ma Vie: journal de jeunesse, correspondance familiale et intime, 1851–1931*. Edited by Marie d'Indy. Paris: Séguier, 2001.

d'Indy, Vincent, et al. *La Schola Cantorum en 1925*. Paris: Bloud et Gay, 1927.

Dorf, Samuel. "Listening between the Classical and the Sensual: Neoclassicism in Parisian Music and Dance Culture, 1870–1935." PhD diss., Northwestern University, 2009.

D'Udine, Jean. *Gluck*. Paris: Renouard, 1906.

Dudley, Sherwood. "Les Premières versions françaises du *Mariage de Figaro* de Mozart." *Revue de musicologie* 69 (1983): 55–83.

Duhem, Jules. *La Question d'Alsace-Lorraine, de 1871 à 1914*. Paris: Alcan, 1917.

Dukas, Paul. *Les Écrits de Paul Dukas sur la musique*. Paris: Société d'éditions françaises et internationales, 1948.

Duncan, Carol, and Alan Wallach. "The University Survey Museum." In Carbonell, *Museum Studies*, 51–70.

Dupêchez, Charles. *Histoire de l'Opéra de Paris: un siècle au Palais Garnier*. Paris: Perrin, 1984.

Durand, Jacques. *Quelques Souvenirs d'un éditeur de musique.* Paris: Durand, 1924.
Einstein, Alfred. *Gluck.* Translated by Eric Blom. London: Dent, 1964.
Ellis, Katharine. "Berlioz, the Sublime, and the *Broderie* Problem." In *Hector Berlioz: Miscellaneous Studies,* edited by Fulvia Morabito and Michela Niccolai, 29–59. Bologna: Ut Orpheus Edizioni, 2005.
———. "A Dilettante at the Opera: Issues in the Criticism of Julien-Louis Geoffroy, 1800–1814." In *Reading Critics Reading: Opera and Ballet Criticism in France from the Revolution to 1848,* edited by Roger Parker and Mary Ann Smart, 46–68. Oxford: Oxford University Press, 2001.
———. "En Route to Wagner: Explaining d'Indy's Early Music Pantheon." In Schwartz, *Vincent d'Indy et son Temps,* 111–21.
———. "Female Pianists and Their Male Critics in Nineteenth-Century Paris." *Journal of the American Musicological Society* 50 (1997): 353–85.
———. *Interpreting the Musical Past: Early Music in Nineteenth-Century France.* Oxford: Oxford University Press, 2005.
———. *Music Criticism in Nineteenth-Century France: "La Revue et Gazette musicale de Paris," 1834–1880.* Cambridge: Cambridge University Press, 1995.
———. "Rameau in Late Nineteenth-Century Dijon: Memorial, Festival, Fiasco." In Kelly, *French Music, Culture, and National Identity,* 197–214.
———. "Rewriting *Don Giovanni,* or 'The Thieving Magpies.'" *Journal of the Royal Musical Association* 119 (1994): 212–50.
———. "Systems Failure in Operatic Paris: The Acid Test of the Théâtre-Lyrique." In Fauser and Everist, *Music, Theater and Cultural Transfer,* 49–71.
———. "Wagner and Anti-Wagnerism in the Paris Periodical Press, 1852–1870." In Fauser and Schwartz, *Von Wagner zum Wagnérisme,* 51–83.
Everist, Mark. "Enshrining Mozart: *Don Giovanni* and the Viardot Circle." *19th-Century Music* 25 (2001–2): 165–89.
———. "Gluck, Berlioz and Castil-Blaze: The Poetics and Reception of French Opera." In Everist, *Giacomo Meyerbeer and Music Drama in Nineteenth-Century Paris,* 65–86. Aldershot, UK: Ashgate, 2005.
———. *Music Drama at the Paris Odéon, 1824–1828.* Berkeley: University of California Press, 2002.
Faguet, Émile. *Rousseau artiste.* Paris: Société française d'imprimerie et de librairie, 1912.
———. *Vie de Rousseau.* Paris: Société française d'imprimerie et de librairie, 1911.
Fauquet, Joël-Marie. "Berlioz and Gluck." Translated by Peter Bloom. In *The Cambridge Companion to Berlioz,* edited by Peter Bloom, 199–210. Cambridge: Cambridge University Press, 2000.
———. "Berlioz's Version of Gluck's *Orphée.*" Translated by Peter Bloom. In *Berlioz Studies,* edited by Peter Bloom, 189–253. Cambridge: Cambridge University Press, 1992.
Fauré, Gabriel. *Gabriel Fauré: A Life in Letters.* Translated and edited by J. Barrie Jones. London: B. T. Batsford, 1988.
———. *Lettres intimes.* Edited by Philippe Fauré-Fremiet. Paris: Grasset, 1951.
———. *Opinions musicales.* Paris: Rieder, 1930.

Fauser, Annegret. "'Cette musique sans tradition': Wagner's *Tannhäuser* and Its French Critics." In Fauser and Everist, *Music, Theater, and Cultural Transfer*, 228–55.

———. "Gendering the Nations: The Ideologies of French Discourse on Music (1870–1914)." In *Musical Constructions of Nationalism: Essays on the History and Ideology of European Music, 1800–1945*, edited by Harry White and Michael Murphy, 72–103. Cork, IR: Cork University Press, 2001.

———. *Musical Encounters at the 1889 Paris World's Fair*. Rochester, NY: University of Rochester Press, 2005.

———. "Phantasmagorie im deutschen Wald? Zur *Freischütz*-Rezeption in London und Paris 1824." In *Deutsche Meister-böse Geister? Nationale Selbstfindung in der Musik*, edited by Hermann Danuser and Herfried Münkler, 245–73. Schliengen: Edition Argus, 2001.

Fauser, Annegret, and Mark Everist, eds. *Music, Theater, and Cultural Transfer: Paris, 1830–1914*. Chicago: University of Chicago Press, 2009.

Fauser, Annegret, and Manuela Schwartz, eds. *Von Wagner zum Wagnérisme: Musik, Literatur, Kunst, Politik*. Leipzig: Leipziger Universitätsverlag, 1999.

Fischer, Jens Malte. "Klassizistischer Wagnérisme? Albéric Magnard und seine 'tragédies en musique.'" In Fauser and Schwartz, *Von Wagner zum Wagnérisme*, 229–63.

Ford, Charles. *Così? Sexual Politics in Mozart's Operas*. Manchester, UK: Manchester University Press, 1991.

Forster, Charles. *Quinze ans à Paris (1832–1848): Paris et les Parisiens*. 2 vols. Paris: 1848.

Fulcher, Jane. *The Composer as Intellectual: Music and Ideology in France, 1914–1940*. Oxford: Oxford University Press, 2005.

———. "The Concert as Political Propaganda in France and the Control of 'Performative Context.'" *Musical Quarterly* 82 (1998): 41–67.

———, ed. *Debussy and His World*. Princeton: Princeton University Press, 2001.

Gallois, Lucien. "Alsace-Lorraine and Europe," *Geographical Review* 6 (1918): 89–115.

Genova, Pamela A. *Symbolist Journals: A Culture of Correspondence*. Aldershot, UK: Ashgate, 2002.

Gerhard, Anselm. *The Urbanization of Opera: Music Theater in Paris in the Nineteenth Century*. Translated by Mary Whitall. Chicago: University of Chicago Press, 1998.

Gibbons, William. "*Iphigénie à Paris*: Positioning Gluck Historically in Early Twentieth-Century France." *Intersections: Canadian Journal of Music* 27 (2006): 3–15.

———. "Music of the Future, Music of the Past: *Tannhäuser* and *Alceste* at the Paris Opéra." *19th-Century Music* 33, no. 3 (Spring 2010): 232–46.

Giger, Andreas. *Verdi and the French Aesthetic: Verse, Stanza, and Melody in Nineteenth-Century Opera*. Cambridge: Oxford University Press, 2008.

Gildea, Robert. *The Past in French History*. New Haven: Yale University Press, 1994.

Gillis, John R. "Memory and Identity: The History of a Relationship." In *Commemorations: The Politics of National Identity*, edited by John R. Gillis, 1–24. Princeton: Princeton University Press, 1994.

Girard, Pauline. "*Don Giovanni* au Théâtre-Italien, 1811–1877." In *Don Juan*, 189–98. Exhibition catalogue. Paris: Bibliothèque Nationale, April 25–July 5, 1991.
Girdlestone, Cuthbert. *Jean-Philippe Rameau: His Life and Word*. Rev. ed. New York: Dover, 1969.
Goehr, Lydia. *The Imaginary Museum of Musical Works*. Oxford: Oxford University Press, 1992.
Goldhill, Simon. *Victorian Culture and Classical Antiquity*. Princeton: Princeton University Press, 2011.
Gounod, Charles. *Le Don Juan de Mozart*. Paris: Ollendorff, 1890.
———. *Mozart's* Don Giovanni*: A Commentary*. Translated by Windeyer Clark and J. T. Hutchinson. New York: Da Capo, 1970.
Greenberg, Resa, Bruce W. Reguson, and Sandy Nairne, eds. *Thinking about Exhibitions*. London: Routledge, 1996.
Gruber, Gernot. *Mozart and Posterity*. Translated by R. S. Furness. Boston: Northeastern University Press, 1994.
Hadlock, Heather. "The Career of Cherubino, or the Trouser Role Grows Up." In Smart, *Siren Songs*, 67–92.
Holford-Strevens, Leofranc. "'Her Eyes Became Two Spouts': Classical Antecedents of Renaissance Laments." *Early Music* 27 (1999): 379–93.
Holomon, D. Kern. *The Société des Concerts du Conservatoire, 1828–1967*. Berkeley: University of California Press, 2004.
Huebner, Steven. *French Opera at the Fin de Siècle: Wagnerism, Nationalism, and Style*. Oxford: Oxford University Press, 1999.
———. "Opera Audiences in Paris, 1830–1870." *Music and Letters* 70 (1989): 206–25.
Humbert-Mougin, Sylvie. *Dionysos revisité: les tragiques grecs en France de Leconte de Lisle à Claudel*. Paris: Belin, 2003.
Hunter, Mary. *Mozart's Operas: A Companion*. New Haven: Yale University Press, 2008.
Imbart de la Tour, Georges. "La Mise en scène d'*Hippolyte et Aricie*." *Bulletin français de la SIM* 4, no. 3 (March 15, 1908): 247–71.
Jansen, Albert. *Jean-Jacques Rousseau als Musiker*. Berlin: Reimer, 1884.
Johnson, James H. *Listening in Paris: A Cultural History*. Berkeley: University of California Press, 1996.
Johnson, Janet Lynn. "The Théâtre Italien and Opera and Theatrical Life in Restoration Paris, 1818–1827." 3 vols. PhD diss., University of Chicago, 1988.
Jullien, Adolphe. *Musique: mélanges d'histoire et de critique musical et dramatique*. Paris: Librairie de l'Art, 1896.
———. *Paris dilettante au commencement du siècle*. Paris: Firmin-Didot, 1884.
Kahan, Syliva. *Music's Modern Muse: A Life of Winnaretta Singer, Princesse de Polignac*. Rochester, NY: University of Rochester Press, 2003.
Kahane, Martine. "Don Juan à l'Opéra." In *Don Juan*, 209–20. Exhibition catalogue. Paris: Bibliothèque Nationale, April 25–July 5, 1991.
Kelly, Barbara L., ed. *French Music, Culture, and National Identity, 1870–1939*. Rochester, NY: University of Rochester Press, 2008.
Kennedy, Michael. *The History of the Royal Manchester College of Music*. Manchester, UK: Manchester University Press, 1971.
Kenyon, Nicholas, ed. *Authenticity and Early Music: A Symposium*. Oxford: Oxford University Press, 1988.

Kosinski, Dorothy M. "Gustave Courbet's *The Sleepers*. The Lesbian Image in Nineteenth-Century French Art and Literature." *Artibus et historiae* 9 (1988): 187–99.

———. *Orpheus in Nineteenth-Century Symbolism.* Ann Arbor, MI: UMI Research Press, 1989.

Kramer, Lloyd S. *Threshold of a New World: Intellectuals and the Exile Experience in Paris, 1830–1848.* Ithaca, NY: Cornell University Press, 1988.

Krauss, Rosalind E. "Postmodernism's Museum without Walls." In Greenberg, Reguson, and Nairne, *Thinking about Exhibitions*, 241–45.

Kushner, Eva. *Mythe d'Orphée dans la littérature française contemporaine.* Paris: A. G. Nizet, 1961.

Labelle, Nicole. "Gabriel Fauré: Music Critic for *Le Figaro*." In *Regarding Fauré.* Edited and translated by Tom Gordon, 15–42. Amsterdam: Gordon and Breach, 1999.

Lacombe, Hervé. *The Keys to French Opera in the Nineteenth Century.* Translated by Edward Schneider. Berkeley: University of California Press, 2001.

Laloy, Louis. *Louis Laloy (1874–1944) on Debussy, Ravel, and Stravinsky.* Translated and edited by Deborah Priest. Aldershot, UK: Ashgate, 1999.

———. *Rameau.* Paris: Alcan, 1908.

Lanson, Gustave. *Corneille.* 3rd ed. Paris: Hachette, 1909.

Large, David C., and William Weber, eds., with Anne Dzamba Sessa. *Wagnerism in European Culture and Politics.* Ithaca, NY: Cornell University Press, 1984.

Lasserre, Pierre. *L'Esprit de la musique française, de Rameau à l'invasion wagnérienne.* Paris: Payot, 1917.

Laurencie, Lionel de la. *Le Goût musical en France.* Paris: Joanin, 1905.

———. *Rameau: Biographie critique.* Paris: Laurens, 1926.

Lavignac, Albert. *The Music Dramas of Richard Wagner and His Festival Theatre in Bayreuth.* Translated by Esther Singleton. New York: Dodd, Mead, 1914.

Lavoix, Henri. *Histoire de la musique.* Paris: Quantin, 1884.

———. *La Musique français.* Paris: Quantin, 1891.

Le Brun, Roger. *Corneille devant trois siècles.* Paris: Sansot, 1906.

Legrand, Raphaëlle, and Nicole Wild. *Regards sur l'opéra-comique: trois siècles de vie théâtrale.* Paris: CNRS, 2002.

Lemaître, Jules. *Jean-Jacques Rousseau.* Paris: Calmann-Lévy, 1907.

Leoussi, Athena S. *Nationalism and Classicism: The Classical Body as National Symbol in Nineteenth-Century England and France.* New York: St. Martin's Press, 1998.

Levin, Alicia. "Musical Theaters in Paris, 1830–1900: A Documentary Overview." In Fauser and Everist, *Music, Theater, and Cultural Transfer,* 379–402.

Levin, David J. *Unsettling Opera: Staging Mozart, Verdi, Wagner, and Zemlinsky.* Chicago: University of Chicago Press, 2007.

Litvinne, Félia. *Mon vie et mon art.* Paris: Plon, 1933.

Macdonald, Sharon, ed. *A Companion to Museum Studies.* Malden, MA: Blackwell, 2006.

Mackaman, Douglas. "Regaining the 'Lost Provinces': Textual Battles for Alsace-Lorraine and the First World War." In Mackaman and Mays, *World War I and the Cultures of Modernity,* 125–34.

Mackaman, Douglas, and Michael Mays, eds. *World War I and the Cultures of Modernity.* Jackson: University of Mississippi Press, 2000.
Makowski, John F. "Bisexual Orpheus: Pederasty and Parody in Ovid." *Classical Journal* 92 (1996): 25–38.
Marty, Laurent. *1805, La création de Don Juan à l'Opéra de Paris.* Paris: Harmattan, 2005.
Marvick, Louis. *Waking the Face That No One Is: A Study in the Musical Context of Symbolist Poetics.* Amsterdam: Rodopi, 2004.
Mathews, Patricia. *Passionate Discontent: Creativity, Gender, and French Symbolist Art.* Chicago: University of Chicago Press, 1999.
Maugue, Annelise. *L'Identité masculine en crise au tournant du siècle: 1871–1914.* Paris: Rivages, 1987.
Maynard, Kelly Jo. "The Enemy Within: Encountering Wagner in Third-Republic France." PhD diss., University of California at Los Angeles, 2007.
McClellan, Andrew, *Inventing the Louvre: Art, Politics, and the Origins of the Modern Museum in Eighteenth-Century Paris.* Berkeley: University of California Press, 1994.
McGahey, Robert. *The Orphic Moment: Shaman to Poet-Thinker in Plato, Nietzsche, and Mallarmé.* Albany: State University of New York Press, 1994.
McMillan, James F. *France and Women, 1789–1914: Gender, Society and Politics.* New York: Routledge, 1999.
Médicis, Catrina Flint de. "Nationalism and Early Music at the French *Fin-de-Siècle*: Three Case Studies." *Nineteenth-Century Music Review* 1, no. 2 (2004): 43–66.
———. "The Schola Cantroum, Early Music and French Political Culture, from 1894–1914." PhD diss., McGill University, 2006.
Messing, Scott. *Neoclassicism in Music: From the Genesis of the Concept through the Schoenberg/Stravinsky Polemic.* Rochester, NY: University of Rochester Press, 1996.
Millington, Barry. *Wagner.* Rev. ed. Princeton: Princeton University Press, 1984.
Mongrédien, Jean. *French Music from the Enlightenment to Romanticism, 1789–1830.* Translated by Sylvain Frémaux. Portland, OR: Amadeus Press, 1996.
———. "*Les Mystères d'Isis* (1801) and Reflections on Mozart from the Parisian Press at the Beginning of the Nineteenth Century." In *Music in the Classic Period: Essays in Honor of Barry S. Brook,* edited by Allan W. Atlas, 195–211. New York: Pendragon Press, 1985.
Myers, Rollo. "The Opera that Never Was: Debussy's Collaboration with Victor Segalen in the Preparation of *Orphée.*" *Musical Quarterly* 64 (1978): 495–506.
Nattiez, Jean-Jacques. *Wagner Androgyne.* Translated by Stewart Spencer. Princeton: Princeton University Press, 1993.
Nedbal, Martin. "Morals Across the Footlights: German Opera, National Identity, and the Aesthetics of Morality." PhD diss., Eastman School of Music, 2009.
———. "Mozart as Viennese Moralist: *Die Zauberflöte* and Its Maxims." *Acta Musicologica* 81 (2009): 125–57.
Nichols, Roger. *The Life of Debussy.* Cambridge: Cambridge University Press, 1998.
Nora, Pierre, ed. *Les Lieux de mémoire.* 3 vols. Paris: Gallimard, 1992.
Nuitter, Charles. *Le Nouvel Opéra.* Paris: Hachette, 1875.

Nye, Robert A. *Masculinity and Male Codes of Honor in Modern France.* Oxford: Oxford University Press, 1993.
Pasler, Jann. "Building a Public for Orchestral Music: Les Concerts Colonne." In *Concert et public: Mutation de la vie musicale en Europe de 1780 à 1914,* edited by Hans-Erich Bödeker, Patrice Veit, and Michael Werner, 209–40. Paris: Editions de la Maison des sciences de l'homme, 2002.
———. *Composing the Citizen: Music and Public Utility in Third Republic France.* Berkeley: University of California Press, 2009.
———. "Concert Programs and Their Narratives as Emblems of Ideology." In Pasler, *Writing through Music,* 365–416.
———. "Countess Greffulhe as Entrepreneur: Negotiating Class, Gender, and Nation." In Pasler, *Writing through Music,* 285–317.
———. "Deconstructing d'Indy, or the Problem of a Composer's Reputation." In Pasler, *Writing through Music,* 135–36.
———. "Material Culture and Postmodern Positivism: Rethinking the 'Popular' in Late Nineteenth-Century French Music." In Pasler, *Writing through Music,* 417–49.
———. "Paris: Conflicting Notions of Progress." In Samson, *The Late Romantic Era,* 389–416.
———. *Writing through Music: Essays on Music, Culture, and Politics.* Oxford: Oxford University Press, 2008.
Patureau, Frederique. *Le Palais Garnier dans la société parisenne, 1875–1914.* Liège: Mardaga, 1991.
Paul, Charles B. "Rameau, d'Indy, and French Nationalism." *Musical Quarterly* 58 (1972): 46–56.
Peraino, Judith. *Listening to the Sirens: Musical Technologies of Queer Identity from Homer to Hedwig.* Berkeley: University of California Press, 2006.
Petrie, Brian. *Puvis de Chavanne.* Edited by Simon Lee. Aldershot, UK: Ashgate, 1997.
Pistone, Danièle. "Rameau à Paris au XIXe siècle." In *Jean-Philippe Rameau: Colloque international, organisé par la Société Rameau,* edited by Jérôme de la Gorce, 131–40. Paris: Champion-Slatkine, 1987.
Pistone, Danièle, and Pierre Brunel, eds. *Musiques d'Orphée.* Paris: Presses Universitaires de France, 1999.
Pomfret, David M. "'A Muse for the Masses': Gender, Age and Nation in France, Fin de Siècle." *American Historical Review* 109 (2004): 1439–75.
Pougin, Arthur. *Jean-Jacques Rousseau musicien.* Paris: Fischbacher, 1901.
———. *Rameau: essai sur sa vie et ses œuvres.* Paris: Decaux, 1876.
Preziosi, Donald. "Art History and Museology: Rending the Visible Legible." In Macdonald, *A Companion to Museum Studies,* 50–63.
———. "The Art of Art History." In *The Art of Art History: A Critical Anthology,* edited by Donald Preziosi, 507–25. Oxford: Oxford University Press, 1998.
Puri, Michael J. "Dandy, Interrupted: Sublimation, Repression, and Self-Portraiture in Maurice Ravel's *Daphnis et Chloé* (1909–1912)." *Journal of the American Musicological Society* 60 (2007): 317–72.
Quittard, Henri. "Exécutions et publications récentes: *Hippolyte et Aricie* à L'Opéra." *Revue musicale* (June 1908): 319–25.

———. "Publications et œuvres récentes: *Iphigénie en Aulide*, de Gluck." *Revue musicale* (January 1908): 16–20.
Rameau, Jean-Philippe. *Hippolyte et Aricie*. Edited by Vincent d'Indy. Vol. 6 of *Œuvres Complètes*. Paris: Durand, 1900.
———. *Pièces de Claveçin*. Edited by Camille Saint-Saëns. Vol. 1 of *Œuvres complètes*. Paris: Durand, 1895.
Rees, Brian. *Camille Saint-Saëns: A Life*. London: Chatto and Windus, 1999.
Régnier, Christian. "The Heart of the King of France: 'Cordial Immortality.'" *Medicographia* 31 (2009): 430–39.
Reid, Roddey. *Families in Jeopardy: Regulating the Social Body in France, 1750–1910*. Stanford: Stanford University Press, 1993.
Roberts, Mary Louise. *Disruptive Acts: The New Woman in Fin-de-Siècle France*. Chicago: University of Chicago Press, 2002.
Rolland, Romain. *Musiciens d'autrefois*. Paris: Hachette, 1908.
———. *Romain Rolland's Essays on Music*. Edited by David Ewen. New York: Dover, 1959.
Rosenberg, Martin. *Raphael and France: The Artist as Paradigm and Symbol*. University Park: Pennsylvania State University Press, 1995.
Sadler, Graham. "Vincent d'Indy and the Rameau *Oeuvres complètes*: A Case of Forgery?" *Early Music* 21 (1993): 415–21.
Saint-Saëns, Camille. *Camille Saint-Saëns on Music and Musicians*. Translated and edited by Roger Nichols. Oxford: Oxford University Press, 2008.
———. *Musical Memories*. Translated by Edwin Gile Rich. Boston: Small, Maynard, 1919.
———. *Outspoken Essays on Music*. Translated by Fred Rothwell. London: Paul, Trench, and Trubner, 1922.
Samson, Jim, ed. *The Late Romantic Era*. London: Macmillan, 1991.
Schneider-Seidel, Kerstin Mira. *Antike Sujets und moderne Musik: Untersuchungen zur französischen Musik um 1900*. Stuttgart and Weimar: Verlag J. B. Metzler, 2002.
Schuré, Édouard. *L'Alsace française: rêves et combats*. Paris: Perrin, 1916.
———. *Le Drame musical*. Rev. ed. 2 vols. Paris: Didier, 1886.
Schwartz, Manuela. "'La question de *Lohengrin*' zwischen 1869 und 1891." In Fauser and Schwartz, *Von Wagner zum Wagnérisme*, 107–36.
———, ed. *Vincent d'Indy et son temps*. Sprimont, Belgium: Mardaga, 2006.
Segal, Charles. *Orpheus: The Myth of the Poet*. Baltimore: Johns Hopkins University Press, 1989.
Ségur, Marquis Anatole-Henri-Philippe de. *Œuvres poétiques*. Paris: Retaux, 1899.
Shaw, Jennifer H. *Dream States: Puvis de Chavannes, Modernism, and the Fantasy of France*. New Haven: Yale University Press, 2002.
Sherman, Daniel J. "Objects of Memory: History and Narrative in French War Museums." *French Historical Studies* 19 (1995): 49–74.
Sherman, Daniel J. *Worthy Monuments: Art Museums and the Politics of Culture in Nineteenth-Century France*. Cambridge, MA: Harvard University Press, 1989.
Silverman, Debora L. *Art Nouveau in Fin-de-Siècle France: Politics, Psychology, and Style*. Berkeley: University of California Press, 1989.
Smart, Mary Ann, ed. *Siren Songs: Representations of Gender and Sexuality in Opera*. Princeton: Princeton University Press, 2000.

Struass, Walter A. *Descent and Return: The Orphic Theme in Modern Literature.* Cambridge, MA: Harvard University Press, 1971.
Suschitzky, Anya. "*Ariane et Barbe-Bleue*: Dukas, the Light, and the Well." *Cambridge Opera Journal* 9 (1997): 133–61.
———. "Debussy's Rameau: French Music and Its Others." *Musical Quarterly* 86 (2002): 398–448.
———. "*Fervaal, Parsifal*, and French National Identity." *19th-Century Music* 25 (2002): 237–65.
———. "The Nation on Stage: Wagner and French Opera at the End of the Nineteenth Century." PhD diss., University of California at Berkeley, 1999.
Taruskin, Richard. "The Pastness of the Present and the Presence of the Past." In Kenyon, *Authenticity and Early Music*, 137–207.
———. *Text and Act: Essays on Music and Performance.* Oxford: Oxford Univeristy Press, 1995.
Theuriet, André. *Poésie de André Theuriet, 1860–1874.* Paris: Lemerre, 1879.
Thomson, Andrew. *Vincent d'Indy and His World.* Oxford: Clarendon Press, 1996.
Tiersot, Julien. *Gluck.* 4th ed. Paris: Alcan, 1919.
———. *Jean-Jacques Rousseau.* Paris: Alcan, 1920.
Tolley, Thomas. *Painting the Cannon's Roar: Music, the Visual Arts, and the Rise of an Attentive Public in the Age of Haydn, c. 1750–1810.* Aldershot, UK: Ashgate, 2001.
Tonnellé, Alfred. *Fragments sur l'art et la philosophie, suivi de notes et pensées diverses.* 2nd ed. Paris: Douinol and Reinwald, 1860.
Turbow, Gerald. "Art and Politics: Wagnerism in France." In Large and Weber, *Wagnerism in European Culture and Politics*, 134–66.
Vallas, Léon. *The Theories of Claude Debussy, Musicien Français.* Translated by Marie O'Brien. London: Oxford University Press, 1929.
Vallas, Léon. *Vincent d'Indy.* 2 vols. Paris: Albin Michel, 1946/1950.
Vançon, Jean-Claire. "Le Temple de la Gloire: Visage et usages de Jean-Philippe Rameau en France entre 1764 et 1895." 3 vols. PhD diss., Université de Paris-Sorbonne, 2009.
Venuti, Lawrence. "Translation, Community, Utopia." In *The Translation Studies Reader*, edited by Lawrence Venuti, 482–502. London: Routledge, 2000.
Wagner, Richard. *Judaism in Music and Other Essays.* Translated by William Ashton Ellis. Lincoln: University of Nebraska Press, 1995.
———. *My Life.* Edited by Mary Whitall. Translated by Andrew Gray. New York: Da Capo Press, 1992.
Walsh, T. J. *Second Empire Opera: The Théâtre Lyrique, Paris, 1851–1870.* New York: Riverrun Press, 1981.
Walton, Benjamin. *Rossini in Restoration Paris: The Sound of Modern Life.* Cambridge: Cambridge University Press, 2007.
Weber, Eugen. *France: Fin de Siècle.* Cambridge, MA: Belknap Press, 1986.
———. *The Nationalist Revival in France, 1905–1914.* Berkeley: University of California Press, 1968.
Weill, Louis. "Le livret de *la Flûte enchantée.*" Pt. 2. *Revue musicale* (August 1909): 391
Wheeldon, Marianne. "Debussy's Legacy: The Controversy over the *Ode à la France.*" *Journal of Musicology* 27 (2010): 304–41.

White, Nicholas. *The Family in Crisis in Late Nineteenth-Century French Fiction.* Cambridge: Cambridge University Press, 1999.
Whittall, Arnold M. "La Querelle des Bouffons." PhD diss., Cambridge University, 1964.
Wild, Nicole. *Dictionnaire des théâtres parisiens au XIXe siècle: les théâtres et la musique.* Paris: Aux Amateurs de Livres, 1989.
Willson, Flora. "Classic Staging: Pauline Viardot and the 1859 *Orphée* Revival." *Cambridge Opera Journal* 22 (2010): 301–26.
Wilss, Wolfram. *The Science of Translation: Problems and Methods.* Tubingen: Gunter Narr, 1982.
Winzer, Dieter. *Claude Debussy und die französische musikalische Tradition.* Wiesbaden: Breiktopf and Härtel, 1981.
Woldu, Gail Hilson. "Debussy, Fauré, and d'Indy and the Conceptions of the Artist: The Institutions, the Dialogues, the Conflicts." In Fulcher, *Debussy and His World*, 235–53.
———. "Gabriel Fauré as Director of the Conservatoire National de Musique et de Declamation, 1905–1920." PhD diss., Yale University, 1983.
Wright, Lesley. "Carvalho and the Opéra-Comique: L'Art de se hâter lentement." In Fauser and Everist, *Stage Music and Cultural Transfer*, 99–126.
Wyzewa, Téodor de, and Georges de Saint-Foix. *Wolfgang Amédée Mozart: sa vie musicale et son œuvre.* 5 vols. Paris: Desclée de Drouwer, 1936–46.

Index

Adam, Adolphe, 148
Alembert, Jean le Rond d', 173
Alsace-Lorraine, 116118. *See also* Franco-Prussian War
ancien régime, 3, 8, 61, 147–48, 162, 179, 190–91
Auber, Daniel François Esprit, 41; *Fra Diavolo*, 41; *Le Domino noir*, 41

Bach, Johann Sebastian, 63, 95–96, 145, 146, 151, 154, 156, 158; *B-Minor Mass*, 151
Bach und Händel Gesellschaft, 95–96
Bachelet, Alfred, 191, 193
Barbedette, Hippolyte, 106, 111, 119, 121
Bauer, Henry, 126
Beaumarchais, Pierre, 25–26
Beaumont, Alexandre, 47–48, 50, 55–57, 93
Beethoven, Ludwig van, 17, 23–24, 69, 70, 95, 96, 111, 121, 141, 145, 148, 169–70, 175; *Fidelio*, 17, 36; "Pastoral" Symphony, 169
Bellaigue, Camille, 66–67, 71–72, 74, 111–12, 125–26
Bellini, Vincenzo, 61
Berlioz, Hector, 10, 17, 36, 72–73, 80, 84–86, 87, 92, 93, 95, 96, 97, 99, 110, 111, 135, 141, 145, 169, 174, 175, 178; *Les Francs-Juges*, 92; *L'Enfance du Christ*, 92; *La Nonne sanglante*, 92; *Symphonie Fantastique*, 169; *Les Troyens*, 36
Bernard, Paul, 31, 37
Berton, Henri Montan, 145
Bertrand, Gustave, 30, 47

Bibesco, Prince Alexander, 93
Bisson, Alexandre, 51, 54, 56–58
Blaze, François-Henri-Joseph. *See* Castil-Blaze
Blaze de Bury, Henri, 31, 32, 64, 72, 121
Bobilier, Marie. *See* Brenet, Michel
Boïeldieu, François-Adrien, 145
Bonnerot, Jean, 96, 156, 158
Bordes, Charles, 177
Borrel, Eugène, 137
Bouyer, Raymond, 134, 142
Brenet, Michel, 122
Bréval, Lucienne, 127
Broussan, Leimistin, 178
Bruneau, Alfred, 101–2, 113, 123, 124–25, 141, 190; *L'Attaque du moulin*, 113

Calvocoressi, M.-D., 103
Calzabigi, Ranieri de', 110
Campra, André, 106, 108, 145, 184
Caron, Rose, 101, 127
Carré, Albert, 41–44, 50–58, 103
Carvalho, Léon, 29, 47, 85, 99
Case, Jules, 75
Castil-Blaze, 28, 29, 31, 38, 39, 43, 84–85
Chantavoine, Jean, 41, 161, 174
Chapuis, August, 157
Chausson, Ernest, 128
Chavannes, Pierre Puvis de, 112, 113–15
Chevigné, Adhéaume de, 51, 57
Chopin, Frédéric, 95
Choquet, Gustave, 66, 69, 108–9
Chuquet, Arthur, 165–66
Clément, Felix, 13, 14, 16, 62, 106, 146–47, 151–52, 177

Comédie-Française. *See* theaters
concert series: Concerts Colonne, 88, 91, 127, 150; Concerts Lamoureux, 10, 88, 91, 103; Concerts Pasdeloup, 10, 88, 91, 148; Société des Concerts du Conservatoire, 10, 85, 88, 89, 91, 148, 149, 153; Société des Grandes Auditions Musicales de France, 91
Corneille, Pierre, 5, 17, 18, 37, 86, 104, 106, 108–10, 147
Cousin, Victor, 109
Curzon, Henri de, 56, 57, 58, 63, 135

Da Ponte, Lorenzo, 25, 28, 42, 43, 64
Damcke, Berthold, 93–96
Daudet, Alphonse, 116
Debay, Victor, 56–57, 104, 188
Debussy, Claude, 15, 19, 63–64, 112, 122–23, 132, 142, 157–62, 167, 169, 171, 172, 176, 185; *La Mer*, 169; *Orphée-roi*, 132; *Pelléas et Mélisande*, 113, 142, 162; *Prélude à l'après-midi d'un faune*, 112; *Syrinx*, 112; *Trois Chansons de Bilitis*, 112
Deldevez, Edme-Marie-Ernest, 89, 91, 153
Delna, Marie, 99, 135, 137
Delville, Jean, 132, 134
Deschamps, Emile, 31
Destouches, André Cardinal, 145
Diderot, Denis, 72, 107, 173
Diémer, Louis, 10
Donizetti, Gaetano, 8, 32, 37, 61; *Lucia di Lammermoor*, 31, 37
Doucet, Camille, 93
Dukas, Paul, 16–17, 18, 19, 36–37, 44, 97–98, 100–101, 103, 147, 154, 157–62 ; *Ariane et Barbe-Bleue*, 161

Eden Théâtre. *See* theaters
Editions. *See Bach und Händel Gesellschaft*; Gluck, Pelletan Edition; Rameau, *Œuvres complètes*
Emmanuel, Maurice, 112
Encyclopedists, 106, 107, 164, 172–74, 175. *See also* Alembert, Jean le Rond de; Diderot, Denis; Grimm, Melchior; Rousseau, Jean-Jacques
Epardaud, Edmond, 190, 193
Escudier, Léon, 86, 108–9

Faguet, Émile, 165–67, 168
Fauré, Gabriel, 18, 19, 39–41, 51, 55–56, 57, 58, 73, 74, 103, 108, 112, 147, 184–85, 188; *La Chanson d'Ève*, 74; *Masques et bergamasques*, 41; *Requiem*, 74
Faure, Jean-Baptiste, 29–30, 33
Ferrier, Paul, 42, 51, 54, 56–58
Fétis, François-Joseph, 16, 28, 30, 60, 87, 148
Fourcaud, Louis de, 186–87
Français, François Louis, 132, 135
Franck, César, 145–46
Franco-Prussian War, 2, 3, 11, 32, 61, 68, 70, 109, 113, 116–18, 146. *See also* Alsace-Lorraine

Gallet, Louis, 124
Gallois, Lucien, 117
Garcia, Manuel, 28, 29
Gide, André, 115–16
Gluck, Christoph Willibald Ritter von, 1, 3–6, 8, 10, 16, 17, 18, 19, 36, 37, 41, 47, 62, 63, 64, 78, 80, 83–142, 146, 147, 148, 149, 154, 156, 159, 161, 163–64, 167, 168, 169, 171, 172, 174–76, 177, 178, 179, 183, 185–86, 189, 194; and antiquity, 110–19; compared to Corneille, 108–10; compared to Rameau, 107–8, 146, 174–76, 177, 186; compared to Wagner, 120–31; early French reception, 83–88; gender roles in operas, 134–39; and national identity, 106–19; Pelletan edition, 83, 91–97, 98, 122, 148, 154, 156, 174; and symbolism), 131–42
Gluck, Christoph Willibald Ritter von, works of: *Alceste*, 3, 8, 9, 10, 17, 36, 83, 85, 86, 87, 93, 95, 96, 99, 100, 101, 103, 104, 110, 111, 113, 115, 117, 119, 120, 121, 123, 124, 126,

128, 164, 169; *Armide*, 17, 36, 84, 87, 93, 94, 97, 101, 103, 117, 126, 127; *Echo et Narcisse*, 84, 94; *Fedra*, 164; *Iphigénie en Aulide*, 17, 36, 84, 87, 93, 96, 97, 101, 103, 103–4, 108, 113, 115, 118–19, 122, 177; *Iphigénie en Tauride*, 3, 17, 36, 87, 91, 93, 96, 97, 100, 101, 103, 113, 115, 118–19, 126; *Orphée et Eurydice*, 3, 10, 17, 36, 83, 85, 87, 93, 94, 95, 96, 97, 98–101, 103, 104, 109, 110, 113, 115, 117–18, 119, 124, 125, 131–42, 169; *Paris et Hélène*, 93; *Siface*, 164
Gounod, Charles, 15, 33–35, 36, 39, 40, 41, 65, 74, 85; *Faust*, 15; *Jeanne d'Arc*, 74; *Mireille*, 41; *Polyeucte*, 74
Grétry, André, 17, 27, 63, 154, 166, 172
Grimm, Melchior, 63, 173
Guilmant, Alexandre, 157

Hahn, Reynaldo, 31, 39, 41, 42, 44, 46, 55, 58, 59, 70, 152–53, 157; *Mozart*, 70
Halévy, Fromental, 15, 31; *La Juive*, 15, 31–32, 37
Halle, Adam de la, 16; *Le Jeu de Robin et de Marion*, 16
Handel, Georg Friedrich, 95–96, 145, 146, 151, 154, 158; *Messiah*, 151
Haydn, Franz Joseph, 26, 95
Hérold, Ferdinand, 145
Hoffmann, E. T. A., 29, 30
Holmès, Augusta, 116
Huegel, Henri. *See* Moreno, H.
Humperdinck, Engelbert, 123

Imbart de la Tour, Georges, 178–79
Imbert, Hughes, 97, 99
Indy, Vincent d', 19, 74, 91, 103, 121–23, 137–39, 150, 153, 155, 157–62, 167, 169, 176, 177, 182–83, 188; *Fervaal*, 74, 161–62
Isouard, Nicolas, 145

Jullien, Adolphe, 23, 26, 27, 29, 32, 33, 34, 56, 57, 58, 145, 152–53, 163–64, 183–84, 193

Kalkbrenner, Friedrich, 26
Krauss, Gabrielle, 91

La Madeleine, Stéphen de, 9, 14
Lalo, Pierre, 185–86
Laloy, Louis, 18, 112, 145–46, 171, 175
Lanson, Gustave, 109
Laprade, Victor de, 109
Lavoix, Henri, 108, 109, 146, 171
Langenevais, François de. *See* Blaze de Bury, Henri
Laurencie, Lionel de la, 172–73, 175
Lemaître, Jules, 75, 165
Lévy, Émile, 132
Lindenlaub, Théodore, 194
Liszt, Franz, 145
Litvinne, Félia, 101, 127–28
Louis XIV, 16. *See also* ancien régime
Louis XV, 191. *See also* ancien régime
Louis XVII, 92. *See also* ancient régime
Louvre, compared to Operatic Museum, 8–9, 10, 13–14, 16–17, 36, 154
Louÿs, Pierre, 137
Lully, Jean-Baptiste, 16, 17, 63, 106, 108, 122, 146, 153, 163, 172, 184

Magnard, Albéric, 153–57
Maillart, Louis-Aimé, 41; *Les Dragons de Villars*, 41
Mallarmé, Stéphane, 132
Malherbe, Charles, 155, 176
Marie Antoinette, 161
Marnold, Jean, 104
Massenet, Jules, 15, 60, 112
Masson, Paul-Marie, 173–74
Méhul, Étienne, 17, 63, 145
Mendelssohn, Felix, 148
Messager, André, 178
Meyerbeer, Giacomo, 9, 15, 32, 37, 106, 161; *Les Huguenots*, 31–32; *Le Prophète*, 15; *Robert le diable*, 15
Michel, Émile, 67
Molière, 17, 18, 27–28, 31, 37, 43, 147
Mondor, Robert, 184
Monsigny, Pierre-Alexandre, 145, 166
Monteverdi, Claudio, 16, 125

Moreau, Gustave, 132
Moreno, H., 32–33, 38–39
Mozart, Wolfgang Amadeus, 1, 3–5, 9, 10, 16, 17, 18, 19, 23–80, 83, 84, 85, 86, 95, 100, 103, 108–9, 110, 135, 145, 147, 148, 153, 175, 178, 185, 191, 194; compared to Raphael, 64–67; early reception in France, 25–31; and frivolity, 70–71, 73; and gender, 68–71; gender roles in operas, 75–80; and national identify, 60–64; and Romanticism/Classicism, 31–46; and sublimity, 71–73
Mozart, Wolfgang Amadeus, works of: *La clemenza di Tito*, 27, 28, 77; *Così fan tutte*, 27, 41, 77; *Don Giovanni/Don Juan*, 3, 5, 16, 19, 23, 26, 27, 28, 29, 30, 31–46, 51, 63, 70, 71, 76–77, 98, 100, 108–9, 153, 183, 191; *Die Entführung aus dem Serail*, 28, 77; *Idomeneo*, 28, 29, 77; *Louis XII, ou La Route de Reims*, 28; *Les Mystères d'Isis*, 26, 29, 56; *Le nozze di Figaro/Les Noces de Figaro*, 23, 25, 26, 27, 28, 29, 41, 63, 72, 76, 135; *Die Zauberflöte/La Flûte enchantée*, 5, 23, 26, 29, 41, 42, 45, 47–59, 71–80, 100, 191

Nicolò. *See* Isouard, Nicolas
Nourrit, Adolphe, 29, 86, 99
Nouveau Théâtre. *See* theaters
Nuitter, Charles, 47, 48, 50, 55, 56, 57, 93

Odéon. *See* theaters
Offenbach, Jacques, 132, 135; *Les Contes d'Hoffmann*, 135; *Orphée aux enfers*, 132
Opéra (Académie nationale de musique). *See* theaters
Opéra-Comique (Théâtre national de l'Opéra-Comique). *See* theaters

Palestrina, Giovanni Pierluigi da, 151
Paris Commune. *See* Franco-Prussian War

Pascal-Estienne, M.-P., 36
Pelletan, Fanny, 92–97
Pergolesi, Giovanni Battista, 175
Perrin, Emile, 32
Philidor, François-André Danican, 145
Piccini, Niccolò, 27, 175, 176; *La Bonne fille*, 27
Pierné, Gabriel, 17, 62–63
Pioch, Georges, 57–58, 73–74, 127, 178
Poisot, Charles, 148
Pougin, Arthur, 43, 163, 167–68, 170–72

Querelle des Bouffons, 107, 162, 163–76, 186
Quittard, Henri, 18, 108, 178, 184–85, 189–90

Racine, Jean, 17, 18, 37, 84, 104, 107, 108, 109, 147
Rameau, Jean-Philippe, 1, 3–4, 6, 14, 16, 17, 18, 19, 36, 37, 51, 63, 83, 96, 106, 107–8, 110, 119, 122–23, 137, 145–95; compared to Gluck, 107–8, 146, 174–76, 177, 186; compared to Rousseau, 164–76
Rameau, Jean-Philippe, works of: *Œuvres complètes*, 16, 19, 96, 148–49, 153–62, 174, 182; *Castor et Pollux*, 3, 6, 106, 148, 149, 150, 156, 161–62, 163, 170, 172, 177, 183, 189–94; *Dardanus*, 150, 177, 183; *La Guirlande*, 150, 176; *Hippolyte et Aricie*, 3, 6, 18, 51, 108, 147, 149, 153, 157, 158, 161, 162, 176, 177–79, 182–85, 187–93; *Les Indes galantes*, 149; *Platée*, 149; *Zoroastre*, 148, 150, 162, 177
Rameau, Paul, 99, 100
Raphael. *See* Mozart, compared to Raphael
Ravel, Maurice, 112
Rolland, Romain, 18, 70, 107, 119
Rossini, Gioachino, 8, 9, 15, 32, 37, 61; *Guillaume Tell*, 9, 15, 31, 37
Rouché, Jacques, 189–90, 191

Rousseau, Jean-Jacques, 6, 107, 162, 164–76; *Le Devin du Village*, 164, 165, 167–68, 173; *Les Muses galantes*, 170

Saint-Foix, Georges de, 69
Séon, Alexandre, 132, 134
Sacchini, Antonio, 27; *La Colonie*, 27
Saint-Saëns, Camille, 8, 15, 19, 39, 93–96, 102, 103, 112, 115, 127, 154–58, 169, 174–75, 187–88; *Antigone*, 115; *Le Déluge*, 169; *Étienne Marcel*, 116
Schikaneder, Emanuel, 26, 47, 48, 54, 55, 56, 57
Schola Cantorum. *See* theaters
Schneider, Louis, 191, 193
Schubert, Franz, 145
Schuré, Edouard, 111, 117, 132
Singer, Winaretta (Princesse de Polignac), 91
Smith, Paul, 120
Spontini, Gaspare, 27, 89; *Fernand Cortez*, 89; *La Vestale*, 89
symbolism. *See* Gluck and symbolism

Théâtre-Lyrique. *See* theaters
theaters: Comédie-Française, 17–18, 115, 131, 147; Eden Théâtre, 124; Nouveau Théâtre, 39; Odéon, 18, 28, 115, 147; Opéra, 6, 8–19, 23–34, 36–39, 40, 41, 43–44, 46, 59, 61, 76, 84–85, 86, 87, 88, 89, 91, 93, 97–98, 101, 108, 113, 117, 119, 120, 121, 124, 126–27, 135, 147, 154–55, 157, 161, 165, 176, 177–79, 182–84, 186–91, 193–94; Opéra-Comique, 5, 8, 10, 14, 15, 16, 17, 18, 19, 23, 24, 34, 36, 37, 39, 40, 41–46, 50–56, 58–59, 61, 62–63, 71, 72, 74, 76, 77, 80, 88, 89, 91, 97, 98–99, 101–2, 103–4, 110, 113, 119, 124, 127, 137, 139, 173, 177, 178–79, 191; Schola Cantorum, 77, 91, 121, 137, 139, 150–51, 153, 155, 176, 177, 188, 189; Théâtre-Italien, 26–29, 42; Théâtre-Lyrique, 10, 29, 30, 47, 85, 86, 99
Thomas, Amboise, 15, 41; *Hamlet*, 15; *Mignon*, 41
Tiersot, Julien, 18, 91, 92, 94, 97, 99–100, 109, 112, 122, 123, 134, 167–70, 172, 173, 175
Thurner, A., 8–9, 10, 11, 16, 87
Trémon, E. de, 139

Udine, Jean d', 23, 66, 123, 127

Valéry, Paul, 132
Vallas, Léon, 103, 122
Vaucorbeil, Auguste, 11, 13
Verdi, Giuseppe, 9, 61
Viardot, Pauline, 10, 30, 31, 86, 93, 99, 135, 139, 148
Voltaire, 3, 4

Wagner, Richard, 5–6, 23–24, 31, 34, 60, 61, 68, 70–71, 74, 86–87, 88–89, 104, 105, 111, 119, 120–31, 132, 134–35, 141, 145–46, 149, 159, 161, 167, 168, 169–70, 172, 174, 175–76, 178; *Der Fliegende Holländer*, 126; *Lohengrin*, 121, 124, 127, 132; *Parsifal*, 74; The *Ring Cycle*, 123, 169; *Siegfried*, 127; *Tannhäuser*, 31, 61, 74, 86–87, 120, 121, 124, 127; *Tristan und Isolde*, 113, 123, 127, 128; *Die Walküre*, 124
War of 1870. *See* Franco-Prussian War
Watteau, Jean-Antoine, 41
Weber, Carl Maria von, 17, 36, 47, 61, 98, 121, 122, 148, 159; *Der Freischütz*, 17, 36, 98
Weber, Johannès, 33
Wilder, Victor, 38
World War I, 4, 6, 24, 69, 70, 89, 96, 113, 151, 155, 189–90, 194
Wyzewa, Téodor de, 44–46, 69

www.ingramcontent.com/pod-product-compliance
Lightning Source LLC
Chambersburg PA
CBHW021658230426
43668CB00008B/660